Caten

COMMENTARY

ON THE

FOUR GOSPELS,

COLLECTED OUT OF THE

WORKS OF THE FATHERS

BY

S. THOMAS AQUINAS.

VOL. IV. PART I.
ST. JOHN.

OXFORD,
JOHN HENRY PARKER;
J. G. F. AND J. RIVINGTON, LONDON.
MDCCCXLV.

BAXTER, PRINTER, OXFORD,

ADVERTISEMENT.

THE following Compilation not being admissible into the
Library of the Fathers from the date of some few. of the
authors introduced into it, the Editors of the latter work
have been led to publish it in a separate form, being assured
that those who have subscribed to their Translations of the
entire Treatises of the ancient Catholic divines, will not feel
less interest, or find less benefit, in the use of so very
judicious and beautiful a selection from them. The Editors
refer to the Preface for some account of the natural and
characteristic excellences of the work, which will be found
as useful in the private study of the Gospels, as it is well
adapted for family reading, and full of thought for those who
are engaged in religious instruction.

Oxford, May 6, 1841.

COMMENTARY

ON THE GOSPEL ACCORDING TO

ST. JOHN.

CHAP. I.

Ver. 1. In the beginning was the Word,

CHRYS. While all the other Evangelists begin with the Chrys.
Incarnation, John, passing over the Conception, Nativity, Hom.iv.
[iii.] in
education, and growth, speaks immediately of the Eternal Joan.
Generation, saying, *In the beginning was the Word.* AUG. Aug.lib.
The Greek word "logos" signifies both Word and Reason. lxxxiii.
Quæst.
But in this passage it is better to interpret it Word ; as refer- q. 63.
ring not only to the Father, but to the creation of things by
the operative power of the Word; whereas Reason, though it
produce nothing, is still rightly called Reason. AUG. Words Aug.
by their daily use, sound, and passage out of us, have become Tract.
super
common things. But there is a word which remaineth inward, Joan. i.
in the very man himself; distinct from the sound which pro- c. 8.
ceedeth out of the mouth. There is a word, which is truly
and spiritually that, which you understand by the sound, not
being the actual sound. Now whoever can conceive the de Trin.
notion of word, as existing not only before its sound, but l. xv.
c.19.(x.)
even before the idea of its sound is formed, may see enigmati-
cally, and as it were in a glass, some similitude of that Word of
Which it is said, *In the beginning was the Word.* For when
we give expression to something which we know, the word
used is necessarily derived from the knowledge thus retained
in the memory, and must be of the same quality with that
knowledge. For a word is a thought formed from a thing
which we know; which word is spoken in the heart, being
neither Greek nor Latin, nor of any language, though, when
we want to communicate it to others, some sign is assumed

Ibid. cap. 20. (xi.) by which to express it. ... Wherefore the word which sounds externally, is a sign of the word which lies hid within, to which the name of word more truly appertains. For that which is uttered by the mouth of our flesh, is the voice of the word; and is in fact called word, with reference to that from which it is taken, when it is developed externally. BASIL; This Word is not a human word. For how was there a human word in the beginning, when man received his being last of all? There was not then any word of man in the beginning, nor yet of Angels; for every creature is within the limits of time, having its beginning of existence from the Creator. But what says the Gospel? It calls the Only-Begotten Himself the Word. CHRYS. But why omitting the Father, does he proceed at once to speak of the Son? Because the Father was known to all; though not as the Father, yet as God; whereas the Only-Begotten was not known. As was meet then, he endeavours first of all to inculcate the knowledge of the Son on those who knew Him not; though neither in discoursing on Him, is he altogether silent on the Father. And inasmuch as he was about to teach that the Word was the Only-Begotten Son of God, that no one might think this a passible generation, he makes mention of the Word in the first place, in order to destroy the dangerous suspicion, and shew that the Son was from God impassibly. And a second reason is, that He was to declare unto us the things of the Father. But he does not speak of the Word simply, but with the addition of the article, in order to distinguish It from other words. For Scripture calls God's laws and commandments words; but this Word is a certain Substance, or Person, an Essence, coming forth impassibly from the Father Himself. BASIL; Wherefore then Word? Because born impassibly, the Image of Him that begat, manifesting all the Father in Himself; abstracting from Him nothing, but existing perfect in Himself. AUG. As our knowledge differs from God's, so does our word, which arises from our knowledge, differ from that Word of God, which is born of the Father's essence; we might say, from the Father's knowledge, the Father's wisdom, or, more correctly, the Father Who is Knowledge, the Father Who is Wisdom. The Word of God then, the Only-Begotten Son of the Father, is in all things like and

Basil. Hom. in princ. Joan.

Chrys. Hom. in Joan. ii. [i.] §. 4.

παθητὴν

John 15, 15.

Basil. Hom. in princ. Joan. c. 3.

Aug. xv. de Trin. c. 22. (xiii.)

c. 23. (xiv.)

equal to the Father; being altogether what the Father is, yet not the Father; because the one is the Son, the other the Father. And thereby He knoweth all things which the Father knoweth; yet His knowledge is from the Father, even as is His being: for knowing and being are the same with Him; and so as the Father's being is not from the Son, so neither is His knowing. Wherefore the Father begat the Word equal to Himself in all things as uttering forth Himself. For had there been more or less in His Word than in Himself, He would not have uttered Himself fully and perfectly. With respect however to our own inner word, which we find, in whatever sense, to be like the Word, let us not object to see how very unlike it is also. A word is a forma- cap. 25. tion of our mind going to take place, but not yet made, and (xv.) something in our mind which we toss to and fro in a slippery circuitous way, as one thing and another is discovered, or occurs to our thoughts. When this, which we toss to and fro, has reached the subject of our knowledge, and been formed therefrom, when it has assumed the most exact likeness to it, and the conception has quite answered to the thing; then we have a true word. Who may not see how great the difference is here from that Word of God, which exists in the Form of God in such wise, that It could not have been first going to be formed, and afterwards formed, nor can ever have been unformed, being a Form absolute, and absolutely equal to Him from Whom It is. Wherefore in speaking of the Word of God here nothing is said about thought in God; lest we should think there was any thing revolving in God, which might first receive form in order to be a Word, and afterwards lose it, and be carried round and round again in an unformed state. AUG. Now the Word Aug. de of God is a Form, not a formation, but the Form of all Verb. Dom. forms, a Form unchangeable, removed from accident, from Serm. failure, from time, from space, surpassing all things, and 38. existing in all things as a kind of foundation underneath, and summit above them. BASIL; Yet has our outward Basil. word some similarity to the Divine Word. For our word Hom. in declares the whole conception of the mind; since what we Joan. conceive in the mind we bring out in word. Indeed our c. 3. heart is as it were the source, and the uttered word the stream which flows therefrom. CHRYS. Observe the spiritual wisdom of the Evangelist. He knew that men honoured most what was most ancient, and that honouring what is before every thing else, they conceived of it as God. On this account he mentions first the beginning, saying, *In the beginning* *was the Word.* ORIGEN; There are many significations of this word *beginning.* For there is a beginning of a journey, and beginning of a length, according to Proverbs, *The be-* *ginning of the right path is to do justice.* There is a beginning too of a creation, according to Job, *He is the* *beginning* [1] *of the ways of God.* Nor would it be incorrect to say, that God is the Beginning of all things. The preexistent material again, where supposed to be original, out of which any thing is produced, is considered as the beginning. There is a beginning also in respect of form: as where Christ is the beginning of those who are made according to the image of God. And there is a beginning of doctrine, according to Hebrews; *When for the time ye* *ought to be teachers, ye have need that one teach you again* *which be the first principles of the oracles of God.* For there are two kinds of beginning of doctrine: one in itself, the other relative to us; as if we should say that Christ, in that He is the Wisdom and Word of God, was in Himself the beginning of wisdom, but to us, in that He was the Word incarnate. There being so many significations then of the word, we may take it as the Beginning through Whom, i. e. the Maker; for Christ is Creator as The Beginning, in that He is Wisdom; so that the Word is in the beginning, i. e. in Wisdom; the Saviour being all these excellences at once. As life then is in the Word, so the Word is in the Beginning, that is to say, in Wisdom. Consider then if it be possible according to this signification to understand the Beginning, as meaning that all things are made according to Wisdom, and the patterns contained therein; or, inasmuch as the Beginning of the Son is the Father, the Beginning of all creatures and existencies, to understand by the text, *In the beginning* *was the Word,* that the Son, the Word, was in the Begin-ning, that is, in the Father. AUG. Or, *In the beginning,* as if it were said, before all things. BASIL; The Holy Ghost foresaw that men would arise, who should envy

Left margin notes:
Orig.
tom. i.
in Joan.
c. 16.
et sq.
Prov.
16.
Vulg.
Job 40,
19.
[1] chief
of, E.T.
princi-
pium,
Vulg.
Col. 1,
18.

Heb. 5,
12.

c. 22.

Aug. de
Trin. vi.
c. 3. (ii)
Basil.
Hom. in
princ.
Joan.

the glory of the Only-Begotten, subverting their hearers by sophistry; as if because He were begotten, He was not; and before He was begotten, He was not. That none might presume then to babble such things, the Holy Ghost saith, *In the beginning was the Word.* HILARY; Years, centuries, ages, are passed over, place what beginning thou wilt in thy imagining, thou graspest it not in time, for He, from Whom it is derived, still *was.* CHRYS. As then when our ship is near shore, cities and port pass in survey before us, which on the open sea vanish, and leave nothing whereon to fix the eye; so the Evangelist here, taking us with him in his flight above the created world, leaves the eye to gaze in vacancy on an illimitable expanse. For the words, *was in the beginning,* are significative of eternal and infinite essence. AUG. They say, however, if He is the Son, He was born. We allow it. They rejoin: if the Son was born to the Father, the Father was, before the Son was born to Him. This the Faith rejects. Then they say, explain to us how the Son could be born from the Father, and yet be coeval with Him from whom He is born: for sons are born after their fathers, to succeed them on their death. They adduce analogies from nature; and we must endeavour likewise to do the same for our doctrine. But how can we find in nature a coeternal, when we cannot find an eternal? However, if a thing generating and a thing generated can be found any where coeval, it will be a help to forming a notion of coeternals. Now Wisdom herself is called in the Scriptures, the brightness of Everlasting Light, the image of the Father. Hence then let us take our comparison, and from coevals form a notion of coeternals. Now no one doubts that brightness proceeds from fire: fire then we may consider the father of the brightness. Presently, when I light a candle, at the same instant with the fire, brightness ariseth. Give me the fire without the brightness, and I will with thee believe that the Father was without the Son. An image is produced by a mirror. The image exists as soon as the beholder appears; yet the beholder existed before he came to the mirror. Let us suppose then a twig, or a blade of grass which has grown up by the water side. Is it not born with its image? If there had always been the twig, there

Marginal notes: Hilar. ii. do Trin. c. 13. Chrys. Hom. i. Aug. de verb. Dom. Serm. 38. [117.] §. 6. Wisd. 7, 26.

would always have been the image proceeding from the twig. And whatever is from another thing, is born. So then that which generates may be coexistent from eternity with that which is generated from it. But some one will say perhaps, Well, I understand now the eternal Father, the coeternal Son: yet the Son is like the emitted brightness, which is less brilliant than the fire, or the reflected image, which is less real than the twig. Not so: there is complete equality between Father and Son. I do not believe, he says; for thou hast found nothing whereto to liken it. However, perhaps we can find something in nature by which we may understand that the Son is both coeternal with the Father, and in no respect inferior also: though we cannot find any one material of comparison that will be sufficient singly, and must therefore join together two, one of which has been employed by our adversaries, the other by ourselves. For they have drawn their comparison from things which are preceded in time by the things which they spring from, man, for example, from man. Nevertheless, man is of the same substance with man. We have then in that nativity an equality of nature; an equality of time is wanting. But in the comparison which we have drawn from the brightness of fire, and the reflexion of a twig, an equality of nature thou dost not find, of time thou dost. In the Godhead then there is found as a whole, what here exists in single and separate parts; and that which is in the creation, existing in a manner suitable to the Creator. Ex Gestis Concilii Ephesini; Wherefore in one place divine Scripture calls Him the Son, in another the Word, in another the Brightness of the Father; names severally meant to guard against blasphemy. For, forasmuch as thy son is of the same nature with thyself, the Scripture wishing to shew that the Substance of the Father and the Son is one, sets forth the Son of the Father, born of the Father, the Only-Begotten. Next, since the terms birth and son, convey the idea of passibleness, therefore it calls the Son the Word, declaring by that name the impassibility of His Nativity. But inasmuch as a father with us is necessarily older than his son, lest thou shouldest think that this applied to the Divine nature as well, it calls the Only-Begotten the Brightness of the Father; for brightness, though arising

Gest.
Conc.
Eph.

from the sun, is not posterior to it. Understand then that *Brightness*, as revealing the coeternity of the Son with the Father; *Word* as proving the impassibility of His birth, and *Son* as conveying His consubstantiality. CHRYS. But they say that *In the beginning* does not absolutely express eternity: for that the same is said of the heaven and the earth: *In the beginning God made the heaven and the earth.* But are not *made* and *was*, altogether different? For in like manner as the word *is*, when spoken of man, signifies the present only, but when applied to God, that which always and eternally is; so too *was*, predicated of our nature, signifies the past, but predicated of God, eternity. ORIGEN; The verb *to be*, has a double signification, sometimes expressing the motions which take place in time, as other verbs do; sometimes the substance of that one thing of which it is predicated, without reference to time. Hence it is also called a substantive verb. HILARY; Consider then the world, understand what is written of it. *In the beginning God made the heaven and the earth.* Whatever therefore is created is made in the beginning, and thou wouldest contain in time, what, as being to be made, is contained in the beginning. But, lo, for me, an illiterate unlearned fisherman is independent of time, unconfined by ages, advanceth beyond all beginnings. For the Word was, what it is, and is not bounded by any time, nor commenced therein, seeing It was not *made* in the beginning, but *was*. ALCUIN; To refute those who inferred from Christ's Birth in time, that He had not been from everlasting, the Evangelist begins with the eternity of the Word, saying, *In the beginning was the Word.*

Marginal notes: Chrys. Hom. in Joan. iii. [ii.] §. 2. Gen. 1, 1. — Orig. Hom. ii. divers. loc. — Hilar. ii. de Trin. c. xiii. — meus piscator (Hil.)

And the Word was with God.

CHRYS. Because it is an especial attribute of God, to be eternal and without a beginning, he laid this down first: then, lest any one on hearing *in the beginning was the Word*, should suppose the Word Unbegotten, he instantly guarded against this; saying, *And the Word was with God.* HILARY; From the beginning He is with God: and though inde-

Marginal notes: Chrys. Hom. iii. [ii.] 3. — Hilar. ii. de Trin.

Basil.
Hom.in
princ.
Joan.
§. 4.

pendent of time, is not independent of an Author. BASIL;
Again he repeats this, *was*, because of men blasphemously
saying, that there was a time when He was not. Where
then was the Word? Illimitable things are not contained
in space. Where was He then? With God. For neither
is the Father bounded by place, nor the Son by aught

Orig.
Hom.ii.
in Joan.
c. l.
¹ *factum*
Vulg.
came
E. T.

circumscribing. ORIGEN; It is worth while noting, that,
whereas the Word is said to come¹ [be made] to some, as to
Hosea, Isaiah, Jeremiah, with God it is not made, as though
it were not with Him before. But, the Word having been
always with Him, it is said, *and the Word was with God:*
for from the beginning it was not separate from the Father.

Chrys.
Hom.iii.

CHRYS. He has not said, was *in* God, but was *with* God:
exhibiting to us that eternity which He had in accordance

Theoph.
in loco.

with His Person. THEOPHYL. Sabellius is overthrown by
this text. For he asserts that the Father, Son, and Holy
Ghost are one Person, Who sometimes appeared as the
Father, sometimes as the Son, sometimes as the Holy Ghost.
But he is manifestly confounded by this text, *and the Word
was with God:* for here the Evangelist declares that the Son
is one Person, God the Father another.

And the Word was God.

Hilar.ii.
de Trin.
c. 15.

HILARY; Thou wilt say, that a word is the sound of the voice,
the enunciation of a thing, the expression of a thought: this
Word was in the beginning with God, because the utterance
of thought is eternal, when He who thinketh is eternal. But
how was that in the beginning, which exists no time either
before, or after, I doubt even whether *in* time at all? For
speech is neither in existence before one speaks, nor after; in
the very act of speaking it vanishes; for by the time a
speech is ended, that from which it began does not exist.
But even if the first sentence, *in the beginning was the Word,*
was through thy inattention lost upon thee, why disputest
thou about the next; *and the Word was with God?* Didst
thou hear it said, " *In* God," so that thou shouldest understand this Word to be only the expression of hidden
thoughts? Or did John say *with* by mistake, and was not

aware of the distinction between being *in,* and being *with,*
when he said, that what was in the beginning, was not
in God, but *with* God? Hear then the nature and name of
the Word; *and the Word was God.* No more then of the
sound of the voice, of the expression of the thought. The
Word here is a Substance, not a sound; a Nature, not an
expression; God, not a nonentity. HILARY; But the title is Hilar.
absolute, and free from the offence of an extraneous subject. Trin. c.
To Moses it is said, *I have given*[1] *thee for a god to* 9,10,11.
Pharaoh: but is not the reason for the name added, when it 1.
is said, *to Pharaoh?* Moses is given for a god to Pharaoh, Vulg.
when he is feared, when he is entreated, when he punishes, *made,*
when he heals. And it is one thing to be *given* for a God, Eng. Tr.
another thing to *be* God. I remember too another applica-
tion of the name in the Psalms, *I have said, ye are gods.* Ps. 82.
But there too it is implied that the title was but bestowed;
and the introduction of, *I said,* makes it rather the phrase
of the Speaker, than the name of the thing. But when I
hear *the Word was God,* I not only hear the Word said to
be, but perceive It proved to be, God. BASIL; Thus cutting Basil.
off the cavils of blasphemers, and those who ask what the in princ.
Word is, he replies, *and the Word was God.* THEOPHYL. Or Joan. c.
combine it thus. From the Word being with God, it follows 4.
plainly that there are two Persons. But these two are of
one Nature; and therefore it proceeds, *In the Word was
God:* to shew that Father and Son are of One Nature, being
of One Godhead. ORIGEN; We must add too, that the Orig.
Word illuminates the Prophets with Divine wisdom, in that in Joan.
He *cometh* to them; but that with God He ever is, because in princ.
He is God[a]. For which reason he placed *and the Word was
with God,* before *and the Word was God.* CHRYS. Not assert- Chrys.
ing, as Plato does, one to be intelligence[1], the other soul[2]; for [i.] §. 4.
the Divine Nature is very different from this. . . . . But you ¹ νοῦς
say, the Father is called God with the addition of the article, iv. [iii.]
the Son without it. What say you then, when the Apostle 3.

---

[a] The Greek has, πρὸς δὲ τὸν Θεὸν ὁ
Θεὸς ἀεὶ τυγχάνων, ἀπὸ τοῦ εἶναι πρὸς
αὐτόν. lit. but with God, God is present
at all times, because He is with Him,
i. e. τυγχάνειν and εἶναι are one with
God. The Word, as God, is always

equally present with God. S. Thomas
avoids the apparent tautology in the
original by substituting " apud Deum
vero est Verbum obtinere ab eo quod
sit Deus."

Tit. 2, 13.
Rom. 9, 5.
Rom. 1, 7. writes, *The great God and our Saviour Jesus Christ;* and again, *Who is over all, God;* and *Grace be unto you and peace from God our Father;* without the article? Besides, too, it were superfluous here, to affix what had been affixed just before. So that it does not follow, though the article is not affixed to the Son, that He is therefore an inferior God.

2. The same was in the beginning with God.

Hilar. ii. de Trin. c. 16. HILARY; Whereas he had said, *the Word was God,* the fearfulness, and strangeness of the speech disturbed me; the prophets having declared that God was One. But, to quiet my apprehensions, the fisherman reveals the scheme of this so great mystery, and refers all to one, without dishonour, without obliterating [the Person], without reference to time [b], saying, *The Same was in the beginning with God;* with One Unbegotten God, from whom He is, the One Only-begotten God. THEOPHYL. Again, to stop any diabolical suspicion, that the Word, because He was God, might have rebelled against His Father, as certain Gentiles fable, or, being separate, have become the antagonist of the Father Himself, he says, *The Same was in the beginning with God;* that is to say, this Word of God never existed separate from Chrys. Hom. iv. [iii.] §. 1. God. CHRYS. Or, lest hearing that *In the beginning was the Word,* you should regard It as eternal, but yet understand the Father's Life to have some degree of priority, he has introduced the words, *The Same was in the beginning with God.* For God was never solitary, apart from Him, but ibid. 3. always God with God. Or forasmuch as he said, *the Word was God,* that no one might think the Divinity of the Son inferior, he immediately subjoins the marks of proper τὸ ἀμετ- αμεγνεὸν Divinity, in that he both again mentions Eternity, *The Same was in the beginning with God;* and adds His attribute of Orig. tom. ii. in Joan. c. 4. Creator, *All things were made by Him.* ORIGEN; Or thus, the Evangelist having begun with those propositions, reunites them into one, saying, *The Same was in the beginning with*

---

[b] Since He was 1) "in the beginning," and 2) "God," and 3) "with God," He was 1) not "in time," nor 2) a word, but The Word, (see p. 8.)   nor 3) in existing in God only, so as to confound or destroy the Personality. [from S. Hil. l. c.]

God. For in the first of the three we learnt *in what* the Word was, that *it was in the beginning;* in the second, *with whom, with God;* in the third *who* the Word was, *God.* Having, then, by the term, The Same, set before us in a manner God the Word of Whom he had spoken, he collects all into the fourth proposition, viz. *In the beginning was the Word, and the Word was with God, and the Word was God;* into, *the Same was in the beginning with God.* It may be asked, however, why it is not said, In the beginning was the Word of God, and the Word of God was with God, and the Word of God was God? Now whoever will admit that truth is one, must needs admit also that the demonstration of truth, that is wisdom, is one. But if truth is one, and wisdom is one, the Word which enuntiates truth and developes wisdom in those who are capable of receiving it, must be One also. And therefore it would have been out of place here to have said, the Word of God, as if there were other words besides that of God, a word of angels, word of men, and so on. We do not say this, to deny that It is the Word of God, but to shew the use of omitting the word God. John himself too in the Apocalypse says, *And his Name is called the Word of God.* Rev. 19, ALCUIN; Wherefore does he use the substantive verb, *was?* [13] That you might understand that the Word, Which is co-eternal with God the Father, was before all time.

3. All things were made by him.

ALCUIN; After speaking of the nature of the Son, he proceeds to His operations, saying, *All things were made by him,* i. e. every thing whether substance, or property. HILARY; Hilar. Or thus: [It is said], the Word indeed was in the beginning, ii. de but it may be that He was not before the beginning. But c. 17. what saith he; *All things were made by him.* He is infinite by Whom every thing, which is, was made: and since all things were made by Him, time is likewise[c]. CHRYS. Moses Chrys. indeed, in the beginning of the Old Testament, speaks to Hom. v. us in much detail of the natural world, saying, *In the*

[c] That is to say, The text, *All things were made by Him,* makes up for the words, *in the beginning,* should these appear to fall short of eternity. For He Who made all things, made time, and so must have existed before time, i. e. from eternity.

beginning God made the heaven and the earth; and then relates how that the light, and the firmament, and the stars, and the various kinds of animals were created. But the Evangelist sums up the whole of this in a word, as familiar to his hearers; and hastens to loftier matter, making the whole of his book to bear not on the works, but on the

Aug. 1. Maker. Aug. Since *all things were made by him,* it is evident
de Gen. that light was also, when God said, *Let there be light.* And
ad lit.
cap. 2. in like manner the rest. But if so, that which God said, viz. *Let there be light,* is eternal. For the Word of God, God with God, is coeternal with the Father, though the world created by Him be temporal. For whereas our *when* and *sometimes* are words of time, in the Word of God, on the contrary, when a thing ought to be made, is eternal; and the thing is then made, when in that Word it is that it ought to be made, which Word hath in It neither *when,* or at *sometime,*

Aug. since It is all eternal. Aug. How then can the Word of God
in Joan. be *made,* when God by the Word made all things? For if the
tract. i.
c. 11. Word Itself were made, by what other Word was It made? If you say it was the Word of the Word by Which That was made, *that* Word I call the Only-Begotten Son of God.

[1] Ver- But if thou dost not call It the Word of the Word [1], then
bum
Verbi grant that that Word was not made, by which all things were
ed. Ben. made. Aug. And if It is not made, It is not a creature; but
Dei Aq.
Aug. de if It is not a creature, It is of the same Substance with the
Trin. i.
c.9.(vi.) Father. For every substance which is not God is a creature;
Theoph. and what is not a creature is God. Theophyl. The Arians
in loc. are wont to say, that all things are spoken of as made by the Son, in the sense in which we say a door is made by a saw, viz. as an instrument; not that He was Himself the Maker. And so they talk of the Son as a thing made, as if He were made for this purpose, that all things might be made by Him. Now we to the inventors of this lie reply simply: If, as ye say, the Father had created the Son, in order to make use of Him as an instrument, it would appear that the Son were less honourable than the things made, just as things made by a saw are more noble than the saw itself; the saw having been made for their sake. In like way do they speak of the Father creating the Son for the sake of the things made, as if, had He thought good to create the universe, neither would He have produced

the Son. What can be more insane than such language? They argue, however, why was it not said that the Word made all things, instead of the preposition *by*[1] being used?[1,A] For this reason, that thou mightest not understand an Unbegotten and Unoriginate Son, a rival God[d]. CHRYS. If the preposition *by* perplex thee, and thou wouldest learn from Scripture that the Word *Itself* made all things, hear David, *Thou, Lord, in the beginning hast laid the foundation of the earth, and the heavens are the work of Thy hands.* That he spoke this of the Only-Begotten, you learn from the Apostle, who in the Epistle to the Hebrews applies these words to the Son. CHRYS. But if you say that the prophet spoke this of the Father, and that Paul applied it to the Son, it comes to the same thing. For he would not have mentioned that as applicable to the Son, unless he fully considered that the Father and the Son were of equal dignity. If again thou dream that in the preposition *by* any subjection is implied, why does Paul use t of the Father? as, *God is faithful, by Whom ye were called into the fellowship of His Son;* and again, *Paul an Apostle by the will of God.* ORIGEN; Here too Valentinus errs, saying, that the Word supplied to the Creator the cause of the creation of the world[*]. If this interpretation is true, it should have been written that all things had their existence from the Word through the Creator, not contrariwise, through the Word from the Creator.

Margin notes: Chrys. Hom. in Joan. v. [iv.]c.2. Ps. 101. Chrys. Hom. v. c. 2. 3. 1 Cor.1, 9. 2 Cor.1, 1. Orig. tom. ii. o. 8.

And without him was not any thing made.

CHRYS. That you may not suppose, when he says, *All things were made by Him,* that he meant only the things Moses had spoken of, he seasonably brings in, *And without Him was not any thing made,* nothing, that is, cognizable either by the senses, or the understanding. Or thus; Lest you should suspect the sentence, *All things were made by Him,* to refer to the miracles which the other Evangelists had related, he adds, *and without Him was not any thing made.* HILARY; Or thus; That *all things were made by him,* is pronouncing

Margin notes: Chrys. Hom. v. in princ. Hilar. lib. ii. de Trin. c. 18.

---

[d] The text of Aug. has et Dei conditorem, perhaps it should be, et Deo contrarium, (as before Patri contrarium.) Theoph. has ἀντίθεον.

[*] τὸν τὴν αἰτίαν παρέχοντα τῆς γενέσεως τοῦ κόσμου τῷ δημιουργῷ. Origen is speaking of Heracleon, a disciple of Valentinus.

too much, it may be said. There is an Unbegotten Who is made of none, and there is the Son Himself begotten from Him Who is Unbegotten. The Evangelist however again implies the Author, when he speaks of Him as Associated; saying, *without Him was not any thing made.* This, that nothing was made without Him, I understand to mean the Son's not being alone, for ' by whom' is one thing, ' not with-out whom' another. ORIGEN: Or thus, that thou mightest not think that the things made by the Word had a separate existence, and were not contained in the Word, he says, *and without Him was not any thing made:* that is, not any thing was made externally of Him; for He encircles all things, as the Preserver of all things. AUG. Or, by saying, *without Him was not any thing made,* he tells us not to suspect Him in any sense to be a thing made. For how can He be a thing made, when God, it is said, made nothing without Him? ORIGEN; If all things were made by the Word, and in the number of all things is wickedness, and the whole influx of sin, these too were made by the Word; which is false. Now ' nothing' and ' a thing which is not,' mean the same. And the Apostle seems to call wicked things, things which are not, *God calleth those things which be not, as though they were.* All wickedness then is called *nothing,* forasmuch as it is made *without* the Word. Those who say however that the devil is not a creature of God, err. In so far as he is the devil, he is not a creature of God; but he, whose character it is to be the devil, is a creature of God. It is as if we should say a murderer is not a creature of God, when, so far as he is a man, he *is* a creature of God. AUG. For sin was not made by Him; for it is manifest that sin is nothing, and that men become nothing when they sin. Nor was an idol made by the Word. It has indeed a sort of form of man, and man himself was made by the Word; but the form of man in an idol was not made by the Word: for it is written, *we know that an idol is nothing.* These then were not made by the Word; but whatever things were made naturally, the whole universe, were; every creature from an angel to a worm. ORIGEN; Valentinus excludes from the things made by the Word, all that were made in the ages which he believes to have existed before the Word. This is plainly false ; inasmuch

Margin notes (left):
Orig. Hom.iii. in div. loc.

Aug. Quæst. Test. N. V. qu. 97.

Orig. in Joh. tom. ii. c. 7.

Rom. 4, 17.

Aug. in Joh. tract. i. c. 13.

1 Cor. 8, 4.

Orig. tom. ii. c. 8.

as the things which he accounts divine are thus excluded from the "all things," and what he deems wholly corrupt are properly ' all things!' Aug. The folly of those men is not to be listened to, who think *nothing* is to be understood here as *something*, because it is placed at the end of the sentence[1]: as if it made any difference whether it was said, without Him nothing was made, or, without Him was made nothing. Origen; If ' the word' be taken for that which is in each man, inasmuch as it was implanted in each by *the Word*, which *was in the beginning*, then also, we commit nothing without this ' word' [reason] taking this word ' nothing' in a popular sense. For the Apostle says that sin was dead without the law, but when the commandment came, sin revived; for sin is not imputed when there is no law. But neither was there sin, when there was no Word, for our Lord says, *If I had not come and spoken to them, they had not had sin.* For every excuse is withdrawn from the sinner, if, with the Word present, and enjoining what is to be done, he refuses to obey Him. Nor is the Word to be blamed on this account; any more than a master, whose discipline leaves no excuse open to a delinquent pupil on the ground of ignorance. All things then were made by the Word, not only the natural world, but also whatever is done by those acting without reason.

Aug. de Natura boni, c. 25.

[1] Vulgate

Orig. tom. ii. c. 9.

John 15, 22.

Vulg. quod factum est in ipso vita erat.

4. In him was life.

Bede; The Evangelist having said that every creature was made by the Word, lest perchance any one might think that His will was changeable, as though He willed on a sudden to make a creature, which from eternity he had not made; he took care to shew that, though a creature was made in time, in the Wisdom of the Creator it had been from eternity arranged what and when He should create. Aug. The passage can be read thus: *What was made in Him was life*[1]. Therefore the whole universe is life: for what was there not made in Him? He is the Wisdom of God, as is said, *In Wisdom hast Thou made them all.* All things therefore are made *in* Him, even as they are by Him. But, if whatever was made in Him is life, the earth is life, a stone is life. We must not interpret it so unsoundly, lest the sect of the

Bede in 1 Joh.

Aug. in Joh. tr. j. c. 16, 17.

[1] Vulg. Ps. 104.

Manicheans creep in upon us, and say, that a stone has life, and that a wall has life; for they do insanely assert so, and when reprehended or refuted, appeal as though to Scripture, and ask, why was it said, *That which was made in Him was life?* Read the passage then thus: make the stop after *What was made,* and then proceed, *In Him was life.* The earth was made; but, the earth itself which was made is not life. In the Wisdom of God however there is spiritually a certain Reason after which the earth is made. This is Life[']. A chest in workmanship is not life, a chest in art is, inasmuch as the mind of the workman lives wherein that original pattern exists. And in this sense the Wisdom of God, by Which all things are made, containeth in art ' all things which are made, according to that art.' And therefore whatever is made, is not in itself life, but is life in Him.

Origen.
Hom. ii.
in div.
loc. ante
med. ORIGEN; It may also be divided thus: *That which was made in him;* and then, *was life;* the sense being, that all things that were made by Him and in Him, are life in Him, and are one in Him. They *were,* that is, in Him; they exist as the cause, before they exist in themselves as effects. If thou ask how and in what manner all things which were made by the Word subsist in Him vitally, immutably, causally, take some examples from the created world. See how that all things within the arch of the world of sense have their causes simultaneously and harmoniously subsisting in that sun which is the greatest luminary of the world: how multitudinous crops of herbs and fruits are contained in single seeds: how the most complex variety of rules, in the art of the artificer, and the mind of the director, are a living unit, how an infinite number of lines coexist in one point. Contemplate these several instances, and thou wilt be able as it were on the wings of physical science, to penetrate with thy intellectual eye the secrets of the Word, and as far as is allowed to a human understanding, to see how all things

---

' The passage continues thus in the Tract. " I will explain my meaning. A workman makes a chest. He first has that chest in his art; for otherwise he could not make it. The chest however does not exist in his art, as a visible chest; it exists there invisibly, and is then brought into visible existence by workmanship. The chest is then first in workmanship; but does it cease to be in art? there it remains still, and there it will continue, the pattern of other chests, when the first visible one has rotted. Mark the distinction between a chest in art, and a chest in workmanship. A chest," &c.

which were made by the Word, live in Him, and were made in Him. HILARY; Or it can be understood thus. In that he had said, *without Him was not any thing made*, one might have been perplexed, and have asked, Was then any thing made by another, which yet was not made without Him? if so, then though nothing is made *without*, all things are not made *by* Him: it being one thing to make, another to be with the maker. On this account the Evangelist declares what it was which was not made without Him, viz. what was made in Him. This then it was which was not made without Him, viz. what was made in Him. And that which was made in Him, was also made by Him. For all things were created in Him and by Him. Now things were made *in* Him, because He was born God the Creator. And for this reason also things that were made in Him, were not made without Him, viz. that God, in that He was born, *was life*, and He who *was life*, was not made life after being born. Nothing then which was made in Him, was made without Him, because He was life, in Whom they were made; because God Who was born of God was God, not after, but in that He was born[b]. CHRYS. Or to give another explanation. We will not put the stop at *without Him was not any thing made*, as the heretics do. For they wishing to prove the Holy Ghost a creature, read, *That which was made in Him, was life*. But this cannot be so understood. For first, this was not the place for making mention of the Holy Ghost. But let us suppose it was; let us take the passage for the present according to their reading, we shall see that it leads to a difficulty. For when it is said, *That which was made in Him, was life;* they say the life spoken of is the Holy Ghost. But this life is also light; for the Evangelist proceeds, *The life was the light of men.* Wherefore according to them, he calls the Holy Ghost the light of all men. But the Word mentioned above, is what he here calls consecutively, God, and Life, and Light. Now *the Word was made flesh*. It follows that the Holy Ghost is incarnate, not the Son. Dismissing then this reading, we adopt a more suitable one, with the following meaning: *All things*

Chrys. Hom. v. [iv.] in Joan. c. 1, 2.

---

[b] i. e. the Son ever being what He is, in that He is, "Living of Living, Perfect of Perfect," not [as man] receiving subsequently, He was the Creator, in that He was, and always equally the Creator, and so of all things, because what He was, He was always, in that He was.

were made by Him, and without Him was not any thing made which was made: there we make a stop, and begin a fresh sentence: *In Him was life. Without Him was not* γινεται *any thing made which was made;* i. e. which could be made. You see how by this short addition, he removes any difficulty which might follow. For by introducing *without Him was not any thing made,* and adding, *which was made,* he includes all things invisible, and excepts the Holy Spirit: for δημιουρ- γιας the Spirit cannot be made. To the mention of creation, succeeds that of providence. *In Him was life¹.* As a fountain which produces vast depths of water, and yet is nothing diminished at the fountain head; so worketh the Only-Begotten. How great soever His creations be, He Himself is none the less for them. By the word *life* here is meant not only creation, but that providence by which the things created are preserved. But when you are told that *in Him was life,* do John 5, not suppose Him compounded; for, *as the Father hath life* 26. *in Himself, so hath He given to the Son to have life in Himself.* As then you would not call the Father compounded, so Orig. neither should you the Son. ORIGEN; Or thus: Our Saviour t.ii.c.12, is said to be some things not for Himself, but for others; 13. others again, both for Himself and others. When it is said then, *That which was made in Him was life;* we must enquire whether the life is for Himself and others, or for others only; and if for others, for whom? Now the Life and the Light are both the same Person: He is the light of men: He is therefore their life. The Saviour is called Life here, not to Himself, but to others; whose Light He also is. This life is inseparable from the Word, from the time it is added on to it. For Reason or the Word must exist before in the soul, cleansing it from sin, till it is pure enough to receive the life, which is thus ingrafted or inborn in every one who renders himself fit to receive the Word of God. Hence observe, that though the Word itself in the beginning was not made, the Beginning never having been without the Word; yet the life of men was not always in the Word. This life of men was *made,* in that It was the light of men; and

¹ τὸν περὶ τῆς προνοίας λόγον. *Life,* he says. The Hom. continues: Life, the Evangelist says, in order that we might not be incredulous as to so many things having come from Him. For as, &c.

this light of men could not be before man was; the light of men being understood relatively to men [k]. And therefore he says, That which was made in the Word was life; not That which *was* in the Word was life. Some copies read, not amiss, " That which *was made, in Him is life*." If we understand the life in the Word, to be He who says below, ' I *am* the life,' we shall confess that none who believe not in Christ live, and that all who live not in God, are dead. John 11, 25; 14, 6.

And the life was the light of men.

THEOPHYL. He had said, *In him was life*, that you might not suppose that the Word was without life. Now he shews that that life is spiritual, and the light of all reasonable creatures. *And the life was the light of men:* i. e. not sensible, but intellectual light, illuminating the very soul. AUG. Life of itself gives illumination to men, but to cattle not: for they have not rational souls, by which to discern wisdom: whereas man, being made in the image of God, has a rational soul, by which he can discern wisdom. Hence that life, by which all things are made, is light, not however of all animals whatsoever, but of men. THEOPHYL. He saith not, the Light of the Jews only, but of all men: for all of us, in so far as we have received intellect and reason, from that Word which created us, are said to be illuminated by Him. For the reason which is given to us, and which constitutes us the reasonable beings we are, is a light directing us what to do, and what not to do. ORIGEN; We must not omit to notice, that he puts the *life* before *the light of men*. For it would be a contradiction to suppose a being without life to be illuminated; as if life were an addition to illumination. But to proceed: if *the life was the light of men*, meaning men only, Christ is the light and the life of men only; an heretical supposition. It does not follow then, when a thing is predicated of any, that it is predicated of those only; for of God it is written, that He is the God of Abraham, Isaac, and Jacob; and yet He is not the God of those fathers' only. In the same way, the *light of men* is not excluded from being the light of others as well. Some moreover contend from

Theoph. in loc.

Aug. in Joh. tr. 1. c. 18.

Orig. non occ.

tom. ii. c. 16.

c. 17.

---

[k] τοῦ φῶτος τῶν ἀνθρώπων κατὰ τὴν πρὸς ἀνθρώπους σχέσιν νοουμένου.

Gen. 1, 26.

Genesis, *Let us make man after our image,* that man means whatever is made after the image and similitude of God. If so, the light of men is the light of any rational creature whatever.

5. And the light shineth in darkness.

Aug. tr. 1. c. 19.

AUG. Whereas that life is the light of men, but foolish hearts cannot receive that light, being so incumbered with sins that they cannot see it; for this cause lest any should think there is no light near them, because they cannot see it, he continues: *And the light shineth in darkness, and the darkness comprehended it not.* For suppose a blind man standing in the sun, the sun is present to him, but he is absent from the sun. In like manner every fool is blind, and wisdom is present to him; but, though present, absent from his sight, forasmuch as sight is gone: the truth being, not that she is absent from him, but that he is absent from her.

Orig. in Joan. t. ii. c. 14.

ORIGEN; This kind of darkness however is not in men by nature, according to the text in the Ephesians, *Ye were some-*

Eph. 5, 8.

time darkness, but now are ye light in the Lord[1]. ORIGEN;

Orig. Hom. ii. in div. loc.

Or thus, The light shineth in the darkness of faithful souls,

[1] Nicolai, for this passage which is incorrectly given, substitutes the following. (Origen, Tom. ii. c. 13. in Joh.) Now if the life is one with the light of men, none who in darkness lives, and none who lives is in darkness; since every one who lives is also in light, and conversely, whoever is in light, also lives. Again, as in thus discoursing on contraries, we may understand the contraries to them which are omitted, and life, and the light of men, are the subjects of our discourse; and the contrary of life is death, and the contrary of the light of men is the darkness of men: we may perceive, that whoever is in darkness, is also in death, and he who does the works of death, is certainly in darkness; whereas he who does the things which are of the light, that is, he whose works shine before men, and who is mindful of God, is not in death, as we read in Ps. vi. He is not in death who remembereth thee. 'Vulg. Quoniam non est in morte qui memor sit tui. Eng. T. In death no man remembereth thee. But whether men's darkness and death are so by nature or not, is another consideration. *We were*

sometime darkness, but now light in the Lord; although we be in some degree holy and spiritual. Whosoever was sometime darkness, did, as Paul, become darkness, although being capable and framed such as to be made light in the Lord. And again, The light of men is our Lord Jesus Christ, Who manifested Himself in human nature to every rational and intelligent creature, and opened to the hearts of the faithful the mysteries of His Divinity, in Which He is equal to the Father; according to the Apostle's saying, (Eph. 5, 8.) Ye were sometime darkness, but now are ye light in the Lord. Hence the light shineth in darkness, because the whole human race, not by nature but as the desert of original sin, was in the darkness of ignorance of the truth; but after His Birth of the Virgin, Christ shineth in the hearts of those who discern Him. But because there are some who still abide in the most profound darkness of impiety and deceit, the Evangelist adds, And the darkness comprehended it not; as though he would say, The Light, &c.

beginning from faith, and drawing onwards to hope; but the
deceit and ignorance of undisciplined souls did not comprehend the light of the Word of God shining in the flesh.
That however is an ethical meaning. The metaphysical
signification of the words is as follows. Human nature, even
though it sinned not, could not shine by its own strength
simply; for it is not naturally light, but only a recipient
of it; it is capable of containing wisdom, but is not wisdom
itself. As the air, of itself, shineth not, but is called by the
name of darkness, even so is our nature, considered in itself,
a dark substance, which however admits of and is made partaker of the light of wisdom. And as when the air receives
the sun's rays, it is not said to shine of itself, but the sun's
radiance to be apparent in it; so the reasonable part of our
nature, while possessing the presence of the Word of God,
does not of itself understand God, and intellectual things, but
by means of the divine light implanted in it. Thus, *The
light shineth in darkness:* for the Word of God, the life and
the light of men, ceaseth not to shine in our nature; though
regarded in itself, that nature is without form and darkness.
And forasmuch as pure light cannot be comprehended by any
creature, hence the text: *The darkness comprehended it not.*
CHRYS. Or thus: throughout the whole foregoing passage he
had been speaking of creation; then he mentions the spiritual
benefits which the Word brought with it: *and the life was the
light of men.* He saith not, the light of Jews, but of all men
without exception; for not the Jews only, but the Gentiles
also have come to this knowledge. The Angels he
omits, for he is speaking of human nature, to whom the
Word came bringing glad tidings. ORIGEN; But they ask,
why is not the Word Itself called the light of men, instead of
the life which is in the Word? We reply, that the life here
spoken of is not that which rational and irrational animals have
in common, but that which is annexed to the Word which is
within us through participation of the primæval Word. For we
must distinguish the external and false life, from the desirable
and true. We are first made partakers of life: and this life with
some is light potentially only, not in act; with those, viz. who
are not eager to search out the things which appertain to
knowledge: with others it is actual light, those who, as the

Chrys.
Hom. v.
[iv.]c.3.

Orig.
tom. ii.
in Joan.
c. 19.

1 Cor. 12, 31. c. 14. Apostle saith, covet earnestly the best gifts, that is to say, the word of wisdom. (If[k] the life and the light of men are the same, whoso is in darkness is proved not to live, and none

Chrys. Hom. v. [iv.]c. 3. who liveth abideth in darkness. CHRYS[l]. Life having come to us, the empire of death is dissolved; a light having shone upon us, there is darkness no longer: but there remaineth ever a life which death, a light which darkness cannot overcome. Whence he continues, *And the light shineth in darkness:* by darkness meaning death and error, for sensible light does not shine in darkness, but darkness must be removed first; whereas the preaching of Christ shone forth amidst the reign of error, and caused it to disappear, and Christ by dying changed death into life, so overcoming it, that, those who were already in its grasp, were brought back again. Forasmuch then as neither death nor error hath overcome his light, which is every where conspicuous, shining forth by its own strength; therefore he adds, *And*

Orig. tom. ii. c. 20. *the darkness comprehended it not*[m]. ORIGEN; As the light of men is a word expressing two spiritual things, so is darkness also. To one who possesses the light, we attribute both the doing the deeds of the light, and also true understanding, inasmuch as he is illuminated by the light of knowledge: and, on the other hand, the term darkness we apply both to unlawful acts, and also to that knowledge, which seems such, but is not. Now as the Father is light, and in Him is no darkness at all, so is the Saviour also. Yet, inasmuch as he underwent the similitude of our sinful flesh, it is not incorrectly said of Him, that in Him there was some darkness; for He took our darkness upon Himself, in order that He might dissipate it. This Light therefore, which was made the life of man, shines in the darkness of our hearts, when the prince of this darkness wars with the human race. This Light the darkness persecuted, as is clear from what our Saviour and His children suffer; the darkness fighting against

---

[k] Nicolai omits this clause, as not being Origen's, nor fitting in with what precedes and substitutes, "which is afterwards followed by the word of knowledge, &c."

[l] Nicolai inserts from S. Chrys., in order to make the connection clear, "The word 'life' means here not only that life which is received by creation, but that perpetual and immortal life which is prepared for us by the Providence of God" Life having, &c.

[m] i. e. could not *get hold* of it; for Chrysostom adds, it is too strong to be contended with.

the children of light. But, forasmuch as God takes up the cause, they do not prevail; nor do they apprehend the light, for they are either of too slow a nature to overtake the light's quick course, or, waiting for it to come up to them, they are put to flight at its approach. We should bear in mind, however, that darkness is not always used in a bad sense, but sometimes in a good, as in Psalm xvii. *He made darkness His* Ps. 18, *secret place :* the things of God being unknown and incompre- ^{11.} hensible. This darkness then I will call praiseworthy, since it tends toward light, and lays hold on it: for, though it were darkness before, while it was not known, yet it is turned to light and knowledge in him who has learned. AUG. A certain Platonist once said, that the beginning of this Aug. de Gospel ought to be copied in letters of gold, and placed Civit. Dei,l.x. in the most conspicuous place in every church. BEDE; c. 29. The other Evangelists describe Christ as born in time; Bede, cire. fin. John witnesseth that He was in the beginning, saying, in loc. *In the beginning was the Word.* The others describe His sudden appearance among men; he witnesseth that He was ever with God, saying, *And the Word was with God.* The others prove Him very man; he very God, saying, *And the Word was God.* The others exhibit Him as man conversing with men for a season; he pronounces Him God abiding with God in the beginning, saying, *The Same was in the beginning with God.* The others relate the great deeds which He did amongst men; he that God the Father made every creature through Him, saying, *All things were made by Him, and without Him was not any thing made.*

6. There was a man sent from God, whose name was John.

7. The same came for a witness, to bear witness of the Light, that all men through him might believe.

8. He was not that Light, but was sent to bear witness of that Light.

AUG. What is said above, refers to the Divinity of Christ. Aug. He came to us in the form of man, but man in such sense, as Tr. ii. c. 2, that the Godhead was concealed within Him. And therefore there was sent before a great man, to declare by his witness that He was more than man. And who was this? He was *a man.* THEOPHYL. Not an Angel, as many have held.

Aug. Tr. ii. The Evangelist here refutes such a notion. AUG. And how could he declare the truth concerning God, unless he were

Chrys. Hom. vi. [v.] c. 1. sent from God. CHRYS. After this esteem nothing that he says as human; for he speaketh not his own, but his that sent him. And therefore the Prophet calls him a messenger,

Mal. 3, 1. *I send My messenger,* for it is the excellence of a messenger, to say nothing of his own. But the expression, *was sent,* does

Isai. 6, 1. not mean his entrance into life, but to his office. As Esaias was sent on his commission, not from any place out of the world, but from where he saw the Lord sitting upon His high and lofty throne; in like manner John was sent from the desert

John 1, 33. to baptize; for he says, *He that sent me to baptize with water, the same said unto me, Upon Whom thou shalt see the Spirit descending, and remaining on Him, the same is He which*

Aug. Tr. ii. *baptizeth with the Holy Ghost.* AUG. What was he called? *whose name was John?* ALCUIN. That is, the grace of God, or one in whom is grace, who by his testimony first made known to the world the grace of the New Testament, that is, Christ. Or John may be taken to mean, to whom it is given: because that through the grace of God, to him it was given, not only to herald, but also to baptize the King of kings.

Aug. Tr. ii. c. 6. Orig. t. ii. c. 28. AUG. Wherefore came he? *The same came for a witness, to bear witness of the Light.* ORIGEN; Some try to undo the testimonies of the Prophets to Christ, by saying that the Son of God had no need of such witnesses; the wholesome words which He uttered and His miraculous acts being sufficient to produce belief; just as Moses deserved belief for his speech and goodness, and wanted no previous witnesses. To this we may reply, that, where there are a number of reasons to make people believe, persons are often impressed by one kind of proof, and not by another, and God, Who for the sake of all men became man, can give them many reasons for belief in Him. And with respect to the doctrine of the Incarnation, certain it is that some have been forced by the Prophetical writings into an admiration of Christ by the fact of so many prophets having, before His advent, fixed the place of His nativity; and by other proofs of the same kind. It is to be remembered too, that, though the display of miraculous powers might stimulate the faith of those who lived in the same age with Christ, they might, in the lapse of time, fail to do so ; as some of them might even get to be regarded as fabulous. Prophecy and miracles together are more convincing than simply past miracles by themselves. We must recollect too that men receive honour themselves from the witness which they bear to God. He deprives the Prophetical choir of immeasurable honour, whoever denies that it was their office to bear witness to Christ. John when he comes to bear witness to the light, follows in the train of those who went before him. CHRYS. Not because the light wanted the testimony, but for the reason which John himself gives, viz. *that all might believe on Him.* For as He put on flesh to save all men from death ; so He sent before Him a human preacher, that the sound of a voice like their own, might the readier draw men to Him. BEDE ; He saith not, that all men should believe *in* him ; for, *cursed be the man that trusteth in man ;* but, *that all men through him might believe ;* i. e. by his testimony believe in the Light. THEOPHYL. Though some however might not believe, he is not accountable for them. When a man shuts himself up in a dark room, so as to receive no light from the sun's rays, he is the cause of the deprivation, not the sun. In like manner John was sent, that all men might believe ; but if no such result followed, he is not the cause of the failure. CHRYS. Forasmuch however as with us, the one who witnesses, is commonly a more important, a more trustworthy person, than the one to whom he bears witness, to do away with any such notion in the present case the Evangelist proceeds ; *He was not that Light, but was sent to bear witness of that Light.* If this were not his intention, in repeating the words, *to bear witness of the Light,* the addition would be superfluous, and rather a verbal repetition, than the explanation of a truth. THEOPHYL. But it will be said, that we do not allow John or any of the saints to be or ever to have been light. The difference is this : If we call any of the saints light, we put light without the article. So if asked whether John is light, without the article, thou mayest allow without hesitation that he is : if with the article, thou allow it not. For he is not

Chrys.
Hom.
vi. [v.]
in Joh.
c. 1.

Bed. in
loc.
Jer. 17,
5.

Chrys.
Hom. vi.
in Joh.
c. 1.

very, original, light, but is only called so, on account of his partaking of the light, which cometh from the true Light.

9. That was the true Light which lighteth every man that cometh into the world.

Aug.
in Joan.
Tr. ii.

Chrys.
Hom.
in Joan.
vii. [vi.]
1.

Aug.
Tract. ii,
in Joh. §.
7.

AUG. What Light it is to which John bears witness, he shews himself, saying, *That was the true Light*. CHRYS. Or thus; Having said above that John had come, and was sent, to bear witness of the Light, lest any from the recent coming of the witness, should infer the same of Him who is witnessed to, the Evangelist takes us back to that existence which is beyond all beginning, saying, *That was the true Light*. AUG. Wherefore is there added, *true?* Because man enlightened is called light, but the true Light is that which lightens. For our eyes are called lights, and yet, without a lamp at night, or the sun by day, these lights are open to no purpose. Wherefore he adds: *which lighteneth every man:* but if every man, then John himself. He Himself then enlightened the person, by whom He wished Himself to be pointed out. And just as we may often, from the reflexion of the sun's rays on some object, know the sun to be risen, though we cannot look at the sun itself; as even feeble eyes can look at an illuminated wall, or some object of that kind: even so, those to whom Christ came, being too weak to behold Him, He threw His rays upon John; John confessed the illumination, and so the Illuminator Himself was discovered. It is said, *that cometh into the world.* Had man not departed from Him, he had not had to be enlightened; but therefore is he to be here enlightened, because he departed thence, when he might have been enlightened.

Theoph.
in loc.

THEOPHYL. Let the Manichean blush, who pronounces us the creatures of a dark and malignant creator: for we should never be enlightened, were

Chrys.
Hom.
viii. c. 2.

we not the children of the true Light. CHRYS. Where are those too, who deny Him to be very God? We see here that He is called very Light. But if He lighteneth every man that cometh into the world, how is it that so many have gone on without light? For all have not known the worship of Christ. The answer is: He only enlighteneth every man, so far as pertains to Him. If men shut their eyes, and will not receive the rays of this light, their darkness arises not from the fault of the light, but from their own wickedness, inasmuch as they voluntarily deprive themselves of the gift of grace. For grace is poured out upon all ; and they, who will not enjoy the gift, may impute it to their own blindness. AUG. Or the words, *lighteneth every man,* may be understood to mean, not that there is no one who is not enlightened, but that no one is enlightened except by Him. BEDE ; Including both natural and divine wisdom ; for as no one can exist of himself, so no one can be wise of himself. ORIGEN ; Or thus : We must not understand the words, *lighteneth every man that cometh into the world,* of the growth from hidden seeds to organized bodies, but of the entrance into the invisible world, by the spiritual regeneration and grace, which is given in Baptism. Those then the true Light lighteneth, who come into the world of goodness, not those who rush into the world of sin. THEOPHYL. Or thus : The intellect which is given in us for our direction, and which is called natural reason, is said here to be a light given us by God. But some by the ill use of their reason have darkened themselves.

Aug. de Pecc. Mer.
Bede; in et Remiss. i. c. xxv.
Orig. Hom. 2, in div. loc.
Theoph. in loc.

10. He was in the world, and the world was made by him, and the world knew him not.

AUG. The Light which lighteneth every man that cometh into the world, came here in the flesh ; because while He was here in His Divinity alone, the foolish, blind, and unrighteous could not discern Him ; those of whom it is said above, *The darkness comprehended it not.* Hence the text ; *He was in the world.* ORIGEN ; For as, when a person leaves off speaking, his voice ceases to be, and vanishes ; so if the Heavenly Father should cease to speak His Word, the effect of that Word, i. e. the universe which is created in the Word, shall cease to exist. AUG. You must not suppose, however, that He was in the world in the same sense in which the earth, cattle, men, are in the world ; but in the sense in which an artificer controls his own work ; whence the text, *And the world was made by Him.* Nor again did He make it after the manner of an artificer ; for whereas an artificer is

Aug. Tr. in Joan. ii. c. 8.
Orig. Hom. 2 in div. loc.
Aug. Tr. ii. c. 10.

external to what he fabricates, God pervades the world,
carrying on the work of creation in every part, and never
absent from any part: by the presence of His Majesty He
both makes and controls what is made. Thus *He was in the*
world, as He by Whom the world was made. CHRYS. And
again, because He was in the world, but not coeval with the
world, for this cause he introduced the words, *and the world*
was made by Him: thus taking you back again to the eternal
existence of the Only-Begotten. For when we are told that
the whole of creation was made by Him, we must be very
dull not to acknowledge that the Maker existed before the
work. THEOPHYL. Here he overthrows at once the insane
notion of the Manichæan°, who says that the world is the work
of a malignant creature, and the opinion of the Arian, that
the Son of God is a creature. AUG. But what meaneth this,
The world was made by Him ? The earth, sky, and sea, and
all that are therein, are called the world. But in another
sense, the lovers of the world are called the world, of whom
he says, *And the world knew Him not.* For did the sky, or
Angels, not know their Creator, Whom the very devils confess, Whom the whole universe has borne witness to ? Who
then did not know Him ? Those who, from their love of the
world, are called the world; for such live in heart in the
world, while those who do not love it, have their body in the
world, but their heart in heaven; as saith the Apostle, *our*
conversation is in heaven. By their love of the world, such
men merit being called by the name of the place where they
live. And just as in speaking of a bad house, or good house,
we do not mean praise or blame to the walls, but to the
inhabitants; so when we talk of the world, we mean those
who live there in the love of it. CHRYS. But they who were
the friends of God, knew Him even before His presence in the
body; whence Christ saith below, *Your father Abraham re-*
joiced to see My day. When the Gentiles then interrupt us with
the question, Why has He come in these last times to work
our salvation, having neglected us so long? we reply, that
He was in the world before, superintending what He had
made, and was known to all who were worthy of Him; and
that, if the world knew Him not, those of whom the world

Chrys. Hom. in Joan. viii. c. 1.

Theoph. in loc.

Aug. Tr. in Joan. ii. c. 11.

Phil. 3, 20.

Chrys. Hom. viii. c. 8. 56.

° So Theoph. Other copies have "of Marcion."

was not worthy knew Him. The reason follows, why *the world knew Him not.* The Evangelist calls those men the world, who are tied to the world, and savour of worldly things; for there is nothing that disturbs the mind so much, as this melting with the love of present things.

11. He came unto his own, and his own received him not.

12. But as many as received him, to them gave he power to become the sons of God, even to them that believe on his name:

13. Which were born, not of blood, nor of the will of the flesh, nor of the will of man, but of God.

CHRYS. When He said that the world knew Him not, he referred to the times of the old dispensation, but what follows has reference to the time of his preaching; *He came unto his own.* AUG. Because all things were made by Him. THEO-PHYL. By *his own,* understand either the world, or Judæa, which He had chosen for His inheritance. CHRYS. He came then unto His own, not for His own good, but for the good of others. But whence did He Who fills all things, and is every where present, come? He came out of condescension to us, though in reality He had been in the world all along. But the world not seeing Him, because it knew Him not, He deigned to put on flesh. And this manifestation and conde-scension is called His advent. But the merciful God so con-trives His dispensations, that we may shine forth in propor-tion to our goodness, and therefore He will not compel, but invites men, by persuasion and kindness, to come of their own accord: and so, when He came, some received Him, and others received Him not. He desires not an unwilling and forced service; for no one who comes unwillingly devotes himself wholly to Him. Whence what follows, *And his own received him not.* He here calls the Jews His own, as being his peculiar people; as indeed are all men in some sense, being made by Him. And as above, to the shame of our common nature, he said, that the world which was made by Him, knew not its Maker: so here again, indignant at the in-

(margin notes:) Chrys. Hom. in Joan. ix. 1. Aug. in Joan. Tr. i. Chrys. Hom. x. [ix.] 2. Hom. ix. [viii.] 1.

gratitude of the Jews, he brings a heavier charge, viz. that *His*

Aug.Tr. in Joan. ii. 12. *own received Him not.* AUG. But if none at all received, none will be saved. For no one will be saved, but he who received Christ at His coming; and therefore he adds, *As*

Chrys. Hom. in Joan. x. [ix.] 2. *many as received Him.* CHRYS. Whether they be bond or free, Greek or Barbarian, wise or unwise, women or men, the young or the aged, all are made meet for the honour, which the Evangelist now proceeds to mention. *To them gave He*

Aug. Tr.ii.13. *power to become the sons of God.* AUG. O amazing goodness! He was born the Only Son, yet would not remain so; but grudged not to admit joint heirs to His inheritance. Nor was

Chrys. Hom. x. [ix.] 2. this narrowed by many partaking of it. CHRYS. He saith not that He made them the sons of God, but gave them power to become the sons of God: shewing that there is need of much care, to preserve the image, which is formed by our adoption in Baptism, untarnished: and shewing at the same time also that no one can take this power from us, except we rob ourselves of it. Now, if the delegates of worldly governments have often nearly as much power as those governments themselves, much more is this the case with us, who derive our dignity from God. But at the same time the Evangelist wishes to shew that this grace comes to us of our own will and endeavour: that, in short, the operation of grace being supposed, it is in the power of our free will to make us the sons of God. THEOPHYL. Or the meaning is, that the most perfect sonship will only be attained at the resurrection, as

Rom. 8, 23. saith the Apostle, *Waiting for the adoption, to wit, the redemption of our body.* He therefore gave us the power to become the sons of God, i. e. the power of obtaining this

Chrys. Hom. x. 2. grace at some future time. CHRYS. And because in the matter of these ineffable benefits, the giving of grace belongs to God, but the extending of faith to man, He subjoins, *even to those who believe on his name.* Why then declarest thou not, John, the punishment of those who received Him not? Is it because there is no greater punishment than that, when the power of becoming the sons of God is offered to men, they should not become such, but voluntarily deprive themselves of the dignity? But besides this, inextinguishable

Aug.Tr. ii. 14. fire awaits all such, as will appear clearly farther on. AUG. To be made then the sons of God, and brothers of Christ,

they must of course be born; for if they are not born, how
can they be sons? Now the sons of men are born of flesh
and blood, and the will of man, and the embrace of wedlock;
but how *these* are born, the next words declare: *Not of
bloods*[1]; that is, the male's and the female's. Bloods is not
correct Latin, but as it is plural in the Greek, the translator
preferred to put it so, though it be not strictly grammatical,
at the same time explaining the word in order not to offend
the weakness of one's hearers. BEDE; It should be understood
that in holy Scripture, blood in the plural number, has the
signification of sin : thus in the Psalms, *Deliver me from blood-
guiltiness*[2]. AUG. In that which follows, *Nor of the will of
the flesh, nor of the will of man*, the flesh is put for the
female; because, when she was made out of the rib, Adam
said, *This is now bone of my bone, and flesh of my flesh.*
The flesh therefore is put for the wife, as the spirit sometimes is for the husband; because that the one ought to
govern, the other to obey. For what is there worse than an
house, where the woman hath rule over the man ? But these
that we speak of are born neither of the will of the flesh,
nor the will of man, *but of God.* BEDE; The carnal birth
of men derives its origin from the embrace of wedlock, but
the spiritual is dispensed by the grace of the Holy Spirit.
CHRYS. The Evangelist makes this declaration, that being
taught the vileness and inferiority of our former birth, which
is through blood, and the will of the flesh, and understanding
the loftiness and nobleness of the second, which is through
grace, we might hence receive great knowledge, worthy of
being bestowed by him who begat us, and after this shew
forth much zeal.

*(margin: ἐξ αἱμά-
των)*

*(margin: Ps. 51,
14.
Aug.
Tr.ii.14.)*

*(margin: Gen. 2,
23.)*

*(margin: Chrys.
Hom. x.
[ix.] 3.)*

14. And the Word was made flesh, and dwelt among us.

AUG. Having said, *Born of God;* to prevent surprise and
trepidation at so great, so apparently incredible a grace,
as that men should be born of God; to assure us, he says,
And the Word was made flesh. Why marvellest thou then
that men are born of God? Know that God Himself
was born of man. CHRYS. Or thus, After saying that they

*(margin: Aug.
Tr.ii.15.)*

*(margin: Chrys.
Hom.
xi. [x.]
1.)*

[1] Plur. in the Vulg. as in the Heb.

were born of God, who received Him, he sets forth the cause
of this honour, viz. the Word being made flesh, God's own
Son was made the son of man, that he might make the sons
of men the sons of God.   Now when thou hearest that
the Word was made flesh, be not disturbed, for He did not
change His substance into flesh, which it were indeed
impious to suppose; but remaining what He was, took upon
Him the form of a servant.   But as there are some who say,
that the whole of the incarnation was only in appearance,
to refute such a blasphemy, he used the expression, *was
made*, meaning to represent not a conversion of substance,
but an assumption of real flesh.   But if they say, God is
omnipotent; why then could He not be changed into flesh?
we reply, that a change from an unchangeable nature is

Aug.
de Trin.
xv. c.20.
(xi.)
a contradiction.   Aug. As our word[q] becomes the bodily
voice, by its assumption of that voice, as a means of developing
itself externally; so the Word of God was made flesh, by
assuming flesh, as a means of manifesting Itself to the world.
And as our word is made voice, yet is not turned into voice;
so the Word of God was made flesh, but never turned into
flesh.   It is by *assuming* another nature, not by *consuming*
themselves in it, that our word is made voice, and the Word,

P. iii.
Hom.
Theod.
Ancyr.
de Nat.
Dom.
flesh.   Ex Gestis Conc. Eph. The discourse which we utter,
which we use in conversation with each other, is incorporeal,
imperceptible, impalpable; but clothed in letters and characters, it becomes material, perceptible, tangible.   So too the
Word of God, which was naturally invisible, becomes visible,
and that comes before us in tangible form, which was by nature

in Joan.
1, 1.
incorporeal.   Alcuin. When we think how the incorporeal
soul is joined to the body, so as that of two is made one
man, we too shall the more easily receive the notion of the
incorporeal Divine substance being joined to the soul in the
body, in unity of person; so as that the Word is not turned
into flesh, nor the flesh into the Word; just as the soul is
not turned into body, nor the body into soul.

Theoph.
in loc.
Theophyl. Apollinarius of Laodicea raised a heresy upon
this text; saying, that Christ had flesh only, not a rational
soul; in the place of which His divinity directed and con-
trolled His body.   Aug. If men are disturbed however by its

Aug.
con.
Serm.
Arian.
c. 7. (9.)

[q] See above, p. 1—3.

being said that *the Word was made flesh*, without mention of a soul; let them know that the flesh is put for the whole man, the part for the whole, by a figure of speech; as in the Psalms, *Unto thee shall all flesh come;* and again in Romans, *By the deeds of the law there shall no flesh be justified.* In the same sense it is said here that *the Word was made flesh;* meaning that the Word was made man. Ps.65,2. Rom. 3, 20.

THEOPHYL. The Evangelist intends by making mention of the flesh, to shew the unspeakable condescension of God, and lead us to admire His compassion, in assuming for our salvation, what was so opposite and incongenial to His nature, as the flesh: for the *soul* has some propinquity to God. If the Word, however, was made flesh, and assumed not at the same time a human soul, our souls, it would follow, would not be yet restored: for what He did not assume, He could not sanctify. What a mockery then, when the soul first sinned, to assume and sanctify the flesh only, leaving the weakest part untouched! This text overthrows Nestorius, who asserted that it was not the very Word, even God, Who the Self-same was made man, being conceived of the sacred blood of the Virgin: but that the Virgin brought forth a man endowed with every kind of virtue, and that the Word of God was united to him: thus making out two sons, one born of the Virgin, i. e. man, the other born of God, that is, the Son of God, united to that man by grace, and relation, and love[r]. In opposition to him the Evangelist declares, that the very Word was made Man, not that the Word fixing upon a righteous man united Himself to him. CYRIL; The Word uniting to Himself a body of flesh animated with a rational soul, substantially, was ineffably and incomprehensibly made Man, and called the Son of man, and that not according to the will only, or good-pleasure, nor again by the assumption of the Person alone. The natures are different indeed which are brought into true union, but He Who is of both, Christ the Son, is One; the difference of the natures, on the Theoph. in loc. Cyril. ad Nes. Ep.

---

[r] The union of the two Natures in our Lord, κατὰ σχέσιν, or σχετικὴ συνάφεια, in the Nestorian heresy, stands opposed to the belief of their "natural" ἕνωσις φυσικὴ in one Person. σχέσις is used for "relation, cognateness, affection, conjunction," to describe a "nearness" of the Manhood, as united *externally,* by dignity, or likeness of honour, or unity of will, or good-pleasure, or love, or affection, or power, instead of being "taken into God." See Petav. de Incarn. iii. 3.

other hand, not being destroyed in consequence of this coa-
Theoph. lition. THEOPHYL. From the text, *The Word was made flesh,*
in v. 14. we learn this farther, that the Word Itself is man, and being
the Son of God was made the Son of a woman, who is rightly
called the Mother of God, as having given birth to God in the
Hil. x. flesh. HILARY; Some, however, who think God the Only-Be-
de Trin.
c. 21,22. gotten, God the Word, Who was in the beginning with God, not
to be God substantially, but a Word sent forth, the Son being
to God the Father, what a word is to one who utters it, these
men, in order to disprove that the Word, being substantially
God, and abiding in the form of God, was born the Man Christ,
argue subtilly, that, whereas that Man (they say) derived His
life rather from human origin than from the mystery of a
spiritual conception, God the Word did not make Himself
Man of the womb of the Virgin; but that the Word of God
was in Jesus, as the spirit of prophecy in the Prophets. And
they are accustomed to charge us with holding, that Christ
was born a Man, not ʳ of our body and soul; whereas we
preach the Word made flesh, and after our likeness born
Man, so that He Who is truly Son of God, was truly born
Son of man; and that, as by His own act He took upon Him
a body of the Virgin, so of Himself He took a soul also, which
in no case is derived from man by mere parental origin.
And seeing He, The Self-same, is the Son of man, how
absurd were it, besides the Son of God, Who is the Word,
to make Him another person besides, a sort of prophet, in-
spired by the Word of God; whereas our Lord Jesus Christ
Chrys. is both the Son of God, and the Son of man. CHRYS. Lest
Hom.
in Joan. from it being said, however, that *the Word was made flesh,*
xi. [x.] you should infer improperly a change of His incorruptible
2. nature, he subjoins, *And dwelt among us.* For that which
inhabits is not the same, but different from the habitation:
different, I say, in nature; though as to union and conjunction,
God the Word and the flesh are one, without confusion or
extinction of substance. ALCUIN; Or, *dwelt among us,*
means, lived amongst men.

14. And we saw his glory, the glory as of the only
begotten of the Father, full of grace and truth.

ʳ non is omitted in some MS; but   throughout guards against Sabellianism.
S. Hilary in writing against the Arians,   Ben.

CHRYS. Having said that we are made the sons of God, and in no other way than because *the Word was made flesh;* he mentions another gift, *And we saw His glory.* Which glory we should not have seen, had He not, by His alliance with humanity, become visible to us. For if they could not endure to look on the glorified face of Moses, but there was need of a veil, how could soiled and earthly creatures, like ourselves, have borne the sight of undisguised Divinity, which is not vouchsafed even to the higher powers themselves. AUG. Or thus; in that *the Word was made flesh and dwelt among us,* His birth became a kind of ointment to anoint the eyes of our heart, that we might through His humanity discern His majesty; and therefore it follows, *And we saw His glory.* No one could see His glory, who was not healed by the humility of the flesh. For there had flown upon man's eye as it were dust from the earth: the eye had been diseased, and earth was sent to heal it again; the flesh had blinded thee, the flesh restores thee. The soul by consenting to carnal affections had become carnal; hence the eye of the mind had been blinded : then the physician made for thee ointment. He came in such wise, as that by the flesh He destroyed the corruption of the flesh. And thus *the Word was made flesh,* that thou mightest be able to say, *We saw His glory.* CHRYS. He subjoins, *As of the Only-Begotten of the Father:* for many prophets, as Moses, Elijah, and others, workers of miracles, had been glorified, and Angels also who appeared unto men, shining with the brightness belonging to their nature; Cherubim and Seraphim too, who were seen in glorious array by the prophets. But the Evangelist withdrawing our minds from these, and raising them above all nature, and every preeminence of fellow servants, leads us up to the summit Himself; as if he said, Not of prophet, or of any other man, or of Angel, or of Archangel, or any of the higher powers, is the glory which we beheld; but as that of the very Lord, very King, very and true Only-Begotten Son. GREG. In Scripture language *as,* and *as it were,* are sometimes put not for likeness but reality ; whence the expression, *As of the Only-Begotten of the Father.* CHRYS. As if he said : We saw His glory, such as it was becoming and proper for the Only-Begotten and true Son to have. We have a

Side notes: Chrys. Hom. xii.[xi.] 1. | Aug. in Joan. Tr. ii. c. 16. | Chrys. Hom. in Joan. xii.[xi.] 1. | Greg. lxviii. Moral. c.6.(12.) | Chrys. Hom. xii.[xi.] 1.

D 2

form of speech, like it, derived from our seeing kings always
splendidly robed.   When the dignity of a man's carriage is
beyond description, we say, *In short, he went as a king.*
So too John says, *We saw His glory, the glory as of the Only
Begotten of the Father.*   For Angels, when they appeared,
did every thing as servants who had a Lord, but He as
the Lord appearing in humble form.   Yet did all creatures
recognise their Lord, the star calling the Magi, the Angels
the shepherds, the child leaping in the womb acknowledged
Him: yea the Father bore witness to Him from heaven, and
the Paraclete descending upon Him: and the very universe
itself shouted louder than any trumpet, that the King of
heaven had come.   For devils fled, diseases were healed, the
graves gave up the dead, and souls were brought out of
wickedness, to the utmost height of virtue.   What shall
one say of the wisdom of precepts, of the virtue of heavenly
laws, of the excellent institution of the angelical life?
Origen. ORIGEN; *Full of grace and truth.* Of this the meaning is two-
Hom. 2. fold.   For it may be understood of the Humanity, and the
Divinity of the Incarnate Word, so that the fulness of grace
has reference to the Humanity, according to which Christ is
the Head of the Church, and the first-born of every creature:
for the greatest and original example of grace, by which
man, with no preceding merits, is made God, is manifested
primarily in Him.   The fulness of the grace of Christ may
also be understood of the Holy Spirit, whose sevenfold
Is.11,2. operation filled Christ's Humanity.   The fulness of truth
applies to the Divinity..........But if you had rather understand the fulness of grace and truth of the New Testament,
you may with propriety pronounce the fulness of the grace of
the New Testament to be given by Christ, and the truth of
Theoph. the legal types to have been fulfilled in Him.   THEOPHYL.
hoc loc. Or, *full of grace,* inasmuch as His word was gracious, as saith
Ps.45,3. David, *Full of grace are thy lips; and truth,* because what
Moses and the Prophets spoke or did in figure, Christ did in
reality.

15. John bare witness of him, and cried, saying,
This was he of whom I spake, He that cometh after
me is preferred before me, for he was before me.

ALCUIN; He had said before that there was a man sent to bear witness; now he gives definitely the forerunner's own testimony, which plainly declared the excellence of His Human Nature and the Eternity of His Godhead. *John bare witness of Him.* CHRYS. Or he introduces this, as if to say, Do not suppose that we bear witness to this out of gratitude, because we were with Him a long time, and partook of His table; for John who had never seen Him before, nor tarried with Him, bare witness to Him. The Evangelist repeats John's testimony many times here and there, because he was held in such admiration by the Jews. Other Evangelists refer to the old prophets, and say, *This was done that it might be fulfilled which was spoken by the prophet.* But he introduces a loftier, and later witness, not intending to make the servant vouch for the master, but only condescending to the weakness of his hearers. For as Christ would not have been so readily received, had He not taken upon Him the form of a servant; so if he had not excited the attention of servants by the voice of a fellow-servant beforehand, there would not have been many Jews embracing the word of Christ. It follows, *And cried;* that is, preached with openness, with freedom, without reservation. He did not however begin with asserting that this one was the natural only-begotten Son of God, but cried, saying, *This was He of whom I spake, He that cometh after me is preferred before me, for He was before me.* For as birds do not teach their young all at once to fly, but first draw them outside the nest, and afterwards try them with a quicker motion; so John did not immediately lead the Jews to high things, but began with lesser flights, saying, that Christ was better than he; which in the mean time was no little advance. And observe how prudently he introduces his testimony; he not only points to Christ when He appears, but preaches Him beforehand; as, *This is He of whom I spake.* This would prepare men's minds for Christ's coming: so that when He did come, the humility of His garb would be no impediment to His being received. For Christ adopted so humble and common an appearance, that if men had seen Him without first hearing John's testimony to His greatness, none of the things spoken of Him would have had any effect. THEOPHYL. He saith,

Chrys. Hom. in Joan. xiii. [xii.] 1, 2, 3.

Who cometh after me, that is, as to the time of His birth. John
was six months before Christ, according to His humanity.

Chrys. Hom. xiii. [xii.] 3. CHRYS. Or this does not refer to the birth from Mary; for
Christ was born, when this was said by John; but to His
coming for the work of preaching. He then saith, *is made*[*]
before me; that is, is more illustrious, more honourable; as if
he said, Do not suppose me greater than He, because I came

Theoph. in loc. 1 γίγονε first to preach. THEOPHYL. The Arians infer from this word[1],
that the Son of God is not begotten of the Father, but made

Aug. in Joan. Tr. 3. like any other creature. AUG. It does not mean—He was
made before I was made; but He is preferred to me. CHRYS.

Chrys. Hom. xiii. [xii.] 3. If the words, *made before me*, referred to His coming into
being, it was superfluous to add, *For He was before me*. For
who would be so foolish as not to know, that if He was *made*
before him, He *was* before him. It would have been more
correct to say, He was before me, because He was made before
me. The expression then, *He was made before me*, must be
taken in the sense of honour: only that which was to take
place, he speaks of as having taken place already, after the
style of the old Prophets, who commonly talk of the future as
the past.

16. And of his fulness have all we received, and
grace for grace.

17. For the law was given by Moses, but grace and
truth came by Jesus Christ.

Orig. in Joan. t. vi. 3. v. 18. ORIGEN; This is to be considered a continuation of the
Baptist's testimony to Christ, a point which has escaped the
attention of many, who think that from this to, *He hath
declared Him*, St. John the Apostle is speaking. But the
idea that on a sudden, and, as it would seem, unseasonably,
the discourse of the Baptist should be interrupted by a
speech of the disciple's, is inadmissible. And any one, able
to follow the passage, will discern a very obvious connexion
here. For having said, *He is preferred before me, for He
was before me*, he proceeds, From this I know that He is
before me, because I and the Prophets who preceded me

---

[*] γίγονε. Vulg. *factus*. Eng. T. *preferred*.

have received of His fulness, and grace for grace, (the second
grace for the first.)   For they too by the Spirit penetrated
beyond the figure to the contemplation of the truth.   And
hence receiving, as we have done, of his fulness, we judge
that the law was given by Moses, but that grace and truth
were made[1], by Jesus Christ—made, not given: the Father ¹ἐγένετο:
gave the law by Moses, but made grace and truth by Jesus. ^{facta}_{Vulg.}
But if it is Jesus who says below, *I am the Truth*, how is E. T.
truth made by Jesus?   We must understand however that ^{came.}John14,
the very substantial Truth[2], from which First Truth and Its ^{6.}
Image many truths are engraven on those who treat of the ²αὐτο-
truth, was not made through Jesus Christ, or through any ^{αλήθεια}
one; but only the truth which is in individuals, such as in
Paul, e. g. or the other Apostles, was made through Jesus
Christ.   CHRYS. Or thus; John the Evangelist here adds Chrys.
his testimony to that of John the Baptist, saying, *And* ^{in Joan.}_{Hom.}
of his fulness have we all received.   These are not the xiv.
words of the forerunner, but of the disciple; as if he meant ^[xiii.] I.
to say, We also the twelve, and the whole body of the
faithful, both present and to come, have received of His
fulness.   AUG. But what have ye received? *Grace for grace.* Aug.
So that we are to understand that we have received a certain ^{in Joan.}_{Tr. iii.}
something from His fulness, and over and above this, *grace for* c. 8.
grace; that we have first received of His fulness, first grace; ^{et seq.}
and again, we have received grace for grace.   What grace
did we first receive?   Faith: which is called grace, because
it is given freely[3].   This is the first grace then which the ³ gratis
sinner receives, the remission of his sins.   Again, we have
grace for grace; i. e. in stead of that grace in which we live
by faith, we are to receive another, viz. life eternal: for life
eternal is as it were the wages of faith.   And thus as faith
itself is a good grace, so life eternal is grace for grace.   There
was not grace in the Old Testament; for the law threatened,
but assisted not, commanded, but healed not, shewed our weakness, but relieved it not.   It prepared the way however for
a Physician who was about to come, with the gifts of grace
and truth: whence the sentence which follows: *For the law*
was given by Moses, but grace and truth were made by Jesus
Christ.   The death of thy Lord hath destroyed death, both
temporal and eternal; that is the grace which was promised,

Chrys.
Hom.
xiv.
[xiii.]
sparsim.
but not contained, in the law.   CHRYS. Or we have received
grace for grace; that is, the new in the place of the old.
For as there is a justice and a justice besides, an adoption
and another adoption, a circumcision and another circumcision; so is there a grace and another grace: only the one
being a type, the other a reality.   He brings in the words to
shew that the Jews as well as ourselves are saved by grace:
it being of mercy and grace that they received the law.
Next, after he has said, *Grace for grace,* he adds something
to shew the magnitude of the gift; *For the law was given
by Moses, but grace and truth were made by Jesus
Christ.*   John when comparing himself with Christ above
had said, *He is preferred before me:* but the Evangelist
draws a comparison between Christ, and one much more
in admiration with the Jews than John, viz. Moses.   And
observe his wisdom.   He does not draw the comparison
between the persons, but the things, contrasting grace and
truth to the law: the latter of which he says *was given,*
a word only applying to an administrator; the former *made,*
as we should speak of a king, who does every thing by
his power: though in this King it would be with grace also,
because that with power He remitted all sins.   Now His
grace is shewn in His gift of Baptism, and our adoption by
the Holy Spirit, and many other things; but to have a better
insight into what the truth is, we should study the figures
of the old law: for what was to be accomplished in the New
Testament, is prefigured in the Old, Christ at His Coming
filling up the figure.   Thus was the figure given by Moses,

Aug.
de Trin.
xiii. c.
24.(xix.)
but the truth made by Christ.   AUG. Or, we may refer
grace to knowledge, truth to wisdom.   Amongst the events
of time the highest grace is the uniting of man to God in
One Person; in the eternal world the highest truth pertains
to God the Word.

18. No man hath seen God at any time; the only
begotten Son, which is in the bosom of the Father, he
hath declared him.

Orig.
in Joan.
t. vi. §.2.
ORIGEN; Heracleon asserts, that this is a declaration of
the disciple, not of the Baptist: an unreasonable supposition;

for if the words, *Of His fulness have we all received*, are the
Baptist's, does not the connexion run naturally, that he
receiving of the grace of Christ, the second in the place of
the first grace, and confessing that the law was given by Moses,
but grace and truth came by Jesus Christ; understood here
that no man had seen God at any time, and that the Only
Begotten, who was in the bosom of the Father, had committed
this declaration of Himself to John, and all who with him
had received of His fulness? For John was not the first
who declared Him; for He Himself who was before Abraham,
tells us, that Abraham rejoiced to see His glory. CHRYS. Or Chrys.
thus; the Evangelist after shewing the great superiority of in Joan.
Christ's gifts, compared with those dispensed by Moses, xiv.
wishes in the next place to supply an adequate reason for [xiii.] 1.
the difference. The one being a servant was made a minister
of a lesser dispensation: but the other Who was Lord, and Son
of the King, brought us far higher things, being ever coexistent
with the Father, and *beholding* Him. Then follows, *No man
hath seen God at any time, &c.* AUG. What is that then Aug.
which Jacob said, *I have seen God face to face;* and that Ep. to Paulina
which is written of Moses, *he talked with God face to face;* (Ep.
and that which the prophet Isaiah saith of himself, *I saw the* 147.
Lord sitting upon a throne? GREG. It is plainly given us to c. 5.)
understand here, that while we are in this mortal state, we Ex. 33.
can see God only through the medium of certain images, not Isa. 6.
in the reality of His own nature. A soul influenced by the grace xviii.
of the Spirit may see God through certain figures, but cannot Moral.
penetrate into his absolute essence. And hence it is that Jacob, (88.)
who testifies that he saw God, saw nothing but an Angel: and rec. 28.
that Moses, who talked with God face to face, says, *Shew me* Exod.
Thy way, that I may know Thee: meaning that he ardently 33, 13.
desired to see in the brightness of His own infinite Nature, Him
Whom he had only as yet seen reflected in images. CHRYS. Chrys.
If the old fathers had seen That very Nature, they would Hom.
not have contemplated It so variously, for It is in Itself simple [xiv.]
and without shape; It sits not, It walks not; these are the
qualities of bodies. Whence he saith through the Prophet,
I have multiplied visions, and used similitudes, by the Hosea
ministry of the Prophets: i. e. I have condescended to them, 12, 10.
I appeared that which I was not. For inasmuch as the Son

of God was about to manifest Himself to us in actual flesh, men were at first raised to the sight of God, in such ways as allowed of their seeing Him. Aug. Now it is said, *Blessed are the pure in heart, for they shall see God;* and again, *When He shall appear, we shall be like unto Him, for we shall see Him as He is.* What is the meaning then of the words here: *No man hath seen God at any time?* The reply is easy: those passages speak of God, as to be seen, not as already seen. *They shall see God,* it is said, not, they *have* seen Him: nor is it, we *have* seen Him, but, *we shall see Him as He is.* For, *No man hath seen God at any time,* neither in this life, nor yet in the Angelic, as He is; in the same way in which sensible things are perceived by the bodily vision.

Greg. If however any, while inhabiting this corruptible flesh, can advance to such an immeasurable height of virtue, as to be able to discern by the contemplative vision, the eternal brightness of God, their case affects not what we say. For whoever seeth wisdom, that is, God, is dead wholly to this life, being no longer occupied by the love of it. Aug. For unless any in some sense die to this life, either by leaving the body altogether, or by being so withdrawn and alienated from carnal perceptions, that he may well not know, as the Apostle says, *whether he be in the body or out of the body,* he cannot be carried away, and borne aloft to that vision. Greg. Some hold that in the place of bliss, God is visible in His *brightness,* but not in His *nature.* This is to indulge in over much subtlety. For in that simple and unchangeable essence, no division can be made between the nature and the brightness. Aug. If we say, that the text, *No one[d] hath seen God at any time,* applies only to men; so that, as the Apostle more plainly interprets it, *Whom no man hath seen nor can see, no one* is to be understood here to mean, no one *of men:* the question may be solved in a way not to contradict what our Lord says, *Their Angels do always behold the face of My Father;* so that we must believe that Angels see, what no one, i. e. of men, hath ever seen. Greg. Some however there are who conceive that not even the Angels see God. Chrys. That very existence which is God, neither Pro-

Aug.
Ep. to
Paulina
sparsim.
Matt. 5,
8.
1 John
3, 2.

Greg.
xviii.
Moral.

Aug. xii.
on Gen.
ad litte-
ram c.
27.

2 Cor.
12, 2.
Greg.
xviii.
Moral.
c. 54. 90.
vet.
xxxviii.

Aug.
to Paul.
c. iv.
1 Tim.
6, 16.

Mat. 18,
10.
Greg.
xviii.
Moral.
c. 54.
(91.) vet.
xxxviii.
Chrys.
Hom.
xv.
(xiv.) 1.

---

[d] εἶδλε: Vulg. nemo: E. T. no man.

phets, nor even Angels, nor yet Archangels, have seen.
For enquire of the Angels; they say nothing concerning His
Substance; but sing, *Glory to God in the highest*, and *Peace* Luke 2,
on earth to men of good will. Nay, ask even Cherubim and ^{1.}
Seraphim; thou wilt hear only in reply the mystic melody of
devotion, and that heaven and earth are full of His glory. Is. 6, 3.
AUG. Which indeed is true so far, that no bodily or even Aug. to
mental vision of man hath ever embraced the fulness of Paulina c. 7.
God; for it is one thing to see, another to embrace the whole
of what thou seest. A thing is seen, if only the sight of it be
caught; but we only see a thing fully, when we have no
part of it unseen, when we see round its extreme limits.
CHRYS. In this complete sense only the Son and the Holy Chrys.
Ghost see the Father. For how can created nature see that in Joan. Hom.
which is uncreated? So then no man knoweth the Father as xv.
the Son knoweth Him: and hence what follows, *The Only-* [xiv.] 1.
*Begotten Son, Who is in the bosom of the Father, He hath
declared Him.* That we might not be led by the identity of
the name, to confound Him with the sons made so by grace,
the article is annexed in the first place; and then, to put
an end to all doubt, the name *Only-Begotten* is introduced. HILARY; The Truth of His Nature did not seem Hil. de
sufficiently explained by the name of Son, unless, in ad- Trin. vi. 39.
dition, its peculiar force as proper to Him were expressed,
so signifying its distinctness from all beside. For in that,
besides *Son*, he calleth Him also *the Only-Begotten*, he cut
off altogether all suspicion of adoption, the Nature of *the
Only-Begotten* guaranteeing the truth of the name. CHRYS. Chrys.
He adds, *Which is in the bosom of the Father.* To dwell Hom. xv.
in the bosom is much more than simply to see. For he who [xiv.] 2.
sees simply, hath not the knowledge thoroughly of that which
he sees; but he who dwells in the bosom, knoweth every
thing. When you hear then that no one knoweth the
Father save the Son, do not by any means suppose that he
only knows the Father more than any other, and does not
know Him fully. For the Evangelist sets forth His residing
in the bosom of the Father on this very account: viz. to
shew us the intimate converse of the Only-Begotten, and His Aug.
coeternity with the Father. AUG. In the bosom of the Father, in Joan.
i. e. in the secret Presence[1] of the Father: for God hath not Tr. iii. c. 17.

¹ secreto

the fold⸰ on the bosom, as we have; nor must be imagined
to sit, as we do; nor is He bound with a girdle, so as to have
a fold: but from the fact of our bosom being placed inner-
most, the secret Presence of the Father is called the bosom
of the Father. He then who, in the secret Presence of the
Father, knew the Father, the same hath declared what He saw.

Chrys.
Hom.
xv.
[xiv.] 3. CHRYS. But what hath He declared? That God is one. But
this the rest of the Prophets and Moses proclaim: what else
have we learnt from the Son Who was in the bosom of the
Father? In the first place, that those very truths, which the
others declared, were declared through the operation of the
Only Begotten: in the next place, we *have* received a far
greater doctrine from the Only Begotten; viz. that God is a
Spirit, and those who worship Him must worship Him in
spirit and in truth; and that God is the Father of the Only

Bede
in loc. Begotten. BEDE; Farther, if the word *declared* have reference
to the past, it must be considered that He, being made man,
declared the doctrine of the Trinity in unity, and how, and by
what acts we should prepare ourselves for the contemplation
of it. If it have reference to the future, then it means that
He will declare Him, when He shall introduce His elect to

Aug.
Tr. lii.
c. 18. the vision of His brightness. AUG. Yet have there been men,
who, deceived by the vanity of their hearts, maintained that
the Father is invisible, the Son visible. Now if they call the
Son visible, with respect to His connexion with the flesh, we
object not; it is the Catholic doctrine. But it is madness in
them to say He was so before His incarnation; i. e. if it be
true that Christ is the Wisdom of God, and the Power of
God. The Wisdom of God cannot be seen by the eye. If
the human word cannot be seen by the eye, how can the

Chrys.
Hom.
xvi.
[xv.] 1. Word of God? CHRYS. The text then, *No man hath seen
God at any time*, applies not to the Father only, but also to
the Son: for He, as Paul saith, is the Image of the invisible
God; but He who is the Image of the Invisible, must Himself
also be invisible.

19. And this is the record of John, when the Jews
sent priests and Levites from Jerusalem to ask him,
Who art thou?

⸰ κολπὸς, sinus, bosom, mean often, fold of the garment on the bosom.

20. And he confessed, and denied not; but confessed, I am not the Christ.

21. And they asked him, What then? Art thou Elias? And he saith, I am not. Art thou that prophet? And he answered, No.

22. Then said they unto him, Who art thou? that we may give an answer to them that sent us. What sayest thou of thyself?

23. He said, I am the voice of one crying in the wilderness, Make straight the way of the Lord, as said the prophet Esaias.

ORIGEN; This is the second testimony of John the Baptist to Christ, the first began with, *This is He of Whom I spake;* and ended with, *He hath declared Him.* THEOPHYL. Or, after the introduction above of John's testimony to Christ, *is preferred before me,* the Evangelist now adds when the above testimony was given, *And this is the record of John, when the Jews sent priests and Levites from Jerusalem.* ORIGEN; The Jews of Jerusalem, as being of kin to the Baptist, who was of the priestly stock, send Priests and Levites to ask him who he is; that is, men considered to hold a superior rank to the rest of their order, by God's election, and coming from that favoured above all cities, Jerusalem. Such is the reverential way in which they interrogate John. We read of no such proceeding towards Christ: but what the Jews did to John, John in turn does to Christ, when he asks Him, through His disciples, *Art thou He that should come, or look we for another?* CHRYS. Such confidence had they in John, that they were ready to believe him on his own words: witness how it is said, *To ask him, Who art thou?* AUG. They would not have sent, unless they had been impressed by his lofty exercise of authority, in daring to baptize. ORIGEN; John, as it appears, saw from the question, that the Priests and Levites had doubts whether it might not be the Christ, who was baptizing; which doubts however they were afraid to profess openly, for fear of incurring the charge of credulity. He wisely determines therefore first to correct their mistake, and then to proclaim the truth. Accordingly, he first of all

Orig.
in Joan.
tom. ii.
c. 29.
Theoph.
in loc.

Orig.
t. vi.
c. 4.

c. 6.

Luke 7,
20.
Chrys.
in Joan.
Hom.
xvi.
[xv.]
Aug.Tr.
4. c. 3.
Orig.
in Joh.
tom. vi.
c. 6.

shews that he is not the Christ: *And he confessed, and denied not; but confessed, I am not the Christ.* We may add here, that at this time the people had already begun to be impressed with the idea that Christ's advent was at hand, in consequence of the interpretations which the lawyers had collected out of the sacred writings to that effect. Thus Theudas had been enabled to collect together a considerable body, on the strength of his pretending to be the Christ; and after him Judas, in the days of the taxation, had done the same. Such being the strong expectation of Christ's advent then prevalent, the Jews send to John, intending by the question, *Who art thou?* to extract from him whether he were the Christ. GREG. He denied directly being what he was not, but he did not deny what he was: thus, by his speaking truth, becoming a true member of Him Whose name he had not dishonestly usurped. CHRYS. Or take this explanation: The Jews were influenced by a kind of human sympathy for John, whom they were reluctant to see made subordinate to Christ, on account of the many marks of greatness about him; his illustrious descent in the first place, he being the son of a chief priest; in the next, his hard training, and his contempt of the world. Whereas in Christ the contrary were apparent; a humble birth, for which they reproach Him; *Is not this the carpenter's son?* an ordinary way of living; a dress such as every one else wore. As John then was constantly sending to Christ, they send to him, with the view of having him for their master, and thinking to induce him, by blandishments, to confess himself Christ. They do not therefore send inferior persons to him, ministers and Herodians, as they did to Christ, but Priests and Levites; and not of these an indiscriminate party, but those of Jerusalem, i. e. the more honourable ones; but they send them with this question, to ask, *Who art thou?* not from a wish to be informed, but in order to induce him to do what I have said. John replies then to their intention, not to their interrogation: *And he confessed, and denied not; but confessed, I am not the Christ.* And observe the wisdom of the Evangelist: he repeats the same thing three times, to shew John's virtue, and the malice and madness of the Jews. For it is the character of a devoted servant, not only to forbear taking to himself

Acts 5.

Greg.
Hom.
vii. in
Evang.
c. 1.
Chrys.
Hom.
xvi.
[xv.] 1,
2.

Mat.13,
55.

his lord's glory, but even, when numbers offer it to him, to reject it. The multitude indeed believed from ignorance that John was the Christ, but in these it was malice; and in this spirit they put the question to him, thinking, by their blandishments to bring him over to their wishes. For unless this had been their design, when he replied, *I am not the Christ*, they would have said, We did not suspect this; we did not come to ask this. When caught, however, and discovered in their purpose, they proceed to another question : *And they asked him, What then ? Art thou Elias?* AUG. For they knew that Elias was to preach Christ; the name of Christ not being unknown to any among the Jews; but they did not think that *He* our Lord was the Christ : and yet did not altogether imagine that there was no Christ about to come. In this way, while looking forward to the future, they mistook at the present.

And he said, I am not. GREG. These words gave rise to a very different question. In another place, our Lord, when asked by His disciples concerning the coming of Elias, replied, *If ye will receive it, this is Elias.* But John says, *I am not* Elias. How is he then a preacher of the truth, if he agrees not with what that very Truth declares ? ORIGEN; Some one will say that John was ignorant that he was Elias; as those say, who maintain, from this passage the doctrine of a second incorporation, as though the soul took up a new body, after leaving its old one. For the Jews, it is said, asking John by the Levites and priests, whether he is Elias, suppose the doctrine of a second body to be already certain; as though it rested upon tradition, and were part of their secret system. To which question, however, John replies, *I am not* Elias: not being acquainted with his own prior existence. But how is it reasonable to imagine, if John were a prophet enlightened by the Spirit, and had revealed so much concerning the Father, and the Only-Begotten, that he could be so in the dark as to himself, as not to know that his own soul had once belonged to Elias? GREG. But if we examine the truth accurately, that which sounds inconsistent, will be found not really so. The Angel told Zacharias concerning John, *He shall go before Him in the spirit and power of Elias.* As Elias then will preach the second

Aug. in Joan. Tr. iv. c. 4.

Greg. Hom. vii. c. 1.

Mat. 11, 14.

Orig. in Joan. tom. vi. c. 7.

Greg. Hom. vii. in Evang. c. 1. Luke 1, 17.

advent of our Lord, so John preached His first; as the former will come as the precursor of the Judge, so the latter was made the precursor of the Redeemer.   John was Elias in spirit, not in person : and what our Lord affirms of the spirit, John denies of the Person: there being a kind of propriety in this; viz. that our Lord to His disciples should speak spiritually of John, and that John, in answering the carnal multitude, should speak of his body, not of his spirit.   ORIGEN; He answers then the Levites and Priests, *I am not,* conjecturing what their question meant : for the purport of their examination was to discover, not whether the spirit in both was the same, but whether John was that very Elias, who was taken up, now appearing again, as the Jews expected, without another birth[1]. But he whom we mentioned above as holding this doctrine of a reincorporation, will say that it is not consistent that the Priests and Levites should be ignorant of the birth of the son of so dignified a priest as Zacharias, who was born too in his father's old age, and contrary to all human probabilities: especially when Luke declares, that *fear came on all that dwelt round about them.*   But perhaps, since Elias was expected to appear before the coming of Christ near the end, they may seem to put the question figuratively, Art thou he who announcest the coming of Christ at the end of the world? to which he answers, *I am not.* But there is in fact nothing strange in supposing that John's birth might not have been known to all.   For as in the case of our Saviour many knew Him to be born of Mary, and yet some wrongly imagined that He was John the Baptist, or Elias, or one of the Prophets; so in the case of John, some were not unacquainted with the fact of his being son of Zacharias, and yet some may have been in doubt whether he were not the Elias who was expected.   Again, inasmuch as many prophets had arisen in Israel, but one was especially looked forward to, of whom Moses had prophesied, *The Lord thy God will raise up unto thee a Prophet from the midst of thee, of thy brethren, like unto me; unto Him shall ye hearken :* they ask him in the third place, not

Orig.
in Joan.
tom. vi.
c. 7.

Luke 1,
65.

Deut.
18, 15.

---

[1] Origen argues again against the re-incorporation from this same passage, in Matt. l. vii. and xiii. §. 1. see Pamph.   Apol. pro Orig. c. 10. p. 45. 46. ed. de la Rue.

simply whether he is a prophet, but with the article prefixed, *Art thou that Prophet?* For every one of the prophets in succession had signified to the people of Israel that he was not the one whom Moses had prophesied of; who, like Moses, was to stand in the midst between God and man, and deliver a testament, sent from God to His disciples. They did not however apply this name to Christ, but thought that He was to be a different person; whereas John knew that Christ was that Prophet, and therefore to this question, *he answered, No.* Aug. Or because John was more than a prophet: for that the prophets announced Him afar off, but John pointed Him out actually present. ^{Ang. in Joan. Tr. iv. c. 8.}

Then said they unto him, Who art thou? that we may give an answer to them that sent us. What sayest thou of thyself? Chrys. You see them here pressing him still more strongly with their questions, while he on the other hand quietly puts down their suspicions, where they are untrue, and establishes the truth in their place: saying, *I am the voice of one crying in the wilderness.* Aug. So spoke Esaias: the prophecy was fulfilled in John the Baptist. Greg. Ye know that the only-begotten Son is called the Word of the Father. Now we know, in the case of our own utterance, the voice first sounds, and then the word is heard. Thus John declares himself to be the voice, i. e. because he precedes the Word, and, through his ministry, the Word of the Father is heard by man. Origen; Heracleon, in his discussion on John and the Prophets, infers that because the Saviour was the Word, and John the voice, therefore the whole of the prophetic order was only sound. To which we reply, that, if the trumpet gives an uncertain sound, who shall prepare himself for the battle? If the voice of prophecy is nothing but sound, why does the Saviour send us to it, saying, *Search the Scriptures?* But John calls himself the voice, not that crieth, but *of one that crieth* in the wilderness; viz. of Him Who stood and cried, *If any man thirst, let him come unto Me and drink.* He *cries,* in order that those at a distance may hear him, and understand from the loudness of the sound, the vastness of the thing spoken of. Theophyl. Or because he declared the truth plainly, while all who were under the law spoke obscurely. Greg. John crieth *in the*

^{Chrys. Hom. xvi. [xv.] 2.}

^{Aug. Tr. iv. c. 7.}

^{Greg. Hom. vii. c. 2.}

^{Orig. in Joan. tom. vi. c. 12.}

^{John 5, 39.}

^{John 7, 37.}

^{in loc.}

^{Greg. Hom. vii. in Ev. c. 2.}

E

wilderness, because it is to forsaken and destitute Judæa that he bears the consolatory tidings of a Redeemer. ORIGEN ; There is need of the voice *crying in the wilderness,* that the soul, forsaken by God, may be recalled to making straight the way of the Lord, following no more the crooked paths of the serpent. This has reference both to the contemplative life, as enlightened by truth, without mixture of falsehood, and to the practical, as following up the correct perception by the suitable action. Wherefore he adds, *Make straight the way of the Lord, as saith the prophet Esaias.* GREG. The way of the Lord is made straight to the heart, when the word of truth is heard with humility; the way of the Lord is made straight to the heart, when the life is formed upon the precept.

Orig.
tom. vi.
c. 10. 11.

Greg.
Hom.
vii. in
Evang.
c. 2.

24. And they which were sent were of the Pharisees.

25. And they asked him, and said unto him, Why baptizest thou then, if thou be not that Christ, nor Elias, neither that prophet?

26. John answered them, saying, I baptize with water : but there standeth one among you, whom ye know not ;

27. He it is, who coming after me is preferred before me, whose shoe's latchet I am not worthy to unloose.

28. These things were done in Bethabara beyond Jordan, where John was baptizing.

Orig.
in Joan.
tom. vi.
c. 13.

ORIGEN ; The questions of the priests and Levites being answered, another mission comes from the Pharisees: *And they that were sent were of the Pharisees.* So far as it is allowable to form a conjecture from the discourse itself here, I should say that it was the third occasion of John's giving his witness. Observe the mildness of the former question, so befitting the priestly and levitical character, *Who art thou?* There is nothing arrogant or disrespectful, but only what becomes true ministers of God. The Pharisees however, being a sectarian body, as their name implies, address the Baptist in an importunate and contumelious way. *And they said, Why baptizest thou then, if thou be not that Christ, neither Elias, neither that Prophet?* not caring about information, but only wishing to prevent him baptizing. Yet the very next thing they did, was to come to John's baptism. The solution of this is, that they came not in faith, but hypocritically, because they feared the people. CHRYS. Or, those very same priests and Levites were of the Pharisees, and, because they could not undermine him by blandishments, began accusing, after they had compelled him to say what he was not. And they asked him, saying, *Why baptizest thou then, if thou art not the Christ, neither Elias, neither that Prophet?* As if it were an act of audacity in him to baptize, when he was neither the Christ, nor His precursor, nor His proclaimer, i. e. *that Prophet.* GREG. A saint, even when perversely questioned, is never diverted from the pursuit of goodness. Thus John to the words of envy opposes the words of life: *John answered them, saying, I indeed baptize with water.* ORIGEN; For how would the question, *Why then baptizest thou,* be replied to in any other way, than by setting forth the carnal nature of his own baptism? GREG. John baptizeth not with the Spirit, but with water; not being able to remit sins, he washes the bodies of the baptized with water, but not their souls with pardon. Why then doth he baptize, when he doth not remit sins by baptism? To maintain his character of forerunner. As his birth preceded our Lord's, so doth his baptism precede our Lord's baptism. And he who was the forerunner of Christ in His preaching, is forerunner also in His baptism, which was the imitation of that Sacrament. And withal he announces the mystery of our redemption, saying that He, the Redeemer, is standing in the midst of men, and they know it not: *There standeth one among you, whom ye know not:* for our Lord, when He appeared in the flesh, was visible in body, but in majesty invisible. CHRYS. *One among you.* It was fitting that Christ should mix with the people, and be one of the many, shewing every where His humility. *Whom ye know not;* i. e. not, in the most absolute and certain sense; not, who He is, and whence He is. AUG. In His low estate He was not seen; and therefore the candle was lighted. THEOPHYL. Or it was, that our Lord was in the midst of the Pharisees; and they not knowing Him. For

Chrys.
Hom.
xvi. (al.
xv.) 2.

Greg.
Hom.
vii. in
Evang.
c. 3.

Orig.
in Joan.
tom. vi.
c. 15.

Greg.
Hom.
vii. in
Evang.
c. 3.

Chrys.
xvi. 3.

Aug.
Tr. iv.
c. 9.

in loc.

they thought that they knew the Scriptures, and therefore, inasmuch as our Lord was pointed out there, He was in the midst of them, i. e. in their hearts. But they knew Him not, inasmuch as they understood not the Scriptures. Or take another interpretation. He was in the midst of them, as mediator between God and man, wishing to bring them, the Pharisees, to God. But they knew Him not. ORIGEN; Or thus; Having said, *I indeed baptize with water*, in answer to the question, *Why baptizest thou then?*—to the next, *If thou be not Christ?* he replies by declaring the preexistent substance of Christ; that it was of such virtue, that though His Godhead was invisible, He was present to every one, and pervaded the whole world; as is conveyed in the words; *There standeth one among you.* For He it is, Who hath diffused Himself through the whole system of nature, insomuch that every thing which is created, is created by Him; *All things were made by Him.* Whence it is evident that even those who enquired of John, *Why baptizest thou then?* had Him among them. Or, the words, *There standeth one among you*, are to be understood of mankind generally. For, from our character as rational beings, it follows that the word* exists in the centre of us, because the heart, which is the spring of motion within us, is situated in the centre of the body. Those then who carry the word within them, but are ignorant of its nature, and the source and beginning and the way in which it resides in them; these, hearing the word within them, know it not. But John recognised Him, and reproached the Pharisees, saying, *Whom ye know not.* For, though expecting Christ's coming, the Pharisees had formed no lofty conception of Him, but supposed that He would only be a holy man: wherefore he briefly refutes their ignorance, and the false ideas that they had of His excellence. He saith, *standeth;* for as the Father standeth, i. e. exists without variation or change, so standeth the Word ever in the work of salvation, though It assume flesh, though It be in the midst of men, though It stand invisible. Lest any one however should think that the invisible One Who cometh to all men, and to

Orig. in Joan. tom. vi. c. 16.

---

* i. e. the λόγος ἐν ἀνθρώποις, reason; the word which is the image of *the* Word.

the universal world, is different from Him Who was made man, and appeared on the earth, he adds, *He that cometh after me*; i. e. Who will appear after me. The *after* however here has not the same meaning that it has, when Christ calls us *after* Him; for there we are told to follow after Him, that by treading in His steps, we may attain to the Father; but here the word is used to intimate what should follow upon John's teaching; for he came that all may believe, having by his ministry been fitted gradually by lesser things, for the reception of the perfect Word. Therefore he saith, *He it is Who cometh after me.* CHRYS. As if he said, Do not think that every thing is contained in my baptism; for if my baptism were perfect, another would not come after me with another baptism. This baptism of mine is but an introduction to the other, and will soon pass away, like a shadow, or an image. There is One coming after me to establish the truth: and therefore this is not a perfect baptism; for, if it were, there would be no room for a second: and therefore he adds, *Who is made before me*: i. e. is more honourable, more lofty. GREG. *Made before me*, i. e. preferred before me. He comes after me, that is, He is born after me; He is made before me, that is, He is preferred to me. CHRYS. But lest thou shouldest think this to be the result of comparison, he immediately shews it to be a superiority beyond all comparison; *Whose shoe's latchet I am not worthy to unloose*: as if He said, He is so much before me, that I am unworthy to be numbered among the lowest of His attendants: the unloosing of the sandal being the very lowest kind of service. AUG. To have pronounced himself worthy even of unloosing His shoe's latchet, he would have been thinking too much of himself. GREG. Or thus: It was a law of the old dispensation, that, if a man refused to take the woman, who of right came to him, to wife, he who by right of relationship came next to be the husband, should unloose his shoe. Now in what character did Christ appear in the world, but as Spouse of the Holy Church? John then very properly pronounced himself unworthy to unloose this shoe's latchet: as if he said, I cannot uncover the feet of the Redeemer, for I claim not the title of spouse, which I have no right to. Or the passage

Chrys. Hom. xvi. (al. xv.) 3.

Greg. Hom. vii. in Ev. c. 3.

Chrys. Hom. xvi. (al. xv.) 3.

Aug. Tr. iv.

Greg. Hom. vii. in Ev. c. 3.

John 3, 29.

may be explained in another way. We know that shoes are
made out of dead animals. Our Lord then, when He came
in the flesh, put on, as it were, shoes; because in His
Divinity He took the flesh of our corruption, wherein we had
of ourselves perished. And the latchet of the shoe, is the
seal upon the mystery. John is not able to unloose the shoe's
latchet; i. e. even he cannot penetrate into the mystery of
the Incarnation. So he seems to say: What wonder that
He is preferred before me, Whom, being born after me, I
contemplate, yet the mystery of Whose birth I comprehend

Orig.
tom. vi.
in Joan.
[1] Hera-
cleon. not. ORIG. The place has been understood not amiss thus
by a certain person [1]; I am not of such importance, as that
for my sake He should descend from this high abode, and
Chrys.
Hom.
xvii. (al.
xvi.) 1.
in Joan. take flesh upon Him, as it were a shoe. CHRYS. John
having preached the thing concerning Christ publicly and
with becoming liberty, the Evangelist mentions the place
of His preaching: *These things were done in Bethany
beyond Jordan, where John was baptizing.* For it was in
no house or corner that John preached Christ, but beyond
Jordan, in the midst of a multitude, and in the presence of
all whom He had baptized. Some copies read more correctly Bethabara: for Bethany was not beyond Jordan, or in
the desert, but near Jerusalem. GLOSS; Or we must suppose
two Bethanies; one over Jordan, the other on this side, not
far from Jerusalem, the Bethany where Lazarus was raised
Chrys.
Hom.
xvii. from the dead. CHRYS. He mentions this too for another
reason, viz. that as He was relating events which had only
recently happened, He might, by a reference to the place,
appeal to the testimony of those who were present and saw
them. ALCUIN. The meaning of Bethany is, house of
obedience; by which it is intimated to us, that all must
Orig.
tom. vi.
c. 24. approach to baptism, through the obedience of faith. ORIG.
Bethabara means house of preparation; which agreeth with
the baptism of Him, who was making ready a people pre-
c. 25.
et seq. pared for the Lord. Jordan, again, means, " their descent."
Now what is this river but our Saviour, through Whom
coming into this earth all must be cleansed, in that He came
down not for His own sake, but for theirs. This river it is
which separateth the lots given by Moses, from those given
c. 29. by Jesus; its streams make glad the city of God. As the

serpent lies hid in the Egyptian river, so doth God in this; for the Father is in the Son. Wherefore whosoever go thither to wash themselves, lay aside the reproach of Egypt, are made meet to receive the inheritance, are cleansed from leprosy, are made capable of a double portion of grace, and ready to receive the Holy Spirit; nor doth the spiritual dove light upon any other river. John again baptizes *beyond* Jordan, as the precursor of Him Who came not to call the righteous, but sinners to repentance. Joshua 5, 9. 2 Kings 5, 14. 2 Kings 2, 9.

29. The next day John seeth Jesus coming to him, and saith, Behold the Lamb of God, which taketh away the sin of the world.

30. This is he of whom I said, After me cometh a man which is preferred before me: for he was before me.

31. And I knew him not: but that he should be made manifest to Israel, therefore am I come baptizing with water.

ORIGEN; After this testimony, Jesus is seen coming to John, not only persevering in his confession, but also advanced in goodness: as is intimated by the second day. Wherefore it is said, *The next day John seeth Jesus coming to him.* Long before this, the Mother of Jesus, as soon as she had conceived Him, went to see the mother of John then pregnant; and as soon as the sound of Mary's salutation reached the ears of Elisabeth, John leaped in the womb: but now the Baptist himself after his testimony seeth Jesus coming. Men are first prepared by hearing from others, and then see with their own eyes. The example of Mary going to see Elisabeth her inferior, and the Son of God going to see the Baptist, should teach us modesty and fervent charity to our inferiors. What place the Saviour came from when He came to the Baptist we are not told here; but we find it in Matthew, *Then cometh Jesus from Galilee to Jordan unto John to be baptized of him.* CHRYS. Or; Matthew relates directly Christ's coming to His baptism, John His coming a second time subsequent to His baptism, as appears from what follows: *I saw the Spirit descending, &c.* The Evangelists

Orig. tom. vi. c. 30.

Matt. 3, 13. Chrys. Hom. xvii.(al. xvi.)

have divided the periods of the history between them; Matthew passing over the part before John's imprisonment, and hastening to that event; John chiefly dwelling on what took place before the imprisonment. Thus he says, *The next day John seeth Jesus coming to him.* But why did He come to him the next day after His baptism? Having been baptized with the multitude, He wished to prevent any from thinking that He came to John for the same reason that others did, viz. to confess His sins, and be washed in the river unto repentance. He comes therefore to give John an opportunity of correcting this mistake; which John accordingly did correct; viz. by those words, *Behold the Lamb of God, which taketh away the sin of the world.* For He Who was so pure, as to be able to absolve other men's sins, evidently could not have come thither for the sake of confessing His own; but only to give John an opportunity of speaking of Him. He came too the next day, that those who had heard the former testimonies of John, might hear them again more plainly; and other besides. For he saith, *Behold the Lamb of God,* signifying that He was the one of old sought after, and reminding them of the prophecy of Isaiah, and of the shadows of the Mosaic law, in order that through the figure he might the easier lead them to the substance. AUG. If the Lamb of God is innocent, and John is the lamb, must he not be innocent? But all men come of that stock of which David sings sorrowing, *Behold, I was conceived in wickedness.* He then alone was the Lamb, who was not thus conceived; for He was not conceived in wickedness, nor in sin did His mother bear Him in her womb, Whom a virgin conceived, a virgin brought forth, because that in faith she conceived, and in faith received. ORIGEN; But whereas five kinds of animals are offered in the temple, three beasts of the field, a calf, a sheep, and a goat; and two fowls of the air, a turtle dove and a pigeon; and of the sheep kind three are introduced, the ram, the ewe, the lamb; of these three he mentions only the lamb; the lamb, as we know, being offered in the daily sacrifice, one in the morning, and one in the evening. But what other daily offering can there be, that can be meant to be offered by a reasonable nature, except the perfect Word, typically called the Lamb? This

Aug. Tr. iv. c. 10.

Ps. 51, 5.

Orig. tom. vi. c. 32. et seq.

sacrifice, which is offered up as soon as the soul begins to
be enlightened, shall be accounted as a morning sacrifice,
referring to the frequent exercise of the mind in divine
things; for the soul cannot continually apply to the highest
objects because of its union with an earthly and gross body.
By this Word too, Which is Christ the Lamb, we shall be able
to reason on many things, and shall in a manner attain to
Him in the evening, while engaged with things of the body[t].
But He Who offered the lamb for a sacrifice, was God hid
in human form, the great Priest, He who saith below, *No* John10,
man taketh it (My life) from Me, but I lay it down of 18.
Myself: whence this name, *the Lamb of God:* for He
carrying our sorrows, and taking away the sins of the whole Isaiah
world, hath undergone death, as it were baptism. For God 53, 4.
suffers no fault to pass uncorrected; but punishes it by the 24.
sharpest discipline. THEOPHYL. He is called the Lamb of 50,
God, because God the Father accepted His death for our salva- in loc.
tion, or, in other words, because He delivered Him up to death
for our sakes. For just as we say, This is the offering of such
a man, meaning the offering made by him; in the same sense
Christ is called the Lamb of God Who gave His Son to die
for our salvation. And whereas that typical lamb did not
take away any man's sin, this one hath taken away the sin
of the whole world, rescuing it from the danger it was in
from the wrath of God. Behold Him[1] *Who taketh away the* [1] Vulg.
sin of the world: he saith not, who *will* take, but, *Who* peated
taketh away the sin of the world; as if He were always
doing this. For He did not then only take it away when He
suffered, but from that time to the present, He taketh it
away; not by being always crucified, for He made one
sacrifice for sins, but by ever washing it by means of that
sacrifice. GREG. But then only will sin be entirely taken Greg.
Moral.

---

[t] Christ the Word is our real daily
sacrifice. He carries on within us what
is outwardly typified by the Mosaic
ritual. As in the Jewish temple the
day began with the one continual sacrifice which was carried on by others in
their turn through the day, (vid. Orig. vi.
c. 34.) till at last the evening sacrifice
put a close to all sacred services: so in
our minds a sacrifice is offered up to God
when the Word (from Whom *our* word,
i. e. reason, is derived) lights up spiritual thoughts, and this is still continued in the Christian, even although
by reason of the infirmity of the flesh,
he cannot always abide in meditation on
the Divinest things, yet is, in Christ,
engaged on many useful things, and so
also when He comes even to the things
of the body, in themselves a sort of
evening and night to the soul, still
doing them also in Christ, he closes all
in Christ.

viii. c.
32.

away from the human race, when our corruption has been
turned to a glorious incorruption. We cannot be free from
sin, so long as we are held in the death of the body. THEO-
PHYL. Why does he say *the sin* of the world, not sins?
Because he wished to express sin universally: just as we say
commonly, that man was cast out of paradise; meaning
the whole human race. GLOSS; Or by the sin of the world is
meant original sin, which is common to the whole world:
which original sin, as well as the sins of every one individually,
Christ by His grace remits. AUG. For He Who took not sin
from our nature, He it is Who taketh away our sin. Some
say, We take away the sins of men, *because* we are holy; for
if he, who baptizes, is not holy, how can he take away the
other's sin, seeing he himself is full of sin? Against these
reasoners let us point to the text; *Behold Him Who taketh
away the sin of the world;* in order to do away with such
presumption in man towards man. ORIGEN; As there was
a connexion between the other sacrifices of the law, and the
daily sacrifice of the lamb, in the same way the sacrifice of
this Lamb has its reflexion in the pouring out of the blood of
the Martyrs, by whose patience, confession, and zeal for
goodness, the machinations of the ungodly are frustrated.
THEOPHYL. John having said above to those who came from
the Pharisees, that there stood one among them whom they
knew not, he here points Him out to the persons thus
ignorant: *This is He of whom I said, After me cometh a
man which is preferred before me.* Our Lord is called *a man*,
in reference to His mature age, being thirty years old when
He was baptized: or in a spiritual sense, as the Spouse of
the Church; in which sense St. Paul speaks, *I have espoused
you to one husband, that I may present you as a chaste
virgin to Christ.* AUG. He *cometh after me*, because he was
born after me: He *is made before me*, because He is preferred
to me. GREG. He explains the reason of this superiority, in
what follows: *For He was before me;* as if his meaning was;
And this is the reason of His being superior to me, though
born after me, viz. that He is not circumscribed by the time
of His nativity. He Who was born of His mother in time,
was begotten of His Father out of time. THEOPHYL. Attend,
O Arius. He saith not, He was created before me, but *He*

was before me. Let the false sect of Paul of Samosata
attend. They will see that He did not derive His original
existence from Mary; for if He derived the beginning of
His being from the Virgin, how could He have been before
His precursor? it being evident that the precursor preceded
Christ by six months, according to the human birth. CHRYS. Chrys.
That He might not seem however to give His testimony from Hom.
any motive of friendship or kindred, in consequence of his being xvi.) 2.
related to our Lord according to the flesh, he says, *I knew
Him not.* John could not of course know Him, having lived
in the desert. And the miraculous events of Christ's childhood, the journey of the Magi, and such like, were now
a long time past; John having been quite an infant, when
they happened. And throughout the whole of the interval,
He had been absolutely unknown: insomuch that John
proceeds, *But that He should be made manifest to Israel,
therefore am I come baptizing with water.* (And hence it is
clear that the miracles said to have been performed by Christ
in His childhood, are false and fictitious. For if Jesus had
performed miracles at this early age, he would not have been
unknown to John, nor would the multitude have wanted
a teacher to point Him out.) Christ Himself then did not
want baptism; nor was that washing for any other reason,
than to give a sign beforehand of faith in Christ. For
John saith not, in order to change men, and deliver from sin,
but, *that he should be made manifest in Israel,* have I come
baptizing. But would it not have been lawful for him to
preach, and bring crowds together, without baptizing? Yes:
but this was the easier way, for he would not have collected
such numbers, had he preached without baptizing. AUG. Aug.
Now when our Lord became known, it was unnecessary to Tr. iv.
prepare a way for Him; for to those who knew Him, He c. 12,13.
became His own way. And therefore John's baptism did
not last long, but only so long as to shew our Lord's
humility. Our Lord received baptism from a servant, in Tr. v.
order to give us such a lesson of humility as might prepare c. 5.
us for receiving the grace of baptism. And that the servant's
baptism might not be set before the Lord's, others were
baptized with it; who after receiving it, had to receive our
Lord's baptism: whereas those who first received our Lord's
baptism, did not receive the servant's after.

32. And John bare record, saying, I saw the Spirit descending from heaven like a dove, and it abode upon him.

33. And I knew him not: but he that sent me to baptize with water, the same said unto me, Upon whom thou shalt see the Spirit descending, and remaining on him, the same is he which baptizeth with the Holy Ghost.

34. And I saw, and bare record that this is the Son of God.

Chrys. Hom. xvii.(al. xvi.) 2. CHRYS. John having made a declaration, so astonishing to all his hearers, viz. that He, whom he pointed out, did of Himself take away the sins of the world, confirms it by a reference to the Father and the Holy Spirit. For John might be asked, how did you know Him? Wherefore he replies beforehand, by the descent of the Holy Spirit: *And John bare record, saying, I saw the Spirit descending from* Aug. de Trin.xv. c. 46. (6.) *heaven like a dove, and it abode upon him.* AUG. This was not however the first occasion of Christ's receiving the unction of the Holy Spirit: viz. Its descent upon Him at His baptism; wherein He condescended to prefigure His body, the Church, wherein those who are baptized receive preeminently the Holy Spirit. For it would be absurd to suppose that at thirty years old, (which was His age, when He was baptized by John,) He received for the first time the Holy Spirit: and that, when He came to that baptism, as He was without sin, so was He without the Holy Spirit. For if even of His servant and forerunner John it is written, *He shall be filled with the Holy Ghost, even from His mother's womb;* if He, though sprung from His father's seed, yet received the Holy Ghost, when as yet He was only formed in the womb; what ought we to think and believe of Christ, whose very flesh had not a carnal but spiritual conception? Aug. deAgon. Chris- tiano, c. 24.(22.) AUG. We do not attribute to Christ only the possession of a real body, and say that the Holy Spirit assumed a false appearance to men's eyes: for the Holy Spirit could no more, in consistency with His nature, deceive men, than could the Son of God. The Almighty God, Who made every creature out of nothing, could as easily form a real body of

a dove, without the instrumentality of other doves, as He
made a real body in the womb of the Virgin, without the
seed of the male. AUG. The Holy Ghost was made to
appear visibly in two ways: as a dove, upon our Lord at His
baptism; and as a flame upon His disciples, when they were
met together: the former shape denoting simplicity, the
latter fervency. The dove intimates that souls sanctified
by the Spirit should have no guile; the fire, that in that
simplicity there should not be coldness. Nor let it disturb
thee, that the tongues are cloven; fear no division; unity is
assured to us in the dove. It was meet then that the Holy
Spirit should be thus manifested descending upon our Lord;
in order that every one who had the Spirit might know, that
he ought to be simple as a dove, and be in sincere peace
with the brethren. The kisses of doves represent this peace.
Ravens kiss, but they tear also; but the nature of the dove is
most alien to tearing. Ravens feed on the dead, but the
dove eats nothing but the fruits of the earth. If doves
moan in their love, marvel not that He Who appeared in the
likeness of a dove, the Holy Spirit, *maketh intercession for*
us with groanings that cannot be uttered. The Holy Spirit
however groaneth not in Himself, but in us: He maketh us
to groan. And he who groaneth, as knowing that, so long
as He is under the burden of this mortality, he is absent from
the Lord, groaneth well: it is the Spirit that hath taught him
to groan. But many groan because of earthly calamities;
because of losses which disquiet them, or bodily sickness
which weigh heavily on them: they groan not, as doth the
dove. What then could more fitly represent the Holy
Spirit, the Spirit of unity, than the dove? as He saith
Himself to His reconciled Church, *My dove is one.* What
could better express humility, than the simplicity and
moaning of a dove? Wherefore on this occasion it was
that there appeared the very most Holy Trinity, the Father
in the voice which said, *Thou art My beloved Son;* the
Holy Spirit in the likeness of the dove. In that Trinity the
Apostles were sent to baptize, i. e. in the name of the Father,
and of the Son, and of the Holy Ghost. GREG. He saith,
Abode upon Him: for the Holy Spirit visits all the faithful;
but on the Mediator alone does He abide for ever in a

Aug.
in Joan.
Tr. vi.
sparsim

Rom. 8,
26.

Cant. 6,
9.

Matt.
28, 19.

Greg.
Moral.
liv. (90.)

peculiar manner; never leaving the Son's Humanity, even as He proceeds Himself from the Son's Divinity. But when the disciples are told of the same Spirit, He shall dwell with you, how is the abiding of the Spirit a peculiar sign of Christ? This will appear if we distinguish between the different gifts of the Spirit. As regards those gifts which are necessary for attaining to life, the Holy Spirit ever abides in all the elect; such are gentleness, humility, faith, hope, charity : but with respect to those, which have for their object, not our own salvation, but that of others, he does not always abide, but sometimes withdraws, and ceases to exhibit them; that men may be more humble in the possession of His gifts. But Christ had all the gifts of the Spirit, un-interruptedly always. CHRYS. Should any however think that Christ really wanted the Holy Spirit, in the way that we do, he corrects this notion also, by informing us that the descent of the Holy Ghost took place only for the purpose of mani-festing Christ: *And I knew Him not : but He that sent me to baptize with water, the same said unto me, Upon whom thou shall see the Spirit descending, and remaining on Him, the same is He which baptizeth with the Holy Ghost.* AUG. But who sent John? If we say the Father, we say true; if we say the Son, we say true. But it would be truer to say, the Father and the Son. How then knew he not Him, by Whom he was sent? For if he knew not Him, by Whom he wished to be baptized, it was rash in him to say, *I have need to be baptized by Thee.* So then he knew Him; and why saith he, *I knew Him not?* CHRYS. When he saith, *I knew Him not,* he is speaking of time past, not of the time of his baptism, when he forbad Him, saying, *I have need to be bap-tized of Thee.* AUG. Let us turn to the other Evangelists, who relate the matter more clearly, and we shall find most satis-factorily, that the dove descended when our Lord ascended from the water. If then the dove descended after baptism, but John said before the baptism, *I have need to be baptized of Thee,* he knew Him before His baptism also. How then said he, *I knew him not, but He which sent me to baptize?* Was this the first revelation made to John of Christ's person, or was it not rather a fuller disclosure of what had been already revealed? John knew the Lord to be the Son

Margin notes:
John 14, 17.

Chrys. Hom. xvii (al. xvi.) 2. in Joan.

Aug. Tr. v. c. i.

Chrys. Hom. xvii. (al. xvi.)c.3. in Joan.
Aug. Tr. iv.v. and vi. sparsim.

of God, knew that He would baptize with the Holy Ghost: for before Christ came to the river, many having come together to hear John, he said unto them, *He that cometh after me is mightier than I: He shall baptize you with the Holy Ghost and with fire.* What then? He did not know that our Lord (lest Paul or Peter might say, my baptism, as we find Paul did say, my Gospel,) would have and retain to Himself the power of baptism, the ministering of it however passing to good and bad indiscriminately. What hindrance is the badness of the minister, when the Lord is good? So then we baptize again after John's baptism; after a homicide's we baptize not: because John gave his own baptism, the homicide gives Christ's; which is so holy a sacrament, that not even a homicide's ministration can pollute it. Our Lord could, had He so willed, have given power to any servant of His to give baptism as it were in His own stead; and to the baptism, thus transferred to the servant, have imparted the same power, that it would have had, when given by Himself. But this He did not choose to do; that the hope of the baptized might be directed to Him, Who had baptized them; He wished not the servant to place hope in the servant. And again, had He given this power to servants, there would have been as many baptisms as servants; as there had been *the baptism of John,* so should we have had the baptism of Paul and of Peter. It is by this power then, which Christ retains in His own possession exclusively, that the unity of the Church is established; of which it is said, *My dove is one.* A man may have a baptism besides the dove; but that any besides the dove should profit, is impossible. CHRYS. The Father having sent forth a voice proclaiming the Son, the Holy Spirit came besides, bringing the voice upon the head of Christ, in order that no one present might think that what was said of Christ, was said of John. But it will be asked: How was it that the Jews believed not, if they saw the Spirit? Such sights however require the mental vision, rather than the bodily. If those who saw Christ working miracles were so drunken with malice, that they denied what their own eyes had seen, how could the appearance of the Holy Spirit in the form of a dove overcome their incredulity? Some say however that the sight was not visible to all, but only to John, and the more

Matt. 3, 11.

Cant. 6, 9.

Chrys. Hom. xvii. (al. xvi.) 3.

devotional part. But even if the descent of the Spirit, as a dove, was visible to the outward eye, it does not follow that because all saw it, all understood it. Zacharias himself, Daniel, Ezechiel, and Moses saw many things, appearing to their senses, which no one else saw: and therefore John adds, *And I saw and bare record that this is the Son of God.* He had called Him the Lamb before, and said that He would baptize with the Spirit; but he had no where called Him the Son before. Aug. It was necessary that the Only Son of God should baptize, not an adopted son. Adopted sons are ministers of the Only Son: but though they have the ministration, the Only one alone has the power.

Aug. Tr. vii. in Joan.

35. Again the next day after John stood, and two of his disciples;

36. And looking upon Jesus as he walked, he saith, Behold the Lamb of God!

Chrys. Chrys. Many not having attended to John's words at Hom. xviii.(al. first, he rouses them a second time: *Again the next day* xvii.) 1. *after John stood, and two of his disciples.* Bede; John Bede. Hom. in stood, because he had ascended that citadel of all excel-Vigil. lences, from which no temptations could cast him down: his S. And. disciples stood with him, as stout-hearted followers of their Chrys. master. Chrys. But wherefore went he not all about, Hom. xviii.(al. preaching in every place of Judæa; instead of standing near xvii.) c. the river, waiting for His coming, that he might point Him 2. out? Because he wished this to be done by the works of Christ Himself. And observe how much greater an effort was produced; He struck a small spark, and suddenly it rose into a flame. Again, if John had gone about and preached, it would have seemed like human partiality, and great suspicion would have been excited. Now the Prophets and Apostles all preached Christ absent; the former before His appearance in the flesh, the latter after His assumption. But He was to be pointed out by the eye, not by the voice only; and therefore it follows: *And looking upon Jesus as He walked, he saith, Behold the Lamb of God!* Theophyl. Looking he saith, as if signifying by his looks his love and admiration for Christ. AUG. John was the friend of the Bridegroom; Aug. he sought not his own glory, but bare witness to the truth. Tr. vii. c. 8. And therefore he wished not his disciples to remain with him, to the hindrance of their duty to follow the Lord; but rather shewed them whom they should follow, saying, *Behold the Lamb of God.* CHRYS. He makes not a long discourse, Chrys. having only one object before him, to bring them and join Hom. xviii. 1. them to Christ; knowing that they would not any further in Joan. need his witness. John does not however speak to his c. 2. disciples alone, but publicly in the presence of all. And so, undertaking to follow Christ, through this instruction common to all, they remained thenceforth firm, following Christ for their own advantage, not as an act of favour to their master[x]. John does not exhort: he simply gazes in admiration on Christ, pointing out the gift[y] He came to bestow, the cleansing from sin: and the mode in which this would be accomplished: both of which the word *Lamb* testifies to. *Lamb* has the article affixed to it, as a sign of preeminence. AUG. For He alone and singly Aug. is the Lamb without spot, without sin; not because His Tr. vii. c. 5. spots are wiped off, but because He never had a spot. He alone is the Lamb of God, for by His blood alone can men be redeemed. This is the Lamb whom the wolves fear; c. 6. even the slain Lamb, by whom the lion was slain. BEDE. Bede. The Lamb therefore he calls Him; for that He was about to Hom 1. give us freely His fleece, that we might make of it a wedding garment; i. e. would leave us an example of life, by which we should be warmed into love. ALCUIN. John *stands* in a mystical sense, the Law having ceased, and Jesus comes, bringing the grace of the Gospel, to which that same Law bears testimony. Jesus *walks*, to collect disciples. BEDE. Bede. The *walking* of Jesus has a reference to the economy of the Hom. in Vigil. Incarnation, by means of which He has condescended to S. And. come to us, and give us a pattern of life.

37. And the two disciples heard him speak, and they followed Jesus.

---

[x] τὸν διδάσκαλον, i. e. John. In the Cat. is substituted "propter gratiam Christi."

[y] τὴν δωρεὰν ἐφ᾽ ἣν συνήγετο καὶ τὸν

τρόπον τοῦ καθαρμοῦ. The Cat. has "præparationem propter quam venit et modum preparationis." Perhaps it should be "purgationis."

F

38. Then Jesus turned, and saw them following, and saith unto them, What seek ye? They said unto Him, Rabbi, (which is to say, being interpreted, Master,) where dwellest thou?

39. He saith unto them, Come and see. They came and saw where he dwelt, and abode with him that day: for it was about the tenth hour.

40. One of the two which heard John speak, and followed him, was Andrew, Simon Peter's brother.

ALCUIN. John having borne witness that Jesus was the Lamb of God, the disciples who had been hitherto with him, in obedience to his command, followed Jesus: *And the two* Chrys. *disciples heard him speak, and they followed Jesus.* CHRYS. Hom. xviii, Observe; when he said, *He that cometh after me is made* 1 et sq. *before me*, and, *Whose shoe's latchet I am not worthy to unloose*, he gained over none; but when he made mention of the economy, and gave his discourse a humbler turn, saying, *Behold the Lamb of God*, then his disciples followed Christ. For many persons are less influenced by the thoughts of God's greatness and majesty, than when they hear of His being man's Helper and Friend; or any thing pertaining to the salvation of men. Observe too, when John says, *Behold the Lamb of God*, Christ says nothing. The Bridegroom stands by in silence; others introduce Him, and deliver the Bride into His hands; He receives her, and so treats her that she no longer remembers those who gave her in marriage. Thus Christ came to unite to Himself the Church; He said nothing Himself; but John, the friend of the Bridegroom, came forth, and put the Bride's right hand in His; i. e. by his preaching delivered into His hands men's souls, whom receiving He so disposed of, that they returned no more to John. And observe farther; As at a marriage the maiden goes not to meet the bridegroom, (even though it be a king's son who weds a humble handmaid,) but he hastens to her; so is it here. For human nature ascended not into heaven, but the Son of God came down to human nature, and took her to His Father's house. Again; There were disciples of John who not only did not follow Christ, but were even onviously disposed toward Him; but the better part heard, and followed; not from contempt of their former master, but by his persuasion; because he promised them that Christ would baptize with the Holy Ghost. And see with what modesty their zeal was accompanied. They did not straightway go and interrogate Jesus on great and necessary doctrines, nor in public, but sought private converse with Him; for we are told that *Jesus turned, and saw them following, and saith unto them, What seek ye?* Hence we learn, that when we once begin to form good resolutions, God gives us opportunities enough of improvement. Christ asks the question, not because He needed to be told, but in order to encourage familiarity and confidence, and shew that He thought them worthy of His instructions. THEOPHYL. Observe then, that it was upon those who followed Him, that our Lord turned His face and looked upon them. Unless thou by thy good works follow Him, thou shalt never be permitted to see His face, or enter into His dwelling. ALCUIN. The disciples followed behind His back, in order to see Him, and did not see His face. So He turns round, and, as it were, lowers His majesty, that they might be enabled to behold His face. ORIGEN. Perhaps it is not without a reason, that after six testimonies John ceases to bear witness, and Jesus asks seventhly, *What seek ye?* CHRYS. And besides following Him, their questions shewed their love for Christ; *They said unto Him, Rabbi, (which is, being interpreted, Master,) where dwellest Thou?* They call Him, Master, before they have learnt any thing from Him; thus encouraging themselves in their resolution to become disciples, and to shew the reason why they followed. ORIGEN. An avowal, befitting persons who came from hearing John's testimony. They put themselves under Christ's teaching, and express their desire to see the dwelling of the Son of God. ALCUIN. They do not wish to be under His teaching for a time only, but enquire where He abides; wishing an immediate initiation in the secrets of His word, and afterwards meaning often to visit Him, and obtain fuller instruction. And, in a mystical sense too, they wish to know in whom Christ dwells, that profiting by their example they may themselves become fit to be His dwelling. Or, their

in loc.

Orig. tom. ii. c. 29.

Chrys. Hom. xviii. in Joan. sparsim

seeing Jesus walking, and straightway enquiring where He resides, is an intimation to us, that we should, remembering His Incarnation, earnestly entreat Him to shew us our eternal habitation. The request being so good a one, Christ promises a free and full disclosure. *He saith unto them, Come and see:* that is to say, My dwelling is not to be understood by words, but by works; *come*, therefore, by believing and working, and then *see* by understanding. ORIGEN. Or perhaps *come*, is an invitation to action; *see*, to contemplation. CHRYS. Christ does not describe His house and situation, but brings them after Him, shewing that he had already accepted them as His own. He says not, It is not the time now, to-morrow ye shall hear if ye wish to learn; but addresses them familiarly, as friends who had lived with him a long time. But how is it that He saith in another place, *The Son of man hath not where to lay His head?* when here He says, *Come and see* where I live? His not having where to lay His head, could only have meant that He had no dwelling of His own, not that He did not live in a house at all: for the next words are, *They came and saw where He dwelt, and abode with Him that day.* Why they stayed the Evangelist does not say: it being obviously for the sake of His teaching. AUG. What a blessed day and night was that! Let us too build up in our hearts within, and make Him an house, whither He may come and teach us. THEOPHYL. *And it was about the tenth hour.* The Evangelist mentions the time of day purposely, as a hint both to teachers and learners, not to let time interfere with their work. CHRYS. It shewed a strong desire to hear Him, since even at sunset they did not turn from Him. To sensual persons the time after meals is unsuitable for any grave employment, their bodies being overloaded with food. But John, whose disciples these were, was not such an one. His evening was a more abstemious one than our mornings. AUG. The number here signifies the law, which was composed of ten commandments. The time had come when the law was to be fulfilled by love, the Jews, who acted from fear, having been unable to fulfil it, and therefore was it at the tenth hour that our Lord heard Himself called, *Rabbi*; none but the giver of the law is the teacher[1] of the law.

Orig. tom. ii. c. 29.

Chrys. Hom. xviii. (al.xvii.) 3.

Matt. 8, 20.

Aug. Tr. vii. c. 9.

Chrys. Hom. xviii. 3.

Aug. Tr. vii. c. 10.

[1] magister

CHRYS. One of the two which *heard John speak and followed* Chrys.
Him was Andrew, Simon Peter's brother. Why is the other $_{\text{xviii. 3.}}^{\text{Hom.}}$
name left out? Some say, because this Evangelist himself was
that other. Others, that it was a disciple of no eminence,
and that there was no use in telling his name any more than
those of the seventy-two, which are omitted. ALCUIN. Or it
would seem that the two disciples who followed Jesus were
Andrew and Philip.

41. He first findeth his own brother Simon, and
saith unto him, We have found the Messias, which is,
being interpreted, the Christ.

42. And he brought him to Jesus. And when Jesus
beheld him, he said, Thou art Simon the son of Jona:
thou shalt be called Cephas, which is by interpretation,
A stone.

CHRYS. Andrew kept not our Lord's words to himself; but Chrys.
ran in haste to his brother, to report the good tidings: *He* $_{\text{xix. 1.}}^{\text{Hom.}}$
first findeth his own brother Simon, and saith unto him, We
have found the Messias, which is, being interpreted, the
Christ. BEDE. This is truly to find the Lord; viz. to have Bede.
fervent love for Him, together with a care for our brother's $_{\text{Vig. St.}}^{\text{Hom. in}}$
salvation. CHRYS. The Evangelist does not mention what Andr.
Christ said to those who followed Him; but we may infer it $_{\text{Hom.}}^{\text{Chrys.}}$
from what follows. Andrew declares in few words what he $_{\text{xix. (al.}}$
had learnt, discloses the power of that Master Who had $^{\text{xviii.)1,}}$
persuaded them, and his own previous longings after Him.
For this exclamation, *We have found,* expresses a longing for
His coming, turned to exultation, now that He was really
come. AUG. Messias in Hebrew, Christus in Greek, Unctus Aug.
in Latin. Chrism is unction, and He had a special unction, $_{\text{c. 13.}}^{\text{Tr. vii.}}$
which from Him extended to all Christians, as appears in the
Psalm, *God, even Thy God, hath anointed Thee with the oil of* Ps. 44,
gladness above Thy fellows[1]. All holy persons are partakers $_{\text{[partici-}}^{\text{(45.)}}$
with Him; but He is specially the Holy of Holies, specially pibus
anointed. CHRYS. And therefore he said not Messias, but Chrys.
the Messias. Mark the obedience of Peter from the $_{\text{xix.1,2.}}^{\text{Hom.}}$
very first; he went immediately without delay, as appears

from the next words: *And he brought him to Jesus.*
Nor let us blame him as too yielding, because he did not
ask many questions, before he received the word. It is
reasonable to suppose that his brother had told him all,
and sufficiently fully; but the Evangelists often make omissions
for the sake of brevity. But, besides this, it is not absolutely
said that he did believe, but only, *He took him to Jesus;*
i. e. to learn from the mouth of Jesus Himself, what Andrew
had reported. Our Lord begins now Himself to reveal the things
of His Divinity, and to exhibit them gradually by prophecy.
For prophecies are no less persuasive than miracles; inasmuch as they are preeminently God's work, and are beyond
the power of devils to imitate, while miracles may be
phantasy or appearance: the foretelling future events with
certainty is an attribute of the incorruptible nature
alone: *And when Jesus beheld him, He said, Thou art
Simon the son of Jonas; thou shalt be called Cephas, which*

Bede. *is by interpretation, A stone.* BEDE. He beheld him not
Hom. i.
Temp. with His natural eye only, but by the insight of His Godhead
Hier. in discerned from eternity the simplicity and greatness of his
Vig. S.
Andr. soul, for which he was to be elevated above the whole
Church. In the word Peter, we must not look for any
additional meaning, as though it were of Hebrew or Syriac
derivation; for the Greek and Latin word Peter, has the
same meaning as Cephas; being in both languages derived
from petra. He is called Peter on account of the firmness of
his faith, in cleaving to that Rock, of which the Apostle
1 Cor. speaks, *And that Rock was Christ;* which secures those
10, 4.
who trust in it from the snares of the enemy, and dispenses
Aug. streams of spiritual gifts. AUG. There was nothing very
Tr. vii.
c. 14. great in our Lord saying whose son he was, for our Lord
knew the names of all His saints, having predestinated them
before the foundation of the world. But it was a great thing
for our Lord to change his name from Simon to Peter.
Peter is from petra, rock, which rock is the Church: so that the
name of Peter represents the Church. And who is safe,
unless he build upon a rock? Our Lord here rouses
our attention: for had he been called Peter before, we
should not have seen the mystery of the Rock, and should
have thought that he was called so by chance, and not pro-

vidcntially.   God therefore made him to be called by another
name before, that the change of that name might give vividness to the mystery.   Chrys. He changed the name too to Chrys.
shew that He was the same who done so before in the Old ^Hom.^
Testament; who had called Abram Abraham, Sarai Sarah, ^xviii.2.)^
Jacob Israel.   Many He had named from their birth, as
Isaac and Samson; others again after being named by their
parents, as were Peter, and the sons of Zebedee.   Those
whose virtue was to be eminent from the first, have names
given them from the first; those who were to be exalted
afterwards, are named afterwards.   Aug. The account ^Aug.^
here of the two disciples on the Jordan, who follow Christ ^de Con. Evang.^
(before he had gone into Galilee) in obedience to John's ^l. ii. c. 17.^
testimony; viz. of Andrew bringing his brother Simon
to Jesus, who gave him, on this occasion, the name of Peter;
disagrees considerably with the account of the other Evangelists, viz. that our Lord found those two, Simon and
Andrew, fishing in Galilee, and then bid them follow Him:
unless we understand that they did not regularly join our
Lord when they saw Him on the Jordan; but only discovered
who He was, and full of wonder, then returned to their occu-
pations.   Nor must we think that Peter first received his
name on the occasion mentioned in Matthew, when our Lord
says, *Thou art Peter, and upon this rock will I build My* ^Mat.16,^
Church; but rather when our Lord says, *Thou shalt be called* ^18.^
Cephas, which is by interpretation, A stone.   Alcuin. Or perhaps He does not actually give him the name now, but only
fixes beforehand what He afterwards gave him when He said,
Thou art Peter, and upon this rock will I build My Church.
And while about to change his name, Christ wishes to shew
that even that which his parents had given him, was not
without a meaning.   For Simon signifies obedience, Joanna
grace, Jona a dove: as if the meaning was; Thou art an
obedient son of grace, or of the dove, i. e. the Holy Spirit;
for thou hast received of the Holy Spirit the humility, to
desire, at Andrew's call, to see Me.   The elder disdained not
to follow the younger; for where there is meritorious faith,
there is no order of seniority.

43. The day following Jesus would go forth into

Galilee, and findeth Philip, and saith unto him, Follow me.

44. Now Philip was of Bethsaida, the city of Andrew and Peter.

45. Philip findeth Nathanael, and saith unto him, We have found him, of whom Moses in the law, and the prophets, did write, Jesus of Nazareth, the son of Joseph.

46. And Nathanael said unto him, Can there any good thing come out of Nazareth? Philip saith unto him, Come and see.

Chrys.
Hom.
xix.

CHRYS. After gaining these disciples, Christ proceeded to convert others, viz. Philip and Nathanael: *The day following, Jesus would go forth into Galilee.* ALCUIN. Leaving, that is, Judæa, where John was baptizing, out of respect to the Baptist, and not to appear to lower his office, so long as it continued. He was going too to call a disciple, and wished to *go forth into Galilee,* i. e. to a place of " transition" or " revelation," that is to say, that as He Himself increased in wisdom or stature, and in favour with God and man, and as He suffered and rose again, and entered into His glory: so He would teach His followers to *go forth,* and increase in virtue, and pass through suffering to joy. He *findeth Philip, and saith unto him, Follow Me.* Every one follows Jesus who imitates His humility and suffering, in order to be

Chrys.
Hom.
xx. 1.

partaker of His resurrection and ascension. CHRYS. Observe, He did not call them, before some had of their own accord joined Him: for had He invited them, before any had joined Him, perhaps they would have started back: but now having determined to follow of their own free choice, they remain firm ever after. He calls Philip, however, because he would be known to him, from living in Galilee. But what made Philip follow Christ? Andrew heard from John the Baptist, and Peter from Andrew; he had heard from no one; and yet on Christ saying, *Follow Me,* was persuaded instantly. It is not improbable that Philip may have heard John: and yet it may have been the mere voice of Christ which produced this effect. THEOPHYL. For the voice of Christ sounded not like a common voice to some, that is, the faithful, but kindled in their inmost soul the love of Him. Philip having been continually meditating on Christ, and reading the books of Moses, so confidently expected Him, that the instant he saw, he believed. Perhaps too he had heard of Him from Andrew and Peter, coming from the same district; an explanation which the Evangelist seems to hint at, when he adds, *Now Philip was of Bethsaida, the city of Andrew and Peter.* CHRYS. The power of Christ appears Chrys. by His gathering fruit out of a barren country. For from Hom. that Galilee, out of which there ariseth no prophet, He takes His most distinguished disciples. ALCUIN. Bethsaida means house of hunters. The Evangelist introduces the name of this place by way of allusion to the characters of Philip, Peter, and Andrew, and their future office, i. e. catching and saving souls. CHRYS. Philip is not persuaded himself, but Chrys. begins preaching to others: *Philip findeth Nathanael, and* Hom. *saith unto him, We have found Him of whom Moses in the xx. 1.* *Law, and the Prophets, did write, Jesus of Nazareth, the Son of Joseph.* See how zealous he is, and how constantly he is meditating on the books of Moses, and looking for Christ's coming. That Christ was coming he had known before; but he did not know that this was the Christ, *of whom Moses and the Prophets did write:* He says this to give credibility to his preaching, and to shew his zeal for the Law and the Prophets, and how that he had examined them attentively. Be not disturbed at his calling our Lord the Son of Joseph; this was what He was supposed to be. AUG. The person to Aug. whom our Lord's mother had been betrothed. The Christians Tr. vii. know from the Gospel, that He was conceived and born of c. 15. an undefiled mother. He adds the place too, *of Nazareth.* THEOPHYL. He was bred up there: the place of His birth could not have been known generally, but all knew that He was bred up in Nazareth.

And Nathanael said unto him, Can there any good thing come out of Nazareth. AUG. However you may understand Aug. these words, Philip's answer will suit. You may read it Tr. vii. either as affirmatory, *Something good can come out of* c. 15, *Nazareth;* to which the other says, *Come and see:* or you 16, 17. may read it as a question, implying doubt on Nathanael's part, *Can any good thing come out of Nazareth? Come and see.* Since either way of reading agrees equally with what follows, we must inquire the meaning of the passage. Nathanael was well read in the Law, and therefore the word Nazareth (Philip having said that he had found Jesus of Nazareth) immediately raises his hopes, and he exclaims, *Something good can come out of Nazareth.* He had searched the Scriptures, and knew, what the Scribes and Pharisees could not, that the Saviour was to be expected thence. ALCUIN. He who alone is absolutely holy, harmless, unde-

Isaiah 11, 1. filed; of whom the prophet saith, *There shall come forth a rod out of the stem of Jesse, and a branch (Nazaræus) shall grow out of his roots.* Or the words may be taken as ex-

Chrys. Hom. xx. 1, 2. pressing doubt, and asking the question. CHRYS. Nathanael knew from the Scriptures, that Christ was to come from Bethlehem, according to the prophecy of Micah, *And thou,*

Micah 5, 2. *Bethlehem, in the land of Judah,—out of thee shall come a Governor, that shall rule my people Israel.* On hearing of *Nazareth,* then, he doubted, and was not able to reconcile Philip's tidings with prophecy. For the Prophets call Him a Nazarene, only in reference to His education and mode of life. Observe, however, the discretion and gentleness with which he communicates his doubts. He does not say, Thou deceivest me, Philip; but simply asks the question, *Can any good thing come out of Nazareth?* Philip too in turn is equally discrete. He is not confounded by the question, but dwells upon it, and lingers in the hope of bringing him to Christ: *Philip saith unto him, Come and see.* He takes him to Christ, knowing that when he had once tasted of His words and doctrine, he will make no more resistance.

47. Jesus saw Nathanael coming to him, and saith of him, Behold an Israelite indeed, in whom is no guile!

48. Nathanael saith unto him, Whence knowest thou me? Jesus answered and said unto him, Before that Philip called thee, when thou wast under the fig tree, I saw thee.

49. Nathanael answered and saith unto him, Rabbi, thou art the Son of God; thou art the King of Israel.

50. Jesus answered and said unto him, Because I said unto thee, I saw thee under the fig tree, believest thou? thou shalt see greater things than these.

51. And he saith unto him, Verily, verily, I say unto you, Hereafter ye shall see heaven open, and the angels of God ascending and descending upon the Son of man.

CHRYS. Nathanael, in difficulty as to Christ coming out of Nazareth, shewed the care with which he had read the Scriptures: his not rejecting the tidings when brought him, shewed his strong desire for Christ's coming. He thought that Philip might be mistaken as to the place. It follows, *Jesus saw Nathanael coming to Him, and saith of him, Behold an Israelite indeed, in whom is no guile!* There was no fault to be found with him, though he had spoken like one who did not believe, because he was more deeply read in the Prophets than Philip. He calls him *guileless*, because he had said nothing to gain favour, or gratify malice. AUG. What meaneth this, *In whom is no guile?* Had he no sin? Was no physician necessary for him? Far from it. No one was ever born, of a temper not to need the Physician. It is guile, when we say one thing, and think another. How then was there no guile in him? Because, if he was a sinner, he confessed his sin; whereas if a man, being a sinner, pretends to be righteous, there is guile in his mouth. Our Lord then commended the confession of sin in Nathanael; He did not pronounce him not a sinner. THEOPHYL. Nathanael however, notwithstanding this praise, does not acquiesce immediately, but waits for further evidence, and asks, *Whence knowest Thou me?* CHRYS. He asks as man, Jesus answers as God: *Jesus answered and said unto him, Before that Philip called thee, when thou wast under the fig tree, I saw thee:* not having beheld him as man, but as God discerning him from above. *I saw thee,* He says, that is, the character of thy life, *when thou wast under the fig tree:* where the two, Philip and Nathanael, had been talking to-

Chrys. Hom. xix.

Aug. Tr. vii. c. 19.

Chrys. Hom. xx.

gether alone, nobody seeing them; and on this account it is said, that on seeing him a long way off, He said, *Behold an Israelite indeed;* whence it appears that this speech was before Philip came near, so that no suspicion could attach to Christ's testimony. Christ would not say, I am not of Nazareth, as Philip told you, but of Bethlehem; in order to avoid an argument: and because it would not have been sufficient proof, had He mentioned it, of His being the Christ. He preferred rather proving this by His having been present at their conversation. AUG. Has this fig tree any meaning? We read of one fig tree which was cursed, because it had only leaves, and no fruit. Again, at the creation, Adam and Eve, after sinning, made themselves aprons of fig leaves. Fig leaves then signify sins; and Nathanael, when he was under the fig tree, was under the shadow of death: so that our Lord seemeth to say, O Israel, whoever of you is without guile, O people of the Jewish faith, before that I called thee by My Apostles, when thou wert as yet under the shadow of death, and sawest Me not, I saw thee. GREG. When thou wast under the fig tree, I saw thee; i. e. when thou wast yet under the shade of the law, I chose thee. AUG. Nathanael remembered that he had been under the fig tree, where Christ was not present corporeally, but only by His spiritual knowledge. Hence, knowing that he had been alone, he recognised our Lord's Divinity. CHRYS. That our Lord then had this knowledge, had penetrated into his mind, had not blamed but praised his hesitation, proved to Nathanael that He was the true Christ: *Nathanael answered and saith unto Him, Rabbi, Thou art the Son of God, Thou art the King of Israel:* as if he said, Thou art He who was expected, thou art He who was sought for. Sure proof being obtained, he proceeds to make confession; herein shewing his devotion, as his former hesitation had shewn his diligence. ID. Many when they read this passage, are perplexed at finding that, whereas Peter was pronounced blessed for having, *after* our Lord's miracles and teaching, confessed Him to be the Son of God, Nathanael, who makes the same confession *before*, has no such benediction. The reason is this. Peter and Nathanael both used the same words, but not in the same meaning. Peter confessed our

[marginal notes:]
ἀμφισβητήσιμος λόγος.

Aug. Tr. vii. c. 21.

Greg. xviii. Mor. c. xxxviii. (59.)

Aug. Serm. 40. (122.)

Chrys. Hom. xx.

Hom. xxi. (al. xx.) 1.

Lord to be the Son of God, in the sense of very God; the latter in the sense of mere man; for after saying, *Thou art the Son of God*, he adds, *Thou art the King of Israel*; whereas the Son of God was not the King of Israel only, but of the whole world. This is manifest from what follows. For in the case of Peter Christ added nothing, but, as if his faith were perfect, said, that he would build the Church upon his confession; whereas Nathanael, as if his confession were very deficient, is led up to higher things: *Jesus answered and said unto him, Because I said unto thee, I saw thee under the fig tree, believest thou? Thou shalt see greater things than these.* As if He said, What I have just said has appeared a great matter to thee, and thou hast confessed Me to be King of Israel; what wilt thou say when thou seest greater things than these? What that greater thing is He proceeds to shew: *And He saith unto him, Verily, verily, I say unto you, Hereafter ye shall see heaven open, and the angels of God ascending and descending upon the Son of man.* See how He raises him from earth for a while, and forces him to think that Christ is not a mere man: for how could He be a mere man, whom angels ministered to? It was, as it were, saying, that He was Lord of the Angels; for He must be the King's own Son, on whom the servants of the King descended and ascended; descended at His crucifixion, ascended at His resurrection and ascension. Angels too before this *came and ministered unto Him*, and angels brought the glad tidings of His birth. Our Lord made the present a proof of the future. After the powers He had already shewn, Nathanael would readily believe that much more would follow. AUG. Let us recollect the Old Testament account. Jacob saw in a dream a ladder reaching from earth to heaven; the Lord resting upon it, and the angels ascending and descending upon it. Lastly, Jacob himself understanding what the vision meant, set up a stone, and poured oil upon it. When he anointed the stone, did he make an idol? No: he only set up a symbol, not an object of worship. Thou seest here the anointing; see the Anointed also. He is the stone which the builders refused. If Jacob, who was named Israel, saw the ladder, and Nathanael was an Israelite indeed, there was

Aug. in Verb. Dom.

Gen. 28, 12.

a fitness in our Lord telling him Jacob's dream; as if he said, Whose name thou art called by, his dream hath appeared unto thee: for thou shalt *see the heaven open, and the angels of God ascending and descending upon the Son of man.* If they descend upon Him, and ascend to Him, then He is both up above and here below at the same time; above in Himself, below in His members. AUG. Good preachers, however, who preach Christ, are as angels of God; i. e. they ascend and descend upon the Son of man; as Paul, who ascended to the third heaven, and descended so far even as to give milk to babes. He saith, *We shall see greater things than these:* because it is a greater thing that our Lord has justified us, whom He hath called, than that He saw us lying under the shadow of death. For had we remained where He saw us, what profit would it have been? It is asked why Nathanael, to whom our Lord bears such testimony, is not found among the twelve Apostles. We may believe, however, that it was because he was so learned, and versed in the law, that our Lord had not put him among the disciples. He chose the foolish, to confound the world. Intending to break the neck of the proud, He sought not to gain the fisherman through the orator, but by the fisherman the emperor. The great Cyprian was an orator; but Peter was a fisherman before him; and through him not only the orator, but the emperor, believed.

Aug.
Tr. vii.
in Joan.
c. 23.

2 Cor.
12, 2.
1 Cor.
3, 2.

c. 17.

CHAP. II.

1. And the third day there was a marriage in Cana of Galilee; and the mother of Jesus was there:

2. And both Jesus was called, and his disciples, to the marriage.

3. And when they wanted wine, the mother of Jesus saith unto him, They have no wine.

4. Jesus saith unto her, Woman, what have I to do with thee? mine hour is not yet come.

CHRYS. Our Lord being known in Galilee, they invite Him to a marriage: *And the third day there was a marriage in Cana of Galilee.* ALCUIN. Galilee is a province; Cana a village in it. CHRYS. They invite our Lord to the marriage, not as a great person, but merely as one they knew, one of the many; for which reason the Evangelist says, *And the mother of Jesus was there.* As they invited the mother, so they invited the Son: and therefore, *Jesus was called, and His disciples to the marriage:* and He came, as caring more for our good, than His own dignity. He who disdained not to take upon Him the form of a servant, disdained not to come to the marriage of servants. AUG. Let the proud man blush to see the humility of God. Lo, among other things, the Son of the Virgin comes to a marriage; He who, when He was with the Father, instituted marriage. BEDE. His condescension in coming to the marriage, and the miracle He wrought there, are, even considering them in the letter only, a strong confirmation of the faith. Therein too are condemned the errors of Tatian, Marcion, and others who detract from the honour of marriage. For if the undefiled bed, and the marriage celebrated with due chastity, partook at all of sin, our Lord would never have

Chrys. Hom. xxi. (al. xx.) 1.

Chrys. Hom. xxi. 1.

Aug. In Verb. Dom. Serm. xli.

Bede. Hom. 2d Sund. after Epiph.

come to one. Whereas now, conjugal chastity being good, the continence of widows better, the perfection of the virgin state best, to sanction all these degrees, but distinguish the merit of each, He deigned to be born of the pure womb of the Virgin; was blessed after birth by the prophetic voice of the widow Anna; and now invited in manhood to attend the celebration of a marriage, honours that also by the presence of His goodness. Aug. What marvel, if He went to that house to a marriage, Who came into this world to a marriage. For here He has His spouse whom He redeemed with His own blood, to whom He gave the pledge of the Spirit, and whom He united to Himself in the womb of the Virgin. For the Word is the Bridegroom, and human flesh the bride, and both together are one Son of God and Son of man. That womb of the Virgin Mary is His chamber, from which he went forth *as a bridegroom.* Bede. Nor is it without some mysterious allusion, that the marriage is related as taking place on the third day. The first age of the world, before the giving of the Law, was enlightened by the example of the Patriarchs; the second, under the Law, by the writings of the Prophets; the third, under grace, by the preaching of the Evangelists, as if by the light of the third day; for our Lord had now appeared in the flesh. The name of the place too where the marriage was held, Cana of Galilee, which means, desire of migrating, has a typical signification, viz. that those are most worthy of Christ, who burn with devotional desires, and have known the passage from vice to virtue, from earthly to eternal things. The wine was made to fail, to give our Lord the opportunity of making better; that so the glory of God in man might be brought out of its hiding place: *And when they wanted wine, the mother of Jesus saith unto Him, They have no wine.* Chrys. But how came it into the mother's mind to expect so great a thing from her Son? for he had done no miracle as yet: as we read afterwards, *This beginning of miracles did Jesus.* His real nature, however, was beginning now to be revealed by John, and His own conversations with His disciples; besides that His conception, and the circumstances of His birth, had from the first given rise to high expectations in her mind: as Luke tells us, *His mother kept all these sayings in her*

Aug.
Tr. viii.
c. 4.

Ps.19,5.
Bede.
in loc.

Chrys.
Hom.
xxi. 1,2.

Luke 2,
51.

heart. Why then did she never ask Him to work a miracle before? Because the time had now come that He should be made known. Before He had lived so much like an ordinary person, that she had not had the confidence to ask Him. But now that she heard that John had borne witness to Him, and that He had disciples, she asks Him confidently. ALCUIN. She represents here the Synagogue, which challenges Christ to perform a miracle. It was customary with the Jews to ask for miracles.

Jesus saith unto her, Woman, what have I to do with thee? Aug. Some who derogate from the Gospel, and say Aug. that Jesus was not born of the Virgin Mary, try to draw an Tr. viii. c. 5. argument for their error from this place; for, how, say they, could she be His mother to whom He said, *What have I to do with thee?* Now who is it who gives this account, and on whose authority do we believe it? The Evangelist John. But he himself says, *The mother of Jesus was there.* Why should He say it, unless both were true. But did He therefore come to the marriage to teach men to despise their mother? CHRYS. That He greatly venerated His mother, we Chrys. know from St. Luke, who tells us that He was subject unto His Hom. parents. For where parents throw no obstacle in the way of xxi. (al. God's commands, it is our duty to be subject to them; but xx.) 2. when they demand any thing at an unseasonable time, or cut us off from spiritual things, we should not be deceived into compliance. Aug. To mark a distinction between His Godhead Aug. de and manhood, that according to His manhood He was Symbolo Serm. ii. inferior and subject, but according to His Godhead supreme, c. 14. He saith, *Woman, what have I to do with thee?* CHRYS. (5.) And for another reason, viz. to prevent any suspicion attach- Chrys. ing to His miracles: for these it was proper should be asked Hom. xxi. (al. for by those who wanted them, not by His mother. He xx.) 2. wished to shew them that He would perform all in their proper time, not all at once, to prevent confusion; for He saith, *Mine hour is not yet come;* i. e. I am not yet known to xxii.(al. the persons present; nay, they know not that the wine hath xxi.) 1. failed; let them find out that first; he who perceives not his want beforehand, will not perceive when his want is Aug. supplied. Aug. Or it was because our Lord as God had not Tr. viii. a mother, though as man He had, and the miracle He was c. 9. et seq.

about to work was the act of His Divinity, not of human
infirmity. When therefore His mother demanded a miracle,
He, as though not acknowledging a human birth, when
about to perform a divine work, said, *Woman, what have I
to do with thee?* As if He said, Thou didst not beget that
in Me, which works the miracle, My Divinity. (She is called
woman, with reference to the female sex, not to any injury
of her virginity.) But because thou broughtest forth My
infirmity, I will acknowledge thee then, when that very infirmity shall hang on the cross. And therefore He adds, *Mine
hour is not yet come:* as if to say, I will acknowledge thee
when the infirmity, of which thou art the mother, shall hang
from the cross. He commended His mother to the disciple,
when about to die, and to rise again, before her death. But
note ; just as the Manicheans have found an occasion of error
and pretext for their faithlessness in our Lord's word, *What
have I to do with thee?* in the same way the astrologers
support theirs from the words, *Mine hour is not yet come.*
For, say they, if Christ had not been under the power of fate,
He would never have said this. But let them believe what God
says below, *I have power to lay it* (my life) *down, and I
have power to take it again:* and then let them ask, why
He says, *Mine hour is not yet come:* nor let them on such a
ground subject the Creator of heaven to fate ; seeing that,
even were there a fatality in the stars, the Maker of the stars
could not be under the dominion of the stars. And not
only had Christ nothing to do with fate, as ye call it ; but
neither hast thou, or any other man. Wherefore said He
then, *Mine hour is not yet come?* Because He had the
power to die when He pleased, but did not think it expedient yet to exert the power. He was to call the disciples,
to proclaim the Kingdom of heaven, to do marvellous works,
to approve His divinity by miracles, His humility by partaking of the sufferings of our mortal state. And when He
had done all, then the hour was come, not of destiny, but of
will, not of obligation, but of power.

John 10, 18.

5. His mother saith unto the servants, Whatsoever
he saith unto you, do it.

6. And there were set there six waterpots of stone,

after the manner of the purifying of the Jews, containing two or three firkins apiece.

7. Jesus saith unto them, Fill the waterpots with water. And they filled them up to the brim.

8. And he saith unto them, Draw out now, and bear unto the governor of the feast. And they bare it.

9. When the ruler of the feast had tasted the water that was made wine, and knew not whence it was: (but the servants which drew the water knew;) the governor of the feast called the bridegroom,

10. And saith unto him, Every man at the beginning doth set forth good wine; and when men have well drunk, then that which is worse: but thou hast kept the good wine until now.

11. This beginning of miracles did Jesus in Cana of Galilee, and manifested forth his glory; and his disciples believed on him.

CHRYS. Although He had said, *Mine hour is not yet come,* He afterwards did what His mother told Him, in order to shew plainly, that He was not under subjection to the hour. For if He was, how could He have done this miracle before the hour appointed for it? In the next place, He wished to shew honour to His mother, and make it appear that He did not go counter to her eventually. He would not put her to shame in the presence of so many; especially as she had sent the servants to Him, that the petition might come from a number, and not from herself only; *His mother saith unto the servants, Whatsoever He saith unto you, do it.* BEDE; As if she said, Though He appear to refuse, He will do it nevertheless. She knew His pity and mercifulness. *And there were set there six waterpots of stone, after the manner of the purifying of the Jews, containing two or three firkins apiece.* Hydriæ[1] are vessels to hold water: hydor being the Greek for water. ALCUIN. Vessels to hold water were there, after the manner of the purifying of Jews. Among other traditions of the Pharisees, they observed fre-

Margin notes: Chrys. Hom. xxii.(al. xxi.) 1. / Bede, in loc. / ὕδωρ.

Chrys. Hom. xxii.(al. xxi) 2. quent washings. CHRYS. Palestine being a dry country, with few fountains or wells, they used to fill waterpots with water, to prevent the necessity of going to the river, if they were unclean, and to have materials for washing at hand. To prevent any unbeliever from suspecting that a very thin wine was made by the dregs having been left in the vessels, and water poured in upon them, He says expressly, *According to the manner of the purifying of the Jews:* which shews that those vessels were never used to hold wine. AUG. A

Aug. Tr. ix. c. 7. firkin is a certain measure; as urn, amphora, and the like.

[1] μετρον αϊ, 'fir- kins.' Metron is the Greek for measure: whence metretæ[1]. *Two or three,* is not to be taken to mean some holding two, others three, but the same vessels holding two or three.

Jesus saith unto them, Fill the waterpots with water. And
Chrys. Hom. xxii. 2. *they filled them up to the brim.* CHRYS. But why did He not work the miracle before they had filled the waterpots, which would have been much more wonderful; inasmuch as it is one thing to change the quality of some existing substance, another to make it that substance out of nothing? The latter miracle would be the more wonderful, but the former would be the more easy of belief. And this principle often acts as a check, to moderate the greatness of our Lord's miracles: He wishes to make them more credible, therefore He makes them less marvellous; a refutation this of the perverse doctrine of some, that He was a different Being from the Maker of the world. For we see He performs most of His miracles upon subject-matter already existing, whereas were He contrary to the Creator of the world, He would not use a material thus alien, to demonstrate His own power. He did not draw out the water Himself which He made wine, but ordered the servants to do so. This was for the sake of having witnesses of the miracle; *And He saith unto them, Draw out now, and bear unto the governor of the feast.* ALCUIN. The Triclinium is a circle of three couches, *cline* signifying couch: the ancients used to recline upon couches. And the Architriclinus is the one at the head of the Triclinium, i. e. the chief of the guests. Some say that among the Jews, He was a priest, and attended the marriage in order to instruct in the duties of the married state.

Chrys. Hom. xxii. 2. CHRYS. Or thus; It might be said that the guests were drunken, and could not, in the confusion of their senses, tell whether it were water or wine. But this objection could not be brought against the attendants, who must have been sober, being occupied wholly in performing the duties of their service gracefully and in order. Our Lord therefore bid the attendants *bear unto the governor of the feast;* who again would of course be perfectly sober. He did not say, Give to the guests to drink. HILARY; Water is poured into the waterpots; wine is drawn out into the chalices; the senses of the drawer out agree not with the knowledge of the pourer in. The pourer in thinks that water is drawn out; the drawer out thinks that wine was poured in. *When the ruler of the feast had tasted the water that was made wine, and knew not whence it was, (but the servants who drew the water knew,) the governor of the feast called the bridegroom.* It was not a mixture, but a creation : the simple nature of water vanished, and the flavour of wine was produced; not that a weak dilution was obtained, by means of some strong infusion, but that which was, was annihilated; and that which was not, came to be. CHRYS. Our Lord wished the power of His miracles to be seen gradually; and therefore He did not reveal what He had done Himself, nor did the ruler of the feast call upon the servants to do so ; (for no credit would have been given to such testimony concerning a mere man, as our Lord was supposed to be,) but He *called the bridegroom,* who was best able to see what was done. Christ moreover did not only make wine, but the best wine. *And (the ruler of the feast) saith unto him, Every man at the beginning doth set forth good wine, and when men have well drunk, then that which is worse; but thou hast kept the good wine until now.* The effects of the miracles of Christ are more beautiful and better than the productions of nature. So then that the water was made wine, the servants could testify; that it was made good wine, the ruler of the feast and the bridegroom. It is probable that the bridegroom made some answer; but the Evangelist omits it, only mentioning what it was necessary for us to know, viz. the water being made wine. He adds, *This beginning of miracles did Jesus in Cana of Galilee.* It was very necessary to work miracles just then, when His devoted

Marginal notes: Hilar. iii. de Trin. c. 5.

Chrys. Hom. xxii. 2, 3.

Hom. xxiii. 1.

disciples were all collected, and present at the place,

attending to what was going on. ID. Should any say that
there is not sufficient proof of this being the beginning of
miracles, because it is added, *in Cana of Galilee*, as if some
had been preferred elsewhere: we answer, as we did before,
that John says below, *That He might be made manifest*
to Israel, therefore have I come baptizing. Now if He
had performed miracles in the earlier part of His life, the
Jews would not have wanted another person to point Him
out. If our Lord in a short time became so distinguished
for the number of His miracles, that His Name was known
to every one, would He not have been much more so, had
He worked miracles from His earliest years? for the things
themselves would have been the more extraordinary, being performed by a Child, and in so long a time must have become
notorious. It was fit and proper however that He should not
begin to work miracles at so early an age : for men would have
thought the Incarnation a phantasy, and in the extremity of
envy would have delivered Him to be crucified before the
appointed time. AUG. This miracle of our Lord's, turning
the water into wine, is no miracle to those who know that
God worked it. For the Same that day made wine in the
waterpots, Who every year makes wine in the vine : only
the latter is no longer wonderful, because it happens uniformly. And therefore it is that God keeps some extraordinary
acts in store for certain occasions, to rouse men out of their
lethargy, and make them worship Him. Thus it follows,
He manifested forth His glory. ALCUIN. He was the King
of glory, and changed the elements because He was their
Lord. CHRYS. He manifests His glory, as far as related to
His own act; and if at the time many knew it not, yet was
it afterwards to be heard and known of all. *And His*
disciples believed on Him. It was probable that these
would believe more readily, and give more attention to what
went on. AUG. If now for the first time they believed on Him,
they were not His disciples when they came to the marriage.
This however is a form of speech, such as saying that the
Apostle Paul was born in Tarsus of Cilicia; not meaning by
this that he was an Apostle then. In the same way when
we hear of Christ's disciples being invited to the marriage,

we should understand not disciples already, but who were to
be disciples. AUG. But see the mysteries which lie hid in that Aug.
miracle of our Lord. It was necessary that all things should $\frac{Tr. ix.}{c. 5.}$
be fulfilled in Christ which were written of Him: those
Scriptures were the water. He made the water wine when
He opened unto them the meaning of these things, and expounded the Scriptures; for thus that came to have a taste
which before had none, and that inebriated, which did not
inebriate before. BEDE; At the time of our Lord's appearing Bede. in
in the flesh, the sweet vinous taste of the law had been $^{v.\ 1.}$
weakened by the carnal interpretations of the Pharisees. AUG. Aug.
Now if He ordered the water to be poured out, and then intro- $\frac{Tr. ix.}{5.\ et\ sq.}$
duced the wine from the hidden recesses[1] of creation, He would [1]sinibus
seem to have rejected the Old Testament. But converting,
as He did, the water into wine, He shewed us that
the Old Testament was from Himself, for it was by His order
that the waterpots were filled. But those Scriptures have
no meaning, if Christ be not understood there. Now we
know from what time the law dates, viz. from the foundation
of the world. From that time to this are six ages; the first,
reckoning from Adam to Noah; the second, from Noah to
Abraham; the third, from Abraham to David; the fourth, from
David to the carrying away into Babylon; the fifth, from
that time to John the Baptist; the sixth, from John the
Baptist to the end of the world. The six waterpots then
denote these six ages of prophecy. The prophecies are
fulfilled; the waterpots are full. But what is the meaning
of their holding two or three firkins apiece? Had He said
three only, our minds would have run immediately to the
mystery of the Trinity. Nor perhaps can we reject it, even
though it is said, *two or three:* for the Father and the Son
being named, the Holy Ghost may be understood by consequence; inasmuch as it is the love between the Father and
the Son, which is the Holy Ghost. Nor should we pass c. 17.
over another interpretation, which makes the two firkins
alluded to the two races of men, the Jews and the Greeks;
and the three to the three sons of Noah. ALCUIN. The
servants are the doctors of the New Testament, who interpret
the holy Scripture to others spiritually; the ruler of the
feast is some lawyer, as Nicodemus, Gamaliel, or Saul.

When to the former then is committed the word of the
Gospel, hid under the letter of the law, it is the water made
wine, being set before the ruler of the feast.   And the three
rows [1] of guests at table in the house of the marriage are
properly mentioned; the Church consisting of three orders
of believers, the married, the continent, and the doctors.
Christ has kept the good wine until now, i. e. He has deferred
the Gospel till this, the sixth age.

1 Tricli-
nium,
three
couches,
see p. 84.

12. After this he went down to Capernaum, he,
and his mother, and his brethren, and his disciples:
and they continued there not many days.

13. And the Jews' passover was at hand, and Jesus
went up to Jerusalem.

Chrys.
Hom.
xxiii.

CHRYS. Our Lord being about shortly to go up to Jerusalem, proceeded to Capernaum, that He might not take His
mother and brethren every where about with Him: *After
this he went down to Capernaum, He, and His mother, and
His brethren, and His disciples, and they continued there not
many days.* AUG. The Lord our God is He, high, that He
might create us; low, that He might create us anew; walking among men, suffering what was human, hiding what was
divine.   So He hath a mother, hath brethren, hath disciples:
whence He hath a mother, thence hath He brethren.   Scripture frequently gives the name of brethren, not to those only
who are born of the same womb, or the same father, but to
those of the same generation, cousins by the father's or
mother's side.   Those who are unacquainted with this way of
speaking, ask, Whence hath our Lord brothers?   Did Mary
bring forth again?   That could not be: with her commenced
the dignity of the virgin state.   Abraham was uncle of Lot,
and Jacob was nephew to Laban the Syrian.   Yet Abraham
and Lot are called brethren; and likewise Jacob and Laban.
ALCUIN. Our Lord's brethren are the relations of Mary and
Joseph, not the sons of Mary and Joseph.   For not only the
blessed Virgin, but Joseph also, the witness of her chastity, abstained from all conjugal intercourse. AUG. *And His disciples;*
it is uncertain whether Peter and Andrew and the sons of

Aug.
Tr. x. in
Joan. 1,
2.

Aug.
de Cons.
Ev. c. ii.
c. xvii.
(39.)

Zebedee, were of their number or not at this time. For Matthew first relates that our Lord came and dwelt at Capernaum, and afterwards that He called those disciples from their boats, as they were fishing. Is Matthew perhaps supplying what he had omitted? For without any mention that it was at a subsequent time, he says, *Jesus walking by the sea of Galilee saw two brethren.* Or is it better to suppose that these were other disciples? For the writings of the Evangelists and Apostles, call not the twelve only, but all who believing in God were prepared for the kingdom of heaven by our Lord's teaching, disciples[a]. How is it too that our Lord's journey to Galilee is placed here before John the Baptist's imprisonment[b], when Matthew says, *Now when Jesus had heard that John was cast into prison, he departed into Galilee:* and Mark the same? Luke too, though he says nothing of John's imprisonment, yet places Christ's visit to Galilee after His temptation and baptism[c], as the two former do. We should understand then that the three Evangelists are not opposed to John, but pass over our Lord's first coming into Galilee after his baptism; at which time it was that He converted the water into wine. EUSEB. When copies of the three Gospels had come to the Evangelist John, he is reported, while he confirmed their fidelity and correctness, to have at the same time noticed some omissions, especially at the opening of our Lord's ministry. Certain it is that the first three Gospels seem only to contain the events of the year in which John the Baptist was imprisoned, and put to death. And therefore John, it is said, was asked to write down those acts of our Saviour's before the apprehension of the Baptist, which the former Evangelists had passed over. Any one then, by attending, will

Marginal notes: Matt. 4, 18. | id. cap. 18. | Euseb. Eccl. Hist. l. iii. c. 24.

---

[a] This supposition agrees best with what follows, which makes out the visit to Galilee, in St. Matthew, St. Mark, and St. Luke, to be the *second* visit. For they all mention the calling of the Apostles as taking place in this visit; which calling therefore had not taken place at the time of this first visit, which St. John is relating now. And it is difficult to imagine that in all three this mention is parenthetical and out of the order of time.

[b] John 3, 23. 24. And John also was baptizing in Enon, near to Salim, because there was much water there: and they came and were baptized. For John was not yet cast into prison."

[c] Comparing Matt. 4, 12. Mark 1, 14. Luke 4, 13. 14. it is evident that the order of events in the three is exactly the same; excepting that St. Luke omits the mention of John the Baptist's imprisonment. The visit to Galilee in St. Luke is meant to be after John's imprisonment, though that event has not been mentioned.

find that the Gospels do not disagree, but that John is relating the events of a different date, from that which the others
refer to.   CHRYS. He did not perform any miracle at Capernaum, the inhabitants of which city were in a very corrupt
state, and not well disposed to Him; He went there however,
and stayed some time out of respect to His mother[d].   BEDE;
He did not stay many days there, on account of the Passover,
which was approaching: *And the Jews' passover was at
hand.*   ORIGEN; But what need of saying, *of the Jews,*
when no other nation had the rite of the Passover? Perhaps[e]
because there are two sorts of Passover, one human, which is
celebrated in a way very different from the design of Scripture; another the true and Divine, which is kept in spirit
and in truth.   To distinguish it then from the Divine, it is
said, *of the Jews.*

ALCUIN. *And He went up to Jerusalem.* The Gospels
mention two journeys of our Lord to Jerusalem, one in the
first year of His preaching, before John was sent to prison,
which is the journey now spoken of; the other in the year of
His Passion.   Our Lord has set us here an example of careful
obedience to the Divine commands.   For if the Son of God
fulfilled the injunctions of His own law, by keeping the
festivals, like the rest, with what holy zeal should we servants prepare for and celebrate them?   ORIGEN; In a mystical sense, it was meet that after the marriage in Cana of
Galilee, and the banquet and wine, our Lord should take
His mother, brethren, and disciples to the land of consolation (as Capernaum signifies[f]) to console, by the fruits that
were to spring up and by abundance of fields, those who

Margin notes:
Chrys. Hom. xxiii. 1.

Orig. tom. x. in Joan. c. 14.

Orig. tom. x. c. 6, 7.

---

[d] Whom, St. Chrys. adds, He was
about to leave behind when He went to
Jerusalem.

[e] Origen literally, It is called the
Jews, as opposed to the *Lord's* Passover.
For as the Jews had made His Father's
house an house of merchandize, not sanc-
tifying it, so had they made the Lord's
passover a human, a Jewish passover,
choosing that which was low and carnal.

[f] Origen literally, that He might
console His disciples, and the soul that
conceived Him of the Holy Ghost, or
them who were there benefited with
the fruits that were to spring up
in their full [replenished] land. And

why is it, went down, and not went
up? Perhaps his 'brethren' are here
to be understood of those powers who
went down with Him, not being called
to the marriage, according to the interpretation we have mentioned, but receiving lower and inferior benefit from
them; and of another sort from those
called the disciples of Christ. For if His
mother he invited, there are some bearing fruit, whom our Lord Himself
goes down to help with the ministers of
the Word, and His disciples; His
mother too accompanying.—The interpretation to which Origen refers is
lost.

received His discipline, and the mind which had conceived
Him by the Holy Ghost; and who were there to be holpen.
For some there are bearing fruit, to whom our Lord Himself
comes down with the ministers of His word and disciples,
helping such, His mother being present. Those however
who are called to Capernaum, do not seem capable of His
presence long: that is, a land which admitteth lower consolation, is not able to take in the enlightenment from many
doctrines; being capable to receive few only. ALCUIN. Or
Capernaum, we may interpret " a most beautiful village," and
so it signifies the world, to which the Word of the Father came
down. BEDE; But He continued there only a few days,
because he lived with men in this world only a short time.
ORIGEN; Jerusalem, as our Saviour Himself saith, is the city Orig.
of the great King, into which none of those who remain on tom. x.
                                                         in Joan.
earth ascend, or enter. Only the soul which has a certain c. 16.
natural loftiness, and clear insight into things invisible, is the
inhabitant of that city. Jesus alone goes up thither*. But His
disciples seem to have been present afterwards. *The zeal of
Thine house hath eaten me up.* But it is as though in every
one of the disciples who went up, it was Jesus who went up.

14. And found in the temple those that sold oxen
and sheep and doves, and the changers of money
sitting :

15. And when he had made a scourge of small
cords, he drove them all out of the temple, and the
sheep, and the oxen; and poured out the changers'
money, and overthrew the tables ;

16. And said unto them that sold doves, Take these
things hence ; make not my Father's house an house
of merchandise.

17. And his disciples remembered that it was
written, The zeal of thine house hath eaten me up.

BEDE; Our Lord on coming to Jerusalem, immediately

---

* He, and His mother, and disciples,   went down to Capernaum. Here Jesus
went to the marriage : He, and His   alone is mentioned.—Orig. in loc.
mother, and brethren, and disciples,

entered the temple to pray; giving us an example that, wheresoever we go, our first visit should be to the house of God to pray. And He found *in the temple those that sold oxen, and sheep, and doves, and the changers of money sitting.* AUG. Such sacrifices were prescribed to the people, in condescension to their carnal minds; to prevent them from turning aside to idols. They sacrificed sheep, and oxen, and doves. BEDE; Those however, who came from a distance, being unable to bring with them the animals required for sacrifice, brought the money instead. For their convenience the Scribes and Pharisees ordered animals to be sold in the temple, in order that, when the people had bought and offered them afterwards, they might sell them again, and thus make great profits. *And changers of money sitting;* changers of money sat at the table to supply change to buyers and sellers. But our Lord disapproving of any worldly business in His house, especially one of so questionable a kind, drove out all engaged in it. AUG. He who was to be scourged by them, was first of all the scourger; *And when He had made a scourge of small cords, He drove them all out of the temple.* THEOPHYL. Nor did He cast out only those who bought and sold, but their goods also: *The sheep, and the oxen, and poured out the changers' money, and overthrew the tables,* i. e. of the money changers, which were coffers of pence. ORIGEN; Should it appear something out of the order of things, that the Son of God should make a scourge of small cords, to drive them out of the temple? We have one answer in which some take refuge, viz. the divine power of Jesus, Who, when He pleased, could extinguish the wrath of His enemies however innumerable, and quiet the tumult of their minds: *The Lord bringeth the counsel of the heathen to nought.* This act indeed exhibits no less power, than His more positive miracles; nay rather, more than the miracle by which water was converted into wine: in that there the subject-matter was inanimate, here, the minds of so many thousands of men are overcome. AUG. It is evident that this was done on two several occasions; the first mentioned by John, the last by the other three. ORIGEN; John says here that He drove out the sellers from the temple; Matthew, the sellers and buyers. The number of buyers was

Margin notes:
Mat. 21.

Aug.
Tr. x.
c. 4.

Aug.
Tr. x.
c. 5.

Orig.
tom. x.
in Joan.
c. 16.

Ps. 32,
33, 10.

Aug.
de Cons.
Ev. l. ii.
c. 67.
Orig.
tom. x.
in Joan.
c. 17.

much greater than of the sellers: and therefore to drive them out
was beyond the power of the carpenter's Son, as He was
supposed to be, had He not by His divine power put all
things under Him, as it is said. BEDE; The Evangelist sets
before us both natures of Christ: the human in that His
mother accompanied Him to Capernaum; the divine, in that
He said, *Make not My Father's house an house of merchandize.* CHRYS. Lo, He speaks of God as His Father, and they
are not angry, for they think He means it in a common
sense. But afterwards when He spoke more openly, and
shewed that He meant equality, they were enraged. In
Matthew's account too, on driving them out, He says, *Ye have
made it* (*My Father's house*) *a den of thieves.* This was just
before His Passion, and therefore He uses severer language.
But the former being at the beginning of His miracles, His
answer is milder and more indulgent. AUG. So that temple
was still a figure only, and our Lord cast out of it all who
came to it as a market. And what did they sell? Things
that were necessary for the sacrifice of that time. What if
He had found men drunken? If the house of God ought
not to be a house of merchandize, ought it to be a house of
drunkenness? CHRYS. But why did Christ use such violence?
He was about to heal on the Sabbath day, and to do many
things which appeared to them transgressions of the Law.
That He might not appear therefore to be acting contrary to
God, He did this at His own peril; and thus gave them to
understand, that He who exposed Himself to such peril to
defend the decency of the house, did not despise the Lord of
that house. For the same reason, to shew His agreement
with God, He said not, the Holy house, but, *My Father's
house.* It follows, *And His disciples remembered what was
written; The zeal of thine house hath eaten me up.* BEDE;
His disciples seeing this most fervent zeal in Him, remembered that it was from zeal for His Father's house that our
Saviour drove the ungodly from the temple. ALCUIN. Zeal,
taken in a good sense, is a certain fervour of the Spirit, by
which the mind, all human fears forgotten, is stirred up to the
defence of the truth. AUG. He then is eaten up with zeal
for God's house, who desires to correct all that he sees
wrong there; and, if he cannot correct, endures and

Chrys.
Hom.
xxiii. in
Joan.
c. 2.

c. xxi.

xxii. 13.

Aug.
Tr. x.
in Joan.
c. 4.

Chrys.
Hom.
xxiii. 2.

in loc.

Aug.
Tr. x.
c. 9.

mourns. In thine house thou busiest thyself to prevent matters going wrong; in the house of God, where salvation is offered, oughtest thou to be indifferent? Hast thou a friend? admonish him gently; a wife? coerce her severely; a maid-servant? even compel her with stripes. Do what thou art able, according to thy station. ALCUIN. To take the passage mystically, God enters His Church spiritually every day, and marks each one's behaviour there. Let us be careful then, when we are in God's Church, that we indulge not in stories, or jokes, or hatreds, or lusts, lest on a sudden He come and scourge us, and drive us out of His Church.

Orig.
tom. x.
in Joan.
c. 16. ORIGEN; It is possible even for the dweller in Jerusalem to incur guilt, and even the most richly endowed may stray. And unless these repent speedily, they lose the capacity wherewith they were endued. He finds them in the temple, i. e. in sacred places, or in the office of enunciating the Church's truths, some who make His Father's house an house of merchandize; i. e. who expose to sale the oxen whom they ought to reserve for the plough, lest by turning back they should become unfit for the kingdom of God: also who prefer the unrighteous mammon to the sheep, from which they have the material of ornament; also who for miserable gain abandon the watchful care of them who are called metaphorically doves, without all gall or bitterness[h]. Our Saviour finding these in the holy house, maketh a scourge of small cords, and driveth them out, together with the sheep and oxen exposed for sale, scatters the heaps of money, as unbeseeming in the house of God, and overthrows the tables set up in the minds of the covetous, forbidding them to sell doves in the house of God any longer. I think too that He meant the above, as a mystical intimation that whatsoever[i] was to be performed with regard to that sacred oblation by the priests, was not to be performed after the manner of material oblations, and that the law was not to be observed as the carnal Jews wished. For our Lord, by driving away the sheep and oxen, and ordering away the doves,

---

[h] Solertiam columbarum privata qui-libet amaritudine vilipendent. The text is not grammatically correct, but soler-tiam is plainly the reading of ἀκμίλιας, and privata &c. of ἀνεπιμθλήτου πάσης πι- κρότητος which applies to the dove.
[i] Orig. literally, " that the Divine service relating to that temple was no longer to be performed," &c.

which were the most common offerings among the Jews, and by overthrowing the tables of material coins, which in a figure only, not in truth, bore the Divine stamp, (i. e. what according to the letter of the law seemed good,) and when with His own hand He scourged the people, He as much as declared that the dispensation was to be broken up and destroyed, and the kingdom translated to the believing from among the Gentiles. AUG. Or, those who sell in the Church, are those who seek their own, not the things of Jesus Christ. They who will not be bought, think they may sell earthly things. Thus Simon wished to buy the Spirit, that he might sell Him: for he was one of those who sell doves. (The Holy Spirit appeared in the form of a dove.) The dove however is not sold, but is given of free grace [1]; for it is called grace. BEDE; They then are the sellers of doves, who, after receiving the free grace of the Holy Spirit, do not dispense it freely [2], as they are commanded, but at a price: who confer the laying on of hands, by which the Holy Spirit is received, if not for money, at least for the sake of getting favour with the people, who bestow Holy Orders not according to merit, but favour. AUG. By the oxen may be understood the Apostles and Prophets, who have dispensed to us the holy Scriptures. Those who by these very Scriptures deceive the people, from whom they seek honour, sell the oxen; and they sell the sheep too, i. e. the people themselves; and to whom do they sell them, but to the devil? For that which is cut off from the one Church, who taketh away, except the roaring lion, who goeth about every where, and seeketh whom he may devour? BEDE; Or, the sheep are works of purity and piety, and they sell the sheep, who do works of piety to gain the praise of men. They exchange money in the temple, who, in the Church, openly devote themselves to secular business. And besides those who seek for money, or praise, or honour from Holy Orders, those too make the Lord's house a house of merchandize, who do not employ the rank, or spiritual grace, which they have received in the Church at the Lord's hands, with singleness of mind, but with an eye to human recompense. AUG. Our Lord intended a meaning to be seen in His making a scourge of small cords, and then scourging those who were carrying on the merchandize in

Aug. Tr. x. c. 6.

[1] gratis

Bede. in loc.

[2] gratis

Aug. Tr. x. c. 7.

1 Pet. 5, 8.

Bede. in loc.

Aug. Tr. x. c. 5.

the temple. Every one by his sins twists for himself a cord, in that he goes on adding sin to sin. So then when men suffer for their iniquities, let them be sure that it is the Lord making a scourge of small cords, and admonishing them to change their lives: which if they fail to do, they will hear at the last, *Bind him hand and foot.* BEDE; With a scourge then made of small cords, He cast them out of the temple; for from the part and lot of the saints are cast out all, who, thrown externally among the Saints, do good works hypocritically, or bad openly. The sheep and the oxen too He cast out, to shew that the life and the doctrine of such were alike reprobate. And He overthrew the change heaps of the money-changers and their tables, as a sign that, at the final condemnation of the wicked, He will take away the form even of those things which they loved. The sale of doves He ordered to be removed out of the temple, because the grace of the Spirit, being freely received, should be freely given. ORIGEN; By the temple we may understand too the soul wherein the Word of God dwelleth; in which, before the teaching of Christ, earthly and bestial affections had prevailed. The ox being the tiller of the soil, is the symbol of earthly affections: the sheep, being the most irrational of all animals, of dull ones; the dove is the type of light and volatile thoughts; and money, of earthly good things; which money Christ cast out by the Word of His doctrine, that His Father's house might be no longer a market.

Mat.23.
Bede.
in loco.

Orig.
tom. x.
in Joan.
c. 16.

18. Then answered the Jews and said unto him, What sign shewest thou unto us, seeing that thou doest these things?

19. Jesus answered and said unto them, Destroy this temple, and in three days I will raise it up.

20. Then said the Jews, Forty and six years was this temple in building, and wilt thou rear it up in three days?

21. But he spake of the temple of his body.

22. When therefore he was risen from the dead, his disciples remembered that he had said this unto

them: and they believed the Scripture, and the word which Jesus had said.

THEOPHYL. The Jews seeing Jesus thus acting with power, hoc loco. and having heard Him say, *Make not My Father's house an house of merchandize*, ask of Him a sign; *Then answered the Jews and said unto Him, What sign shewest Thou unto us, seeing that Thou doest these things?* CHRYS. But were Chrys. signs necessary for His putting a stop to evil practices? Was xxiii. 2. not the having such zeal for the house of God, the greatest sign of His virtue? They did not however remember the prophecy, but asked for a sign; at once irritated at the loss of their base gains, and wishing to prevent Him from going further. For this dilemma, they thought, would oblige Him either to work miracles, or give up His present course. But He refuses to give them the sign, as He did on a like occasion, when He answers, *An evil and adulterous gene-* Mat.12, *ration seeketh after a sign, and there shall no sign be given* 39. *it, but the sign of Jonas the prophet;* only the answer is more open there than here. He however who even anticipated men's wishes, and gave signs when He was not asked, would not have rejected here a positive request, had He not seen a crafty design in it. As it was, *Jesus answered and said unto them, Destroy this temple, and in three days I will raise it up.* BEDE; For inasmuch as they sought a sign from our Lord of His right to eject the customary merchan-dize from the temple, He replied, that that temple signified the temple of His Body, in which was no spot of sin; as if He said, As by My power I purify your inanimate temple from your merchandize and wickedness; so the temple of My Body, of which that is the figure, destroyed by your hands, on the third day I will raise again. THEOPHYL. He does not however provoke them to commit murder, by saying, *Destroy;* but only shews that their intentions were not hidden from Him. Let the Arians observe how our Lord, as the destroyer of death, says, *I will raise it up;* that is to say, by My own power. AUG. The Father also raised Him up again; Aug. to Whom He says, *Raise Thou me up, and I shall reward* Tr. x. in Joan. *them.* But what did the Father do without the Word? As c. 11. Ps. 41, then the Father raised Him up, so did the Son also: even as 10.

H

John 10, He saith below, *I and My Father are one.* CHRYS. But
30.
Chrys. why does He give them the sign of His resurrection? Because
Tract. this was the greatest proof that He was not a mere man;
xxiii. 3.
shewing, as it did, that He could triumph over death, and in
Orig. a moment overthrow its long tyranny. ORIGEN. Both those,
tom. x.
in Joan. i. e. both the Body of Jesus and the temple, seem to me to
c. 20. be a type of the Church, which with lively stones is built up
into a spiritual house, into an holy priesthood; according to
1 Cor. St. Paul, *Ye are the body of Christ, and members in*
12, 27.
particular. And though the structure of stones seem to be
broken up, and all the bones of Christ scattered by adversities
and tribulations, yet shall the temple be restored, and raised up
again in three days, and stablished in the new heaven and the
new earth. For as that sensible body of Christ was crucified
and buried, and afterward rose again; so the whole body of
Christ's saints was crucified with Christ, (each glorying in
that cross, by which He Himself too was crucified to the
world,) and, after being buried with Christ, hath also risen
with Him, walking in newness of life. Yet have we not
risen yet in the power of the blessed resurrection, which is
still going on, and is yet to be completed. Whence it is not
said, On the third day *I will build it up,* but, *in three days;*
for the erection is being in process throughout the whole of
the three days. THEOPHYL. The Jews, supposing that He
spoke of the material temple, scoffed: *Then said the Jews,
Forty and six years was this temple in building, and wilt
Thou rear it up in three days?* ALCUIN. Note, that they
allude here not to the first temple under Solomon, which was
finished in seven years, but to the one rebuilt under Zoro-
Ezra 4, babel. This was forty-six years building, in consequence of
5.
Orig. the hindrance raised by the enemies of the work. ORIGEN.
tom. x. Or some will reckon perhaps the forty and six years from the
c. 22.
time that David consulted Nathan the Prophet on the building of the temple. David from that time was busy in
collecting materials. But perhaps the number forty may
with reference to the four corners of the temple allude to the
four elements of the world, and the number six, to the creation
Aug. iv. of man on the sixth day. AUG. Or it may be that this
de Trin.
c. 9. (v.) number fits in with the perfection of the Lord's Body. For
six times forty-six are two hundred and seventy-six days,

which make up nine months and six days, the time that our
Lord's Body was forming in the womb; as we know by
authoritative traditions handed down from our fathers, and
preserved by the Church. He was, according to general
belief, conceived on the eighth of the Kalends of April, the March
24.
day on which He suffered, and born on the eighth of the
Kalends of January[1]. The intervening time contains two Dec. 25.
hundred and seventy-six days, i. e. six multiplied by forty-
six. AUG. The process of human conception is said to be Aug. b.
this. The first six days produce a substance like milk, which lxxxiii.
Quaest.
in the following nine is converted into blood; in twelve more 2. 5. f.
is consolidated, in eighteen more is formed into a perfect set
of limbs, the growth and enlargement of which fills up the
rest of the time till the birth. For six, and nine, and twelve,
and eighteen, added together are forty-five, and with the
addition of one (which[1] stands for the summing up, all these [1] added
numbers being collected into one) forty-six. This multiplied from
S. Aug.
by the number six, which stands at the head of this calculation[2], makes two hundred and seventy-six, i. e. nine months [2] hujus
ordina-
and six days. It is no unmeaning information then that the tionis
temple was forty and six years building; for the temple pre- caput
tenet.
figured His Body, and as many years as the temple was in
building, so many days was the Lord's Body in forming.
AUG. Or thus, if you take the four Greek words, anatole, the Aug.
in Joan.
east; dysis, the west; arctos, the north; and mesembria, the Tr. x.
south; the first letters of these words make Adam. And our c. 12.
Lord says that He will gather together His saints from the
four winds, when He comes to judgment. Now these letters
of the word Adam, make up, according to Greek figuring, the
number of the years during which the temple was building.
For in Adam we have alpha, one; delta, four; alpha again,
one; and mi, forty; making up together forty-six. The
temple then signifies the body derived from Adam; which
body our Lord did not take in its sinful state, but renewed
it, in that after the Jews had destroyed it, He raised it again
the third day. The Jews however, being carnal, understood
carnally; He spoke spiritually. He tells us, by the Evangelist,
what temple He means; *But He spake of the temple of His
Body*. THEOPHYL. From this Apollinarius draws an heretical Theoph.
ad loc.
inference: and attempts to shew that Christ's flesh was fin.

inanimate, because the temple was inanimate. In this way you will prove the flesh of Christ to be wood and stone, because the temple is composed of these materials. Now if you refuse to allow what is said, *Now is My soul troubled;* and, *I have power to lay it* (My life) *down,* to be said of the rational soul, still how will you interpret, *Into Thy hands, O Lord, I commend My spirit?* you cannot understand this of an irrational soul: or again, the passage, *Thou shalt not leave My soul in hell.* ORIGEN. Our Lord's Body is called the temple, because as the temple contained the glory of God dwelling therein, so the Body of Christ, which represents the Church, contains the Only-Begotten, Who is the image and glory of God. CHRYS. Two things there were in the mean time very far removed from the comprehension of the disciples: one, the resurrection of our Lord's Body: the other, and the greater mystery, that it was God who dwelt in that Body: as our Lord declares by saying, *Destroy this temple, and in three days I will raise it up.* And thus it follows, *When therefore He had risen from the dead, His disciples remembered that He had said this unto them: and they believed the Scripture, and the word which Jesus had said.* ALCUIN. For before the resurrection they did not understand the Scriptures, because they had not yet received the Holy Ghost, *Who was not yet given, because Jesus was not yet glorified.* But on the day of the resurrection our Lord appeared and opened their meaning to His disciples; that they might understand what was said of Him in the Law and the Prophets. And then they believed the prediction of the Prophets that Christ would rise the third day, and the word which Jesus had spoken to them: *Destroy this temple, &c.* ORIGEN. But (in the mystical interpretation) we shall attain to the full measure of faith, at the great resurrection of the whole body of Jesus, i. e. His Church; inasmuch as the faith which is from sight, is very different from that which seeth as through a glass darkly.

Marginal notes:
John 12, 27.
ib. 10,
18.
Luke 23, 46.
Ps. 16, 11.
Orig. tom. x. in Joan. c. 23.
Chrys. Hom. xxiii. in Joan. 3.
John 7, 39.
Orig. Tr. x. c. 27.

23. Now when he was in Jerusalem at the passover, in the feast day, many believed in his name, when they saw the miracles which he did.

24. But Jesus did not commit himself unto them, because he knew all men.

25. And needed not that any should testify of man: for he knew what was in man.

BEDE. The Evangelist has related above what our Lord Bede. did on his way to Jerusalem; now He relates how others in loc. were affected towards Him at Jerusalem; *Now when He was in Jerusalem at the Passover, in the feast day, many believed in His Name, when they saw the miracles which He did.* ORIGEN. But how was it that many believed on Him from Orig. seeing His miracles? for he seems to have performed no tom. x. c. 30. supernatural works at Jerusalem, except we suppose Scripture to have passed them over. May not however the act of His making a scourge of small cords, and driving all out of the temple, be reckoned a miracle? CHRYS. Those had been Chrys. wiser disciples, however, who were brought to Christ not by Hom. xxiv. 1. His miracles, but by His doctrine. For it is the duller sort who are attracted by miracles; the more rational are convinced by prophecy, or doctrine. And therefore it follows, *But Jesus did not commit Himself unto them.* AUG. What Aug. Tr. xi. meaneth this, *Many believed in His Name—but Jesus did not* in Joan. *commit Himself unto them?* Was it that they did not believe c. 2. 2. in Him, but only pretended that they did? In that case the Evangelist would not have said, *Many believed in His Name.* Wonderful this, and strange, that men should trust Christ, and Christ trusts not Himself to men; especially considering that He was the Son of God, and suffered voluntarily, or else need not have suffered at all. Yet such are all catechumens. If we say to a catechumen, Believest thou in Christ? he answers, I do believe, and crosses himself. If we ask him, Dost thou eat the flesh of the Son of man? he knows not what we say[k], for Jesus has not committed Himself to him. ORIGEN. Or, it was those who believed *in His Name*, not Orig. *on Him*, to whom Jesus would not commit Himself. They tom. x. c. 28. believe *on Him*, who follow the narrow way which leadeth unto life; they believe *in His Name*, who only believe the miracles. CHRYS. Or it means that He did not place confidence in them, Chrys. Hom. xxv. 1.

[k] Catechumens in the early Church not being taught the mystery of the Eucharist. Nic.

as perfect disciples, and did not, as if they were brethren of confirmed faith, commit to them all His doctrines, for He did not attend to their outward words, but entered into their hearts, and well knew how short-lived was their zeal[1]. *Because He knew all men, and needed not that any should testify of man, for He knew what was in man.* To know what is in man's heart, is in the power of God alone, who fashioned the heart. He does not want witnesses, to inform Him of that mind, which was of His own fashioning. AUG. The Maker knew better what was in His own work, than the work knew what was in itself. Peter knew not what was in himself when he said, *I will go with Thee unto death;* but our Lord's answer shewed that He knew what was in man ; *Before the cock crow, thou shalt thrice deny Me.* BEDE. An admonition to us not to be confident of ourselves, but ever anxious and mistrustful ; knowing that what escapes our own knowledge, cannot escape the eternal Judge.

Aug. Tr. xi. c. 2.

Luke 22, 33.

ver. 61.

---

[1] εἰδὼς τὴν πρόσκαιρον αὐτῶν θερμότητα   Aq. tempus opportunum manifestè sciens.

CHAP. III.

1. There was a man of the Pharisees, named Nicodemus, a ruler of the Jews:

2. The same came to Jesus by night, and said unto him, Rabbi, we know that thou art a teacher come from God: for no man can do these miracles that thou doest, except God be with him.

3. Jesus answered and said unto him, Verily, verily, I say unto thee, Except a man be born again, he cannot see the kingdom of God.

AUG. He had said above that, *when He was at Jerusalem—* Aug. Tr. xi. *many believed in His Name, when they saw the miracles which He did.* Of this number was Nicodemus, of whom we are told; *There was a man of the Pharisees, Nicodemus, a ruler of the Jews.* BEDE. His rank is given, *A ruler of the Jews;* and then what he did, *This man came to Jesus by night:* hoping, that is, by so secret an interview, to learn more of the mysteries of the faith; the late public miracles having given him an elementary knowledge of them. CHRYS. Chrys. Hom. As yet however he was withheld by Jewish infirmity: and xxiv. 1. therefore he came in the night, being afraid to come in the day. Of such the Evangelist speaks elsewhere, *Nevertheless,* John 12, *among the chief rulers also many believed on Him; but* 42. *because of the Pharisees they did not confess Him, lest they should be put out of the synagogue.* AUG. Nicodemus was Aug. Tr. xi. one of the number who believed, but were not as yet born c. 3, 4. again. Wherefore he came to Jesus by night. Whereas those who are born of water and the Holy Ghost, are Eph. 5, addressed by the Apostle, *Ye were sometimes darkness, but* 8. *now are ye light in the Lord.* HAYMO. Or, well may it be Haymo. Hom. said that he came in the night, enveloped, as he was, in the in Oct. Pent.

darkness of ignorance, and not yet come to the light, i. e. the belief that our Lord was very God. Night in the language of Holy Writ is put for ignorance. *And said unto him, Rabbi, we know that Thou art a teacher come from God.* The Hebrew Rabbi, has the meaning of Magister in Latin. He calls him, we see, a Master, but not God: he does not hint at that; he believes Him to be sent from God, but does not see that He is God. AUG. What the ground of his belief was, is plain from what immediately follows: *For no one can do these miracles that Thou doest, except God be with him.* Nicodemus then was one of the many who *believed in His Name, when they saw the signs that He did.*

CHRYS. He did not however conceive any great idea of them from His miracles; and attributed to Him as yet only a human character, speaking of Him as a Prophet, sent to execute a commission, and standing in need of assistance to do His work; whereas the Father had begotten Him perfect, selfsufficient, and free from all defect. It being Christ's design however for the present not so much to reveal His dignity, as to prove that He did nothing contrary to the Father; in words He is often humble, while His acts ever testify His power. And therefore to Nicodemus on this occasion He says nothing expressly to magnify Himself; but He imperceptibly corrects his low views of Him, and teaches him that He was Himself all-sufficient, and independent in His miraculous works. Hence He answers, *Verily, verily, I say unto you, Except a man be born again, he cannot see the kingdom of God.* AUG. Those then are the persons to whom Jesus commits Himself, those born again, who come not in the night to Jesus, as Nicodemus did. Such persons immediately make professsion. CHRYS. He says therefore, *Except a man be born again, he cannot see the kingdom of God:* as if He said, Thou art not yet born again, i. e. of God, by a spiritual begetting; and therefore thy knowledge of Me is not spiritual, but carnal and human. But I say unto thee, that neither thou, nor any one, except he be born again of God, shall be able to see the glory which is around me, but shall be out of the kingdom: for it is the begetting by baptism, which enlightens the mind. Or the meaning is, Except thou art born from above, and

Aug.
Tr. xi.
c. 3.

Chrys.
Hom.
xxiv. 2.
in Joan.

Aug.Tr.
xi. c. 4.

Chrys.
Hom.
xxiv. 2.

hast received the certainty of my doctrines, thou wanderest
out of the way, and art far from the kingdom of heaven.
By which words our Lord discloses His nature, shewing that
He is more than what He appears to the outward eye.   The
expression, *From above**, means, according to some, from
heaven, according to others, from the beginning.   Had the
Jews heard it, they would have left Him in scorn; but Nicodemus shews the love of a disciple, by staying to ask more
questions.

4. Nicodemus saith unto him, How can a man be
born when he is old? can he enter the second time
into his mother's womb, and be born?

5. Jesus answered, Verily, verily, I say unto thee,
Except a man be born of water and of the Spirit, he
cannot enter into the kingdom of God.

6. That which is born of the flesh is flesh; and that
which is born of the Spirit is spirit.

7. Marvel not that I said unto thee, Ye must be
born again.

8. The wind bloweth where it listeth, and thou
hearest the sound thereof, but canst not tell whence it
cometh, and whither it goeth; so is every one that is
born of the Spirit.

CHRYS. Nicodemus coming to Jesus, as to a man, is startled on learning greater things than man could utter, things too lofty for him.   His mind is darkened, and he does not stand firm, but reels like one on the point of falling away from the faith.   Therefore he objects to the doctrine as being impossible, in order to call forth a fuller explana-tion.   Two things there are which astonish him, such a birth, and such a kingdom; neither yet heard of among the Jews.   First he urges the former difficulty, as being the greatest marvel.   *Nicodemus saith unto him, How can a man be born when he is old? can he enter a second time into his mother's womb, and be born?*   BEDE. The question

Chrys. Hom. xxiv. 3.

Bede. in loc.

* Desuper Aq. denuo Vulg. see Tr. 67 on Holy Baptism, p. 45 note.

put thus sounds as if a boy *might* enter a second time into his mother's womb and be born. But Nicodemus, we must remember, was an old man, and took his instance from himself; as if he said, I am an old man, and seek my salvation; how can I enter again into my mother's womb, and be born?

Chrys. Hom. xxiv. 2. CHRYS. Thou callest Him Rabbi, and sayest that He comes from God, and yet receivest not His sayings, but usest to thy master a word which brings in endless confusion; for that *how*, is the enquiry of a man who has no strong belief; and many who have so enquired, have fallen from the faith; some asking, how God became incarnate? others, how He was born[b]? Nicodemus here asks from anxiety. But observe when a man trusts spiritual things to reasonings of his own,

Aug. Tr. xi. c. 6. how ridiculously he talks. AUG. It is the Spirit that speaketh, whereas he understandeth carnally; he knew of no birth save one, that from Adam and Eve; from God and the Church he knows of none. But do thou so understand the birth of the Spirit, as Nicodemus did the birth of the flesh; for as the entrance into the womb cannot be repeated,

Chrys. Hom. xxiv. 3. so neither can baptism. CHRYS. While Nicodemus stumbles, dwelling upon our birth here, Christ reveals more clearly the manner of our spiritual birth; Jesus answered, *Verily, verily, I say unto you, Except a man be born of water and of the*

Aug. Tr. xii. c. 5. *Spirit, he cannot enter into the kingdom of God.* AUG. As if He said, Thou understandest me to speak of a carnal birth; but a man must be born of water and of the Spirit, if he is to enter into the kingdom of God. If to obtain the temporal inheritance of his human father, a man must be born of the womb of his mother; to obtain the eternal inheritance of his heavenly Father, he must be born of the womb of the Church. And since man consists of two parts, body and soul, the mode even of this latter birth is twofold; water the visible part cleansing the body; the Spirit by His

Chrys. Hom. xxv. 1. invisible cooperation, changing the invisible soul. CHRYS. If any one asks how a man is born of water, I ask in return, how Adam was born from the ground. For as in the beginning though the element of earth was the subject-matter, the man was the work of the fashioner; so now too, though the element of water is the subject-matter, the whole work is

---

[b] So S. Chrys. and how He remained impassible. Aq.

done by the Spirit of grace. He then gave Paradise for a place to dwell in; now He hath opened heaven to us. But what need is there of water, to those who receive the Holy c. 2. Ghost? It carries out the divine symbols of burial, mortification, resurrection, and life. For by the immersion of our heads in the water, the old man disappears and is buried as it were in a sepulchre, whence he ascends a new man. Thus shouldest thou learn, that the virtue of the Father, and of the Son, and of the Holy Ghost, filleth all things. For which reason also Christ lay three days in the grave before His resurrection. That then which the Hom. womb is to the offspring, water is to the believer; he is xxvi. 1. fashioned and formed in the water. But that which is fashioned in the womb needeth time; whereas the water all is done in an instant. For the nature of the body is such as to require time for its completion; but spiritual creations are perfect from the beginning. From the time that our Lord ascended out of the Jordan, water produces no longer reptiles, i. e. living souls; but souls rational and endued with the Spirit. AUG. Because He does not say, Except Aug. a man be born again[1] of water and of the Spirit, he shall lib. i. de Bapt. not have salvation, or eternal life; but, *he shall not enter* *into the kingdom of God;* from this, some infer that children c. 30. i Vulg. are to be baptized in order to be with Christ in the kingdom of God, where they would not be, were they not baptized; but that they will obtain salvation and eternal life even if they die without baptism, not being bound with any chain of sin. But why is a man born again, except to be changed from his old into a new state? Or why doth the image of God not enter into the kingdom of God, if it be not by reason of sin? HAYMO. But Nicodemus being unable to Haymo. take in so great and deep mysteries, our Lord helps him by Hom. in Oct. the analogy of our carnal birth, saying, *That which is born* Pent. *of the flesh is flesh, and that which is born of the Spirit is* *spirit.* For as flesh generates flesh, so also doth spirit spirit. CHRYS. Do not look then for any material pro-Chrys. duction, or think that the Spirit generates flesh; for even the Hom. xxvi. in Lord's flesh is generated not by the Spirit only, but also by Joan. 1. the flesh. That which is born of the Spirit is spiritual. The birth here spoken of takes place not according to our substance, but according to honour and grace. But the birth of the Son of God is otherwise; for else what would He have been more than all who are born again? And He would be proved too inferior to the Spirit, inasmuch as His birth would be by the grace of the Spirit. How does this differ from the Jewish doctrine?—But mark next the part c. 1, 13. of the Holy Spirit, in the divine work. For whereas above some are said to be *born of God*, here, we find, the Spirit generates them.—The wonder of Nicodemus being roused again by the words, *He who is born of the Spirit is spirit*, Christ meets him again with an instance from nature; *Marvel not that I said unto thee, Ye must be born again.* The expression, *Marvel not*, shews that Nicodemus was surprised at His doctrine. He takes for this instance some thing, not of the grossness of other bodily things, but still removed from the incorporeal nature, the wind; *The wind bloweth where it listeth, and thou hearest the sound thereof, but canst not tell whence it cometh, and whither it goeth: so is every one that is born of the Spirit.* That is to say, if no one can restrain the wind from going where it will; much less can the laws of nature, whether the condition of our natural birth, or any other, restrain the action of the Spirit. That He speaks of the wind here is plain, from His saying, *Thou hearest the sound thereof*, i. e. its noise when it strikes objects. He would not in talking to an unbeliever and ignorant person, so describe the action of the Spirit. He says, *Bloweth where it listeth[e]*; not meaning any power of choice in the wind, but only its natural movements, in their uncontrolled power. *But canst not tell whence it cometh or whither it goeth;* i. e. If thou canst not explain the action of this wind which comes under the cognizance both of thy feeling and hearing, why examine into the operation of the Divine Spirit? He adds, *So is every one that is born of the Spirit.* Aug. But who of us does not see, for example, that

Aug.
Tr. xii.
c. 7.

the south wind blows from south to north, another wind from the east, another from the west? And how then do we not

---

[e] S. Chrys. adds §. 2. that the whole applies à fortiori to the Holy Spirit; "It bloweth where It listeth" is spoken also to express the power of the Spirit. If no one restraineth the wind, but it is borne whither it will, much more shall not the laws of nature or the rules of earthly birth, or any thing of this sort, hold the might of the Spirit.

know whence the wind cometh, and whither it goeth? BEDE. Bede.
It is the Holy Spirit therefore, Who bloweth where He listeth. in Hom. in part.
It is in His own power to choose, whose heart to visit with Invent.
His enlightening grace. *And thou hearest the sound thereof.* S. Cruc. Ed.Nic.
When one filled with the Holy Spirit is present with thee
and speaks to thee. AUG. The Psalm soundeth, the Gospel Aug.
soundeth, the Divine Word soundeth; it is the sound of the Tr. xii. c. 5.
Spirit. This means that the Holy Spirit is invisibly present
in the Word and Sacrament, to accomplish our birth. ALCUIN.
Therefore, *Thou knowest not whence it cometh, or whither it
goeth;* for, although the Spirit should possess a person in
thy presence at a particular time, it could not be seen how
He entered into him, or how He went away again, because
He is invisible. HAYMO. Or, *Thou canst not tell whence it* Haymo.
cometh; i. e. thou knowest not how He brings believers to Hom. in Oct.
the faith; *or whither it goeth,* i. e. how He directs the Pent.
faithful to their hope. And *so is every one that is born
of the Spirit;* as if He said, The Holy Spirit is an invisible
Spirit; and in like manner, every one who is born of the
Spirit is born invisibly. AUG. Or thus: If thou art born of Aug.
the Spirit, thou wilt be such, that he, who is not yet born of Tr. xii. c. 5.
the Spirit, will not know whence thou comest, or whither
thou goest. For it follows, *So is every one that is born of
the Spirit.* THEOPHYL. This completely refutes Macedonius in loc.
the impugner of the Spirit, who asserted that the Holy Ghost
was a servant. The Holy Ghost, we find, works by His
own power, where He will, and what He will.

9. Nicodemus answered and said unto him, How
can these things be?

10. Jesus answered and said unto him, Art thou a
master of Israel, and knowest not these things?

11. Verily, verily, I say unto thee, We speak that
we do know, and testify that we have seen; and ye receive not our witness.

12. If I have told you earthly things, and ye believe
not, how shall ye believe, if I tell you of heavenly
things.

HAYMO. Nicodemus cannot take in the mysteries of the Divine Majesty, which our Lord reveals, and therefore asks how it is, not denying the fact, not meaning any censure, but wishing to be informed: *Nicodemus answered and said unto Him, How can these things be?*

CHRYS. Forasmuch then as he still remains a Jew, and, after such clear evidence, persists in a low and carnal system, Christ addresses him henceforth with greater severity: *Jesus answered and said unto him, Art thou a master in Israel, and knowest not these things?*

AUG. What think we? that our Lord wished to insult this master in Israel? He wished him to be born of the Spirit: and no one is born of the Spirit except he is made humble; for this very humility it is, which makes us to be born of the Spirit. He however was inflated with his eminence as a master, and thought himself of importance because he was a doctor of the Jews. Our Lord then casts down his pride, in order that he may be born of the Spirit.

CHRYS. Nevertheless He does not charge the man with wickedness, but only with want of wisdom, and enlightenment. But some one will say, What connexion hath this birth, of which Christ speaks, with Jewish doctrines? Thus much. The first man that was made, the woman that was made out of his rib, the barren that bare, the miracles which were worked by means of water, I mean, Elijah's bringing up the iron from the river, the passage of the Red Sea, and Naaman the Syrian's purification in the Jordan, were all types and figures of the spiritual birth, and of the purification which was to take place thereby. Many passages in the Prophets too have a hidden reference to this birth: as that in the Psalms, *Making thee young and lusty as an eagle:* and, *Blessed is he whose unrighteousness is forgiven.* And again, Isaac was a type of this birth. Referring to these passages, our Lord says, *Art thou a master in Israel, and knowest not these things?* A second time however He condescends to his infirmity, and makes use of a common argument to render what He has said credible: *Verily, verily, I say unto thee, We speak that we do know, and testify that we have seen, and ye receive not our testimony.* Sight we consider the most certain of all the senses; so that when we say, we saw such a thing with our

Marginal references:
Chrys. Hom. xxvi. 2.
Aug. Tr. xii. c. 6.
Chrys. Hom. xxvi. 2.
Ps. 102, 5. Ps. 31, 1.
ver. 11.

eyes, we seem to compel men to believe us. In like manner Christ, speaking after the manner of men, does not indeed say that he has seen actually, i. e. with the bodily eye, the mysteries He reveals; but it is clear that He means it of the most certain absolute knowledge. This then, viz. *That we do know*, he asserts of Himself alone. HAYMO. Why, it is asked, does He speak in the plural number, *We speak that we do know?* Because the speaker being the Only-Begotten Son of God, He would shew that the Father was in the Son, and the Son in the Father, and the Holy Ghost from both, proceeding indivisibly. ALCUIN. Or, the plural number may have this meaning; I, and they who are born again of the Spirit, alone understand what we speak; and having seen the Father in secret, this we testify openly to the world; and ye, who are carnal and proud, receive not our testimony. THEO-PHYL. This is not said of Nicodemus, but of the Jewish race, who to the very last persisted in unbelief. CHRYS. They are words of gentleness, not of anger; a lesson to us, when we argue and cannot converse, not by sore and angry words, but by the absence of anger and clamour, (for clamour is the material of anger,) to prove the soundness of our views. Jesus in entering upon high doctrines, ever checks Himself in compassion to the weakness of His hearer: and does not dwell continuously on the most important truths, but turns to others more humble. Whence it follows: *If I have told you earthly things, and ye believe not, how shall ye believe if I tell you of heavenly things.* AUG. That is: If ye do not believe that I can raise up a temple, which you have thrown down, how can ye believe that men can be regenerated by the Holy Ghost? CHRYS. Or thus: Be not surprised at His calling Baptism earthly. It is performed upon earth, and is compared with that stupendous birth, which is of the substance of the Father, an earthly birth being one of mere grace. And well hath He said, not, Ye understand not, but, Ye believe not: for when the understanding cannot take in certain truths, we attribute it to natural deficiency or ignorance: but where that is not received which it belongs to faith only to receive, the fault is not deficiency, but unbelief. These truths, however, were revealed that posterity

Haymo. Hom. in Oct. Pent.

Chrys. Hom. xxvi. 3.

Aug. Tr. xii. in Joan. c. 7.

Chrys. Hom. xxvii. 1.

might believe and benefit by them, though the people of that age did not.

13. And no man hath ascended up to heaven, but he that came down from heaven, even the Son of man which is in heaven.

Aug.
DePecc.
mer. et
remiss.
c. xxxi.

AUG. After taking notice of this lack of knowledge in a person, who, on the strength of his magisterial station, set himself above others, and blaming the unbelief of such men, our Lord says, that if such as these do not believe, others will: *No one hath ascended into heaven, but He that came down from heaven, even the Son of man who is in heaven.* This may be rendered: The spiritual birth shall be of such sort, as that men from being earthly shall become heavenly: which will not be possible, except they are made members of Me; so that he who ascends, becomes one with Him who descended. Our Lord accounts His body, i. e.

Greg.
xxvii.
Mor.c.8.
al. 11.

His Church, as Himself. GREG. Forasmuch as we are made one with Him, to the place from which He came alone in Himself, thither He returns alone in us; and He who is ever in heaven, daily ascendeth to heaven.

Aug.
nt sup.

AUG. Although He was made the Son of man upon earth, yet His Divinity with which, remaining in heaven, He descended to earth, He hath declared not to disagree with the title of Son of man, as He hath thought His flesh worthy the name of Son of God. For through the Unity of person, by which both substances are one Christ, He walked upon earth, being Son of God; and remained in heaven, being Son of man. And the belief of the greater, involves belief in the less. If then the Divine substance, which is so far more removed from us, and could for our sake take up the substance of man so as to unite them in one person; how much more easily may we believe, that the Saints united with the man Christ, become with Him one Christ; so that while it is true of all, that they ascend by grace, it is at the same time true, that He alone ascends to

Chrys.
Hom.
xxvii. 1.

heaven, Who came down from heaven. CHRYS. Or thus: Nicodemus having said, *We know that Thou art a teacher sent from God;* our Lord says, *And no man hath ascended, &c.* in that He might not appear to be a teacher only like one of the Prophets. THEOPHYL. But when thou in loc. hearest that the Son of man came down from heaven, think not that His flesh came down from heaven; for this is the doctrine of those heretics, who hold that Christ took His Body from heaven, and only passed through the Virgin. CHRYS. Chrys. By the title Son of man here, He does not mean His flesh, Hom. xxvii. 1. but Himself altogether; the lesser part of His nature being put to express the whole. It is not uncommon with Him to name Himself wholly from His humanity, or wholly from His divinity. BEDE; If a man of set purpose descend naked to the valley, and there providing himself with clothes and armour, ascend the mountain again, he who ascended may be said to be the same with him who descended. HILARY; Hilar. Or, His descending from heaven is the source of His origin de Trin. c. 16. as conceived by the Spirit: Mary gave not His body its origin, though the natural qualities of her sex contributed its birth and increase. That He is the Son of man is from the birth of the flesh which was conceived in the Virgin. That He is in heaven is from the power of His everlasting nature, which did not contract the power of the Word of God, which is infinite, within the sphere of a finite body. Our Lord remaining in the form of a servant, far from the whole circle, inner and outer, of heaven and the world, yet as Lord of heaven and the world, was not absent therefrom. So then He came down from heaven because He was the Son of man; and He was in heaven, because the Word, which was made flesh, had not ceased to be the Word. AUG. But thou wonderest that He was at once here, and in Aug. heaven. Yet such power hath He given to His disciples. Tr. xii. c. 8. Hear Paul, *Our conversation is in heaven.* If the man Paul Phil. 3, walked upon earth, and had his conversation in heaven; 20. shall not the God of heaven and earth be able to be in heaven and earth? CHRYS. That too which seemeth very lofty is Chrys. still unworthy of His vastness. For He is not in heaven only, Hom. xxvii. 1. but every where, and filleth all things. But for the present He accommodates Himself to the weakness of His hearer, that by degrees He may convert him.

14. And as Moses lifted up the serpent in the wilderness, even so must the Son of man be lifted up:

15. That whosoever believeth in him should not perish, but have eternal life.

Chrys. Hom. xxvii. 1. CHRYS. Having made mention of the gift of baptism, He proceeds to the source of it, i. e. the cross: *And as Moses lifted up the serpent in the wilderness, even so must the Son of man be lifted up.* BEDE; He introduces the teacher of the Mosaic law, to the spiritual sense of that law; by a passage from the Old Testament history, which was intended **Aug.** to be a figure of His Passion, and of man's salvation. AUG. **de Pecc. mer. et remiss. c. xxxii.** Many dying in the wilderness from the attack of the serpents, Moses, by commandment of the Lord, lifted up a brazen serpent: and those who looked upon it were immediately healed. The lifting up of the serpent is the death of Christ; the cause, by a certain mode of construction, being put for the effect. The serpent was the cause of death, inasmuch as he persuaded man into that sin, by which he merited death. Our Lord, however, did not transfer sin, i. e. the poison of the serpent, to his flesh, but death; in order that in the likeness of sinful flesh, there might be punishment without sin, by virtue of which sinful flesh might be delivered **in loc.** both from punishment and from sin. THEOPHYL. See then the aptness of the figure. The figure of the serpent has the appearance of the beast, but not its poison: in the same way Christ came in the likeness of sinful flesh, being free from sin. By Christ's being *lifted up,* understand His being suspended on high, by which suspension He sanctified the air, even as He had sanctified the earth by walking upon it. Herein too is typified the glory of Christ: for the height of the cross was made His glory: for in that He submitted to be judged, He judged the prince of this world; for Adam died justly, because he sinned; our Lord unjustly, because He did no sin. So He overcame him, who delivered Him over to death, and thus delivered Adam from death. And in this the devil found himself vanquished, that he could not upon the cross torment our Lord into hating His murderers: but only made Him love and pray for them the more. In this way the cross of Christ was made His lifting up, and glory.

Chrys. Hom. xxvii. 2. CHRYS. Wherefore He does not say, ' The Son of man must be suspended, but *lifted up,* a more honourable term, but

coming near the figure. He uses the figure to shew that the
old dispensation is akin to the new, and to shew on His
hearers' account that He suffered voluntarily; and that His
death issued in life. Aug. As then formerly he who looked
to the serpent that was lifted up, was healed of its poison,
and saved from death; so now he who is conformed to the
likeness of Christ's death by faith and the grace of baptism,
is delivered both from sin by justification, and from death by
the resurrection: as He Himself saith; *That whosoever
believeth on Him should not perish, but have everlasting
life.* What need then is there that the child should be conformed by baptism to the death of Christ, if he be not
altogether tainted by the poisonous bite of the serpent?
Chrys. Observe; He alludes to the Passion obscurely, in
consideration to His hearer; but the fruit of the Passion He
unfolds plainly; viz. that they who believe in the Crucified
One should not perish. And if they who believe in the
Crucified live, much more shall the Crucified One Himself.
Aug. But there is this difference between the figure and the
reality, that the one recovered from temporal death, the other
from eternal.

Aug. Tr. xii. c. 11.

Chrys. Hom. xxvii. 2.

Aug. Tr. xii. c. 11.

16. For God so loved the world, that he gave his
only begotten Son, that whosoever believeth in him
should not perish, but have everlasting life.

17 For God sent not his Son into the world to
condemn the world; but that the world through him
might be saved.

18. He that believeth on him is not condemned:
but he that believeth not is condemned already, because
he hath not believed in the name of the only begotten
Son of God.

Chrys. Having said, *Even so must the Son of man be lifted
up,* alluding to His death; lest His hearer should be cast down
by His words, forming some human notion of Him, and
thinking of His death as an evil[1], He corrects this by saying,
that He who was given up to death was the Son of God, and
that His death would be the source of life eternal; *So God*

*1 ἀπ-
ταξίαν,
destruc-
tion,
Nicolai,
non sa-
lutarem.*

loved the world, that He gave His only begotten Son, that whosoever believeth in Him should not perish, but have everlasting life; as if He said, Marvel not that I must be lifted up, that you may be saved: for so it seemeth good to the Father, who hath so loved you, that He hath given His Son to suffer for ungrateful and careless servants. The text, *God so loved the world,* shews intensity of love. For great indeed and infinite is the distance between the two. He who is without end, or beginning of existence, Infinite Greatness, loved those who were of earth and ashes, creatures laden with sins innumerable. And the act which springs from the love is equally indicative of its vastness. For God gave not a servant, or an Angel, or an Archangel, but His Son. Again, had He had many sons, and given one, this would have been a very great gift; but now He hath given His Only Begotten

Hilar. vi. de Trin. c. 40.

Son. HILARY; If it were only a creature given up for the sake of a creature, such a poor and insignificant loss were no great evidence of love. They must be precious things which prove our love, great things must evidence its greatness. God, in love to the world, gave His Son, not an adopted Son, but His own, even His Only Begotten. Here is proper Sonship, birth, truth: no creation, no adoption, no lie: here is the test of love and charity, that God sent His

n loc.

own and only begotten Son to save the world. THEOPHYL. As He said above, that the Son of man came down from heaven, not meaning that His flesh did come down from heaven, on account of the unity of person in Christ, attributing to man what belonged to God: so now conversely what belongs to man, he assigns to God the Word. The Son of God was impassible; but being one in respect of person with man, who was passible, the Son is said to be given up to death; inasmuch as He truly suffered, not in His own nature, but in His own flesh. From this death follows an exceeding great and incomprehensible benefit: viz. that *whosoever believeth in Him should not perish, but have everlasting life.* The Old Testament promised to those who obeyed it, length of days: the Gospel promises life eternal, and imperishable.

¹ Ed. Nicolai.

BEDE[1]; Note here, that the same which he before said of the Son of man, lifted up on the cross, he repeats of the only begotten Son of God: viz. *That whosoever believeth in*

Him, &c. For the same our Maker and Redeemer, who was Son of God before the world was, was made at the end of the world the Son of man; so that He who by the power of His Godhead had created us to enjoy the happiness of an endless life, the same restored us to the life we have lost by taking our human frailty upon Him. ALCUIN. Truly through the Son of God shall the world have life; for for no other cause came He into the world, except to save the world. *God sent not His Son into the world to condemn the world, but that the world through Him might be saved.* AUG. For why is He called the Saviour of the world, but because He saves the world? The physician, so far as his will is concerned, heals the sick. If the sick despises or will not observe the directions of the physician, he destroys himself. CHRYS. Because however He says this, slothful men in the multitude of their sins, and excess of carelessness, abuse God's mercy, and say, There is no hell, no punishment; God remits us all our sins. But let us remember, that there are two advents of Christ; one past, the other to come. The former was, not to judge but to pardon us: the latter will be, not to pardon but to judge us. It is of the former that He says, I have not come to judge the world. Because He is merciful, instead of judgment, He grants an internal remission of all sins by baptism; and even after baptism opens to us the door of repentance, which had He not done all had been lost; *for all have sinned, and come short of the glory of God.* Afterwards, however, there follows something about the punishment of unbelievers, to warn us against flattering ourselves that we can sin with impunity. Of the unbeliever He says, ' he is judged already.'—But first He says, *He that believeth on Him is not judged.* He who believeth, He says, not who enquires. But what if his life be impure? Paul very strongly declares that such are not believers: *They confess,* he says, *that they know God, but in works deny Him.* That is to say, Such will not be judged for their belief, but will receive a heavy punishment for their works, though unbelief will not be charged against them. ALCUIN. He who believes on Him, and cleaves to Him as a member to the head, will not be condemned. AUG. What didst thou expect Him to say of him who believed not, except that he is condemned. Yet

Aug. Tr. xii. c. 12.

Chrys. Hom. xxviii.1.

Rom. 3, 23.

Tit. 1, 16.

Aug. Tr. x'i. c. 12.

mark His words: *He that believeth not is condemned already.*
The Judgment hath not appeared, but it is already given.
For the Lord knows who are His; who are awaiting the
Chrys. crown, and who the fire. CHRYS. Or the meaning is, that
Hom. disbelief itself is the punishment of the impenitent: inasmuch
xxviii.1. as that is to be without light, and to be without light is of
itself the greatest punishment. Or He is announcing what is
to be. Though a murderer be not yet sentenced by the
Judge, still his crime has already condemned him. In like
manner he who believes not, is dead, even as Adam, on the
Greg. day that he ate of the tree, died. GREG. Or thus: In the
l. xxvi. last judgment some perish without being judged, of whom it
Mor. c. is here said, *He that believeth not is condemned already.*
xxvii. For the day of judgment does not try those who for unbelief
(50.) are already banished from the sight of a discerning judge,
are under sentence of damnation; but those, who retaining
the profession of faith, have no works to shew suitable to that
profession. For those who have not kept even the sacraments
of faith, do not even hear the curse of the Judge at the last
trial. They have already, in the darkness of their unbelief,
received their sentence, and are not thought worthy of being
convicted by the rebuke of Him whom they had despised
Again; For an earthly sovereign, in the government of his state,
has a different rule of punishment, in the case of the dis-
affected subject, and the foreign rebel. In the former case,
he consults the civil law; but against the enemy he proceeds
at once to war, and repays his malice with the punishment it
deserves, without regard to law, inasmuch as he who never
submitted to law, has no claim to suffer by the law. ALCUIN.
He then gives the reason why he who believeth not is
condemned, viz. *because he believeth not in the name of the
only begotten Son of God.* For in this name alone is there
salvation. God hath not many sons who can save; He by
Aug. de whom He saves is the Only Begotten. AUG. Where then
Pecc. do we place baptized children? Amongst those who believe?
mer. et This is acquired for them by the virtue of the Sacrament, and
Rem. the pledges of the sponsors. And by this same rule we
l.1.c. 33. reckon those who are not baptized, among those who believe
not.

19. And this is the condemnation, that light is come into the world, and men loved darkness rather than light, because their deeds were evil.

20. For every one that doeth evil hateth the light, neither cometh to the light, lest his deeds should be reproved.

21. But he that doeth truth cometh to the light, that his deeds may be made manifest, that they are wrought in God.

ALCUIN. Here is the reason why men believed not, and why they are justly condemned; *This is the condemnation, that light is come into the world.* CHRYS. As if He said, So far from their having sought for it, or laboured to find it, light itself hath come to them, and they have refused to admit it; *Men loved darkness rather than light.* Thus He leaves them no excuse. He came to rescue them from darkness, and bring them to light; who can pity him who does not choose to approach the light when it comes unto him? BEDE. He calls *Himself* the light, whereof the Evangelist speaks, *That was the true light;* whereas sin He calls darkness. CHRYS. Then because it seemed incredible that man should prefer light to darkness, he gives the reason of the infatuation, viz. that *their deeds were evil.* And indeed had He come to Judgment, there had been some reason for not receiving Him; for he who is conscious of his crimes, naturally avoids the judge. But criminals are glad to meet one who brings them pardon. And therefore it might have been expected that men conscious of their sins would have gone to meet Christ, as many indeed did; for the publicans and sinners came and sat down with Jesus. But the greater part being too cowardly to undergo the toils of virtue for righteousness' sake, persisted in their wickedness to the last; of whom our Lord says, *Every one that doeth evil, hateth the light.* He speaks of those who choose to remain in their wickedness. ALCUIN. *Every one that doeth evil, hateth the light;* i. e. he who is resolved to sin, who delights in sin, hateth the light, which detects his sin. AUG. Because they dislike being deceived, and like to deceive, they love light for discovering

Chrys. Hom. xxviii.2.

Bede. in loc. c. 1.

Chrys. Hom. xxviii.2.

Aug. Conf. c. xxiii.

(34.)

herself, and hate her for discovering them. Wherefore it shall be their punishment, that she shall manifest them against their will, and herself not be manifest unto them. They love the brightness of truth, they hate her discrimination; and therefore it follows, *Neither cometh to the light, that*

Chrys. Hom. xxvii. 2.

his deeds should be reproved. CHRYS. No one reproves a Pagan, because his own practice agrees with the character of his gods; his life is in accordance with his doctrines. But a Christian who lives in wickedness all must condemn. If there are any Gentiles whose life is good, I know them not. But are there not Gentiles? it may be asked. For do not tell me of the naturally amiable and honest; this is not virtue. But shew me one who has strong passions, and lives with wisdom. You cannot. For if the announcement of a kingdom, and the threats of hell, and other inducements, hardly keep men virtuous when they are so, such calls will hardly rouse them to the attainment of virtue in the first instance. Pagans, if they do produce any thing which looks well, do it for vain-glory's sake, and will therefore at the same time, if they can escape notice, gratify their evil desires as well. And what profit is a man's sobriety and decency of conduct, if he is the slave of vain-glory? The slave of vain-glory is no less a sinner than a fornicator; nay, sins even oftener, and more grievously. However, even supposing there are some few Gentiles of good lives, the exceptions so rare do not affect my argument. BEDE; Morally too they love darkness rather than light, who when their preachers tell them their duty, assail them with calumny.

But he that doeth truth cometh to the light, that his deeds may be made manifest, that they are wrought in God. CHRYS. He does not say this of those who are

Chrys. Hom. xxviii. 3.

brought up under the Gospel, but of those who are converted to the true faith from Paganism or Judaism. He shews that no one will leave a false religion for the true faith, till he first resolve to follow a right course of life. AUG. He calls

Aug. de Pecc. mer. et Remiss. l.i. c. 53.

the works of him who comes to the light, *wrought in God;* meaning that his justification is attributable not to his own merits, but to God's grace. AUG. But if God hath dis-

Aug. Tr. xii. 13, 14.

covered all men's works to be evil, how is it that any have done the truth, and come to the light, i. e. to Christ? Now

what He saith is, that *they loved darkness rather than light;*
He lays the stress upon that. Many have loved their sins,
many have confessed them. God accuseth thy sins; if thou
accuse them too, thou art joined to God. Thou must hate
thine own work, and love the work of God in thee. The
beginning of good works, is the confession of evil works,
and then thou doest the truth: not soothing, not flattering
thyself. And thou art come to the light, because this very
sin in thee, which displeaseth thee, would not displease thee,
did not God shine upon thee, and His truth shew it unto
thee. And let those even who have sinned only by word
or thought, or who have only exceeded in things allowable,
do the truth, by making confession, and come to the light
by performing good works. For little sins, if suffered to
accumulate, become mortal. Little drops swell the river:
little grains of sand become an heap, which presses and
weighs down. The sea coming in by little and little, unless
it be pumped out, sinks the vessel. And what is to pump
out, but by good works, mourning, fasting, giving and
forgiving, to provide against our sins overwhelming us?

22. After these things came Jesus and his disciples
into the land of Judæa; and there he tarried with them,
and baptized.

23. And John also was baptizing in Ænon near to
Salim, because there was much water there: and they
came, and were baptized.

24. For John was not yet cast into prison.

25. Then there arose a question between some
of John's disciples and the Jews about purifying.

26. And they came unto John, and said unto him,
Rabbi, he that was with thee beyond Jordan, to whom
thou barest witness, behold, the same baptizeth, and
all men come to him.

CHRYS. Nothing is more open than truth, nothing bolder; Chrys.
it neither seeks concealment, or avoids danger, or fears the Hom.
xxix. 1.
snare, or cares for popularity. It is subject to no human
weakness. Our Lord went up to Jerusalem at the feasts, not

from ostentation or love of honour, but to teach the people
His doctrines, and shew miracles of mercy. After the
festival He visited the crowds who were collected at the
Jordan. *After these things came Jesus and His disciples
into the land of Judæa; and there he tarried with them, and
baptized.* BEDE; *After these things*, is not immediately
after His dispute with Nicodemus, which took place at
Jerusalem; but on His return to Jerusalem after some time
spent in Galilee. ALCUIN. By Judæa are meant those who
confess, whom Christ visits; for wherever there is confession
of sins, or the praise of God, thither cometh Christ and His
disciples, i. e. His doctrine and enlightenment; and there
He is known by His cleansing men from sin: *And there He
tarried with them, and baptized.* CHRYS. As the Evangelist
says afterwards, that Jesus baptized not but His disciples,
it is evident that he means the same here, i. e. that the
disciples only baptized. AUG. Our Lord did not baptize
with the baptism wherewith He had been baptized; for He
was baptized by a servant, as a lesson of humility to us, and
in order to bring us to the Lord's baptism, i. e. His own;
for Jesus baptized, as the Lord, the Son of God. BEDE;
John still continues baptizing, though Christ has begun;
for the shadow remains still, nor must the forerunner cease,
till the truth is manifested. *And John also was baptizing in
Ænon, near to Salim.* Ænon is Hebrew for water; so that
the Evangelist gives, as it were, the derivation of the name,
when he adds, *For there was much water there.* Salim is a
town on the Jordan, where Melchisedec once reigned.
JEROME; It matters not whether it is called Salem, or
Salim; since the Jews very rarely use vowels in the middle
of words; and the same words are pronounced with different
vowels and accents, by different readers, and in different
places.

And they came, and were baptized. BEDE; The same
kind of benefit which catechumens receive from instruction
before they are baptized, the same did John's baptism
convey before Christ's. As John preached repentance,
announced Christ's baptism, and drew all men to the
knowledge of the truth now made manifest to the world:
so the ministers of the Church first instruct those who come

Marginalia: Chrys. Hom. xxix. 1. — Aug. Tr. xiii. c. 4. — Hierom. Ep. c. xxiii. ad Evag.

to the faith, then reprove their sins; and lastly, drawing them to the knowledge and love of the truth, offer them remission by Christ's baptism. CHRYS. Notwithstanding the disciples of Jesus baptized, John did not leave off till his imprisonment; as the Evangelist's language intimates, *For John was not yet cast into prison.* BEDE; He evidently here is relating what Christ did before John's imprisonment; a part which has been passed over by the rest, who commence after John's imprisonment. AUG. But why did John baptize? Because it was necessary that our Lord should be baptized. And why was it necessary that our Lord should be baptized? That no one might ever think himself at liberty to despise baptism. CHRYS. But why did he go on baptizing now? Because, had he left off, it might have been attributed to envy or anger: whereas, continuing to baptize, he got no glory for himself, but sent hearers to Christ. And he was better able to do this service, than were Christ's own disciples; his testimony being so free from suspicion, and his reputation with the people so much higher than theirs. He therefore continued to baptize, that he might not increase the envy felt by his disciples against our Lord's baptism. Indeed, the reason, I think, why John's death was permitted, and, in his room, Christ made the great preacher, was, that the people might transfer their affections wholly to Christ, and no longer be divided between the two. For the disciples of John did become so envious of Christ's disciples, and even of Christ Himself, that when they saw the latter baptizing, they threw contempt upon their baptism, as being inferior to that of John's; *And there arose a question from some of John's disciples with the Jews about purifying.* That it was they who began the dispute, and not the Jews, the Evangelist implies by saying, that *there arose a question from John's disciples,* whereas he might have said, The Jews put forth a question. AUG. The Jews then asserted Christ to be the greater person, and His baptism necessary to be received. But John's disciples did not understand so much, and defended John's baptism. At last they come to John, to solve the question: *And they came unto John, and said unto him, Rabbi, He that was with thee beyond Jordan, behold, the Same baptizeth.* CHRYS.

Marginal notes:
Chrys. Hom. xxix. 1.
Aug. Tr. xiii. c. 6.
Chrys. Hom. xx. 1.
Aug. Tr. xiii. c. 8.
Chrys. Hom. xxix. 2.

Meaning, He, Whom thou baptizedst, baptizeth. They did not say expressly, Whom thou baptizedst, for they did not wish to be reminded of the voice from heaven, but, *He Who was with thee,* i. e. Who was in the situation of a disciple, who was nothing more than any of us, He now separateth Himself from thee, and baptizeth. They add, *To Whom thou barest witness;* as if to say, Whom thou shewedst to the world, Whom thou madest renowned, He now dares to do as thou dost. *Behold, the Same baptizeth.* And in addition to this, they urge the probability that John's doctrines would fall into discredit. *All men come to Him.* ALCUIN. Meaning, Passing by thee, all men run to the baptism of Him Whom thou baptizedst.

27. John answered and said, A man can receive nothing, except it be given him from heaven.

28. Ye yourselves bear me witness, that I said, I am not the Christ, but that I am sent before him.

29. He that hath the bride is the bridegroom; but the friend of the bridegroom, which standeth and heareth him, rejoiceth greatly because of the bridegroom's voice: this my joy therefore is fulfilled.

30. He must increase, but I must decrease.

Chrys.
Hom.
xxix. 2.

CHRYS. John, on this question being raised, does not rebuke his disciples, for fear they might separate, and turn to some other school, but replies gently, *John answered and said, A man can receive nothing, except it be given him from heaven;* as if he said, No wonder that Christ does such excellent works, and that all men come to Him; when He Who doeth it all is God. Human efforts are easily seen through, are feeble, and short-lived. These are not such: they are not therefore of human, but of divine originating. He seems however to speak somewhat humbly [k] of Christ, which will not surprise us, when we consider that it was not fitting to tell the whole truth, to minds prepossessed with such a passion as envy. He only tries for the present to alarm

[k] Referring to, " *A man can receive nothing,*" &c. ver. 27.

them, by shewing that they are attempting impossible things,
and fighting against God. Aug. Or perhaps John is speaking ^{Aug.}
here of himself: I am a mere man, and have received all ^{Tr. xiii.}_{c. 9.}
from heaven, and therefore think not that, because it has
been given me to be somewhat, I am so foolish as to speak
against the truth. Chrys. And see; the very argument ^{Chrys.}
by which they thought to have overthrown Christ, *To whom* ^{Hom.}_{xxix. 2.}
thou barest witness, he turns against them; *Ye yourselves*
bear me witness, that I said, I am not the Christ; as if he
said, If ye think my witness true, ye must acknowledge Him
more worthy of honour than myself. He adds, *But that I*
was sent before Him; that is to say, I am a servant, and
perform the commission of the Father which sent me; my
witness is not from favour or partiality; I say that which was
given me to say. Bede; Who art thou then, since thou art'
not the Christ, and who is He to Whom thou bearest witness? John replies, He is the Bridegroom; I am the friend
of the Bridegroom, sent to prepare the Bride for His approach:
He that hath the Bride, is the Bridegroom. By the Bride
he means the Church, gathered from amongst all nations; a
Virgin in purity of heart, in perfection of love, in the bond
of peace, in chastity of mind and body; in the unity of the
Catholic faith; for in vain is she a virgin in body, who con-
tinueth not a virgin in mind. This Bride hath Christ joined
unto Himself in marriage, and redeemed with the price of
His own Blood. Theophyl. Christ is the spouse of every
soul; the wedlock, wherein they are joined, is baptism; the
place of that wedlock is the Church; the pledge of it, remission of sins, and the fellowship of the Holy Ghost; the
consummation, eternal life; which those who are worthy
shall receive. Christ alone is the Bridegroom: all other
teachers are but the friends of the Bridegroom, as was the
forerunner. The Lord is the *giver* of good; the rest are the
despisers of His gifts. Bede; His Bride therefore our Lord
committed to His friend, i. e. the order of preachers, who
should be jealous of her, not for themselves, but for Christ;
The friend of the Bridegroom which standeth and heareth
Him, rejoiceth greatly because of the Bridegroom's voice.
Aug. As if He said, She is not My spouse. But dost thou ^{Aug.}
therefore not rejoice in the marriage? Yea, I rejoice, he ^{Tr. xiii.}_{c. 12.}

Chrys.
Hom.
xxviii.2. saith, because I am the friend of the Bridegroom. CHRYS. But how doth he who said above, *Whose shoe's latchet I am not worthy to unloose,* call himself a friend? As an expression not of equality, but of excess of joy: (for the friend of the Bridegroom is always more rejoiced than the servant,) and also, as a condescension to the weakness of his disciples, who thought that he was pained at Christ's ascendancy. For he hereby assures them, that so far from being pained, he was right glad that the Bride recognised her Spouse.

Aug.
Tr. xiii. AUG. But wherefore doth he stand? Because he falleth not, by reason of his humility. A sure ground this to stand upon, *Whose shoe's latchet I am not worthy to unloose.* Again; He standeth, and heareth Him. So then if he falleth, he heareth Him not. Therefore the friend of the Bridegroom ought to stand and hear, i. e. to abide in the grace which he hath received, and to hear the voice in which he rejoiceth. I rejoice not, he saith, because of my own voice, but because of the Bridegroom's voice. I rejoice; I in hearing, He in speaking; I am the ear, He the Word. For he who guards the bride or wife of his friend, takes care that she love none else; if he wish to be loved himself in the stead of his friend, and to enjoy her who was entrusted to him, how detestable doth he appear to the whole world? Yet many are the adulterers I see, who would fain possess themselves of the spouse who was bought at so great a price, and who aim by their words at being loved themselves instead of

Chrys.
Hom.
xxix. 3. the Bridegroom. CHRYS. Or thus; The expression, *which standeth,* is not without meaning, but indicates that his part is now over, and that for the future he must stand and listen. This is a transition from the parable to the real subject. For having introduced the figure of a bride and bridegroom, he shews how the marriage is consummated, viz. by word and

Rom.
10, 17. doctrine. *Faith cometh by hearing, and hearing by the word of God.* And since the things he had hoped for had come to pass, he adds, *This my joy therefore is fulfilled;* i. e. The work which I had to do is finished, and nothing more is left, that I can do. THEOPHYL. For which cause I rejoice now, that all men follow Him. For had the bride, i. e. the people, not come forth to meet the Bridegroom, then I,

Aug.
Tr. xiv.
c. 3. as the friend of the Bridegroom, should have grieved. AUG.

Or thus; *This my joy is fulfilled,* i. e. my joy at hearing the Bridegroom's voice. I have my gift; I claim no more, lest I lose that which I have received. He who would rejoice in himself, hath sorrow; but he who would rejoice in the Lord, shall ever rejoice, because God is everlasting. BEDE; He rejoiceth at hearing the Bridegroom's voice, who knows that he should not rejoice in his own wisdom, but in the wisdom which God giveth him. Whoever in his good works seeketh not his own glory, or praise, or earthly gain, but hath his affections set on heavenly things; this man is the friend of the Bridegroom. CHRYS. He next dis- Chrys. misses the motions of envy, not only as regards the present, Hom. xxix. 3. but also the future, saying, *He must increase, but I must decrease:* as if he said, My office hath ceased, and is ended; but His advanceth. AUG. What meaneth this, *He must in-* Aug. *crease?* God neither increases, nor decreases. And John c. 4, 5. and Jesus, according to the flesh, were of the same age: for the six months' difference between them is of no conse- quence. This is a great mystery. Before our Lord came, men gloried in themselves; He came in no man's nature, that the glory of man might be diminished, and the glory of God exalted. For He came to remit sins upon man's confession: a man's confession, a man's humility, is God's pity, God's exaltation. This truth Christ and John proved, even by their modes of suffering: John was beheaded, Christ was lifted up on the cross. Then Christ was born, when the days begin to lengthen; John, when they begin to shorten. Let God's glory then increase in us, and our own decrease, that ours also may increase in God. But it is because thou understandest God more and more, that He seemeth to in- crease in thee: for in His own nature He increaseth not, but is ever perfect: even as to a man cured of blindness, who beginneth to see a little, and daily seeth more, the light seemeth to increase, whereas it is in reality always at the full, whether he seeth it or not. In like manner the inner man maketh advancement in God, and it seemeth as if God were increasing in Him; but it is He Himself that decreaseth, falling from the height of His own glory, and rising in the glory of God. THEOPHYL. Or thus; As, on the sun rising, the light of the other heavenly bodies seems to be extin-

guished, though in reality it is only obscured by the greater
light: thus the forerunner is said to decrease; as if he
were a star hidden by the sun. Christ increases in propor-
tion as he gradually discloses Himself by miracles; not in
the sense of increase, or advancement in virtue, (the opinion
of Nestorius,) but only as regards the manifestation of His
divinity.

31. He that cometh from above is above all: he
that is of the earth is earthly, and speaketh of the
earth: he that cometh from heaven is above all.

32. And what he hath seen and heard, that he
testifieth;

Chrys.
Hom.
xxx. 1. CHRYS. As the worm gnaws wood, and rusts iron, so vain-
glory destroys the soul that cherishes it. But it is a most
obstinate fault. John with all his arguments can hardly
subdue it in his disciples: for after what he has said above,
he saith yet again, *He that cometh from above is above all:*
meaning, Ye extol my testimony, and say that the witness
is more worthy to be believed, than He to whom he bears
witness. Know this, that He who cometh from heaven,
cannot be accredited by an earthly witness. He *is above all;*
being perfect in Himself, and above comparison. THE-
OPHYL. Christ cometh from above, as descending from the
Father; and is above all, as being elected in preference to
all. ALCUIN. Or, *cometh from above;* i. e. from the height
of that human nature which was before the sin of the first
man. For it was that human nature which the Word of God
assumed: He did not take upon Him man's sin, as He did
his punishment.

He that is of the earth is of the earth; i. c. is earthly,
Chrys.
Hom.
xxx. 1. *and speaketh of the earth,* speaketh earthly things. CHRYS.
And yet he was not altogether of the earth; for he had a
soul, and partook of a spirit, which was not of the earth.
What means he then by saying that he is of the earth?
Only to express his own worthlessness, that he is one born
on the earth, creeping on the ground, and not to be com-
pared with Christ, Who cometh from above. *Speaketh of the*

earth, does not mean that he spoke from his own understanding; but that, in comparison with Christ's doctrine, he spoke of the earth: as if he said, My doctrine is mean and humble, compared with Christ's; as becometh an earthly teacher, compared with Him, in Whom are hid all the treasures of wisdom and knowledge. Aug. Or, *speaketh of the earth*, he saith of the man, i. e. of himself, so far as he speaks merely humanly. If he says ought divine, he is enlightened by God to say it: as saith the Apostle; *Yet not I, but the grace of God which was with me.* John then, so far as pertains to John, *is of the earth*, and *speaketh of the earth*: if ye hear ought divine from him, attribute it to the Enlightener, not to him who hath received the light. Chrys. Having corrected the bad feeling of his disciples, he comes to discourse more deeply upon Christ. Before this it would have been useless to reveal the truths which could not yet gain a place in their minds. It follows therefore, *He that cometh from heaven.* Gloss. That is, from the Father. He is above all in two ways; first, in respect of His humanity, which was that of man before he sinned: secondly, in respect of the loftiness of the Father, to whom He is equal. Chrys. But after this high and solemn mention of Christ, his tone lowers: *And what he hath seen and heard, that he testifieth.* As our senses are our surest channels of knowledge, and teachers are most depended on who have apprehended by sight or hearing what they teach, John adds this argument in favour of Christ, that, *what he hath seen and heard, that he testifieth:* meaning that every thing which He saith is true. I want, saith John, to hear what things He, Who cometh from above, hath seen and heard, i. e. what He, and He alone, knows with certainty. Theophyl. When ye hear then, that Christ speaketh what He saw and heard from the Father, do not suppose that He needs to be taught by the Father; but only that that knowledge, which He has naturally, is from the Father. For this reason He is said to have heard, whatever He knows, from the Father. Aug. But what is it, which the Son hath heard from the Father? Hath He heard the word of the Father? Yea, but He *is* the Word of the Father. When thou conceivest a word, wherewith to name a thing, the very con-

Col. 2, 3.

Aug. Tr. xiv. c. 6.

1 Cor. 15, 10.

Chrys. Hom. xxx. 1.

Chrys. Hom. xxx. 1.

Aug. Tr. xiv. c. 7.

K

ception of that thing in the mind is a word. Just then as
thou hast in thy mind and with thee thy spoken word; even
so God uttered the Word, i. e. begat the Son. Since then the
Son is the Word of God, and the Son hath spoken the Word
of God to us, He hath spoken to us the Father's word.
What John said is therefore true.

32. —and no man receiveth his testimony.

33. He that hath received his testimony hath set to
his seal that God is true.

34. For he whom God hath sent speaketh the
words of God: for God giveth not the Spirit by measure unto him.

35. The Father loveth the Son, and hath given all
things into his hand.

36. He that believeth on the Son hath everlasting
life: and he that believeth not the Son shall not see
life; but the wrath of God abideth on him.

Chrys.
Hom.
xxx. 1. CHRYS. Having said, *And what he hath seen and heard,
that he testifieth,* to prevent any from supposing, that what
he said was false, because only a few for the present
believed, he adds, *And no man receiveth his testimony;* i. e.
only a few; for he had disciples who received his testimony.
John is alluding to the unbelief of his own disciples, and to
the insensibility of the Jews, of whom we read in the beginning of the Gospel, *He came unto His own, and His own
Aug.
Tr. xiv.
c. 8. received Him not.* AUG. Or thus; There is a people reserved
for the wrath of God, and to be condemned with the devil;
of whom none receiveth the testimony of Christ. And others
there are ordained to eternal life. Mark how mankind are
divided spiritually, though as human beings they are mixed
up together: and John separated them by the thoughts of
their heart, though as yet they were not divided in respect of
place, and looked on them as two classes, the unbelievers,
and the believers. Looking to the unbelievers, he saith,
No man receiveth his testimony. Then turning to those on
the right hand he saith, *He that hath received his testimony,*

hath set to his seal. CHRYS. i. e. hath shewn *that God is* Chrys. *true.* This is to alarm them: for it is as much as saying, no $_{xxx. 2.}^{Hom.}$ one can disbelieve Christ without convicting God, Who sent Him, of falsehood: inasmuch as He speaks nothing but what is of the Father. *For He,* it follows, *Whom God hath sent, speaketh the words of God.* ALCUIN. Or, *Hath put to his seal,* i. e. hath put a seal on his heart, for a singular and special token, that this is the true God, Who suffered for the salvation of mankind. AUG. What is it, *that God is true,* $_{c. 8.}^{Aug. Tr. xiv.}$ except that God is true, and every man a liar? For no man can say what truth is, till he is enlightened by Him who cannot lie. God then is true, and Christ is God. Wouldest thou have proof? Hear His testimony, and thou wilt find it so. But if thou dost not yet understand God, thou hast not yet received His testimony. Christ then Himself is God the true, and God hath sent Him; God hath sent God, join both together; they are One God. For John saith, *Whom God hath sent,* to distinguish Christ from himself. What then, was not John himself sent by God? Yes; but mark what follows, *For God giveth not the Spirit by measure unto Him.* To men He giveth by measure, to His only Son He giveth not by measure. To one man is given by the Spirit the word of wisdom, to another the word of knowledge: one has one thing, another another; for *measure* implies a kind of division of gifts. But Christ did not receive by measure, though He gave by measure. CHRYS. By Spirit here is meant the operation of the Holy Chrys. Spirit. He wishes to shew that all of us have received $_{xxx. 2.}^{Hom.}$ the operation of the Spirit by measure, but that Christ contains within Himself the whole operation of the Spirit. How then shall He be suspected, Who saith nothing, but what is from God, and the Spirit? For He makes no mention yet of God the Word, but rests His doctrine on the authority of the Father and the Spirit. For men knew that there was God, and knew that there was the Spirit, (although they had not right belief about His nature;) but that there was the Son they did not know. AUG. Aug. Having said of the Son, *God giveth not the Spirit by mea-* $_{c. 11.,}^{Tr. xiv.}$ *sure unto Him;* he adds, *The Father loveth the Son,* and farther adds, *and hath given all things into His hand;*

K 2

in order to shew that *the Father loveth the Son*, in a peculiar sense. For the Father loveth John, and Paul, and yet hath not given all things into their hands. But *the Father loveth the Son*, as the Son, not as a master his servant: as an only, not as an adopted, Son. Wherefore He hath given all things into His hand; so that, as great as the Father is, so great is the Son; let us not think then that, because He hath deigned to send the Son, any one inferior to the Father has been sent. THEOPHYL. The Father then hath given all things to the Son in respect of His divinity; of right, not of grace. Or; He *hath given all things into His hand*, in respect of His humanity: inasmuch as He is made Lord of all things that are in heaven, and that are in earth. ALCUIN. And because all things are in His hand, the life everlasting is too: and therefore it follows, *He that believeth on the Son hath everlasting life.* BEDE. We must understand here not a faith in words only, but a faith which is developed in works. CHRYS. He means not here, that to believe on the Son is sufficient to gain everlasting life, for elsewhere He says, *Not every one that saith unto Me, Lord, Lord, shall enter into the kingdom of heaven.* And the blasphemy against the Holy Ghost is of itself sufficient to send into hell. But we must not think that even a right belief on Father, Son, and Holy Ghost, is sufficient for salvation; for we have need of a good life and conversation. Knowing then that the greater part are not moved so much by the promise of good, as by the threat of punishment, he concludes, *But He that believeth not the Son, shall not see life; but the wrath of God abideth on him.* See how He refers to the Father again, when He speaketh of punishment. He saith not, the wrath of the Son, though the Son is judge; but maketh the Father the judge, in order to alarm men more. And He does not say, in Him, but *on Him*, meaning that it will never depart from Him; and for the same reason He says, *shall not see life*, i. e. to shew that He did not mean only a temporary death. AUG. Nor does He say, *The wrath of God cometh to him*, but, *abideth on him.* For all who are born, are under the wrath of God, which the first Adam incurred. The Son of God came without sin, and was clothed with mortality:

Chrys. Hom. xxxi. 1.

Matt. 7.

Aug. Tr. xiv. c. 13.

He died that thou mightest live. Whosoever then will not believe on the Son, on him abideth the wrath of God, of which the Apostle speaks, *We were by nature the children* Eph. 2, *of wrath.*   3.

1. When therefore the Lord knew how the Pharisees had heard that Jesus made and baptized more disciples than John,

2. (Though Jesus himself baptized not, but his disciples,)

3. He left Judæa, and departed again into Galilee.

4. And he must needs go through Samaria.

5. Then cometh he to a city of Samaria, which is called Sychar, near to the parcel of ground that Jacob gave to his son Joseph.

6. Now Jacob's well was there. Jesus therefore, being wearied with his journey, sat thus on the well: and it was about the sixth hour.

GLOSS.[1] The Evangelist, after relating how John checked the envy of his disciples, on the success of Christ's teaching, comes next to the envy of the Pharisees, and Christ's retreat from them. *When therefore the Lord knew that the Pharisees had heard, &c.* AUG. Truly had the Pharisees' knowledge that our Lord was making more disciples, and baptizing more than John, been such as to lead them heartily to follow Him, He would not have left Judæa, but would have remained for their sake: but seeing, as He did, that this knowledge of Him was coupled with envy, and made them not followers, but persecutors, He departed thence. He could too, had He pleased, have stayed amongst them, and escaped their hands; but He wished to shew His own example to believers in time to come, that it was no sin for a servant of God to fly from the fury of persecutors. He did it like a good teacher, not out of fear for Himself, but for our instruction. CHRYS. He did it too to pacify the envy of men, and perhaps to avoid bringing the dispensation of the incarnation into suspicion. For had he been taken and

[1] The nearest passage is one of S. Cyril. (Nic.)

Aug. Tr. xv. c. 2.

Chrys. Hom. xxxi. 1.

escaped, the reality of His flesh would have been doubted.
AUG. It may perplex you, perhaps, to be told that Jesus *Aug.* *baptized more than John,* and then immediately after, *Though* *Tr. xv.* *c. 3.* *Jesus Himself baptized not.* What? Is there a mistake made, and then corrected? CHRYS. Christ Himself did not *Chrys.* baptize, but those who reported the fact, in order to raise the *Hom.* *xxxi. 1.* envy of their hearers, so represented it as to appear that Christ Himself baptized. The reason why He baptized not *non occ.* Himself, had been already declared by John, *He shall* *Luke 3,* *16.* *baptize you with the Holy Ghost and with fire.* Now He had not yet given the Holy Spirit: it was therefore fitting that He should not baptize. But His disciples baptized, as an efficacious mode of instruction; better than gathering up believers here and there, as had been done in the case of Simon and his brother. Their baptism, however, had no more virtue than the baptism of John; both being without the grace of the Spirit, and both having one object, viz. that of bringing men to Christ. AUG. Or, both are true; *Aug.* for Jesus both baptized, and baptized not. He baptized, *Tr. xv.* *o. 3.* in that He cleansed: He baptized not, in that He dipped not. The disciples supplied the ministry of the body, He the aid of that Majesty of which it was said, *The Same is* *ver. 33.* *He which baptizeth.* ALCUIN. The question is often asked, whether the Holy Ghost was given by the baptism of the disciples; when below it is said, *The Holy Ghost was not* *c. 7.* *yet given, because Jesus was not yet glorified.* We reply, that the Spirit was given, though not in so manifest a way as he was after the Ascension, in the shape of fiery tongues. For, as Christ Himself in His human nature ever possessed the Spirit, and yet afterwards at His baptism the Spirit descended visibly upon Him in the form of a dove; so before the manifest and visible coming of the Holy Spirit, all saints might possess the Spirit secretly. AUG. But we must *Aug.* believe that the disciples of Christ were already baptized *Ad Se-* *leuciam* themselves, either with John's baptism, or, as is more *Ep.xviii.* probable, with Christ's. For He who had stooped to the humble service of washing His disciples' feet, had not failed to administer baptism to His servants, who would thus be enabled in their turn to baptize others. CHRYS. Christ on *Chrys.* withdrawing from Judæa, joined those whom He was with *Hom.* *xxxi. 2.*

before, as we read next, *And departed again into Galilee.*
As the Apostles, when they were expelled by the Jews, went
to the Gentiles, so Christ goes to the Samaritans. But, to
deprive the Jews of all excuse, He does not go to stay there,
but only takes it on His road, as the Evangelist implies by
saying, *And he must needs go through Samaria.* Samaria receives its name from Somer, a mountain there, so called from
the name of a former possessor of it. The inhabitants of the
country were formerly not Samaritans, but Israelites. But
in process of time they fell under God's wrath, and the king
of Assyria transplanted them to Babylon and Media; placing
Gentiles from various parts in Samaria in their room. God
however, to shew that it was not for want of power on His
part that He delivered up the Jews, but for the sins of the
people themselves, sent lions to afflict the barbarians. This
was told the king, and he sent a priest to instruct them in
God's law. But not even then did they wholly cease from
their iniquity, but only half changed. For in process of
time they turned to idols again, though they still worshipped God, calling themselves after the mountain,
Samaritans. BEDE. He must needs pass through Samaria;
because that country lay between Judea and Galilee.
Samaria was the principal city of a province of Palestine, and
gave its name to the whole district connected with it. The
particular place to which our Lord went is next given: *Then
cometh He to a city of Samaria which is called Sychar.*
CHRYS. It was the place where Simeon and Levi made a
great slaughter for Dinah. THEOPHYL. But after the sons
of Jacob had desolated the city, by the slaughter of the
Sychemites, Jacob annexed it to the portion of his son Joseph,
as we read in Genesis, *I have given to thee one portion above
thy brethren, which I took out of the hand of the Amorite
with my sword, and with my bow.* This is referred to in
what follows, *Near to the place of ground which Jacob gave
to his son Joseph.*

Now Jacob's well was there. AUG. It was a well. Every
well is a spring, but every spring is not a well. Any water
that rises from the ground, and can be drawn for use, is a
spring: but where it is ready at hand, and on the surface, it
is called a spring only; where it is deep and low down, it is

called a well, not a spring. THEOPHYL. But why does the
Evangelist make mention of the parcel of ground, and the
well? First, to explain what the woman says, *Our father
Jacob gave us this well:* secondly, to remind you that what
the Patriarchs obtained by their faith in God, the Jews had lost
by their impiety. They had been supplanted to make room
for Gentiles. And therefore there is nothing new in what
has now taken place, i. e. in the Gentiles succeeding to the
kingdom of heaven in the place of the Jews. CHRYS. Christ *Chrys.*
prefers labour and exercise to ease and luxury, and therefore *Hom. xxxi. 3.*
travels to Samaria, not in a carriage but on foot; until at
last the exertion of the journey fatigues Him; a lesson to us,
that so far from indulging in superfluities, we should often
even deprive ourselves of necessaries: *Jesus therefore being
wearied with His journey, &c.* AUG. Jesus, we see, is strong *Aug.*
and weak: strong, because *in the beginning was the Word;* *Tr. xv, c. 6.*
weak, because *the Word was made flesh.* Jesus thus weak,
being wearied with his journey, sat on the well. CHRYS. As *Chrys.*
if to say, not on a seat, or a couch, but on the first place He saw *Hom. xxx. 3.*
—upon the ground. He sat down because He was wearied, and
to wait for the disciples. The coolness of the well would be
refreshing in the midday heat: *And it was about the sixth
hour.* THEOPHYL. He mentions our Lord's sitting and
resting from His journey, that none might blame Him for
going to Samaria Himself, after He had forbidden the
disciples going. ALCUIN. Our Lord left Judæa also mystically, i. e. He left the unbelief of those who condemned
Him, and by His Apostles, went into Galilee, i. e. into the
fickleness* of the world; thus teaching His disciples to pass
from vices to virtues. The parcel of ground I conceive to
have been left not so much to Joseph, as to Christ, of whom
Joseph was a type; whom the sun, and moon, and all the
stars truly adore. To this parcel of ground our Lord came,
that the Samaritans, who claimed to be inheritors of the
Patriarch Israel, might recognise Him, and be converted to
Christ, the legal heir of the Patriarch. AUG. His journey *Aug.*
is His assumption of the flesh for our sake. For whither *Tr. xv. c. 7.*
doth He go, Who is every where present? What is this,

---

* The Heb. root signifying to roll, revolve, &c. as applied to idols, it is a
term of shame.

except that it was necessary for Him, in order to come to us, to take upon Him visibly a form of flesh? So then His being wearied with His journey, what meaneth it, but that He is wearied with the flesh? And wherefore is it the sixth hour? Because it is the sixth age of the world. Reckon severally as hours, the first age from Adam to Noah, the second from Noah to Abraham, the third from Abraham to David, the fourth from David unto the carrying away into Babylon, the fifth from thence to the baptism of John; on this calculation the present age is the sixth hour. AUG. At the sixth hour then our Lord comes to the well. The black abyss of the well, methinks, represents the·lowest parts of this universe, i. e. the earth, to which Jesus came at the sixth hour, that is, in the sixth age of mankind, the old age, as it were, of the old man, which we are bidden to put off, that we may put on the new. For so do we reckon the different ages of man's life: the first age is infancy, the second childhood, the third boyhood, the fourth youth, the fifth manhood, the sixth old age. Again, the sixth hour, being the middle of the day, the time at which the sun begins to descend, signifies that we, who are called by Christ, are to check our pleasure in visible things, that by the love of things invisible refreshing the inner man, we may be restored to the inward light which never fails. By His sitting is signified His humility, or perhaps His magisterial character; teachers being accustomed to sit.

Marginalia: Aug. l. lxxxiii. Quæst. qu. 64.

Marginalia: Col. 3, 9.

7. There cometh a woman of Samaria to draw water: Jesus saith unto her, Give me to drink.

8. (For his disciples were gone away unto the city to buy meat.)

9. Then saith the woman of Samaria unto him, How is it that thou, being a Jew, askest drink of me, which am a woman of Samaria? for the Jews have no dealings with the Samaritans.

10. Jesus answered and said unto her, If thou knewest the gift of God, and who it is that saith to thee, Give me to drink; thou wouldest have asked of him, and he would have given thee living water.

11. The woman saith unto him, Sir, thou hast nothing to draw with, and the well is deep: from whence then hast thou that living water?

12. Art thou greater than our father Jacob, which gave us the well, and drank thereof himself, and his children, and his cattle?

CHRYS. That this conversation might not appear a violation of His own injunctions against talking to the Samaritans, the Evangelist explains how it arose; viz. for He did not come with the intention beforehand of talking with the woman, but only would not send the woman away, when she had come. *There came a woman of Samaria to draw water.* Observe, she comes quite by chance. AUG. The woman here is the type of the Church, not yet justified, but just about to be. And it is a part of the resemblance, that she comes from a foreign people. The Samaritans were foreigners, though they were neighbours; and in like manner the Church was to come from the Gentiles, and to be alien from the Jewish race. THEOPHYL. The argument with the woman arises naturally from the occasion: *Jesus saith unto her, Give me to drink.* As man, the labour and heat He had undergone had made Him thirsty. AUG. Jesus also thirsted after that woman's faith? He thirsteth for their faith, for whom He shed His blood. CHRYS. This shews us too not only our Lord's strength and endurance as a traveller, but also his carelessness about food; for His disciples did not carry about food with them, since it follows, *His disciples were gone away into the city to buy food.* Herein is shewn the humility of Christ; He is left alone. It was in His power, had He pleased, not to send away all, or, on their going away, to leave others in their place to wait on Him. But He did not choose to have it so: for in this way He accustomed His disciples to trample upon pride of every kind. However some one will say, Is humility in fishermen and tent-makers so great a matter? But these very men were all on a sudden raised to the most lofty situation upon earth, that of friends and followers of the Lord of the whole earth. And men of humble origin, when they arrive at dignity, are on this very account more liable

Marginal notes: Chrys. Hom. xxxi. 4. / Aug. Tract. xv. c. 19. / Aug. l. lxxxiii. Quæst. qu. 64. Chrys. Hom. xxxi. 3.

than others to be lifted up with pride; the honour being so
new to them. Our Lord therefore to keep His disciples
humble, taught them in all things to subdue themselves.
The woman on being told, *Give Me to drink,* very naturally
asks, *How is it that Thou, being a Jew, askest drink of me,
who am a woman of Samaria?* She knew Him to be a Jew
from His figure and speech. Here observe her simpleness.
For even had our Lord been bound to abstain from dealing
with her, that was His concern, not hers; the Evangelist
saying not that the Samaritans would have no dealings with
the Jews, but that *the Jews have no dealings with the
Samaritans.* The woman however, though not in fault herself, wished to correct what she thought a fault in another.
The Jews after their return from the captivity entertained
a jealousy of the Samaritans, whom they regarded as aliens,
and enemies; and the Samaritans did not use all the Scriptures, but only the writings of Moses, and made little of the
Prophets. They claimed to be of Jewish origin, but the Jews
considered them Gentiles, and hated them, as they did the
rest of the Gentile world. AUG. The Jews would not even
use their vessels. So it would astonish the woman to hear
a Jew ask to drink out of her vessel; a thing so contrary to
Jewish rule. CHRYS. But why did Christ ask what the
law allowed not? It is no answer to say that He knew she
would not give it, for in that case, He clearly ought not
to have asked for it. Rather His very reason for asking,
was to shew His indifference to such observances, and to
abolish them for the future. AUG. He who asked to drink,
however, out of the woman's vessel, thirsted for the woman's
faith: *Jesus answered and said unto her, If thou knewest
the gift of God, or Who it is that saith to thee, Give Me to
drink, thou wouldest have asked of Him, and He would have
given thee living water.* ORIGEN. For it is as it were a doctrine, that no one receives a divine gift, who seeks not for it.
Even the Saviour Himself is commanded by the Father to
ask, that He may give it Him, as we read, *Require of
Me, and I will give Thee the heathen for Thine inheritance.*
And our Saviour Himself says, *Ask, and it shall be given
you.* Wherefore He says here emphatically, *Thou wouldest
have asked of Him, and He would have given thee.* AUG.

Aug.
Tract.
xiii.

Aug.
Tract.
xv.

Origen.
tom.xiv.
in Joan.

Ps.2,8.

Luke11,
9.

He lets her know that it was not the water, which she meant, Aug. 1. that He asked for; but that knowing her faith, He wished to satisfy her thirst, by giving her the Holy Spirit. For so must we interpret the living water, which is the gift of God; as He saith, *If thou knewest the gift of God.* AUG. Living water is that which comes out of a spring, in distinction to what is collected in ponds and cisterns from the rain. If spring water too becomes stagnant, i. e. collects into some spot, where it is quite separated from its fountain head, it ceases to be living water. CHRYS. In Scripture the grace of the Holy Spirit is sometimes called fire, sometimes water, which shews that these words are expressive not of its substance, but of its action. The metaphor of fire conveys the lively and sin-consuming property of grace; that of water the cleansing of the Spirit, and the refreshing of the souls who receive Him. THEOPHYL. The grace of the Holy Spirit then He calls living water; i. e. lifegiving, refreshing, stirring. For the grace of the Holy Spirit is ever stirring him who does good works, directing the risings of his heart. CHRYS. These words raised the woman's notions of our Lord, and make her think Him no common person. She addresses Him reverentially by the title of Lord; *The woman saith unto Him, Lord, Thou hast nothing to draw with, and the well is deep: from whence then hast Thou that living water?* AUG. She understands the living water to be the water in the well; and therefore says, Thou wishest to give me living water; but Thou hast nothing to draw with as I have: Thou canst not then give me this living water; *Art Thou greater than our father Jacob, who gave us the well, and drank thereof himself, and his children, and his cattle?* CHRYS. As if she said, Thou canst not say that Jacob gave us this spring, and used another himself; for he, and they that were with him drank thereof, which would not have been done, had he had another better one. Thou canst not then give me of this spring; and Thou hast not another better spring, unless Thou confess Thyself greater than Jacob. Whence then hast Thou the water, which Thou promisest to give us? THEOPHYL. The addition, *and his cattle,* shews the abundance of the water; as if she said, Not only is the water sweet, so that Jacob and his sons drank of it,

Marginal notes: Aug. lxxxiii. Quæst. qu. 64. / Aug. Tr. xv. / Chrys. Hom. xxxii. / Chrys. Hom. xxxi. 4. / Aug. Tr. xv. c. 13. / Chrys. Hom. xxxi. 4.

but so abundant, that it satisfied the vast multitude of the
Chrys.
Hom.
xxxi. 4. Patriarchs' cattle. CHRYS. See how she thrusts herself upon
the Jewish stock. The Samaritans claimed Abraham as their
ancestor, on the ground of his having come from Chaldea;
and called Jacob their father, as being Abraham's grandson.
BEDE. Or she calls Jacob their father, because she lived
under the Mosaic law, and possessed the farm which Jacob
Orig.
t. xiii. 6. gave to his son Joseph. ORIGEN. In the mystical sense,
Jacob's well is the Scriptures. The learned then drink
like Jacob and his sons; the simple and uneducated, like
Jacob's cattle.

13. Jesus answered and said unto her, Whosoever
drinketh of this water shall thirst again :

14. But whosoever drinketh of the water that I shall
give him shall never thirst; but the water that I
shall give him shall be in him a well of water springing
up into everlasting life.

15. The woman saith unto him, Sir, give me this
water, that I thirst not, neither come hither to draw.

16. Jesus saith unto her, Go, call thy husband, and
come hither.

17. The woman answered and said, I have no husband. Jesus said unto her, Thou hast well said, I
have no husband :

18. For thou hast had five husbands; and he whom
thou now hast is not thy husband : in that saidst thou
truly.

Chrys.
Hom.
xxxii.1. CHRYS. To the woman's question, *Art Thou greater than
our father Jacob ?* He does not reply, I am greater, lest He
should seem to boast; but His answer implies it; *Jesus
answered and said to her, Whosoever drinketh of this water
shall thirst again : but whosoever drinketh of the water that
I shall give him shall never thirst;* as if He said, If Jacob
is to be honoured because he gave you this water, what wilt
thou say, if I give thee far better than this ? He makes the
comparison however not to depreciate Jacob, but to exalt

Himself. For He does not say, that this water is vile and counterfeit, but asserts a simple fact of nature, viz. that *whosoever drinketh of this water shall thirst again.* AUG. Which is true indeed both of material water, and of that of which it is the type. For the water in the well is the pleasure of the world, that abode of darkness. Men draw it with the waterpot of their lusts; pleasure is not relished, except it be preceded by lust. And when a man has enjoyed this pleasure, i. e. drunk of the water, he thirsts again; but if he have received water from Me, he shall never thirst. For how shall they thirst, who are drunken with the abundance of the house of God? But He promised this fulness of the Holy Spirit. CHRYS. The excellence of this water, viz. that he that drinketh of it never thirsts, He explains in what follows, *But the water that I shall give him shall be in him a well of water springing up into everlasting life.* As a man who had a spring within him, would never feel thirst, so will not he who has this water which I shall give him. THEOPHYL. For the water which I give him is ever multiplying. The saints receive through grace the seed and principle of good; but they themselves make it grow by their own cultivation. CHRYS. See how the woman is led by degrees to the highest doctrine. First, she thought He was some lax Jew. Then hearing of the living water, she thought it meant material water. Afterwards she understands it as spoken spiritually, and believes that it can take away thirst, but she does not yet know what it is, only understands that it was superior to material things: *The woman saith unto Him, Sir, give me this water, that I thirst not, neither come hither to draw.* Observe, she prefers Him to the patriarch Jacob, for whom she had such veneration. AUG. Or thus; The woman as yet understands Him of the flesh only. She is delighted to be relieved for ever from thirst, and takes this promise of our Lord's in a carnal sense. For God had once granted to His servant Elijah, that he should neither hunger nor thirst for forty days; and if He could grant this for forty days, why not for ever? Eager to possess such a gift, she asks Him for the living water; *The woman saith unto Him, Sir, give me this water, that I thirst not, neither come hither to draw.* Her poverty obliged her

Aug. Tr. xv. c. 16.

Ps.36,8.

Chrys. Hom. xxxii. 1.

Chrys. Hom. xxxii.1.

Aug. Tr. xv. c.15-18.

to labour more than her strength could well bear; would

Mat.11, 28. that she could hear, *Come unto Me, all that labour and are heavy laden, and I will refresh you.* Jesus had said this very thing, i. e. that she need not labour any longer; but she did not understand Him. At last our Lord was resolved that she should understand: *Jesus saith unto her, Go call thy husband, and come hither.* What meaneth this? Did He wish to give her the water through her husband? Or, because she did not understand, did He wish to teach her by means of her husband? The Apostle indeed saith of

1 Cor. 14, 35. women, *If they will learn any thing, let them ask their husbands at home.* But this applies only where Jesus is not present. Our Lord Himself was present here; what need then that He should speak to her through her husband? Was it through her husband that He spoke to Mary, who

Chrys. Hom. xxxii. 2. sat at His feet? CHRYS. The woman then being urgent in asking for the promised water, *Jesus saith unto her, Go call thy husband;* to shew that he too ought to have a share in these things. But she was in a hurry to receive the gift, and wished to conceal her guilt, (for she still imagined she was speaking to a man:) *The woman answered and said, I have no husband.* Christ answers her with a seasonable reproof; exposing her as to former husbands, and as to her present one, whom she had concealed; *Jesus said unto her, Thou*

Aug. Tr. xv. c. 20. *hast well said, I have no husband.* AUG. Understand, that the woman had not a lawful husband, but had formed an irregular connexion with some one. He tells her, *Thou hast had five husbands,* in order to shew her His miraculous

Orig. tom.xiii. in Joan. c. 5, 6. knowledge. ORIGEN. May not Jacob's well signify mystically the letter of Scripture; the water of Jesus, that which is above the letter, which all are not allowed to penetrate into? That which is written was dictated by men, whereas the things which the eye hath not seen, nor ear heard, neither have entered into the heart of man, cannot be reduced to writing, but are from the fountain of water, that springeth up unto everlasting life, i. e. the Holy Ghost. These truths are unfolded to such as carrying no longer a human heart within

1 Cor. 11, 16. them, are able to say with the Apostle, *We have the mind of Christ.* Human wisdom indeed discovers truths, which are handed down to posterity; but the teaching of the Spirit is

a well of water which springeth up into everlasting life. The woman wished to attain, like the angels, to angelic and super-human truth without the use of Jacob's water. For the angels have a well of water within them, springing from the Word of God Himself. She says therefore, *Sir, give me this water.* But it is impossible here to have the water which is given by the Word, without that which is drawn from Jacob's well; and therefore Jesus seems to tell the woman that He cannot supply her with it from any other source than Jacob's well; If we are thirsty, we must first drink from Jacob's well. *Jesus saith unto her, Go, call thy husband, and come hither.* According to the Apostle, the Law is the husband of the soul. AUG. The five husbands some interpret to be the five books which were given by Moses. And the words, *He whom thou now hast is not thy husband,* they understand as spoken by our Lord of Himself; as if He said, Thou hast served the five books of Moses, as five husbands; but now *he whom thou hast,* i. e. whom thou hearest, *is not thy husband;* for thou dost not yet believe in him. But if she did not believe in Christ, she was still united to those five husbands, i. e. five books, and therefore why is it said, *Thou hast had five husbands,* as if she no longer had them? And how do we understand that a man must have these five books, in order to pass over to Christ, when he who believes in Christ, so far from forsaking these books, embraces them in this spiritual meaning the more strongly? Let us turn to another interpretation. AUG. Jesus seeing that the woman did not understand, and wishing to enlighten her, says, *Call thy husband;* i. e. apply thine understanding. For when the life is well ordered, the understanding governs the soul itself, pertaining to the soul. For though it is indeed nothing else than the soul, it is at the same time a certain part of the soul. And this very part of the soul which is called the understanding and the intellect, is itself illuminated by a light superior to itself. Such a Light was talking with the woman; but in her there was not understanding to be enlightened. Our Lord then, as it were, says, I wish to enlighten, and there is not one to be enlightened; *Call thy husband,* i. e. apply thine understanding, through which thou must be

Rom. 7, 1.
Aug. lib. lxxxiii. Quaest. qu. 64.

Aug. Tr. xv. c. 19.

L

taught, by which governed. The five former husbands may
be explained as the five senses, thus: a man before he has
the use of his reason, is entirely under the government of
his bodily senses. Then reason comes into action; and
from that time forward he is capable of entertaining ideas,
and is either under the influence of truth or error. The
woman had been under the influence of error, which error
was not her lawful husband, but an adulterer. Wherefore
our Lord says, Put away that adulterer which corrupts thee,
and call thy husband, that thou mayest understand Me.

Origen. ORIGEN. And what more proper place than Jacob's well,
tom.xiii. for exposing the unlawful husband, i. e. the perverse law?
c. 8. For the Samaritan woman is meant to figure to us a soul,
that has subjected itself to a kind of law of its own, not the
divine law. And our Saviour wishes to marry her to a
lawful husband, i. e. Himself; the Word of truth which was
to rise from the dead, and never again to die.

19. The woman saith unto him, Sir, I perceive that
thou art a prophet.

20. Our fathers worshipped in this mountain; and
ye say, that in Jerusalem is the place where men
ought to worship.

21. Jesus saith unto her, Woman, believe me, the
hour cometh, when ye shall neither in this mountain,
nor yet at Jerusalem, worship the Father.

22. Ye worship ye know not what: we know what
we worship: for salvation is of the Jews.

23. But the hour cometh, and now is, when the
true worshippers shall worship the Father in spirit and
in truth: for the Father seeketh such to worship him.

24. God is a Spirit: and they that worship him
must worship him in spirit and in truth.

Chrys. CHRYS. The woman is not offended at Christ's rebuke.
Hom. She does not leave Him, and go away. Far from it: her
xxxii. admiration for Him is raised: *The woman saith unto Him,
Sir, I perceive that Thou art a Prophet:* as if she said, Thy
knowledge of me is unaccountable, Thou must be a prophet.

Aug. The husband was beginning to come to her, though He had not yet fully come. She thought our Lord a prophet, and He was a prophet: for He says of Himself, *A prophet is not without honour, save in his own country.* Chrys. And having come to this belief she asks no questions relating to this life, the health or sickness of the body: she is not troubled about thirst, she is eager for doctrine. Aug. And she begins enquiries on a subject that perplexed her; *Our fathers worshipped in this mountain; and ye say that in Jerusalem is the place where men ought to worship.* This was a great dispute between the Samaritans and the Jews. The 'Jews worshipped in the temple built by Solomon, and made this a ground of boasting over the Samaritans. The Samaritans replied, Why boast ye, because ye have a temple which we have not? Did our fathers, who pleased God, worship in that temple? Is it not better to pray to God in this mountain, where our fathers worshipped? Chrys. By, *our fathers*, she means Abraham, who is said to have offered up Isaac here. Origen. Or thus; The Samaritans regarded Mount Gerizim, near which Jacob dwelt, as sacred, and worshipped upon it; while the sacred place of the Jews was Mount Sion, God's own choice. The Jews being the people from whom salvation came, are the type of true believers; the Samaritans of heretics. Gerizim, which signifies division, becomes the Samaritans; Sion, which signifies watch-tower, becomes the Jews. Chrys. Christ however does not solve this question immediately, but leads the woman to higher things, of which He had not spoken till she acknowledged Him to be a prophet, and therefore listened with a more full belief: *Jesus saith unto her, Woman, believe Me, the hour cometh, when ye shall neither in this mountain, nor yet at Jerusalem, worship the Father.* He says, *Believe me*, because we have need of faith, the mother of all good, the medicine of salvation, in order to obtain any real good. They who endeavour without it, are like men who venture on the sea without a boat, and, being able to swim only a little way, are drowned. Aug. *Believe Me*, our Lord says with fitness, as the husband is now present. For now there is one in thee that believes, thou hast begun to be present in the understanding; but *if ye will not believe, surely ye shall not be established.*

Side notes:
Aug. Tr. xv. c. 23.
Mat. 13, 57.
Chrys. Hom. xxxii. 2.
Aug. Tr. xv. c. 23.
Chrys. Hom. xxxii. 2.
Origen. tom. xiii. c. 13.
Chrys. Hom. xxxii. 3.
Aug. Tr. xv. c. 24.
Isa. 7, 9.

ALCUIN. In saying, *the hour cometh,* He refers to the Gospel dispensation, which was now approaching; under which the shadows of types were to withdraw, and the pure light of truth was to enlighten the minds of believers. CHRYS. There was no necessity for Christ to shew why the fathers worshipped in the mountain, and the Jews in Jerusalem. He therefore was silent on that question; but nevertheless asserted the religious superiority of the Jews on another ground, the ground not of place, but of knowledge; *Ye worship ye know not what, we know what we worship; for salvation is of the Jews.* ORIGEN. *Ye,* literally refers to the Samaritans, but mystically, to all who understand the Scriptures in an heretical sense. *We* again literally means the Jews, but mystically, I the Word, and all who conformed to My Image, obtain salvation from the Jewish Scriptures. CHRYS. The Samaritans worshipped they knew not what, a local, a partial God, as they imagined, of whom they had the same notion that they had of their idols. And therefore they mingled the worship of God with the worship of idols. But the Jews were free from this superstition: indeed they knew God to be the God of the whole world; wherefore He says, *We worship what we know.* He reckons Himself among the Jews, in condescension to the woman's idea of Him; and says as if He were a Jewish prophet, *We worship,* though it is certain that He is the Being who is worshipped by all. The words, *For salvation is of the Jews,* mean that every thing calculated to save and amend the world, the knowledge of God, the abhorrence of idols, and all other doctrines of that nature, and even the very origin of our religion, comes originally from the Jews. In salvation too He includes His own presence, which He says is of the Jews, as we are told by the Apostle, *Of whom as concerning the flesh Christ came.* See how He exalts the Old Testament, which He shews to be the root of every thing good; thus proving in every way that He Himself is not opposed to the Law. AUG. It is saying much for the Jews, to declare in their name, *We worship what we know.* But He does not speak for the reprobate Jews, but for that party from whom the Apostles and the Prophets came. Such were all those saints who laid the prices of their possessions at the Apostle's feet.

Chrys.
Hom.
xxxiii.
1.

Orig.
tom. xiii.
c. 17.

Chrys.
Hom.
xxxiii. 1.

Rom. 9,
5.

Aug.
in Joan.
Tr. xv.
c. 26.

CHRYS. The Jewish worship then was far higher than the Samaritan; but even it shall be abolished; *The hour cometh, and now is, when the true worshippers shall worship the Father in spirit and in truth.* He says, *and now is,* to shew that this was not a prediction, like those of the ancient Prophets, to be fulfilled in the course of ages. The event, He says, is now at hand, it is approaching your very doors. The words, *true worshippers,* are by way of distinction: for there are false worshippers who pray for temporal and frail benefits, or whose actions are ever contradicting their prayers. CHRYS. Or by saying, *true,* he excludes the Jews together with the Samaritans. For the Jews, though better than the Samaritans, were yet as much inferior to those who were to succeed them, as the type is to the reality. The true worshippers do not confine the worship of God to place, but worship in the spirit; as Paul saith, *Whom I serve with my spirit.* ORIGEN. Twice it is said, *The hour cometh,* and the first time without the addition, *and now is.* The first seems to allude to that purely spiritual worship which is suited only to a state of perfection; the second to earthly worship, perfected as far as is consistent with human nature. When that hour cometh, which our Lord speaks of, the mountain of the Samaritans must be avoided, and God must be worshipped in Sion, where is Jerusalem, which is called by Christ the city of the Great King. And this is the Church, where sacred oblations and spiritual victims are offered up by those who understand the spiritual law. So that when the fulness of time shall have come, the true worship, we must suppose, will no longer be attached to Jerusalem, i. e. to the present Church: for the Angels do not worship the Father at Jerusalem: and thus those who have obtained the likeness of the Jews, worship the Father better than they who are at Jerusalem. And when this hour is come, we shall be accounted by the Father as sons. Wherefore it is not said, Worship God, but, *Worship the Father.* But for the present the true worshippers worship the Father in spirit and in truth*. CHRYS. He speaks here

Chrys. Hom. xxxiii. 1.

C'rys. Hom. xxiii. 2.

Rom. 1, 9.

Origen. tom.xiii. c. 14.

Chrys. Hom. xxxiii. 2.

---

* Origen literally. The words *the hour cometh* are repeated; the second time with the addition *and now is.* I think that the first expression signifies the most perfect worship that human nature is capable of in this life. So until the hour shall have come which the Lord speaks of, the mountain of the Samaritans (who represent those who separate themselves from the Church) is to be

of the Church; wherein there is true worship, and such as becometh God; and therefore adds, *For the Father seeketh such to worship Him.* For though formerly He willed that mankind should linger under a dispensation of types and figures, this was only done in condescension to human frailty, and to prepare men for the reception of the truth.

Origen. tom.xiii. c. 20. ORIGEN. But if the Father seeks, He seeks through Jesus, Who came to seek and to save that which was lost, and to teach men what true worship was. *God is a Spirit;* i. e. He constitutes our real life, just as our breath (spirit) con-

Chrys. Hom. xxxii. 2. stitutes our bodily life. CHRYS. Or it signifies that God is incorporeal; and that therefore He ought to be worshipped not with the body, but with the soul, by the offering up a pure mind, i. e. that *they who worship Him, must worship Him in spirit and in truth.* The Jews neglected the soul, but paid great attention to the body, and had various kinds of purification. Our Lord seems here to refer to this, and to say, not by cleansing of the body, but by the incorporeal nature within us, i. e. the understanding, which He calls the spirit, that we must worship the incorporeal God.

Hilar. ii. de Trin. c. 31. HILARY. Or, by saying that God being a Spirit ought to be worshipped in spirit, He indicates the freedom and knowledge of the worshippers, and the uncircumscribed nature of the

2 Cor. 3, 17. Chrys. Hom. xxxii. 2. worship: according to the saying of the Apostle, *Where the Spirit of the Lord is, there is liberty.* CHRYS. And that we are to worship in truth, means that whereas the former ordinances were typical; that is to say, circumcision, burnt offerings, and sacrifices; now, on the contrary, every thing is real. THEOPHYL. Or, because many think that they worship God in the spirit, i, e. with the mind, who yet held heretical doctrines concerning Him, for this reason He adds, *and in truth.* May not the words too refer to the two kinds of philosophy among us, i. e. active and contemplative; the

Rom. 8, 14. spirit standing for action, according to the Apostle, *As many*

avoided and God must be worshipped in Sion at Jerusalem, which Christ calls the city of the Great King. What is this but the Church where the holy offerings of spiritual victims are presented by men of spiritual minds? But when the fulness of time shall have come, the true worship will no longer be performed in Jerusalem, that is, in the present Church. For the Angels do not worship the Father at Jerusalem: and so those who are like them worship the Father better than those who are in Jerusalem, even though for the sake of the latter they abide with them, and become Jews to the Jews, that they may gain the Jews. And when &c. Nicolai has missed the meaning of the last sentence.

as are led by the Spirit of God; truth, on the other hand, for contemplation. Or, (to take another view,) as the Samaritans thought that God was confined to a certain place, and ought to be worshipped in that place; in opposition to this notion, our Lord may mean to teach them here, that the true worshippers worship not locally, but spiritually. Or again, all being a type and shadow in the Jewish system, the meaning may be that the true worshippers will worship not in type, but in truth. God being a Spirit, seeketh for spiritual worshippers; being the truth, for true ones. AUG. O for a mountain to pray on, thou criest, high and inaccessible, that I may be nearer to God, and God may hear me better, for He dwelleth on high. Yes, God dwelleth on high, but He hath respect unto the humble. Wherefore descend that thou mayest ascend. "Ways on high are in their heart," it is said, " passing in the valley of tears," and in " tears" is humility. Wouldest thou pray in the temple? pray in thyself; but first do thou become the temple of God.

Aug. Tr. xv. c. 23.

Ps.74,7.

25. The woman saith unto him, I know that Messias cometh, which is called Christ: when he is come, he will tell us all things.

26. Jesus saith unto her, I that speak unto thee am he.

CHRYS. The woman was struck with astonishment at the loftiness of His teaching, as her words shew: *The woman saith unto Him, I know that Messias cometh, which is called Christ.* AUG. Unctus in Latin, Christ in Greek, in the Hebrew Messias. She knew then who *could* teach her, but did not know Who *was* teaching her. *When He is come, He will tell us all things:* as if she said, The Jews now contend for the temple, we for the mountain; but He, when He comes, will level the mountain, overthrow the temple, and teach us how to pray in spirit and in truth. CHRYS. But what reason had the Samaritans for expecting Christ's coming? They acknowledged the books of Moses, which foretold it. Jacob prophesies of Christ, *The sceptre shall not depart from Judah, nor a lawgiver from beneath his feet, until Shiloh come.* And Moses says, *The Lord thy God shall raise up a Prophet from the*

Chrys. Hom. xxxii. 2.

Aug. Tr. xv. c. 27.

Chrys. Hom. xxxii. 2.

Gen.49, 10.

Deut.18, 15.

midst of thee, of thy brethren. ORIGEN. It should be known,

that as Christ rose out of the Jews, not only declaring but proving Himself to be Christ; so among the Samaritans there arose one Dositheus by name, who asserted that he was the Christ prophesied of.

AUG. It is a confirmation to discerning minds that the five senses were what were signified by the five husbands, to find the woman making five carnal answers, and then mentioning the name of Christ.

CHRYS. Christ now reveals Himself to the woman: *Jesus saith unto her, I that speak unto thee am He.* Had He told the woman this to begin with, it would have appeared vanity. Now, having gradually awakened her to the thought of Christ, His disclosure of Himself is perfectly opportune. He is not

equally open to the Jews, who ask Him, *If Thou be the Christ, tell us plainly;* for this reason, that they did not ask in order to learn, but to do Him injury; whereas she spoke in the simplicity of her heart.

27. And upon this came his disciples, and marvelled that he talked with the woman: yet no man said, What seekest thou? or, Why talkest thou with her?

28. The woman then left her waterpot, and went her way into the city, and saith to the men,

29. Come, see a man, which told me all things that ever I did: is not this the Christ?

30. Then they went out of the city, and came unto him.

CHRYS. The disciples arrive opportunely, and when the teaching is finished: *And upon this came His disciples, and marvelled that He talked with the woman.* They marvelled at the exceeding kindness and humility of Christ, in condescending to converse with a poor woman, and a Samaritan.

AUG. He who came to seek that which was lost, sought the lost one. This was what they marvelled at: they marvelled at His goodness; they did not suspect evil.

CHRYS. But notwithstanding their wonder, they asked Him no questions, *No man said, What seekest Thou? or, Why talkest Thou with her?* So careful were they to observe the rank of disciples, so great was their awe and veneration for Him.

On subjects indeed which concerned themselves, they did not hesitate to ask Him questions. But this was not one. ORIGEN. The woman is almost turned into an Apostle. So forcible are His words, that she leaves her waterpot to go to the city, and tell her townsmen of them. *The woman then left her waterpot,* i. e. gave up low bodily cares, for the sake of benefitting others. Let us do the same. Let us leave off caring for things of the body, and impart to others of our own. AUG. Hydria answers to our word aquarium; hydor being Greek for water. CHRYS. As the Apostles, on being called, left their nets, so does she leave her waterpot, to do the work of an Evangelist, by calling not one person, but a whole city: *She went her way into the city, and saith to the men, Come, see a man which told me all things that ever I did: is not this the Christ?* ORIGEN. She calls them together to see a man, whose words were deeper than man's. She had had five husbands, and then was living with the sixth, not a lawful husband. But now she gives him up for a seventh, and she leaving her waterpot, is converted to chastity. CHRYS. She was not prevented by shame-facedness from spreading about what had been said to her. For the soul, when it is once kindled by the divine flame, regards neither glory, nor shame, nor any other earthly thing, only the flame which consumes it. But she did not wish them to trust to her own report only, but to come and judge of Christ for themselves. *Come, see a man,* she says. She does not say, Come and believe, but, *Come and see;* which is an easier matter. For well she knew that if they only tasted of that well, they would feel as she did. ALCUIN. It is only by degrees, however, that she comes to the preaching of Christ. First she calls Him *a man,* not Christ; for fear those who heard her might be angry, and refuse to come. CHRYS. She then neither openly preaches Christ, nor wholly omits Him, but says, *Is not this the Christ?* This wakened their attention, *Then they went out of the city, and came unto Him.* AUG. The circumstance of the woman's leaving her waterpot on going away, must not be overlooked. For the waterpot signifies the love of this world, i. e. concupiscence, by which men from the dark depth, of which the well is the image, i. e. from an earthly conversation, draw up pleasure.

Orig. tom. xiii. in Joan. c. 28.

Aug.

Tr. xv. Chrys. Hom. xxxiv. 1.

Orig. tom. xiii. in Joan. c. 29.

Chrys. Hom. xxxiv. 1.

Chrys. Hom. xxxiv. 1.

It was right then for one who believed in Christ to renounce
the world, and, by leaving her waterpot, to shew that she had
parted with worldly desires. AUG. She cast away therefore
concupiscence, and hastened to proclaim the truth. Let
those who wish to preach the Gospel, learn, that they should
first leave their waterpots at the well. ORIGEN. The woman
having become a vessel of wholesome discipline, lays aside
as contemptible her former tastes and desires.

Aug.
Tr. xv.
c. 30.

Orig.
tom. xiii.
c. 29.

31. In the mean while his disciples prayed him,
saying, Master, eat.

32. But he said unto them, I have meat to eat that
ye know not of.

33. Therefore said the disciples one to another,
Hath any man brought him ought to eat?

34. Jesus saith unto them, My meat is to do the
will of him that sent me, and to finish his work.

AUG. His disciples had gone to buy food, and had returned. They offered Christ some: *In the mean while His
disciples prayed Him, saying, Master, eat.* CHRYS. They
all ask Him at once, Him so fatigued with the journey and
heat. This is not impatience in them, but simply love, and
tenderness to their Master. ORIGEN. They think the present time convenient for dining; it being after the departure
of the woman to the city, and before the coming of the
Samaritans; so that they sit at meat by themselves. This
explains, *In the mean while.* THEOPHYL. Our Lord, knowing that the woman of Samaria was bringing the whole town
out to Him, tells His disciples, *I have meat that ye know
not of.* CHRYS. The salvation of men He calls His food,
shewing His great desire that we should be saved. As food
is an object of desire to us, so was the salvation of men to
Him. Observe, He does not express Himself directly, but
figuratively; which makes some trouble necessary for His
hearers, in order to comprehend His meaning, and thus
gives a greater importance to that meaning when it is
understood. THEOPHYL. *That ye know not of,* i. e. know
not that I call the salvation of men food; or, know not that

Aug.
Tr. xv.
c. 31.

Orig.
tom. xiii.
c. 31.

Chrys.
Hom.
xxxiv.1.

the Samaritans are about to believe and be saved. The disciples however were in perplexity: *Therefore said the disciples one to another, Hath any man brought Him ought to eat?* AUG. What wonder that the woman did not under- Aug. Tr. xv. c. 31. stand about the water? Lo, the disciples do not under- stand about the meat. CHRYS. They shew, as usual, the Chrys. Hom. xxxiv. honour and reverence in which they hold their Master, by talking among themselves, and not presuming to question[1]. Him. THEOPHYL. From the question of the disciples, *Hath any man brought Him ought to eat,* we may infer that our Lord was accustomed to receive food from others, when it was offered Him: not that He who giveth food to all flesh, Ps. 146. needed any assistance; but He received it, that they who gave it might obtain their reward, and that poverty thenceforth might not blush, nor the support of others be esteemed a disgrace. It is proper and necessary that teachers should depend on others to provide them with food, in order that, being free from all other cares, they may attend the more to the ministry of the word. AUG. Our Lord heard His Aug. Tr. xv. c. 31. doubting disciples, and answered them as disciples, i. e. plainly and expressly, not circuitously, as He answered the women; *Jesus saith unto them, My meat is to do the will of Him that sent Me.* ORIGEN. Fit meat for the Son of God, Orig. tom. xiii. c. 6. who was so obedient to the Father, that in Him was the same will that was in the Father: not two wills, but one will in both. The Son is capable of first accomplishing the whole will of the Father. Other saints do nothing against the Father's will; He does that will. That is His meat in an especial sense. And what means, *To finish His work?* It would seem easy to say, that a work was what was ordered by him who set it; as where men are set to build or dig. But some who go deeper ask whether a work being finished does not imply that it was before incomplete; and whether God could originally have made an incomplete work? The completing of the work, is the completing of a rational creature: for it was to complete this work, which was as yet imperfect, that the Word made flesh come. THEOPHYL. He finished the work of God, i. e. man, He, the Son of God, finished it by exhibiting our nature in Himself without sin, perfect and uncorrupt. He finished also the work of God,

Rom.
10, 4.
i. e. the Law, (for Christ is the end of the Law,) by abolish-
ing it, when every thing in it had been fulfilled, and chang-
Orig.
tom.xiii.
c. 31. ing a carnal into a spiritual worship. ORIGEN. The matter
of spiritual drink and living water being explained, the subject of meat follows. Jesus had asked the woman of Samaria,
and she could give Him none good enough. Then came the
disciples, having procured some humble food among the
people of the country, and offered it Him, beseeching Him
to eat. They fear perhaps lest the Word of God, deprived
of His own proper nourishment, fail within them; and
therefore with such as they have found, immediately propose
to feed Him, that being confirmed and strengthened, He
may abide with His nourishers. Souls require food as well
as bodies. And as bodies require different kinds of it, and
in different quantities, so is it in things which are above the
Heb. 5,
12. body. Souls differ in capacity, and one needs more nourishment, another less. So too in point of quality, the same
nourishment of words and thoughts does not suit all.
Infants just born need the milk of the word; the grown up,
solid meat. Our Lord says, *I have meat to eat.* For one
who is over the weak who cannot behold the same things
with the stronger, may always speak thus [b].

35. Say not ye, There are yet four months, and
then cometh harvest? behold, I say unto you, Lift up
your eyes, and look on the fields; for they are white
already to harvest.

36. And he that reapeth receiveth wages, and
gathereth fruit unto life eternal: that both he that
soweth and he that reapeth may rejoice together.

37. And herein is that saying true, One soweth,
and another reapeth.

38. I sent you to reap that whereon ye bestowed
no labour: other men laboured, and ye are entered
into their labours.

[b] i. e. those of weak faith cannot
understand the spiritual gifts and nourishment of the strong. It is " meat
they know not of." So S. Aug , when
unconverted, of S. Ambrose, " What
comfort he had in adversities, and what
sweet joys Thy Bread had for the
hidden mouth of his spirit—I neither
could conjecture nor had experienced."
Conf. vi. 3.

CHRYS. What is the will of the Father He now proceeds to explain: *Say ye not, There are yet four months, and then cometh harvest?* THEOPHYL. Now ye are expecting a material harvest. But I say unto you, that a spiritual harvest is at hand: *Lift up your eyes, and look on the fields; for they are white already to harvest.* He alludes to the Samaritans who are approaching. CHRYS. He leads them, as his custom is, from low things to high. *Fields* and *harvest* here express the great number of souls, which are ready to receive the word. The *eyes* are both spiritual, and bodily ones, for they saw a great multitude of Samaritans now approaching. This expectant crowd he calls very suitably white fields. For as the corn, when it grows white, is ready for the harvest; so were these ready for salvation. But why does He not say this in direct language? Because by making use in this way of the objects around them, he gave greater vividness and power to His words, and brought the truth home to them; and also that His discourse might be more pleasant, and might sink deeper into their memories. AUG. He was intent now on beginning the work, and hastened to send labourers: *And he that reapeth receiveth wages, and gathereth fruit unto life eternal, that both he that soweth and he that reapeth may rejoice together.* CHRYS. Again, He distinguishes earthly from heavenly things, for as above He said of the water, that he who drank of it should never thirst, so here He says, *He that reapeth gathereth fruit unto life eternal;* adding, *that both he that soweth and he that reapeth may rejoice together.* The Prophets sowed, the Apostles reaped, yet are not the former deprived of their reward. For here a new thing is promised; viz. that both sowers and reapers shall rejoice together. How different this from what we see here. Now he that soweth grieveth because he soweth for others, and he only that reapeth rejoiceth. But in the new state, the sower and reaper share the same wages. AUG. The Apostles and Prophets had different labours, corresponding to the difference of times; but both will attain to like joy, and receive together their wages, even eternal life. CHRYS. He confirms what He says by a proverb, *And herein is that saying true, one soweth and another reapeth,* i. e. one party has the labour,

Chrys.
Hom.
xxxiv.1.

Chrys.
Hom.
xxxiv.2.

Aug.
Tr. xv.
c. 32.

Chrys.
Hom.
xxxiv.2.

Aug.
Tr. xv.
c. 32.

Chrys.
Hom.
xxxiv.2.

and another reaps the fruit. The saying is especially applicable here, for the Prophets had laboured, and the disciples reaped the fruits of their labours: *I sent you to reap that whereon* Aug. Tr. xv. c. 32. *ye bestowed no labour.* AUG. So then He sent reapers, no sowers. The reapers went where the Prophets had preached. Read the account of their labours: they all contain prophecy of Christ. And the harvest was gathered on that occasion when so many thousands brought the prices of their possessions, and laid them at the Apostles' feet; relieving their shoulders from earthly burdens, that they might follow Christ. Yea verily, and from that harvest were a few grains scattered, which filled the whole world. And now ariseth another harvest, which will be reaped at the end of the world, not by Apostles, Mat. 13. but by Angels. *The reapers,* He says, *are the Angels.* CHRYS. Chrys. Hom. xxxiv.2. *I sent you to reap that whereon ye bestowed no labour,* i. e. I have reserved you for a favourable time, in which the labour is less, the enjoyment greater. The more laborious part of the work was laid on the Prophets, viz. the sowing of the seed: *Other men laboured, and ye are entered into their labours.* Christ here throws light on the meaning of the old prophecies. He shews that both the Law and the Prophets, if rightly interpreted, led men to Him; and that the Prophets were sent in fact by Himself. Thus the intimate connexion is established between the Old Testament Orig. tom. xv. in Joan. c.39-40. and the New. ORIGEN. How can we consistently give an allegorical meaning to the words, *Lift up your eyes, &c.* and only a literal one to the words, *There are yet four months, and then cometh harvest?* The same principle of interpretation surely must be applied to the latter, that is to the former. The four months represent the four elements, i. e. our natural life; the harvest, the end of the world, when all conflict shall have ceased, and truth shall prevail. The disciples then regard the truth as incomprehensible in our natural state, and look forward to the end of the world for attaining the knowledge of it. But this idea our Lord condemns: *Say not ye, there are four months, and then cometh harvest? Behold, I say unto you, Lift up your eyes.* In many places of Holy Scripture, we are commanded in the same way to raise the thoughts of our minds, which cling so obstinately to earth. A difficult task this for one who

indulges his passions, and lives carnally. Such an one will
not see if the fields be white to the harvest. For when are
the fields white to the harvest? When the Word of God
comes to light up and make fruitful the fields of Scripture.
Indeed, all sensible things are as it were fields made white
for the harvest, if only reason be at hand to interpret them.
We lift up our eyes, and behold the whole universe over-
spread with the brightness of truth. And he that reapeth
those harvests, has a double reward of his reaping; first, his
wages; *And he that reapeth receiveth wages;* meaning his
reward in the life to come; secondly, a certain good state
of the understanding, which is the fruit of contemplation, *And
gathereth fruit unto life eternal.* The man who thinks out
the first principles of any science, is as it were the sower in
that science; others taking them up, pursuing them to their
results, and engrafting fresh matter upon them, strike out
new discoveries, from which posterity reaps a plentiful harvest. And how much more may we perceive this in the art
of arts? The seed there is the whole dispensation of the
mystery, now revealed, but formerly hidden in darkness;
for while men were unfit for the advent of the Word, the
fields were not yet white to their eyes, i. e. the legal and
prophetical Scriptures were shut up. Moses and the Prophets, who preceded the coming of Christ, were the sowers of
this seed; the Apostles who came after Christ and saw His
glory were the reapers. They reaped and gathered into
barns the deep meaning which lay hid under the prophetic
writings; and did in short what those do who succeed to a
scientific system which others have discovered, and who with
less trouble attain to clearer results than they who originally
sowed the seed. But they that sowed and they that reaped
shall rejoice together in another world, in which all sorrow
and mourning shall be done away. Nay, and have they not
rejoiced already? Did not Moses and Elias, the sowers,
rejoice with the reapers Peter, James, and John, when they
saw the glory of the Son of God at the Transfiguration?
Perhaps in, *one soweth and another reapeth, one and another*
may refer simply to those who live under the Law, and those
who live under the Gospel. For these may both rejoice

together, inasmuch as the same end is laid up for them by one God, through one Christ, in one Holy Spirit.

39. And many of the Samaritans of that city believed on him for the saying of the woman, which testified, He told me all that ever I did.

40. So when the Samaritans were come unto him, they besought him that he would tarry with them: and he abode there two days.

41. And many more believed because of his own word;

42. And said unto the woman, Now we believe, not because of thy saying: for we have heard him ourselves, and know that this is indeed the Christ, the Saviour of the world.

Orig. tom.xiii. in Joan. c. 50.   ORIGEN. After this conversation with the disciples, Scripture returns to those who had believed on the testimony of the woman, and were come to see Jesus. Chrys.
Chrys. Hom. xxxiv.2.   CHRYS. It is now, as it were, harvest time, when the corn is gathered, and a whole floor soon covered with sheaves; *And many of the Samaritans of that city believed on Him, for the saying of the woman which testified, He told me all that ever I did.* They considered that the woman would never of her own accord have conceived such admiration for one Who had reproved her offences, unless He were really some great and wonderful person.
Hom. xxxv.1.   And thus relying solely on the testimony of the woman, without any other evidence, they went out to beseech Christ to stay with them: *So when the Samaritans were come to Him, they besought Him that He would tarry with them.* The Jews when they saw His miracles, so far from begging Him to stay, tried in every way to get rid of His presence. Such is the power of malice, and envy, and vain-glory, that obstinate vice which poisons even goodness itself. Though the Samaritans however wished to keep Him with them, He would not consent, but only *tarried there two days.*
Orig. tom.xiii. c. 51.   ORIGEN. It is natural to ask, why our Saviour stays with the Samaritans, when He had given a command to His disciples

not to enter into any city of the Samaritans.   But we must
explain this mystically.   To go the way of the Gentiles, is
to be imbued with Gentile doctrine ; to go into a city of the
Samaritans, is to admit the doctrines of those who believe
the Scriptures, but interpret them heretically.   But when
men have given up their own doctrines, and come to Jesus,
it is lawful to stay with them.   CHRYS. The Jews disbelieved Chrys.
in spite of miracles, while these exhibited great faith, be- Hom.
fore even a miracle was wrought, and when they had only xxxv. 1.
heard our Lord's words. *And many more believed because of
His own word.*   Why then do not the Evangelists give these
words ?   To shew that they omit many important things, and
because the result shews what they were; the result being
that the whole city was convinced.   On the other hand,
when the hearers are not convinced, the Evangelists are
obliged to give our Lord's words, that the failure may be
seen to be owing to the indifference of the hearers, not to
any defect in the preacher.   And now, having become
Christ's disciples, they dismiss their first instructor; *And
they said unto the woman, Now we believe not because of
thy saying : for we have heard Him ourselves, and know
that this is indeed the Christ, the Saviour of the world.*
How soon they understand that He was come for the
deliverance of the whole world, and could not therefore
confine His purposes to the Jews, but must sow the Word
every where.   Their saying too, *The Saviour of the world,*
implies that they looked on this world as miserable and
lost; and that, whereas Prophets and Angels had come
to save it, this was the only real Saviour, the Author not
only of temporal but eternal salvation.   And, observe,
whereas the woman had spoken doubtfully, *Is not this the
Christ?* they do not say, we suspect, but *we know,* know,
that this is indeed the Saviour of the world, not one Christ
out of many.   Though they had only heard His words, they
said as much as they could have done, had they seen ever
so many and great miracles.   ORIGEN. With the aid of our Orig.
former observations on Jacob's well, and the water, it will tom.xvii.
not be difficult to see, why, when they find the true word, c. 50.
they leave other doctrines, i. e. the city, for a sound faith. c. 51.
Observe, they did not ask our Saviour only to enter Samaria,

St. John particularly remarks, or enter that city, but to tarry
there. Jesus tarries with those who ask Him, and especially
with those who go out of the city to Him. ORIGEN. They
were not ready yet for the third day; having no anxiety to
see a miracle, as those had who supped with Jesus in Cana
of Galilee. (This supper was after He had been in Cana three
days.) The woman's report was the ground of their belief.
The enlightening power of the Word itself was not yet visible
to them. AUG. So then they knew Christ first by report of
another, afterwards by His own presence; which is still the
case of those that are without the fold, and not yet Christians.
Christ is announced to them by some charitable Christians,
by the report of the woman, i. e. the Church; they come to
Christ, they believe on Him, through the instrumentality of
that woman; He stays withthem two days, i. e. gives them
two precepts of charity. And thenceforth their belief is
stronger. They believe that He is indeed the Saviour of
the world. ORIGEN. For it is impossible that the same
impression should be produced by hearing from one who
has seen, and seeing one's self; walking by sight is different
from walking by faith. The Samaritans now do not believe only from testimony, but from really seeing the truth.

*Orig.
tom.xiii.
c. 53.*

*Aug.
Tr. xv.
c. 33.*

*Orig.
tom.xiii.
c. 52.*

43. Now after two days he departed thence, and
went into Galilee.

44. For Jesus himself testified, that a prophet hath
no honour in his own country.

45. Then when he was come into Galilee, the
Galilæans received him, having seen all the things
that he did at Jerusalem at the feast: for they also
went unto the feast.

*Aug.
Tr. xvi.*

AUG. After staying two days in Samaria, He departed into
Galilee, where He resided: *Now after two days He departed
thence, and went into Galilee.* AUG. Why then does the
Evangelist say immediately, *For Jesus Himself testified,
that a prophet hath no honour in his own country.* For
He would seem to have testified more to the truth, had He
remained in Samaria, and not gone into Galilee. Not so:

He stayed two days in Samaria, and the Samaritans believed on Him: He stayed the same time in Galilee, and the Galileans did not believe on Him, and therefore He said, that *a prophet hath no honour in his own country*. CHRYS. Or consider this the reason that He went, not to Capernaum, but to Galilee and Cana, as appears below, His country being, I think, Capernaum. As He did not obtain honour there, hear what He says; *And thou, Capernaum, which art exalted unto heaven, shalt be brought down to hell*. He calls it His own country, because He had most resided here. THEOPHYL. Or thus: Our Lord on leaving Samaria for Galilee, explains why He was not always in Galilee: viz. because of the little honour He received there. *A prophet hath no honour in his own country*. ORIGEN. The country of the prophets was Judæa, and every one knows how little honour they received from the Jews, as we read, *Whom of the prophets have not your fathers persecuted?* One cannot but wonder at the truth of this saying, exemplified not only in the contempt cast upon the holy prophets and our Lord Himself, but also in the case of other teachers of wisdom who have been despised by their fellow-citizens and put to death [c]. CHRYS. But do we not see many held in admiration by their own people? We do; but we cannot argue from a few instances. If some are honoured in their own country, many more are honoured out of it, and familiarity generally subjects men to contempt. The Galileans however received our Lord: *Then when He was come into Galilee, the Galileans received Him*. Observe how those who are spoken ill of, are always the first to come to Christ. Of the Galileans we find it said below, *Search and look, for out of Galilee ariseth no prophet*. And He is reproached with being a Samaritan, *Thou art a Samaritan, and hast a devil*. And yet the Samaritans and Galileans believe, to the condemnation of the Jews. The Galileans however are superior to the Samaritans; for the latter believed from hearing the woman's words, the former from seeing the signs which He did: *Having seen all the things that He did at Jerusalem at the feast*. ORIGEN. Our Lord by ejecting those who sold sheep and oxen from the temple, had impressed the Galileans with a strong idea of His

Marginal notes:
Chrys. Hom. xxxv. 1.

Mat. 11, 23.

Orig. tom. xvii. c. 54.
Mat. 23.

Chrys. Hom. xxxv. 2.

Orig. tom. xvii. c. 55.

---

[c] In allusion to the persecution of some Greek philosophers.

Majesty, and they received Him. His power was shewn no less in this act, than in making the blind to see, and the deaf to hear. But probably He had performed some other miracles as well. BEDE. They had seen Him at Jerusalem, *For they also went unto the feast.* Our Lord's return has a mystical meaning, viz. that, when the Gentiles have been confirmed in the faith by the two precepts of love, i. e. at the end of the world, He will return to His country, i. e. Judæa. ORIGEN. The Galilæans were allowed to keep the feast at Jerusalem, where they had seen Jesus. Thus they were prepared to receive Him, when He came: otherwise they would either have rejected Him; or He, knowing their unprepared state, would not have gone near them.

Orig. tom.xiii. c. 55.

46. So Jesus came again into Cana of Galilee, where he made the water wine. And there was a certain nobleman, whose son was sick at Capernaum.

47. When he heard that Jesus was come out of Judæa into Galilee, he went unto him, and besought him that he would come down, and heal his son: for he was at the point of death.

48. Then said Jesus unto him, Except ye see signs and wonders, ye will not believe.

49. The nobleman saith unto him, Sir, come down ere my child die.

50. Jesus saith unto him, Go thy way; thy son liveth. And the man believed the word that Jesus had spoken unto him, and he went his way.

51. And as he was now going down, his servants met him, and told him, saying, Thy son liveth.

52. Then enquired he of them the hour when he began to amend. And they said unto him, Yesterday at the seventh hour the fever left him.

53. So the father knew that it was at the same hour, in the which Jesus said unto him, Thy son liveth: and himself believed, and his whole house.

54. This is again the second miracle that Jesus did, when he was come out of Judæa into Galilee.

CHRYS. On a former occasion our Lord attended a marriage in Cana of Galilee, now He goes there to convert the people, and confirm by His presence the faith which His miracle had produced. He goes there in preference to His own country. AUG. There, we are told, *His disciples believed on Him.* Though the house was crowded with guests, the only persons who believed in consequence of this great miracle, were His disciples. He therefore visits the city again, in order to try a second time to convert them. THEO-PHYL. The Evangelist reminds us of the miracle in order to express the praise due to the Samaritans [d]. For the Galileans in receiving Him were influenced as well by the miracle He had wrought with them, as by those they had seen at Jerusalem. The nobleman certainly believed in consequence of the miracle performed at Cana, though he did not yet understand Christ's full greatness; *And there was a certain nobleman whose son was sick at Capernaum.* ORIGEN. Some think that this was an officer of King Herod's; others, that he was one of Cæsar's household, then employed on some commission in Judæa. It is not said that He was a Jew. AUG. He is called a nobleman, either as being of the royal family, or as having some office of government. CHRYS. Some think that he is the same centurion, who is mentioned in Matthew. But that he is a different person is clear from this; that the latter, when Christ wished to come to his house, entreated Him not; whereas the former brought Christ to his house, though he had received no promise of a cure. And the latter met Jesus on His way from the mountain to Capernaum; whereas the former came to Jesus in Cana. And the latter servant was laid up with the palsy, the former's son with a fever. Of this nobleman then we read, *When he heard that Jesus was come out of Judæa into Galilee, he went unto Him, and besought Him that He would heal his son: for he was at the point of death.* AUG. Did not he who made this request believe? Mark what our Lord says; *Then said Jesus unto him, Except ye see*

Margin notes: Chrys. Hom. xxxv. 2.
Aug. Tr. xvi. c. 3.
Orig. tom. xvii. c. 57.
βασιλικὸς
Chrys. Hom. xxxv. 2.
Matt. 8, 5.
Aug. Tr. xvi. c. 3.

[d] διὰ τὸ εἰζῆσαι Σαμαρείτας τὸ ἐγκώμιον. But in the Lat. it is, ut augeret Christi præconium.

signs and wonders, ye will not believe. This is to charge
the man either with lukewarmness, or coldness of faith, or
with want of faith altogether: as if his only object was to
put Christ's power to the test, and see who and what kind
of person Christ was, and what He could do. The word
prodigy (wonder) signifies something *far off*, in futurity.
Aug. Our Lord would have the mind of the believer so
raised above all mutable things, as not to seek even for
miracles. For miracles, though sent from heaven, are, in

Greg. their subject matter, mutable. GREG. Remember what He
Hom. in asked for, and you will plainly see that he doubted. He
Evang.
xxviii. 1. asked Him to come down and see his son: *The nobleman
saith unto him, Sir, come down, ere my child die.* His
faith was deficient; in that he thought that our Lord could

Chrys. not save, except He were personally present. CHRYS. And
Hom.
xxxv. 2. mark his earthly mind, shewn in hurrying Christ along with
him; as if our Lord could not raise his son after death.
Indeed it is very possible that he may have asked
in unbelief. For fathers often are so carried away by their
affection, as to consult not only those they depend upon, but
even those they do not depend upon at all: not wishing to
leave any means untried, which might save their children.
But had he had any strong reliance upon Christ, he would

Greg. have gone to Him in Judæa. GREG. Our Lord in His answer
Hom. in
Evang. implies that He is in a certain sense where He is invited
xxviii. present, even when He is absent from a place. He saves by
1, 2. His command simply, even as by His will He created all
things: *Jesus saith unto him, Go thy way, thy son liveth.*
Here is a blow to that pride which honours human wealth
and greatness, and not that nature which is made after the
image of God. Our Redeemer, to shew that things made
much of among men, were to be despised by Saints, and
things despised made much of, did not go to the nobleman's

Chrys. son, but was ready to go to the centurion's servant. CHRYS.
Hom.
xxxv. 2. Or thus; In the centurion there was confirmed faith and true
devotion, and therefore our Lord was ready to go. But the
nobleman's faith was still imperfect, as he thought our Lord
could not heal in the absence of the sick person. But
Christ's answer enlightened him. *And the man believed the
word which Jesus had spoken to him, and went his way.* He
did not believe, however, wholly or completely. ORIGEN. His

rank appears in the fact of his servants meeting him: *And as he was now going down, his servants met him, and told him, saying, Thy son liveth.* CHRYS. They met him, to announce what had happened, and prevent Christ from coming, as He was no longer wanted. That the nobleman did not fully believe, is shewn by what follows: *Then enquired he of them at what hour he began to amend.* He wished to find out whether the recovery was accidental, or owing to our Lord's word. *And they said unto him, Yesterday at the seventh hour the fever left him.* How obvious is the miracle? His recovery did not take place in an ordinary way, but all at once; in order that it might be seen to be Christ's doing, and not the result of nature: *So the father knew that it was at the same hour, in the which Jesus said unto him, Thy son liveth; and himself believed, and his whole house.* AUG. If he only believed when he was told that his son was well again, and had compared the hour according to his servant's account, with the hour predicted by Christ, he did not believe when he first made the petition. BEDE. So, we see, faith, like the other virtues, is formed gradually, and has its beginning, growth, and maturity. His faith had its beginning, when he asked for his son's recovery; its growth, when he believed our Lord's words, *Thy son liveth;* its maturity, after the announcement of the fact by his servants. AUG. The Samaritans believed on the strength of His words only: that whole house believed on the strength of the miracle which had been brought in it. The Evangelist adds, *This is again the second miracle which Jesus did, when He was come out of Judæa into Galilee.* CHRYS. *The second miracle,* he says markedly. The Jews had not come to the more perfect faith of the Samaritans, who saw no miracle. ORIGEN. The sentence is ambiguous. Taken one way, it means that Jesus after coming to Galilee, performed two miracles, of which that of healing the nobleman's son was the second: taken another, it means, that of the two miracles which Jesus performed in Galilee, the second was done after coming from Judæa into Galilee. The latter is the true and received meaning. Mystically, the two journeys of Christ into Galilee signify His two advents; at the first of which He makes us His guest at supper, and

Chrys.
Hom.
xxxv. 3.

Aug.
Tr. xvi.
c. 3.

Aug.
Tr. xvi.
c. 3.

Chrys.
Hom.
xxxvi. 1.

Orig.
tom. xvii.
c. 60.

c. 56.

gives us wine to drink; at the second, He raises up the nobleman's son who was at the point of death, i. e. the Jewish people, who, after the fulness of the Gentiles, attain themselves to salvation. For, as the great King of Kings is He, whom God hath seated upon His holy hill of Sion, so the lesser king is he, who saw his day, and was glad, i. e. Abraham'. And therefore his sick son is the Jewish people fallen from the true religion, and thrown into a fever in consequence by the fiery darts of the enemy. And we know that the saints of old, even when they had put off the covering of the flesh, made the people the object of their care: for we read in Maccabees, after the death of Jeremiah, *This is Jeremias the prophet of the Lord, who prayeth much for the people.* Abraham therefore prays to our Saviour to succour his diseased people. Again, the word of power, *Thy son liveth,* comes forth from Cana, i. e. the work of the Word, the healing of the nobleman's son, is done in Capernaum, i. e. the land of consolation. The nobleman's son signifies the class of believers who though diseased are yet not altogether destitute of fruits. The words, *Except ye see signs and wonders, ye will not believe,* are spoken of the Jewish people in general, or perhaps of the nobleman, i. e. Abraham himself, in a certain sense. For as John waited for a sign; *on Whom thou shalt see the Spirit descending;* so too the Saints who died before the coming of Christ in the flesh, expected Him to manifest Himself by signs and wonders. And this nobleman too had servants as well as a son; which servants stand for the lower and weaker class of believers. Nor is it chance that the fever leaves the son at the *seventh hour;* for seven is the number of rest. ALCUIN. Or it was the seventh hour, because all remission of sins is through the sevenfold Spirit; for the number seven divided into three and four, signifies the Holy Trinity, in the four seasons of the world, in the four elements. ORIGEN. There may be an allusion in the two journeys to the two advents of Christ in the soul, the first supplying a spiritual banquet of wine, the second taking away all remains of weakness and death. THEOPHYL. The little king stands for man generally; man not only deriving his soul from the King of the

2 Macc. 12.

Orig. t. xviii. c. 56.

' The same word as nobleman: a more literal translation.

universe, but having Himself dominion over all things. His
son, i. e. his mind, labours under a fever of evil passion
and desires. He goes to Jesus and entreats Him to come
down; i. e. to exercise the condescension of His pity, and
pardon his sins, before it is too late. Our Lord answers;
Go thy way, i. e. advance in holiness, and then thy son will
live; but if thou stop short in thy course, thou wilt destroy
the power of understanding and doing right.

CHAP. V.

1. After this there was a feast of the Jews; and Jesus went up to Jerusalem.

2. Now there is at Jerusalem by the sheep market a pool, which is called in the Hebrew tongue Bethesda, having five porches.

3. In these lay a great multitude of impotent folk, of blind, halt, withered, waiting for the moving of the water.

4. For an angel went down at a certain season into the pool, and troubled the water: whosoever then first after the troubling of the water stepped in, was made whole of whatsoever disease he had.

5. And a certain man was there, which had an infirmity thirty and eight years.

6. When Jesus saw him lie, and knew that he had been now a long time in that case, he saith unto him, Wilt thou be made whole?

7. The impotent man answered him, Sir, I have no man, when the water is troubled, to put me into the pool: but while I am coming, another steppeth down before me.

8. Jesus saith unto him, Rise, take up thy bed, and walk.

9. And immediately the man was made whole, and took up his bed, and walked: and on the same day was the sabbath.

10. The Jews therefore said unto him that was cured, It is the sabbath day: it is not lawful for thee to carry thy bed.

11. He answered them, He that made me whole, the same said unto me, Take up thy bed, and walk.

12. Then asked they him, What man is that which said unto thee, Take up thy bed, and walk?

13. And he that was healed wist not who it was: for Jesus had conveyed himself away, a multitude being in that place.

Aug. After the miracle in Galilee, He returns to Jerusalem: *After this there was a feast of the Jews, and Jesus went up to Jerusalem.* Chrys. The feast of Pentecost. Jesus always went up to Jerusalem at the time of the feasts, that it might be seen that He was not an enemy to, but an observer of, the Law. And it gave Him the opportunity of impressing the simple multitude by miracles and teaching: as great numbers used then to collect from the neighbouring towns.

Now there is at Jerusalem by the sheep-market a pool, which is called in the Hebrew tongue Bethesda, having five porches. Alcuin. The pool by the sheep-market, is the place where the priest washed the animals that were going to be sacrificed. Chrys. This pool was one among many types of that baptism, which was to purge away sin. First God enjoined water for the cleansing from the filth of the body, and from those defilements, which were not real, but legal, e. g. those from death, or leprosy, and the like. Afterwards infirmities were healed by water, as we read: *In these (the porches) lay a great multitude of impotent folk, of blind, halt, withered, waiting for the moving of the water.* This was a nearer approximation to the gift of baptism, when not only defilements are cleansed, but sicknesses healed. Types are of various ranks, just as in a court, some officers are nearer to the prince, others farther off. The water, however, did not heal by virtue of its own natural properties, (for if so the effect would have followed uniformly,) but by the descent of an Angel: *For an Angel went down at a certain season into the pool, and troubled the water.* In the same way, in Baptism, water does not act simply as water, but receives first the grace of the Holy Spirit, by means of which it cleanses us from all our sins. And the Angel troubled the

Margin notes: Aug. de Con. Evang. Liv.c.10. Chrys. Hom. xxxvi.1. Chrys. Hom. xxxvi.1.

water, and imparted a healing virtue to it, in order to prefigure to the Jews that far greater power of the Lord of the
Angels, of healing the diseases of the soul. But then their
infirmities prevented their applying the cure; for it follows,
*Whosoever then first after the troubling of the water stepped
in, was made whole of whatsoever disease he had.* But now
every one may attain this blessing, for it is not an Angel
which troubleth the water, but the Lord of Angels, which
worketh every where. Though the whole world come, grace
fails not, but remains as full as ever; like the sun's rays
which give light all day, and every day, and yet are not
spent. The sun's light is not diminished by this bountiful
expenditure: no more is the influence of the Holy Spirit by
the largeness of its outpourings. Not more than one could be
cured at the pool; God's design being to put before men's
minds, and oblige them to dwell upon, the healing power of
water; that from the effect of water on the body, they might
believe more readily its power on the soul. Aug. It was a
greater act in Christ, to heal the diseases of the soul, than
the sicknesses of the perishable body. But as the soul itself
did not know its Restorer, as it had eyes in the flesh to
discern visible things, but not in the heart wherewith to
know God; our Lord performed cures which could be seen,
that He might afterwards work cures which could not be
seen. He went to the place, where lay a multitude of sick,
out of whom He chose one to heal: *And a certain man was
there, which had an infirmity thirty and eight years.* CHRYS.
He did not, however, proceed immediately to heal him, but
first tried by conversation to bring him into a believing
state of mind. Not that He required faith in the first
instance, as He did from the blind man, saying, *Believe ye
that I am able to do this?* for the lame man could not well
know who He was. Persons who in different ways had had
the means of knowing Him, were asked this question, and
properly so. But there were some who did not and could
not know Him yet, but would be made to know Him by His
miracles afterwards. And in their case the demand for faith
is reserved till after those miracles have taken place: *When
Jesus saw him lie, and knew that he had been a long time
in that case, He saith unto him, Wilt thou be made whole?*

Aug.
Tr. xvii.
c. 1.

Chrys.
Hom.
xxxiii.
1, 2.

Matt. 9,
28.

He does not ask this question for His own information, (this were unnecessary,) but to bring to light the great patience of the man, who for thirty and eight years had sat year after year by the place, in the hope of being cured; which sufficiently explains why Christ passed by the others, and went to him.   And He does not say, Dost thou wish Me to heal thee? for the man had not as yet any idea that He was so great a Person.   Nor on the other hand did the lame man suspect any mockery in the question, to make him take offence, and say, Hast thou come to vex me, by asking me if I would be made whole; but he answered mildly, *Sir, I have no man, when the water is troubled, to put me into the pool; but while I am coming, another steppeth down before me.* He had no idea as yet that the Person who put this question to him would heal him, but thought that Christ might probably be of use in putting him into the water.   But Christ's word is sufficient, *Jesus saith unto him, Rise, take up thy bed, and walk.*   Aug.   Three distinct biddings.   *Rise,* however, is not a command, but the conferring of the cure.   Two commands were given upon his cure, *take up thy bed, and walk.* Chrys.   Behold the richness of the Divine Wisdom.   He not only heals, but bids him carry his bed also.   This was to shew the cure was really miraculous, and not a mere effect of the imagination; for the man's limbs must have become quite sound and compact, to allow him to take up his bed. The impotent man again did not deride and say, The Angel cometh down, and troubleth the water, and he only cureth one each time; dost Thou, who art a mere man, think that Thou canst do more than an Angel?   On the contrary, he heard, believed Him who bade him, and was made whole: *And immediately the man was made whole, and took up his bed, and walked.*   Bede;   There is a wide difference between our Lord's mode of healing, and a physician's.   He acts by His word, and acts immediately: the other's requires a long time for its completion.   Chrys.   This was wonderful, but what follows more so.   As yet he had no opposition to face. It is made more wonderful when we see him obeying Christ afterwards in spite of the rage and railing of the Jews: *And on the same day was the sabbath.   The Jews therefore said unto him that was cured, It is the sabbath day, it is not*

Aug.
Tr. xvii.
c. 7.

Chrys.
Hom.
xxxvi.
1, 2.

Chrys.
Hom.
xxxvii.
2.

Aug.
Tr. xvii.
c. 10.

lawful for thee to carry thy bed. Aug. They did not charge our Lord with healing on the sabbath, for He would have replied that if an ox or an ass of theirs had fallen into a pit, would not they have taken it out on the sabbath day: but they addressed the man as he was carrying his bed, as if to say, Even if the healing could not be delayed, why enjoin the work? He shields himself under the authority of his Healer: *He that made me whole, the Same said unto me, Take up thy bed, and walk:* meaning, Why should not I

Chrys.
Hom.
xxxvii.
2.

receive a command, if I received a cure from Him? Chrys. Had he been inclined to deal treacherously, he might have said, If it is a crime, accuse Him Who commanded it, and I will lay down my bed. And he would have concealed his cure, knowing, as he did, that their real cause of offence was not the breaking of the Sabbath, but the miracle. But he neither concealed it, nor asked for pardon, but boldly confessed the cure. They then ask spitefully; *What man is that who said unto thee, Take up thy bed, and walk.* They do not say, Who is it, who made thee whole? but only mention the offence. It follows, *And he that was healed wist not who it was, for Jesus had conveyed Himself away, a multitude being in that place.* This He had done first, because the man who had been made whole, was the best witness of the cure, and could give his testimony with less suspicion in our Lord's absence; and secondly, that the fury of men might not be excited more than was necessary. For the mere sight of the object of envy, is no small incentive to envy. For these reasons He departed, and left them to examine the fact for themselves. Some are of opinion, that this is the same with the one who had the palsy, whom Matthew mentions. But he is not. For the latter had many to wait upon, and carry him, whereas this man had none. And the place where the miracle was performed, is different.

Aug.
Tr. xvii.
c. 1.

Aug. Judging on low and human notions of this miracle, it is not at all a striking display of power, and only a moderate one of goodness. Of so many, who lay sick, only one was healed; though, had He chosen, He could have restored them all by a single word. How must we account for this? By supposing that His power and goodness were asserted more for imparting a knowledge of eternal salvation to the

soul, than working a temporal cure on the body. That
which received the temporal cure was certain to decay at
last, when death arrived: whereas the soul which believed
passed into life eternal. The pool and the water seem to
me to signify the Jewish people: for John in the Apocalypse Rev. 17,
obviously uses water to express people. BEDE. It is fitly
described as a sheep pool. By sheep are meant people,
according to the passage, *We are Thy people, and the* Ps. 95,7.
sheep of Thy pasture. AUG. The water then, i. e. the people, Aug.
was enclosed within five porches, i. e. the five books of
Moses. But those books only betrayed the impotent, and
did not recover them; that is to say, the Law convicted the
sinner, but did not absolve him. BEDE. Lastly, many kinds
of impotent folk lay near the pool: the blind, i. e. those who
are without the light of knowledge; the lame, i. e. those who have
not strength to do what they are commanded; the withered,
i. e. those who have not the marrow of heavenly love. AUG. Aug.
So then Christ came to the Jewish people, and by means of Tr. xvii.
mighty works, and profitable lessons, troubled the sinners, c. 3.
i. e. the water, and the stirring continued till He brought
on His own passion. But He troubled the water, unknown
to the world. *For had they known Him, they would not* 1 Cor.
have crucified the Lord of glory. But the troubling of the 11.
water came on all at once, and it was not seen who troubled
it. Again, to go down into the troubled water, is to believe
humbly on our Lord's passion. Only one was healed, to
signify the unity of the Church: whoever came afterwards
was not healed, to signify that whoever is out of this unity
cannot be healed. Wo to them who hate unity, and raise
sects. Again, he who was healed had had his infirmity
thirty and eight years: this being a number which belongs
to sickness, rather than to health. The number forty has a
sacred character with us, and is significative of perfection.
For the Law was given in Ten Commandments, and was to
be preached throughout the whole world, which consists of
four parts; and four multiplied into ten, make up the number forty. And the Law too is fulfilled by the Gospel,
which is written in four books. So then if the number
forty possesses the perfectness of the Law, and nothing
fulfils the Law, except the twofold precept of love, why

Side notes:
Rev. 17, 15.
Bede. in v. cap. Joan.
Ps. 95, 7.
Aug. Tr. xvii. c. 2.
Aug. Tr. xvii. c. 3.
1 Cor. 11.

wonder at the impotence of him, who was two less than forty? Some man was necessary for his recovery; but it was a man who was God. He found the man falling short by the number two, and therefore gave two commandments, to fill up the deficiency. For the two precepts of our Lord signify love; the love of God being first in order of command, the love of our neighbour, in order of performance. *Take up thy bed*, our Lord saith, meaning, When thou wert impotent, thy neighbour carried thee; now thou art made whole, carry thy neighbour. *And walk;* but whither, except to the Lord thy God. BEDE. What mean the words, *Arise*, and *walk;* except that thou shouldest raise thyself from thy torpor and indolence, and study to advance in good works. *Take up thy bed,* i. e. thy neighbour by which thou art carried, and bear him patiently thyself. AUG. Carry him then with whom thou walkest, that thou mayest come to Him with Whom thou desirest to abide. As yet however he wist not who Jesus was; just as we too believe in Him though we see Him not. Jesus again does not wish to be seen, but conveys Himself out of the crowd. It is in a kind of solitude of the mind, that God is seen: the crowd is noisy; this vision requires stillness.

Bede. c.v.num. 30.

Aug. Tr.xvii. c. 9.

14. Afterward Jesus findeth him in the temple, and said unto him, Behold, thou art made whole: sin no more, lest a worse thing come unto thee.

15. The man departed, and told the Jews that it was Jesus, which had made him whole.

16. And therefore did the Jews persecute Jesus, and sought to slay him, because he had done these things on the sabbath day.

17. But Jesus answered them, My Father worketh hitherto, and I work.

18. Therefore the Jews sought the more to kill him, because he not only had broken the sabbath, but said also that God was his Father, making himself equal with God.

CHRYS. The man, when healed, did not proceed to the market place, or give himself up to pleasure or vain glory, but, which was a great mark of religion, went to the temple: *Afterward Jesus findeth him in the temple.* AUG. The Lord Jesus saw him both in the crowd, and in the temple. The impotent man does not recognise Jesus in the crowd; but in the temple, being a sacred place, he does. ALCUIN[c]. For if we would know our Maker's grace, and attain to the sight of Him, we must avoid the crowd of evil thoughts and affections, convey ourselves out of the congregation of the wicked, and flee to the temple; in order that we may make ourselves the temple of God, souls whom God will visit, and in whom He will deign to dwell.

And (He) said unto him, *Behold, thou art made whole; sin no more, lest a worse thing come upon thee.* CHRYS. Here we learn in the first place, that his disease was the consequence of his sins. We are apt to bear with great indifference the diseases of our souls; but, should the body suffer ever so little hurt, we have recourse to the most energetic remedies. Wherefore God punishes the body for the offences of the soul. Secondly, we learn, that there is really a Hell. Thirdly, that it is a place of lasting and infinite punishment. Some say indeed, Because we have corrupted ourselves for a short time, shall we be tormented eternally? But see how long this man was tormented for his sins. Sin is not to be measured by length of time, but by the nature of the sin itself. And besides this we learn, that if, after undergoing a heavy punishment for our sins, we fall into them again, we shall incur another and a heavier punishment still: and justly; for one, who has undergone punishment, and has not been made better by it, proves himself to be a hardened person, and a despiser; and, as such, deserving of still greater torments. Nor let it embolden us, that we do not see all punished for their offences here: for if men do not suffer for their offences here, it is only a sign that their punishment will be the greater hereafter. Our diseases however do not always arise from sins; but only most commonly so. For some spring from other lax habits: some are sent for the sake of trial, as Job's were. But why

Chrys.
Hom.
xxxvii.

Aug.
Tr. xvii.
c. 11.

in loc.

Chrys.
Hom.
xxxviii.
1.

---

[c] Alcuin's commentary on St. John's Gospel is the work always referred to.

N

does Christ make mention of this palsied man's sins? Some
say, because he had been an accuser of Christ. And shall
we say the same of the man afflicted with the palsy?
Matt. 9, 2. For he too was told, *Thy sins are forgiven thee?* The truth
is, Christ does not find fault with the man here for his past sins,
but only warns him against future. In healing others,
however, He makes no mention of sins at all: so that it
would seem to be the case that the diseases of these
men had arisen from their sins; whereas those of the
others had come from natural causes only. Or perhaps
through these, He admonishes all the rest. Or he may have
admonished this man, knowing his great patience of mind, and
that he would bear an admonition. It is a disclosure too of
His divinity, for He implies in saying, *Sin no more*, that He
Aug. Tr.xvii. c. 12. knew what sins He had committed. AUG. Now that the
man had seen Jesus, and knew Him to be the author of his
recovery, he was not slow in preaching Him to others: *The
man departed, and told the Jews that it was Jesus which
Chrys. Hom. xxxviii. 2. had made him whole.* CHRYS. He was not so insensible to
the benefit, and the advice he had received, as to have any
malignant aim in speaking this news. Had it been done to
disparage Christ, he could have concealed the cure, and put
forward the offence. But he does not mention Jesus's
saying, *Take up thy bed*, which was an offence in the eyes
of the Jews; but *told the Jews that it was Jesus which had
Aug. Tr.xviii. c. 13. made him whole.* AUG. This announcement enraged them,
*And therefore did the Jews persecute Jesus, because He had
done these things on the sabbath day.* A plain bodily work
had been done before their eyes, distinct from the healing of
the man's body, and which could not have been necessary,
even if healing was; viz. the carrying of the bed.
Wherefore our Lord openly says, that the sacrament of the
Sabbath, the sign of observing one day out of seven, was
only a temporary institution, which had attained its fulfil-
ment in Him: *But Jesus answered them, My Father worketh
hitherto, and I work:* as if He said, Do not suppose that
My Father rested on the Sabbath in such a sense, as that
from that time forth, He has ceased from working; for He
worketh up to this time, though without labour, and so
work I. God's resting means only that He made no other

creature, after the creation. The Scripture calls it rest, to
remind us of the rest we shall enjoy after a life of good
works here. And as God only when He had made man in
His own image and similitude, and finished all His works,
and seen that they were very good, rested on the seventh
day: so do thou expect no rest, except thou return to the
likeness in which thou wert made, but which thou hast lost by
sin; i. e. unless thou doest good works. AUG. It may be said Aug.
then, that the observance of the sabbath was imposed on the ^{iv. super} Gen. ad
Jews, as the shadow of something to come; viz. that spiritual litteram
rest, which God, by the figure of His own rest promised ^(c. xi.)
to all who should perform good works. AUG. There will be
a sabbath of the world, when the six ages, i. e. the six days,
as it were, of the world, have passed: then will come that
rest which is promised to the saints. AUG. The mystery of Aug.
which rest the Lord Jesus Himself sealed by His burial: for ^{iv. Gen. ad lit}
He rested in His sepulchre on the sabbath, having on c. xi.
the sixth day finished all His work, inasmuch as He said,
It is finished. What wonder then that God, to prefigure the c. 19.
day on which Christ was to rest in the grave, rested one
day from His works, afterwards to carry on the work of
governing the world. We may consider too that God, when
He rested, rested from the work of creation simply, i. e.
made no more new kinds of creatures: but that from that time
till now, He has been carrying on the government of those
creatures. For His power, as respects the government of
heaven and earth, and all the things that He had made, did
not cease on the seventh day: they would have perished
immediately, without His government: because the power of
the Creator is that on which the existence of every creature
depends. If it ceased to govern, every species of creation
would cease to exist: and all nature would go to nothing.
For the world is not like a building, which stands after the
architect has left it; it could not stand the twinkling of an
eye, if God withdrew His governing hand. Therefore when
our Lord says, *My Father worketh hitherto,* he means the
continuation of the work; the holding together, and governing
of the creation. It might have been different, had He said,
Worketh even now. This would not have conveyed the sense
of continuing. As it is we find it, *Until now;* i. e. from the

Aug.
Tr. xvii.
s. 15.

time of the creation downwards. Aug. He says then, as it were, to the Jews, Why think ye that I should not work on the sabbath? The sabbath day was instituted as a type[d] of Me. Ye observe the works of God: by Me all things were made. The Father made light, but He spoke,.that it might be made. If He spoke, then He made it by the Word; and I am His Word. My Father worked when He made the world, and He worketh until now, governing the world: and as He made the world by Me, when He made it, so He governs it by Me, now He governs it. Chrys. Christ

Chrys.
Hom.
xxxviii.
2.

defended His disciples, by putting forward the example of their fellow-servant David: but He defends Himself by a reference to the Father. We may observe too that He does not defend Himself as man, nor yet purely as God, but sometimes as one, sometimes as the other; wishing both to be believed, both the dispensation of His humiliation, and the dignity of His Godhead; wherefore He shews His equality to the Father, both by calling Him His Father emphatically, (*My* Father,) and by declaring that He doeth the same things, that the Father doth, (*And I work*.) *Therefore*, it follows, *the Jews sought the more to kill Him, because he not only had broken the sabbath, but said also that God was His Father*.

Aug.
Tr. xviii.
s. 16.

Aug. i. e. not in the secondary sense in which it is true of all of us, but as implying equality. For we all of

Matt. 6.

us say to God, *Our Father, Which art in heaven*. And the

Isaiah
63, 16.

Jews say, *Thou art our Father*. They were not angry then because He called God His Father, but because He called

Aug.
de Con.
Ev. l. iv.
c. x.

Him so in a sense different from men. Aug. The words, *My Father worketh hitherto, and I work*, suppose Him to be equal to the Father. This being understood, it followed from the Father's working, that the Son worked: inasmuch

Chrys.
Hom.
xxxviii.
s. 3.

as the Father doth nothing without the Son. Chrys. Were He not the Son by nature, and of the same substance, this defence would be worse than the former accusation made. For no prefect could clear Himself from a transgression of the king's law, by urging that the king broke it also. But, on the supposition of the Son's equality to the Father, the defence is valid. It then follows, that as the Father worked

---

d Since our everlasting rest, which the sabbath foreshadowed, is in Him. see Conf. fin. de Civ. D. xi. 8. &c.

on the Sabbath without doing wrong: the Son could do so likewise. AUG. So, the Jews understood what the Arians do not. For the Arians say that the Son is not equal to the Father, and hence sprang up that heresy which afflicts the Church. CHRYS. Those however who are not well-disposed to this doctrine, do not admit that Christ made Himself equal to the Father, but only that the Jews thought He did. But let us consider what has gone before. That the Jews persecuted Christ, and that He broke the sabbath, and said that God was His Father, is unquestionably true. That which immediately follows then from these premises, viz. His *making Himself equal with God*, is true also. HILARY. The Evangelist here explains why the Jews wished to kill Him. CHRYS. And again, had it been that our Lord Himself did not mean this, but that the Jews misunderstood Him, He would not have overlooked their mistake. Nor would the Evangelist have omitted to remark upon it, as he does upon our Lord's speech, *Destroy this temple*. AUG. The Jews however did not understand from our Lord that He was the Son of God, but only that He was equal with God; though Christ gave this as the result of His being the Son of God. It is from not seeing this, while they saw at the same time that equality was asserted, that they charged Him with *making Himself equal with God:* the truth being, that He did not *make* Himself equal, but the Father had begotten Him equal.

19. Then answered Jesus and said unto them, Verily, verily, I say unto you, The Son can do nothing of himself, but what he seeth the Father do: for what things soever he doeth, these also doeth the Son likewise.

20. For the Father loveth the Son, and sheweth him all things that himself doeth: and he will shew him greater works than these, that ye may marvel.

HILARY. He refers to the charge of violating the sabbath, brought against Him. *My Father worketh hitherto, and I work;* meaning that He had a precedent for claiming the

Margin notes: Aug. Tr. xvii. s. 16. — Chrys. Hom. xxxviii. 3. — Hilar. vii. de Trin. c. 15. — c. 11. — Aug. Tr. xvii. s. 16. — Hilar. vii. de Trin. c. 17.

right He did; and that what He did was in reality His
Father's doing, who acted in the Son.   And to quiet the
jealousy which had been raised, because by the use of His
Father's name He had made Himself equal with God, and
to assert the excellency of His birth and nature, He says,
Verily, verily, I say unto you, The Son can do nothing of
Himself, but what He seeth the Father do.   Aug. Some who
would be thought Christians, the Arian heretics, who say that
the very Son of God who took our flesh upon Him, was inferior to the Father, take advantage of these words to throw
discredit upon our doctrine, and say, You see that when our
Lord perceived the Jews to be indignant, because He seemed
to make Himself equal with God, He gave such an answer
as shewed that He was not equal.   For they say, he who
can do nothing but what he sees the Father do is not equal
but inferior to the Father.   But if there is a greater God,
and a less God, (the Word being God,) we worship two
Gods, and not one[e].   HILARY. Lest then that assertion of
His equality, which must belong to Him, as by Name and
Nature the Son, might throw doubt upon His Nativity[f],
He says that the Son *can do nothing of Himself.*   Aug. As
if He said: Why are ye offended that I called God *My*
Father, and that I make Myself equal with God?   I am
equal, but equal in such a sense as is consistent with His
having begotten Me; with My being from Him, not Him
from Me.   With the Son, being and power are one and the
same thing.   The Substance of the Son then being of the
Father, the power of the Son is of the Father also: and as the
Son *is* not of Himself, so He *can* not of Himself.   *The Son*
can do nothing of Himself, but what He seeth the Father do.—
His seeing and His being born of the Father are the same.
His vision is not distinct from His Substance, but the whole

Marginal notes:
Aug.
Tr.xviii.
3, 5.

Hilar.
vii. de
Tr.c.17.

Aug.
Tr. xx.
4.

xxi. 4.

---

[e] This is the answer of the Catholic
to the Arian argument, and is drawn
out more fully in Augustin's text,
where the Arian blasphemy, that there
was a greater and a lesser God, is said
to savour of Paganism.   Nic.

[f] i. e. left to themselves, people
would be vacillating between the
thought our Lord was not equal to the
Father or not the Son, and therefore
our Lord at once conveys the doctrine
of His Equality with the Father, and
yet that He was the Son, "The Only-
Begotten God operating by the operations of the power of the Father, and
so He wrought that, which He knew
in His own intrinsic knowledge that the
Nature of God the Father, inseparable
from Himself, Which He possessed
through His true Nativity, could
work."   S. Hil. l. c.

together is of the Father. HILARY. That the wholesome Hilar. order of our confession, i. e. that we believe in the Father vii. de Tr.c.17. and the Son, might remain, He shews the nature of His birth; viz. that He derived the power of acting not from an accession of strength supplied for each work, but by His own knowledge in the first instance. And this knowledge He derived not from any particular visible precedents, as if what the Father had done, the Son could do afterwards; but that the Son being born of the Father, and consequently conscious of the Father's virtue and nature within Him, could do nothing but what He saw the Father do: as he here testifies; God does not see by bodily organs, but by the virtue of His nature. AUG. If we understand this subordination of the Son Aug. to arise from the human nature, it will follow that the Father ii.de Tr. c. 3. walked first upon the water, and did all the other things which the Son did in the flesh, in order that the Son might do them. Who can be so insane as to think this [d]? AUG. Yet Aug. that walking of the flesh upon the sea was done by the Father Tr. xx. s. 6. through the Son. For when the flesh walked, and the Divinity of the Son guided, the Father was not absent, as the Son Himself saith below, *The Father that dwelleth in Me,* c. 14. *He doeth the works.* He guards however against the carnal s. 9. interpretation of the words, *The Son can do nothing of Him* (v. 10.) *self.* As if the case were like that of two artificers, master and disciple, one of whom made a chest, and the other made another like it, by adding, *For whatsoever things he doeth, these doeth the Son likewise.* He does not say, Whatsoever the Father doeth, the Son does *other* things like them, but the very same things. The Father made the world, the Son made the world, the Holy Ghost made the world. If the Father, Son, and Holy Ghost are one, it follows that one and the same world was made by the Father, through the Son, in the Holy Ghost. Thus it is the very same thing that the Son doeth. He adds *likewise,* to prevent another error arising. For the body seems to do the same things with the mind, but it does not do them in a like way, inas-

---

[d] *The Son can do nothing of Himself, but what He seeth the Father do.* If this arises from His human nature, then He must have seen in His human nature, i. e. visibly, with the natural eye, each several act of His done beforehand by the Father. It follows that the subordination here mentioned arises from the Sonship itself of the Son's, not from His human nature.

much as the body is subject, the soul governing, the body visible, the soul invisible. When a slave does a thing at the command of his master, the same thing is done by both; but is it in a like way? Now in the Father and Son there is not this difference; they do the same things, and in a like way. Father and Son act with the same power; so that the Son is equal to the Father. HILARY. Or thus; *All things* and *the same*, He says, to shew the virtue of His nature, its being the same with God's. That is the same nature, which can do all the same things. And as the Son does all the same things in a like way, the likeness of the works excludes the notion of the worker existing alone [g]. Thus we come to a true idea of the Nativity, as our faith receives it: the likeness of the works bearing witness to the Nativity, their sameness to the Nature. CHRYS. Or thus; That *the Son can do nothing of Himself*, must be understood to mean, that He can do nothing contrary to, or displeasing to, the Father. And therefore He does not say that He *does* nothing contrary, but that He *can* do nothing; in order to shew His perfect likeness, and absolute equality to the Father. Nor is this a sign of weakness in the Son, but rather of goodness. For as when we say that it is impossible for God to sin, we do not charge Him with weakness, but bear witness to a certain ineffable goodness; so when the Son says, I can do nothing of myself, it only means, that He can do nothing contrary to the Father. AUG. This is not a sign of failing in Him, but of His abiding in His birth from the Father. And it is as high an attribute of the Almighty that He does not change, as it is that He does not die. The Son could do what He had not seen the Father doing, if He could do what the Father does not do through Him; i. e. if He could sin: a supposition inconsistent with the immutably good nature which was begotten from the Father. That He cannot do; this then is to be understood of Him, not in the sense of deficiency, but of power. CHRYS. And this is confirmed by what follows: *For whatsoever he doeth, these also doeth the Son likewise.* For if the Father does all things by Himself,

Marginal notes:
Hilar. vii. de Tr.c.18.

Chrys. Hom. xxxviii. 4.

Aug. contra Serm. Arianorum,c.9. (xiv.)

Chrys. Hom. xxxviii. 4.

---

g "Similitudo operum solitudinem operantis exclusit." Bened. and edd. i. e. as before, the Son is equal to The Father, since He doeth *all* the same things. Yet the very expression "sameness" implies a plurality of Persons. Nic. reads similitudinem, which does not belong to the argument here.

so does the Son also, if this *likewise* is to stand good. You
see how high a meaning these humble words bear. He
gives His thoughts a humble dress purposely. For whenever He expressed Himself loftily, He was persecuted, as an
enemy of God. Aug. Having said that He did the same Aug.
things that the Father did, and in a like way, He adds, *For* Tr. xxi.
the Father loveth the Son, and sheweth Him all things that s. 2.
Himself doeth. And sheweth Him all things that Himself
doeth: this has a reference to the words above; *But what*
He seeth the Father do. But again, our human ideas are
perplexed, and one may say, So then the Father first does
something, that the Son may see what He does; just as an
artificer teaches his son his art, and shews him what he
makes, that he may be able to make the same after him.
On this supposition, when the Father does a thing, the
Son does not do it; in that the Son is beholding what His
Father doeth. But we hold it as a fixed and incontrovertible
truth, that the Father makes all things through the Son, and
therefore He must shew them to the Son, *before* He makes
them. And where does the Father shew the Son what He
makes, except in the Son Himself, by whom He makes
them? For if the Father makes a thing for a pattern, and
the Son attends to the workmanship as it goes on, where is
the indivisibility of the Trinity? The Father therefore does
not shew the Son what He doeth by doing it, but by shewing
doeth it, through the Son. The Son seeth, and the Father
sheweth, before a thing is made, and from the shewing of the
Father, and the seeing of the Son, that is made which is
made; made by the Father, through the Son. But thou wilt
say, I shew my Son what I wish him to make, and he makes
it, and I make it through him. True; but before thou doest
any thing, thou shewest it to thy son, that he may do it for
thy example, and thou by him; but thou speakest to thy
son words which are not thyself; whereas the Son Himself is
the Word of the Father; and could He speak by the Word to
the Word? Or, because the Son was the great Word, were
lesser words to pass between the Father and the Son, or a
certain sound and temporary creation, as it were, to go out of
the mouth of the Father, and strike the ear of the Son? Put
away these bodily notions, and if thou art simple, see the

truth in simplicity. If thou canst not comprehend what God is, comprehend at least what He is not. Thou wilt have advanced no little way, if thou thinkest nothing that is untrue of God. See what I am saying exemplified in thine own mind. Thou hast memory, and thought, thy memory sheweth to thy thought Carthage: before thou perceivest what is in her, she sheweth it to thought, which is turned toward her: the memory then hath shewn, the thought hath perceived, and no words have passed between them, no outward sign been used. But whatever is in thy memory, thou receivest from without: that which the Father sheweth to the Son, He doth not receive from without; the whole goes on within; there being no creature existing without, but what the Father hath made by the Son. And the Father maketh by shewing, in that He maketh by the Son who sees. The Father's shewing begets the Son's seeing, as the Father begets the Son? Shewing begets seeing, not seeing shewing. But it would be more correct, and more spiritual, not to view the Father as distinct from His shewing, or the Son from His seeing. HILARY. It must not be supposed that the Only Begotten God needed such shewing on account of ignorance. For the shewing here is only the doctrine of the nativity [h]; the self-existing Son, from the self-existing Father. AUG. For to see the Father is to see His Son. The Father so shews all His works to the Son, that the Son sees them from the Father [i]. For the birth of the Son is in His seeing: He sees from the same source, from which He is, and is born, and remains. HILARY. Nor did the heavenly discourse lack the caution, to guard against our inferring from these words any difference in the nature of the Son and the Father. For He says that the works of the Father were shewn to Him, not that strength was supplied Him for the doing of them, in order to teach that this shewing is substantially nothing else than His birth; for that simultaneously with the Son Himself is born the Son's knowledge of the works the Father will do through Him. AUG. But now from Him whom we called coeternal with the Father, who saw

Margin notes:

Hilar. vii. de Trin. c. 19.

Aug. Tr. xxi.

Hilar. vii. de Trin. c. 19.

Aug. Tr. xxi. s. 5.

---

[h] i. e. implying another person (who shews) who is the *author*: first in order of succession, i. e. the Father. It is explained by the Aug. following.

[i] i. e. not looking *toward* the Father, but from Him; i. e. being in the Father at the time.

the Father, and existed in that He saw, we return to the things of time, *And He will shew him greater works than these.* But if He will shew him, i. e. is about to shew him, He hath not yet shewn him: and when He does shew him, others also will see; for it follows, *That ye may believe.* It is difficult to see what the eternal Father can shew in time to the coeternal Son, Who knows all that exists within the Father's mind. *For as the Father raiseth up the dead, and quickeneth them, even so the Son quickeneth whom He will.* To raise the dead was a greater work than to heal the sick. But this is explained by considering that He Who a little before spoke as God, now begins to speak as man. As man, and therefore living in time, He will be shewn greater works in time. Bodies will rise again by the human dispensation by which the Son of God assumed manhood in time; but souls by virtue of the eternity of the Divine Substance. For which reason it was said before that the Father loved the Son, and shewed Him what things soever He did. For the Father shews the Son that souls are raised up; for they are raised up by the Father and the Son, even as they cannot live, except God give them life. Or the Father is about to shew this to us, not to Him; according to what follows, *That ye may believe.* This being the reason why the Father would *shew Him greater things than these.* But why did He not say, shall shew you, instead of the Son? Because we are members of the Son, and He, as it were, learns in His members, even as He suffers in us. For as He says, *Inasmuch as ye have done it unto one of the least of these My brethren, ye have done it unto Me:* so, if we ask Him, how He, the Teacher of all things, learns, He replies, When one of the least of My brethren learns, I learn.

Tr. xix.

Tr. xxi.

Matt. 25, 40.

21. For as the Father raiseth up the dead, and quickeneth them; even so the Son quickeneth whom he will.

22. For the Father judgeth no man, but hath committed all judgment unto the Son:

23. That all men should honour the Son, even as

they honour the Father. He that honoureth not the Son honoureth not the Father which hath sent him.

Aug.
Tr. xxi.
s. 5, 6. AUG. Having said that the Father would shew the Son greater works than these, He proceeds to describe these greater works: *For as the Father raiseth up the dead, and quickeneth them, even so the Son quickeneth whom He will.* These are plainly greater works, for it is more of a miracle that a dead man should rise again, than that a sick man should recover. We must not understand from the words, that some are raised by the Father, others by the Son; but that the Son raises to life the same whom the Father raiseth. And to guard against any one saying, The Father raises the dead by the Son, the former by His own power, the latter, like an instrument, by another power, He asserts distinctly the power of the Son: *The Son quickeneth whom he will.* Observe here not only the power of the Son, but also His will. Father and Son have the same power and will. The Father willeth nothing distinct from the Son; but both have the same will, even as they have the same substance.

Hilar.
de Trin.
vii.c.19. HILARY. For to will is the free power of a nature, which by the act of choice, resteth in the blessedness of perfect excellence.

Aug.
Tr. xxi.
s. 11. AUG. But who are these dead, whom the Father and Son raise to life? He alludes to the general resurrection which is to be; not to the resurrection of those few, who were raised to life, that the rest might believe; as Lazarus, who rose again, to die afterwards. Having said then, *For as the Father raiseth up the dead, and quickeneth them,* to prevent our taking the words to refer to the dead whom He raised up for the sake of the miracle, and not to the resurrection to life eternal, He adds, *For the Father judgeth no man;* thus shewing that He spoke of that resurrection of the dead which would take place at the judgment.

Tr.xxiii.
s. 13. Or the words, *As the Father raiseth up the dead, &c.* refer to the resurrection of the soul; *For the Father judgeth no man, but hath committed all judgment unto the Son,* to the resurrection of the body. For the resurrection of the soul takes place by the substance of the

Father and the Son[k], and therefore it is the work of the Father and the Son together: but the resurrection of the body takes place by a dispensation of the Son's humanity, which is a temporal dispensation, and not coeternal with the Father. But see how the Word of Christ leads the mind in different directions, not allowing it any carnal resting place; but by variety of motion exercising it, by exercise purifying it, by purifying enlarging its capacity, and after enlarging filling it. He said just before that the Father shewed what things soever He did to the Son. So I saw, as it were, the Father working, and the Son waiting: now again I see the Son working, the Father resting. AUG. For this, viz. that the Father *hath given all judgment unto the Son,* does not mean that He *begat* the Son with this attribute, as is meant in the words, *So hath He given to the Son to have life in Himself.* For if so, it would not be said, *The Father judgeth no man,* because, in that the Father begat the Son equal, He judgeth with the Son. What is meant is, that in the judgment, not the form of God but the form of the Son of man will appear; not because He will not judge Who hath given all judgment to the Son; since the Son says of Him below, *There is one that seeketh and judgeth,* but *the Father judgeth no man;* i. e. no one will see Him in the judgment, but all will see the Son, because He is the Son of man, even the ungodly who *will look on Him Whom they pierced.* HILARY. Having said that *the Son quickeneth whom He will,* in order that we might not lose sight of the nativity, and think that He stood upon the ground of His own unborn power, He immediately adds, *For the Father judgeth no man, but hath given all judgment unto the Son.* In that all judgment is given to Him, both His nature, and His nativity are shewn; because only a self-existent nature can possess all things, and nativity cannot have any thing, except what is given it. CHRYS. As He gave Him life, i. e. begot Him living; so He gave Him judgment, i. e. begot Him a judge. *Gave,* it is said, that thou mayest not think Him unbegotten, and imagine

Marginal notes:
Tr. xxi. s. 12.

Aug. de Trin. c. 30. (xiii.)

c. 19.

Zech. 12. Hilar. de Trin. vii-c. 20.

Chrys. Hom. xxxviii. 1.

---

[k] For the soul becomes blessed from partaking of God, not from partaking of another blessed soul, nor by partaking in any Angelic nature. For as the soul being inferior to God gains life to that which is inferior to itself, i. e. the body; so the soul again cannot be endowed with heavenly life, but by Him who is superior to the soul, even God.

two Fathers: *All judgment,* because He has the awarding

Hilar.
vii. de
Trin. c.
20.
both of punishment and reward. HILARY. All judgment is given to Him, because He quickens whom He will. Nor can the judgment be looked on as taken away from the Father, inasmuch as the cause of His not judging is, that the judgment of the Son is His. For all judgment is given from the Father. And the reason for which He gives it, appears immediately after: *That all men may honour the Son even as*

Chrys.
Hom.
xxxix.
2.
they honour the Father. CHRYS. For, lest you should infer from hearing that the Author of His power was the Father, any difference of substance, or inequality of honour, He connects the honour of the Son with the honour of the Father, shewing that both have the same. But shall men then call Him the Father? God forbid; he who calls Him the Father, does not honour the Son equally with the Father, but confounds

Aug.
xxi. 8.
13.
both. AUG. First indeed, the Son appeared as a servant, and the Father was honoured as God. But the Son will be seen to be equal to the Father, *that all men may honour the*

1 ref. not
found
Son, even as they honour the Father. [1]But what if persons are found, who honour the Father, and do not honour the Son? It cannot be: *He that honoureth not the Son, honoureth not the Father which hath sent Him.* It is one thing to acknowledge God, as God; and another to acknowledge Him as the Father. When thou acknowledgest God the Creator, thou acknowledgest an almighty, supreme, eternal, invisible, immutable Spirit. When thou acknowledgest the Father, thou dost in reality acknowledge the Son; for He could not be the Father, had He not the Son. But if thou honour the Father as greater, the Son as less, so far as thou givest less honour to the Son, thou takest away from the honour of the Father. For thou in reality thinkest that the Father could not or would not beget the Son equal to Himself; which if He would not do, He was envious, if He

Tr.xxiii.
s. 13.
could not, He was weak. Or, *That all men should honour the Son even as they honour the Father;* has a reference to the resurrection of souls, which is the work of the Son, as well as of the Father. But the resurrection of the body is meant in what comes after: *He that honoureth not the Son, honoureth not the Father that sent Him.* Here is no *as;* the man Christ is honoured, but not as the Father Who sent

Him, since with respect to His manhood He Himself saith, *My Father is greater than I.* But some one will say, Tr. xxi. if the Son is sent by the Father, He is inferior to the Father. s. 17. Leave thy fleshly actions, and understand a mission, not a separation. Human things deceive, divine things make clear; although even human things give testimony against thee, e. g. if a man offers marriage to a woman, and cannot obtain her by himself, he sends a friend, greater than himself, to urge his suit for him. But see the difference in human things. A man does not go with him whom he sends; but the Father Who sent the Son, never ceased to be with the Son; as we read, *I am not alone, but the Father is with Me.* c. 21. Aug. It is not, however, as being born of the Father, that Aug. the Son is said to be sent, but from His appearing in this iv. de world, as the Word made flesh; as He says, *I went forth* Trin.c. *from the Father, and am come into the world:* or from His 28.(xx.) being received into our minds individually, as we read[1], *Send* John 16, *her, that she may be with me, and may labour with me.* 28. Hilary. The conclusion then stands good against all the Hilar. fury of heretical minds. He is the Son, because He does vii. de nothing of Himself: He is God, because, whatsoever things Trin. c. the Father doeth, He doeth the same; They are one, because 21. They are equal in honour: He is not the Father, because He is sent.

24. Verily, verily, I say unto you, He that heareth my word, and believeth on him that sent me, hath everlasting life, and shall not come into condemnation; but is passed from death unto life.

Gloss. Having said that the Son quickeneth whom He will, He next shews that we attain to life through the Son: *Verily, verily, I say unto you, He that heareth My word, and believeth on Him that sent Me, hath everlasting life.* Aug. If Aug. in hearing and believing is eternal life, how much more in Tr.xxii understanding? But the step to our piety is faith, the fruit s. 2. of faith, understanding. It is not, Believeth on Me, but *on Him that sent Me.* Why is one to hear His word, and believe another? Is it not that He means to say, His word is in

[1] Wisd. 9, 10. The Vulgate is: Mitte illam ut mecum sit, et mecum laboret.

Me? And what is, *Heareth My word*, but heareth Me? And it is, *Believeth on Him that sent Me:* as to say, He that believeth on Him, believeth on His Word, i. e. on Me, because I am the Word of the Father. CHRYS. Or, He did not say, He that heareth My words, and believeth on Me ; as they would have thought this empty boasting and arrogance. To say, *Believeth on Him that sent Me*, was a better way of making His discourse acceptable. To this end He says two things: one, that he who hears Him, believes on the Father; the other, that he who hears and believes *shall not come into condemnation*. AUG. But who is this favoured Person? Will there be any one better than the Apostle Paul, who says, *We must all appear before the judgment-seat of Christ?* Now judgment sometimes means punishment, sometimes trial. In the sense of trial, we must all appear before the judgment-seat of Christ: in the sense of condemnation we read, some *shall not come into judgment ;* i. e. shall not be condemned. It follows, *but is passed from death into life:* not, is now passing, but hath passed from the death of unbelief, into the life of faith, from the death of sin, unto the life of righteousness. Or, it is so said perhaps, to prevent our supposing that faith would save us from bodily death, that penalty which we must pay for Adam's transgression. He, in whom we all then were, heard the divine sentence, *Thou shalt surely die ;* nor can we evade it. But when we have suffered the death of the old man, we shall receive the life of the new, and by death make a passage to life. But to what life? To life everlasting : the dead shall rise again at the end of the world, and enter into everlasting life. For this life does not deserve the name of life; only that life is true which is eternal. AUG. We see the lovers of this present transitory life so intent on its welfare, that when in danger of death, they will take any means to delay its approach, though they can not hope to drive it off altogether. If so much care and labour then is spent on gaining a little additional length of life, how ought we to strive after life eternal ? And if they are thought wise, who endeavour in every way to put off death, though they can live but a few days longer ; how foolish are they who so live, as to lose the eternal day ?

Chrys. Hom. xxxix. 2.

Aug. Tr.xxii. s.4.et sq. 1 Cor. 6.

Gen. 2.

Tr. xix.

Tr.xxii.

Aug. deVerb. Dom. Serm. lxiv.

25. Verily, verily, I say unto you, The hour is coming, and now is, when the dead shall hear the voice of the Son of God: and they that hear shall live.

26. For as the Father hath life in himself; so hath he given to the Son to have life in himself.

AUG. Some one might ask thee, The Father quickeneth him who believes on Him; but what of thee? dost thou not quicken? Observe thou that the Son also quickens whom He will: *Verily, verily, I say unto you, The hour is coming, and now is, when the dead shall hear the voice of the Son of God; and they that hear shall live.* CHRYS. After, *The hour cometh*, He adds, *and now is;* to let us know that it will not be long before it comes. For as in the future resurrection we shall be roused by hearing His voice speaking to us, so is it now. THEOPHYL. Here He speaks with a reference to those whom He was about to raise from the dead: viz. the daughter of the ruler of the synagogue, the son of the widow, and Lazarus. AUG. Or, He means to guard against our thinking, that the being passed from death to life, refers to the future resurrection; its meaning being, that he who *believes* is passed: and therefore He says, *Verily, verily, I say unto you, The hour cometh,* (what hour?) *and now is, when the dead shall hear the voice of the Son of God, and they that hear shall live.* He saith not, because they live, they hear; but in consequence of hearing, they come to life again. But what is hearing, but obeying? For they who believe and do according to the true faith, live, and are not dead; whereas those who believe not, or, believing, live a bad life, and have not love, are rather to be accounted dead. And yet that hour is still going on, and will go on, the same hour, to the end of the world: as John says, *It is the last hour.* AUG. *When the dead*, i. e. unbelievers, *shall hear the voice of the Son of God*, i. e. the Gospel: *and they that hear*, i. e. who obey, *shall live*, i. e. be justified, and no longer remain in unbelief. AUG. But some one will ask, Hath the Son life, whence those who believe will live? Hear His own words: *As the Father hath life in Himself, so*

Aug. Tr. xxiii. s. 14.

Chrys. Hom. xxxix. 2.

Aug. Tr. xxii. s. 12.

1 John 2, 13.

Aug. Tr. xxii. s. 9.

o

hath He given to the Son to have life in Himself. Life is original and absolute in Him, cometh from no other source, dependeth on no other power. He is not as if He were partaker of a life, which is not Himself; but has life in Himself: so as that He Himself is His own life. Hear, O dead soul, the Father, speaking by the Son: arise, that thou mayest receive that life which thou hast not in thyself, and enter into the first resurrection. For this life, which the Father and the Son are, pertaineth to the soul, and is not perceived by the body. The rational mind only discovers the life of wisdom. HILARY. The heretics, driven hard by Scripture proofs, are obliged to attribute to the Son at any rate a likeness, in respect of virtue, to the Father. But they do not admit a likeness of nature, not being able to see that a likeness of virtue, could not arise but from a likeness of nature; as an inferior nature can never attain to the virtue of a higher and better one. And it cannot be denied that the Son of God has the same virtue with the Father, when He says, *What things soever (the Father) doeth, the same doeth the Son likewise.* But an express mention of the likeness of nature follows: *As the Father hath life in Himself, so hath He given to the Son to have life in Himself.* In life are comprehended nature and essence. And the Son, as He hath it, so hath He it given to Him. For the same which is life in both, is essence in both; and the life, i. e. essence, which is begotten from life, is born; though not born unlike the other. For, being life from life, it remains like in nature to its origin.

Aug.
xv. de
Trin.
c. 47.
(xxvi.)
Hilar.
vii. de
Triu.
c. 27,28. AUG. The Father must be understand not to have given life to the Son, who was existing without life, but so to have begotten Him, independently of time, that the life which He gave Him in begetting, was coeternal with His own. HILARY. Living born from living, hath the perfection of nativity, without the newness of nature. For there is nothing new implied in generation from living to living, the life not coming at its birth from nothing. And the life which derives its birth from life, must by the unity of nature, and the sacrament of a perfect birth, both be in the living being, and have the being who lives it, in itself. Weak human nature indeed is made up of unequal elements, and brought to life out of inanimate matter; nor does the human offspring

live for some time after it is begotten. Neither does it wholly live from life, since much grows up in it insensibly, and decays insensibly. But in the case of God, the whole of what He is, lives : for God is life, and from life, can nothing be but what is living. AUG. *Given to the Son,* then, has the meaning of, begat the Son; for He gave Him the life, by begetting. As He gave Him being, so He gave Him to have life in Himself; so that the Son did not stand in need of life to come to Him from without; but was in Himself the fulness of life, whence others, i. e. believers, received their life. What then is the difference between Them? This, that one gave, the other received. CHRYS The likeness is perfect in all but one respect, viz. that, in point of essence, one is the Father, the other the Son. HILARY. For the person of the receiver, is distinct from that of the giver: it being inconceivable that one and the same person, should give to and receive from Himself. He who lives of Himself is one person : He who acknowledges an Author of His life is another.

Aug. Tr. xxii. s. 10.

Chrys. Hom. xxxix. 3.

27. And hath given him authority to execute judgment also, because he is the Son of man.

28. Marvel not at this : for the hour is coming, in the which all that are in the graves shall hear his voice,

29. And shall come forth ; they that have done good, unto the resurrection of life ; and they that have done evil, unto the resurrection of damnation.

THEOPHYL. The Father granted the Son power not only to give life, but also to execute judgment. *And hath given Him authority to execute judgment.* CHRYS. But why does He dwell so constantly on these subjects ; judgment, resurrection, and life? Because these are the most powerful arguments for bringing men over to the faith, and the most likely ones to prevail with obstinate hearers. For one who is persuaded that he shall rise again, and be called by the Son to account for his misdeeds, will, though he know nothing more than this, be anxious to propitiate his Judge.

Chrys. Hom. xxxix. s. 3.

It follows, *Because He is the Son of man, marvel not at this.*
Paul of Samosata reads it, *Hath given Him power to execute*
judgment also, because He is the Son of man.   But this connexion has no meaning; for He does not receive the power
to judge because He is man, (as, on this supposition, what
would prevent all men from being judges:) but because He
is the ineffable Son of God; therefore is He Judge.   We
must read it then, *Because He is the Son of man, marvel*
not at this.   As Christ's hearers thought him a mere man,
and as what He asserted of Himself was too high to be true
of men, or even angels, or any being short of God Himself,
there was a strong obstacle in the way of their believing,
which our Lord notices in order to remove it: Marvel not,
He says, that He is the Son of man: and then adds the
reason why they should not marvel: *For the hour is coming,*
in the which all that are in the graves shall hear the voice
of the Son of God.   And why did He not say, Marvel not
that He is the Son of man: because in truth He is the Son
of God?   Because, having given out that it was He who
should raise men from the dead, the resurrection being a
strictly divine work, He leaves His hearers to infer that He is
God, and the Son of God.   Persons in arguing often do this.
When they have brought out grounds amply sufficient to
prove the conclusion they want, they do not draw that conclusion themselves; but, to make the victory greater, leave
the opponent to draw it.   In referring above to the resurrection of Lazarus and the rest, he said nothing about judgment,
for Lazarus did not rise again for judgment; whereas now,
that He is speaking of the general resurrection, He brings in
the mention of the judgment: *And (they) shall come forth,* He
says, *they that have done good unto the resurrection of life,*
and they that have done evil unto the resurrection of damna-
tion.   Having said above, *He that heareth My words, and*
believeth on Him that sent Me, hath everlasting life; that
men might not suppose from this, that belief was sufficient
for salvation, He proceeds to speak of works: *And they that*
have done good,—and they that have done evil.   AUG. Or
thus: Inasmuch as the Word was in the beginning with God,
the Father gave Him to have life in Himself; but inasmuch
as the Word was made flesh of the Virgin Mary, being made

Aug.
Tr.xxii.
in Joan.
s. 10,11.

man, He became the Son of man: and as the Son of man,
He received power to execute judgment at the end of the
world; at which time the bodies of the dead shall rise again.
The souls then of the dead God raises by Christ the Son of
God; their bodies by the same Christ, the Son of man.
Wherefore He adds, *Because He is the Son of man:* for, as
to the Son of God, He always had the power. Aug. At the Aug.
judgment will appear the form of man, that form will judge, de Ver.
which was judged; He will sit a Judge Who stood before the Ser. 64.
judge; He will condemn the guilty, Who was condemned
innocent. For it is proper that the judged should see their
Judge. Now the judged consist of both good and bad; so
that the form of the servant will be shewn to good and bad
alike; the form of God to the good only. *Blessed are the* Matt. 5,
pure in heart, for they shall see God. Aug. None if the 8.
                                                        Aug.
founders of false religious sects have been able to deny the Tr. xix.
resurrection of the soul, but many have denied the resur- s. 14.
rection of the body; and, unless Thou, Lord Jesus, hadst
declared it, what answer could we give the gainsayer? To
set forth this truth, He says, *Marvel not at this;* (i. e. that
He hath given power to the Son of man to execute judgment,)
for the hour is coming, &c. Aug. He does not add, *And* Aug.
now is, here; because this hour would be at the end of the de Ver.
                                                         Dom.
world. Marvel not, i. e. marvel not, men will all be judged Ser. 64.
by a man. But what men? Not those only, whom He will
find alive, *For the hour cometh, in which all that are in their*
graves shall hear His voice. Aug. What can be plainer? Aug.
Men's bodies are in their graves, not their souls. Above Sup. †
                                                          Joan.
when He said, *The hour cometh,* and added, *and now is;* Tr. xix.
He proceeds, When the dead shall hear the voice of the s. 17,18.
Son of God. He does not say, All the dead; for by the
dead are meant the wicked, and the wicked have not all
been brought to obey the Gospel. But in the end of the
world all that are in their graves shall hear His voice, and
come forth. He does not say, *Shall live,* as He said above,
when He spoke of the eternal and blessed life; which all
will not have, who shall come forth from their graves. This
judgment was committed to Him because He was the Son
of man. But what takes place in this judgment? *They that*
have done good shall go unto the resurrection of life, i. e. to

live with the Angels of God; *they that have done evil unto the resurrection of judgment.* Judgment here meaning damnation.

30. I can of mine own self do nothing: as I hear, I judge: and my judgment is just; because I seek not mine own will, but the will of the Father which hath sent me.

Aug. Tr. xix. s. 19.
AUG. We were about to ask Christ, Thou wilt judge, and the Father not judge: wilt not Thou then judge according to the Father? He anticipates us by saying, *I can of Mine own Self do nothing.*

Chrys. Hom. xxxix. 4.
CHRYS. That is, nothing that is a departure from, or that is unlike to, what the Father wishes, shall ye see done by Me, but *as I hear, I judge.* He is only shewing that it was impossible He should ever wish any thing but what the Father wished. I judge, His meaning

Aug. Tr. xxiii. s. 15. v. 19.
is, as if it were My Father that judged. AUG. When He spoke of the resurrection of the soul, He did not say, Hear, but, See. Hear implies a command issuing from the Father.

Aug. Serm. contr. Arrian. c. 9. (xiv.)
He speaks as man, who is inferior to the Father. AUG. *As I hear, I judge,* is said with reference either to His human subordination, as the Son of man, or to that immutable and simple nature of the Sonship derived from the Father; in which nature hearing and seeing is identical

at sup. c. xvii.
with being. Wherefore as He hears, He judges. The Word is begotten one with the Father, and therefore judges ac-

c. xvii.
cording to truth. It follows, *And My judgment is just, because I seek not Mine own will, but the will of the Father which hath sent Me.* This is intended to take us back to

sc. Adam.
that man who, by seeking his own will, not the will of Him who made him, did not judge himself justly, but had a just judgment pronounced upon him. He did not believe that, by doing his own will, not God's, he should die. So he did his own will, and died; because the judgment of God is just, which judgment the Son of God executes, by not seeking His own will, i. e. His will as being the Son of man. Not that He has no will in judging, but His will is not His own in such sense, as to be different from the Father's. AUG.

Aug. Tr. xix. s19.
I seek not then Mine own will, i. e. the will of the Son of man, in opposition to God: for men do their own will, not

God's, when, to do what they wish, they violate God's commands. But when they so do what they wish, as at the
same time to follow the will of God, they do not their own
will. Or, *I seek not Mine own will:* i. e. because I am not
of myself, but of the Father. CHRYS. He shews that the Chrys.
Father's will is not a different one from His own, but one and ˣˣˣⁱˣ.4.
the same, as a ground of defence. Nor marvel if being
hitherto thought no more than a mere man, He defends
Himself in a somewhat human way, and shews his judgment
to be just on the same ground which any other person would
have taken; viz. that one who has his own ends in view,
may incur suspicion of injustice, but that one who has not
cannot. AUG. The only Son says, *I seek not Mine own* Aug.
will: and yet men wish to do their own will. Let us do the ᵀʳ· ˣˣⁱ·
will of the Father, Christ, and Holy Ghost: for these have
one will, power, and majesty.

31. If I bear witness of myself, my witness is not
true.

32. There is another that beareth witness of me;
and I know that the witness which he witnesseth of me
is true.

33. Ye sent unto John, and he bare witness unto
the truth.

34. But I receive not testimony from man: but
these things I say, that ye might be saved.

35. He was a burning and a shining light: and ye
were willing for a season to rejoice in his light.

36. But I have greater witness than that of John:
for the works which the Father hath given me to finish,
the same works that I do, bear witness of me, that the
Father hath sent me.

37. And the Father himself, which hath sent me,
hath borne witness of me. Ye have neither heard his
voice at any time, nor seen his shape.

38. And ye have not his word abiding in you: for
whom he hath sent, him ye believe not.

39. Search the Scriptures; for in them ye think ye

have eternal life: and they are they which testify of me.

40. And ye will not come to me, that ye might have life.

Chrys. Hom. xl. 1. CHRYS. He now brings proof of those high declarations respecting Himself. He answers an objection: *If I bear witness of Myself, My witness is not true.* These are Christ's own words. But does not Christ in many places bear witness of Himself? And if all this is false, where is our hope of salvation? Whence shall we obtain truth, when the Truth Itself says, *My witness is not true.* We must believe then that *true*, here, is said, not with reference to the intrinsic value of His testimony, but to their suspicions; for the Jews might say, We do not believe Thee, because no one who bears witness to himself is to be depended on. In answer then, he puts forth three clear and irrefragable proofs, three witnesses as it were, to the truth of what He had said; the works which He had done, the testimony of the Father, and the preaching of John: putting the least of these foremost, i. e. the preaching of John: *There is another that beareth witness of Me: and I know that the witness which he witnesseth of Me is true.* Aug. de Verb. Dom. x. 43. AUG. He knew Himself that His witness of Himself was true, but in compassion to the weak and unbelieving, the Sun sought for candles, that their weak sight might not be dazzled by His full blaze. And therefore John was brought forward to give his testimony to the truth. Not that there is such testimony really, for whatever witnesses bear witness to Him, it is really He who bears witness to Himself; as it is His dwelling in the witnesses, which moves them so to give their witness to the truth. ALCUIN. Or thus; Christ, being both God and man, He shews the proper existence of both, by sometimes speaking according to the nature he took from man, sometimes according to the majesty of the Godhead. *If I bear witness of Myself, My witness is not true:* this is to be understood of His humanity; the sense being, *If I*, a man, *bear witness of Myself*, i. e. without God, *My witness is not true:* and then follows, *There is another that beareth witness of Me.* The Father bore witness of Christ, by the voice which was heard at the baptism, and at the transfiguration on the mount. *And I know that His witness is true;* because He is the God of truth. How then can His witness be otherwise than true? CHRYS. But according to the former interpretation, they might say to Him, Chrys. Hom. xl. 2. If Thy witness is not true, how sayest Thou, I know that the witness of John is true? But His answer meets the objection: *Ye sent unto John, and he bare witness of the truth:* as if to say: Ye would not have sent to John, if ye had not thought him worthy of credit. And what is more remarkable, they did send to him, not to ask Him about Christ, but about himself. For they who were sent out did not say, What sayest thou of Christ? but, *Who art thou? what sayest thou* c. 1, 22. *of thyself?* In so great admiration did they hold him. ALCUIN. But he bore witness not to himself, but to the truth: as the friend of the truth, he bore witness to the truth, i. e. Christ. Our Lord, on His part, does not reject the witness of John, as not being necessary, but shows only that men ought not to give such attention to John as to forget that Christ's witness was all that was necessary to Himself. *But I receive not,* He says, *testimony from men.* BEDE. Because I do not want it. John, though he bore witness, did it not that Christ might increase, but that men might be brought to the knowledge of Him. CHRYS. Even the witness Chrys. Hom. xl. 2. of John was the witness of God: for what he said, God taught him. But to anticipate their asking how it appeared that God taught John, as if the Jews had objected that John's witness might not be true, our Lord anticipates them by saying, "Ye sought him yourselves to enquire of him; that is why I use his testimony, for I need it not." He adds, *But these things I say that ye might be saved.* As if He said, I being God, needed not this human kind of testimony. But, since ye attend more to him, and think him more worthy of credit than any one else, while ye do not believe me, though I work miracles; for this cause I remind you of his testimony. But had they not received John's testimony? Before they have time to ask this, He answers it: *He was a burning and a shining light, and ye were willing for a season to rejoice in his light.* He says this to shew, how lightly they had held by John, and how soon they had left him, thus preventing him from leading them to Christ. He calls him a candle, because John had not his light from himself, but from the grace of the Holy Spirit. ALCUIN. John was a candle lighted by Christ, the Light, burning with faith and love, shining in word and deed. He was sent before, to confound the enemies

Ps. 131. of Christ, according to the Psalm, *I have ordained a lantern for Mine Anointed; as for His enemies, I shall clothe them with*

Chrys. *shame*[m]. CHRYS. I therefore direct you to John, not because
Hom.
xl. 2. I want his testimony, but that ye may be saved: for *I have greater witness than that of John*, i. e. that of my works; *The works which the Father hath given Me to finish, the same works that I do bear witness of Me, that the Father hath sent Me.* ALCUIN. That He enlightens the blind, that He opens the deaf ear, looses the mouth of the dumb, casts out devils,

Hilar. raises the dead; these works bear witness of Christ. HILARY.
vi, de
Trin. c. The Only-begotten God shews Himself to be the Son, on
27. the testimony not of man only, but of His own power. The works which He does, bear witness to His being sent from the Father. Therefore the obedience of the Son and the authority of the Father are set forth in Him who was sent. But the testimony of works not being sufficient evidence, it follows, *And the Father Himself which hath sent Me, hath borne witness of Me.* Open the Evangelic volumes, and examine their whole range: no testimony of the Father to the Son is given in any of the books, other than that He is the Son. So what a calumny is it in men now saying that this is only a name of adoption: thus making God

Bede. a liar, and names unmeaning. BEDE. By His mission we
v. Joan. must understand His incarnation. Lastly, He shews that God is incorporeal, and cannot be seen by the bodily eye: *Ye have neither heard His voice at any time, nor seen His shape.* ALCUIN. The Jews might say, We heard the voice of the Lord at Sinai, and saw Him under the appearance of fire. If God then bears witness of Thee, we should know His voice. To which He replies, I have the witness of the Father, though ye understand it not; because ye never heard

Chrys. His voice, or saw His shape. CHRYS. How then says Moses,
Hom.xl.
3

---

[m] Alcuin literally, John bore witness of Christ, like a candle, not in order to heal his friends, but to confound his enemies .... John was not a candle, as if lighted from himself, but lighted by Christ. The words in the text are taken from an interlineary gloss and a sermon of St Bernard on John. Nic.

Ask—whether there hath been any such thing as this great Deut. 4, 32. 33. *thing is: did ever people hear the voice of God, speaking out of the midst of the fire, as thou hast heard and seen?* Isaiah too, and many others, are said to have seen Him. So what does Christ mean here? He means to impress upon them the philosophical doctrine, that God has neither voice, or appearance, or shape; but is superior to such modes of speaking of Him. For as in saying, *Ye have never heard His voice,* He does not mean to say that He has a voice, only not an audible one to them; so when He says, *Nor have even His shape,* no tangible, sensible, or visible shape is implied to belong to God: but all such mode of speaking is pronounced inapplicable to God. ALCUIN. For it is not by the carnal ear, but by the spiritual understanding, through the grace of the Holy Spirit, that God is heard. And they did not hear the spiritual voice, because they did not love or obey Him, nor saw they His shape; inasmuch as that is not to be seen by the outward eye, but by faith and love. CHRYS. But it Chrys. Hom. xl. 3. was impossible for them to declare that they had received, and obeyed God's commands: and therefore He adds, *Ye have not His word abiding in you;* i. e. the commandments, the law, and the prophets; though God instituted them, ye have them not. For if the Scriptures every where tell you to believe on Me, and ye believe not, it is manifest that His word is gone from you: *For whom He hath sent, Him ye believe not.* ALCUIN. Or thus; they cannot have abiding in them the Word which was in the beginning, who came not to keep in mind, or fulfil in practice, that word of God which they hear. Having mentioned the testimonies of John, and the Father, and of His works, He adds now that of the Mosaic Law: *Search the Scriptures, for in them ye think ye have eternal life; and they are they which testify of Me:* as if He said, Ye think ye have eternal life in the Scriptures, and reject Me as being opposed to Moses: but you will find that Moses himself testifies to My being God, if you search the Scripture carefully. All Scripture indeed bears witness of Christ, whether by its types, or by prophets, or by the ministering of Angels. But the Jews did not believe these intimations of Christ, and therefore could not obtain eternal life: *Ye will not come to Me, that ye may have life;* meaning, The Scriptures bear witness of Me, but ye will not come to Me notwithstanding, i. e. ye will not believe on Me, and seek for salvation at My hands. CHRYS. Or the connection may be given thus. They might say to Him, How, if we have never heard God's voice, has God borne witness to you? So He says, *Search the Scriptures;* meaning that God had borne witness of Him by the Scriptures. He had borne witness indeed at the Jordan, and on the mount. But they did not hear the voice on the mount, and did not attend to it at the Jordan. Wherefore He sends them to the Scriptures, when they would also find the Father's testimony. He did not send them however to the Scriptures simply to read them, but to examine them attentively, because Scripture ever threw a shade over its own meaning, and did not display it on the surface. The treasure was, as it were, hidden from their eye. He does not say, For in them ye have eternal life, but, For in them ye *think* ye have eternal life; meaning that they did not reap much fruit from the Scriptures, thinking, as they did, that they should be saved by the mere reading of them, without faith. For which reason He adds, *Ye will not come to Me;* i. e. ye will not believe on Me. BEDE. That coming is put for believing we know, *Come unto Him, and be lightened.*[a] He adds, *That ye might have life;* For, if the soul which sinneth dies, they were dead in soul and mind. And therefore He promises the *life* of the soul, i. e. eternal happiness.

Chrys. Hom. xl. 3.

Hom. xli. 1.

Bede. in v. Joan. Ps. 33.

41. I receive not honour from men.

42. But I know you, that ye have not the love of God in you.

43. I am come in my Father's name, and ye receive me not: if another shall come in his own name, him ye will receive.

44. How can ye believe, which receive honour one of another, and seek not the honour that cometh from God only?

45. Do not think that I will accuse you to the

---

[a] Vulg. They had an eye unto Him, and were lightened.

Father: there is one that accuseth you, even Moses,
in whom ye trust.

46. For had ye believed Moses, ye would have
believed me : for he wrote of me.

47. But if ye believe not his writings, how shall ye
believe my words?

CHRYS. Our Lord having made mention of John, and the
witness of God, and His own works, many, who did not see
that His motive was to induce them to believe, might suspect
Him of a desire for human glory, and therefore He says,
I receive not honour from men: i. e. I do not want it. My
nature is not such as to want that glory, which cometh from
men. For if the Son receives no addition from the light of
a candle, much more am not I in want of human glory.
ALCUIN. Or, *I receive not honour from men:* i. e. I seek
not human praise; for I came not to receive carnal honour
from men, but to give spiritual honour *to* men. I do not
bring forward this testimony then, because I seek my own
glory; but because I compassionate your wanderings, and
wish to bring you back to the way of truth. Hence what
follows, *But I know you that ye have not the love of God
in you.* CHRYS. As if to say, I said this to prove that
it is not from your love of God, that you persecute Me; for
He bears witness to Me, by My own works, and by the
Scriptures. So that, if ye loved God, as ye rejected Me,
thinking Me against God, so now ye would come to Me.
But ye do not love Him. And He proves this, not only
from what they do now, but from what they will do in
time to come: *I am come in My Father's name, and ye
receive Me not; if another shall come in his own name, him
ye will receive.* He says plainly, *I am come in the Father's
name,* that they might never be able to plead ignorance as
an excuse   ALCUIN. As if He said, For this cause came I
into the world, that through Me the name of the Father might
be glorified; for I attribute all to Him. As then they would
not receive Him, Who came to do His Father's will; they
had not the love of God. But Antichrist will come not in
the Father's name, but in his own, to seek, not the Father's
glory, but his own. And the Jews having rejected Christ, it

Chrys.
Hom.
xli. 1.

Chrys.
Hom.
xli. 1.

was a fit punishment on them, that they should receive Antichrist, and believe a lie, as they would not believe the Truth. Aug. Hear John, *As ye have heard that Antichrist shall come, even now are there many Antichrists.* But what dost thou dread in Antichrist, except that he will exalt his own name, and despise the name of the Lord? And what else does he do, who says, " I justify;" or those who say, " Unless we are good, ye must perish°?" Wherefore my life shall depend on Thee, and my salvation shall be fastened to Thee. Shall I so forget my foundation? Is not my rock Christ? Chrys. Here is the crowning proof of their impiety. He says, as it were, If it was the love of God that made you persecute me, you would persecute Antichrist much more : for he does not profess to be sent by the Father, or to come according to His will ; but, on the contrary, usurping what does not belong to him, will proclaim himself to be God over all. It is manifest that your persecution of Me is from malice and hatred of God. Then He gives the reason of their unbelief: *How can ye believe, which receive honour one of another, and seek not the honour that cometh from God only?* another proof this, that theirs was not a zeal for God, but a gratification of their own passions. Alcuin. How faulty then is the boasting temper, and that eagerness for human praise, which likes to be thought to have what it has not, and would fain be thought to have all that it has, by its own strength. Men of such temper cannot believe ; for in their hearts, they are bent solely on gaining praise, and setting themselves up above others. Bede. The best way of guarding against this sin, is to bring to our consciences the remembrance, that we are dust, and should ascribe all the good that we have not to ourselves, but to God. And we should endeavour always to be such, as we wish to appear to others. Then, as they might ask, Wilt thou accuse us then to the Father? He anticipates this question : *Do not think that I will accuse you to the Father.* Chrys. For I am not come to condemn, but to save. *There is one that accuseth you, even Moses, in whom you trust.* As He had said of the

Aug. de Verb. Dom. Serm. 45. a med. 1 John 2, 18.

Chrys. Hom. xli. 13.

Chrys. Hom. xli. 2.

° Alluding to the Donatists, who made baptismal justification to depend on the goodness of the minister, and   denied the efficacy of any but their own Baptism. Nic.

Scriptures above : *In them ye think ye have eternal life.* So now of Moses He says, *In whom ye trust,* always answering them out of their authorities. But they will say, How will he accuse us ? What hast Thou to do with Moses, Thou who hast broken the sabbath ? So He adds : *For had ye believed Moses, ye would perhaps have believed Me, for he wrote of me.* This is connected with what was said before. For where evidence that He came from God had been forced upon them by His words, by the voice of John, and the testimony of the Father, it was certain that Moses would condemn them; for he had said, If any one shall come, ^{alluding to Deut. 13, 1.} doing miracles, leading men to God, and foretelling the future with certainty, you must obey him. Christ did all this, and they did not obey Him. ALCUIN. *Perhaps,* He says, in accommodation to our way of speaking, not because there is really any doubting in God. Moses prophesied of Christ, *A Prophet shall the Lord your God raise up from among* ^{Deut. 18, 18.} *your brethren like unto me: Him shall ye hear.* AUG. But, ^{Aug.} in fact, the whole that Moses wrote, was written of Christ, ^{cont.} i. e. it has reference to Him principally ; whether it point ^{Faust. l. xvi. c. 9.} to Him by figurative actions, or expression; or set forth His grace and glory.

But if ye believe not his writings, how shall ye believe My words. THEOPHYL. As if He said, He has even written, and has left his books among you, as a constant memento to you, lest you forget His words. And since you believe not his writings, how can ye believe My unwritten words ? ALCUIN. From this we may infer too, that he who knows the commandments against stealing, and other crimes, and neglects them, will never fulfil the more perfect and refined precepts of the Gospel. CHRYS. Indeed had they attended ^{Chrys.} to His words, they ought and would have tried to learn from ^{Hom. xli. 2.} Him, what the things were which Moses had written of Him. But they are silent. For it is the nature of wickedness to defy persuasion. Do what you will, it retains its venom to the last.

CHAP. VI.

1. After these things Jesus went over the sea of Galilee, which is the sea of Tiberias.

2. And a great multitude followed him, because they saw his miracles which he did on them that were diseased.

3. And Jesus went up into a mountain, and there he sat with his disciples.

4. And the Passover, a feast of the Jews, was nigh.

5. When Jesus then lifted up his eyes, and saw a great company come unto him, he saith unto Philip, Whence shall we buy bread, that these may eat?

6. And this he said to prove him: for he himself knew what he would do.

7. Philip answered him, Two hundred pennyworth of bread is not sufficient for them, that every one of them may take a little.

8. One of his disciples, Andrew, Simon Peter's brother, saith unto him,

9. There is a lad here, which hath five barley loaves, and two small fishes: but what are they among so many?

10. And Jesus said, Make the men sit down. Now there was much grass in the place. So the men sat down, in number about five thousand.

11. And Jesus took the loaves; and when he had given thanks, he distributed to the disciples, and the disciples to them that were set down; and likewise of the fishes as much as they would.

12. When they were filled, he said unto his disciples, Gather up the fragments that remain, that nothing be lost.

13. Therefore they gathered them together, and filled twelve baskets with the fragments of the five barley loaves, which remained over and above unto them that had eaten.

14. Then those men, when they had seen the miracle that Jesus did, said, This is of a truth that Prophet that should come into the world.

CHRYS. As missiles rebound with great force from a hard body, and fly off in all directions, whereas a softer material retains and stops them; so violent men are only excited to greater rage by violence on the side of their opponents, whereas gentleness softens them. Christ quieted the irritation of the Jews by retiring from Jerusalem. He went into Galilee, but not to Cana again, but beyond the sea: *After these things Jesus went over the sea of Galilee, which is the sea of Tiberias.* ALCUIN. This sea hath different names, from the different places with which it is connected; the sea of Galilee, from the province; the sea of Tiberias, from the city of that name. It is called a sea, though it is not salt water, that name being applied to all large pieces of water, in Hebrew. This sea our Lord often passes over, in going to preach to the people bordering on it. THEOPHYL. He goes from place to place to try the dispositions of people, and excite a desire to hear Him: *And a great multitude followed Him, because they saw His miracles which He did on them that were diseased.* ALCUIN. viz. His giving sight to the blind, and other like miracles. And it should be understood, that all, whom He healed in body, He renewed likewise in soul. CHRYS. Though favoured with such teaching, they were influenced less by it, than by the miracles; a sign of their low state of belief: for Paul says of tongues, that *they are for a sign, not to them that believe, but to them that believe not.* They were wiser of whom it is said, that *they were astonished at His doctrine.* The

P

Marginal notes: Chrys. Hom. xlii. 1. — Chrys. Hom. xlii. 1. — 1 Cor. 14, 22. — Matt. 7, 28.

Evangelist does not say what miracles He wrought, the great object of his book being to give our Lord's discourses. It follows: *And Jesus went up into a mountain, and there sat with His disciples.* He went up into the mountain, on account of the miracle which was going to be done. That the disciples alone ascended with Him, implies that the people who stayed behind were in fault for not following. He went up to the mountain too, as a lesson to us to retire from the tumult and confusion of the world, and leave wisdom in solitude. *And the passover, a feast of the Jews, was nigh.* Observe, in a whole year, the Evangelist has told us of no miracles of Christ, except His healing the impotent man, and the nobleman's son. His object was to give not a regular history, but only a few of the principal acts of our Lord. But why did not our Lord go up to the feast? He was taking occasion, from the wickedness of the Jews, gradually to abolish the Law. THEOPHYL. The persecutions of the Jews gave Him reason for retiring, and thus setting aside the Law. The truth being now revealed, types were at an end, and He was under no obligation to keep the Jewish feasts. Observe the expression, *a feast of the Jews,* not a feast of Christ. BEDE. If we compare the accounts of the different Evangelists, we shall find very clearly, that there was an interval of a year between the beheading of John, and our Lord's Passion. For, since Matthew says that our Lord, on hearing of the death of John, withdrew into a desert place, where He fed the multitude; and John says that the Passover was nigh, when He fed the multitude; it is evident that John was beheaded shortly before the Passover. And at the same feast, the next year Christ suffered. It follows, *When Jesus then lifted up His eyes, and saw a great company come unto Him, He saith unto Philip, Whence shall we buy bread, that these may eat?* When Jesus lifted up His eyes, this is to shew us, that Jesus was not generally with His eyes lifted up, looking about Him, but sitting calm and attentive, surrounded by His disciples. CHRYS. Nor did He only sit with His disciples, but conversed with them familiarly, and gained possession of their minds. Then He looked, and saw a crowd advancing. But why did He ask Philip that question? Because He knew

Mat. 14, 13.

Chrys. Hom. xlii. 1.

that His disciples, and he especially, needed further teaching. For this Philip it was who said afterwards, *Shew us the* c. 14, 8. *Father, and it sufficeth us.* And if the miracle had been performed at once, without any introduction, the greatness of it would not have been seen. The disciples were made to confess their own inability, that they might see the miracle more clearly; *And this He said to prove him.* AUG. One kind of temptation leads to sin, with which God never tempts any one; and there is another kind by which faith is tried. In this sense it is said that Christ proved His disciple. This is not meant to imply that He did not know what Philip would say; but is an accommodation to men's way of speaking. For as the expression, *Who searcheth the hearts of men,* does not mean the searching of ignorance, but of absolute knowledge; so here, when it is said that our Lord proved Philip, we must understand that He knew him perfectly, but that He tried him, in order to confirm his faith. The Evangelist himself guards against the mistake which this imperfect mode of speaking might occasion, by adding, *For He Himself knew what He would do.* ALCUIN. He asks him this question, not for His own information, but in order to shew His yet unformed disciple his dulness of mind, which he could not perceive of himself. THEOPHYL. Or to shew others it. He was not ignorant of His disciple's heart Himself. AUG. But if our Lord, according to John's account, on seeing the multitude, asked Philip, tempting him, whence they could buy food for them, it is difficult at first to see how it can be true, according to the other account, that the disciples first told our Lord, to send away the multitude; and that our Lord replied, *They need not depart; give ye them to eat.* We must understand then it was after saying this, that our Lord saw the multitude, and said to Philip what John had related, which has been omitted by the rest. CHRYS. Or they are two different occasions altogether. THEOPHYL. Thus tried by our Lord, Philip was found to be possessed with human notions, as appears from what follows, *Philip answered Him, Two hundred pennyworth of bread is not sufficient for them, that every one of them may take a little.* ALCUIN. Wherein he shews his dulness: for, had he perfect ideas of his Creator, he would not be thus doubting

Aug. de Verb. Dom. Serm. 17.

James i. 13.

Deut. 13, 3.

Aug. de Con. Evang. l. ii. c. xlvi.

Matt. 25, 16.

Chrys. Hom. xlii. s. 1.

His power. AUG. The reply, which is attributed to Philip by John, Mark puts in the mouth of all the disciples, either meaning us to understand that Philip spoke for the rest, or else putting the plural number for the singular, which is often done. THEOPHYL. Andrew is in the same perplexity that Philip is; only he has rather higher notions of our Lord: *There is a lad here which hath five barley loaves and two small fishes.* CHRYS. Probably He had some reason in his mind for this speech. He would know of Elijah's miracle, by which a hundred men were fed with twenty loaves. This was a great step; but here he stopped. He did not rise any higher. For his next words are, *But what are these among so many?* He thought that less could produce less in a miracle, and more more; a great mistake; inasmuch as it was as easy for Christ to feed the multitude from a few fishes as from many. He did not really want any material to work from, but only made use of created things for this purpose in order to shew that no part of the creation was severed from His wisdom. THEOPHYL. This passage confounds the Manicheans, who say that bread and all such things were created by an evil Deity. The Son of the good God, Jesus Christ, multiplied the loaves. Therefore they could not have been naturally evil; a good God would never have multiplied what was evil. AUG. Andrew's suggestion about the five loaves and two fishes, is given as coming from the disciples in general, in the other Evangelists, and the plural number is used. CHRYS. And let those of us, who are given to pleasure, observe the plain and abstemious eating of those great and wonderful men [b]. He made the men sit down before the loaves appeared, to teach us that with Him, things that are not are as things that are; as Paul says, *Who calleth those things that be not, as though they were.* The passage proceeds then: *And Jesus said, Make the men sit down.* ALCUIN. *Sit down,* i. e. lie down, as the ancient custom was, which they could do, as *there was much grass in the place.* THEOPHYL. i. e. green grass. It was the time of the Passover, which was kept the first month of the spring. *So the men sat down in number about five thousand.* The Evangelist only counts the *men,* following

Marginal notes:
Aug. de Con. Evan. l. ii. c. xlvi.

Chrys. Hom. xlii. 11.

Aug. de Con. Evang. ii.c.xlvi.

Chrys. Hom. xlii. 11.

Rom. 25, 17.

---

[b] Alluding to the five loaves and two fishes.

the direction in the law. Moses numbered the people from twenty years old and upwards, making no mention of the women; to signify that the manly and juvenile character is especially honourable in God's eyes. *And Jesus took the loaves; and when He had given thanks, He distributed[c] to them that were sat down: and likewise of the fishes as much as they would.* CHRYS. But why when He is going Chrys. to heal the impotent, to raise the dead, to calm the sea, Hom. xlii. 11. does He *not* pray, but here does give thanks? To teach us to give thanks to God, whenever we sit down to eat. And He prays more in lesser matters, in order to shew that He does not pray from any motive of need. For had prayer been really necessary to supply His wants, His praying would have been in proportion to the importance of each particular work. But acting, as He does, on His own authority, it is evident, He only prays out of condescension to us. And, as a great multitude was collected, it was an opportunity of impressing on them, that His coming was in accordance with God's will. Accordingly, when a miracle was private, He did not pray; when numbers were present, He did. HILARY. Five loaves are then set before the Hilar. multitude, and broken. The broken portions pass through iii. de into the hands of those who break, that from which they are c. 18. broken all the time not at all diminishing. And yet there they are, the bits taken from it, in the hands of the persons breaking[d]. There is no catching by eye or touch the miraculous operation: that is, which was not, that is seen, which is not understood. It only remains for us to believe that God can do all things. AUG. He multiplied in His Aug. hands the five loaves, just as He produces harvest out of a Tr.xxiv. few grains. There was a power in the hands of Christ; and s. 1. those five loaves were, as it were, seeds, not indeed committed to the earth, but multiplied by Him who made the earth. CHRYS. Observe the difference between the servant Chrys. and the lord. The Prophets received grace, as it were, by Hom. xlii. 3.

---

[c] Vulgate omits, *to the disciples, and the disciples.*

[d] Hilary literally. The operation escapes the sight; whilst you follow with your eyes one hand filled with fragments, you see that the other has

not lost its portion; meantime the heap of fragments increases; those who break are engaged in supplying, those who eat in receiving, the hungry are satisfied; twelve baskets are filled with what remains. Nic.

measure, and according to that measure performed their
miracles: whereas Christ, working this by His own absolute
power, produces a kind of superabundant result. *When
they were filled, He said unto His disciples, Gather up the
fragments that remain, that nothing be lost. Therefore they
gathered them together, and filled twelve baskets with the
fragments.* This was not done for needless ostentation, but
to prevent men from thinking the whole a delusion; which
was the reason why He made use of an existing material to
work from. But why did He give the fragments to His
disciples to carry away, and not to the multitude? Because
the disciples were to be the teachers of the world, and therefore it was most important that the truth should be impressed
upon them. Wherefore I admire not only the multitude of
the loaves which were made, but the definite quantity of the
fragments: neither more nor less than twelve baskets full, and
corresponding to the number of the twelve Apostles. THE-
OPHYL. We learn too from this miracle, not to be pusillani-
mous in the greatest straits of poverty. BEDE. When the
multitude saw the miracle our Lord had done, they marvelled; as they did not know yet that He was God. *Then
those men*, the Evangelist adds, i. e. *carnal* men, whose
understanding was carnal, *when they had perceived the
miracle that Jesus did, said, This is of a truth that Prophet
that should come into the world.* ALCUIN. Their faith
being as yet weak, they only call our Lord a Prophet,
not knowing that He was God. But the miracle had produced considerable effect upon them, as it made them
call our Lord *that Prophet*, singling Him out from the
rest. They call Him a Prophet, because some of the
Prophets had worked miracles; and properly, inasmuch as
our Lord calls Himself a Prophet; *It cannot be that a
prophet perish out of Jerusalem.* AUG. Christ is a Prophet,
and the Lord of Prophets; as He is an Angel, and the Lord
of Angels. In that He came to announce something, He
was an Angel; in that He foretold the future, He was a
Prophet; in that He was the Word made flesh, He was
Lord both of Angels and Prophets; for none can be a
Prophet without the word of God. CHRYS. Their expression, *that should come into the world*, shews that they

Luke
13, 33.
Aug.
Tr.xxiv.
s. 7.

expected the arrival of some great Prophet. And this is why they say, *This is of a truth that Prophet:* the article being put in the Greek, to shew that He was distinct from other Prophets. Aug. But let us reflect a little here. For-asmuch as the Divine Substance is not visible to the eye, and the miracles of the divine government of the world, and ordering of the whole creation, are overlooked in consequence of their constancy; God has reserved to Himself acts, beside the established course and order of nature, to do at suitable times; in order that those who overlooked the daily course of nature, might be roused to wonder by the sight of what was different from, though not at all greater, than what they were used to. The government of the world is a greater miracle, than the satisfying the hunger of five thousand with five loaves; and yet no one wonders at this: the former excited wonder; not from any real superiority in it, but because it was uncommon. But it would be wrong to gather no more than this from Christ's miracles: for, the Lord who is on the mount[e], and the Word of God which is on high, the same is no humble person to be lightly passed over, but we must look up to Him reverently. ALCUIN. Mystically, the sea signifies this tumultuous world. In the fulness of time, when Christ had entered the sea of our mortality by His birth, trodden it by His death, passed over it by His resurrection[f], then followed Him crowds of believers, both from the Jews and Gentiles. BEDE. Our Lord went up to the mountain, when He ascended to heaven, which is signified by the mountain. ALCUIN. His leaving the multitude below, and ascending the heights with His disciples, signifies, that lesser precepts are to be given to beginners, higher to the more matured. His refreshing the people shortly before the Passover signifies our refreshment by the bread of the divine word; and the body and blood, i. e. our spiritual passover, by which we pass over from vice to virtue. And the Lord's eyes are spiritual gifts, which he mercifully bestows on His Elect. He turns His eyes upon them, i. e. has compassionate respect unto them. Aug. The five barley loaves signify the old law; either because the law was given to men not as yet spiritual, but carnal, i. e. under the

Margin notes: Aug. Tr. xxiv. s. 1, 2.

Aug. lib. lxxxiii. Quæst. q. 61. In princ.

---

[e] V. 15. departed into a mountain Himself alone. [f] V. 1. Jesus went over the sea of Galilee.

dominion of the five senses, (the multitude itself consisted of five thousand:) or because the Law itself was given by Moses in five books. And the loaves being of barley is also an allusion to the Law, which concealed the soul's vital nourishment, under carnal ceremonies. For in barley the corn itself is buried under the most tenacious husk. Or, it alludes to the people who were not yet freed from the husk of carnal appetite, which cling to their heart. BEDE. Barley is the food of cattle and slaves: and the old law was given to slaves and cattle, i. e. to carnal men. AUG. The two fishes again, that gave the pleasant taste to the bread, seem to signify the two authorities by which the people were governed, the Royal, viz. and the Priestly; both of which prefigure our Lord, who sustained both characters. BEDE. Or, by the two fishes are meant the saying or writings of the Prophets, and the Psalmist. And whereas the number five refers to the five senses, a thousand stands for perfection. But those who strive to obtain the perfect government of their five senses, are called men, in consequence of their superior powers: they have no womanly weaknesses; but by a sober and chaste life, earn the sweet refreshment of heavenly wisdom. AUG. The boy who had these is perhaps the Jewish people, who, as it were, carried the loaves and fishes after a servile fashion, and did not eat them. That which they carried, while shut up, was only a burden to them; when opened became their food. BEDE. And well is it said, *But what are these among so many?* The Law was of little avail, till He took it into His hand, i. e. fulfilled it, and gave it a spiritual meaning. *The Law made nothing perfect.* AUG. By the act of breaking He multiplied the five loaves. The five books of Moses, when expounded by breaking, i. e. unfolding them, made many books. AUG. Our Lord by breaking, as it were, what was hard in the Law, and opening what was shut, that time when He opened the Scriptures to the disciples after the resurrection, brought the Law out in its full meaning. AUG. Our Lord's question proved the ignorance of His disciples, i. e. the people's ignorance of the Law. They lay on the grass, i. e. were carnally minded, rested in carnal things, *for all flesh is grass.* Men are filled with the loaves, when what they hear with the ear, they fulfil in practice. AUG. And what are the fragments, but the

Margin notes:
Bede. Hom. in Luc. c. vi.
Aug.lib. lxxxiv. Quæst. qu. 61.
Aug. Tr.xxiv. 5.
Bede. Aug. xxiv. 5.
Heb. 7, 19.
Aug. Tr.xxiv. s. 5.
Aug.lib. lxxxiii. Quæst. qu. 61.
Aug. Tr.xxiv. s. 5.
Isa. 40, 6.
Aug. Tr.xxiv. s. 6.

parts which the people could not eat? An intimation, that those deeper truths, which the multitude cannot take in, should be entrusted to those who are capable of receiving them, and afterwards teaching them to others; as were the Apostles. For which reason twelve baskets were filled with them. ALCUIN. Baskets are used for servile work. The baskets here are the Apostles and their followers, who, though despised in this present life, are within filled with the riches of spiritual sacraments. The Apostles too are represented as baskets, because, that through them, the doctrine of the Trinity was to be preached in the four parts of the world. His not making new loaves, but multiplying what there were, means that He did not reject the Old Testament, but only developed and explained it.

15. When Jesus therefore perceived that they would come and take him by force, to make him a king, he departed again into a mountain himself alone.

16. And when even was now come, his disciples went down unto the sea,

17. And entered into a ship, and went over the sea toward Capernaum. And it was now dark, and Jesus was not come to them.

18. And the sea arose by reason of a great wind that blew.

19. So when they had rowed about five and twenty or thirty furlongs, they see Jesus walking on the sea, and drawing nigh unto the ship: and they were afraid.

20. But he saith unto them, It is I; be not afraid.

21. Then they willingly received him into the ship: and immediately the ship was at the land whither they went.

BEDE. The multitude concluding, from so great a miracle, that He was merciful and powerful, wished to make Him a king. For men like having a merciful king to rule over them, and a powerful one to protect them. Our Lord knowing this, retired to the mountain: *When Jesus therefore perceived that they would come and take Him by force to make Him a king, He departed again into a mountain Himself alone.* From this we gather, that our Lord went down from the mountain before, where He was sitting with His disciples, when He saw the multitude coming, and had fed them on the plain below. For how could He go up to the mountain again, unless He had come down from it.

Aug. de Con. Ev. ii. c. xlvii. Mat.14, 23.

AUG. This is not at all inconsistent with what we read, that *He went up into a mountain apart to pray:* the object of escape being quite compatible with that of prayer. Indeed our Lord teaches us here, that whenever escape is necessary, there is great necessity for prayer.

Aug. Tr. xxv. 2.

AUG. Yet He who feared to be made a king, was a king; not made king by men, (for He ever reigneth with the Father, in that He is the Son of God,) but making men kings: which kingdom of His the Prophets had foretold. Christ by being made man, made the believers in Him Christians, i. e. members of His kingdom, incorporated and purchased by His Word. And this kingdom will be made manifest, after the judgment; when the brightness of His saints shall be revealed. The disciples however, and the multitude who believed on Him, thought that He had come to reign now; and so would have taken Him by force, to make Him a king, wishing to anticipate His time, which He kept secret.

Chrys. Hom. xiii. 3.

CHRYS. See what the belly can do. They care no more for the violation of the Sabbath; all their zeal for God is fled, now that their bellies are filled: Christ has become a Prophet, and they wish to enthrone Him as king. But Christ makes His escape; to teach us to despise the dignities of the world. He dismisses His disciples, and goes up into

Hom. xliii. 1.

the mountain.—These, when their Master had left them, went down in the evening to the sea; as we read; *And when even was now come, His disciples went down unto the sea.* They waited till evening, thinking He would come to them; and then, as He did not come, delayed no longer searching for Him, but in the ardour of love, *entered into a ship, and went over the sea toward Capernaum.* They went

Aug. Tr. xxv. s. 5.

to Capernaum thinking they should find Him there. AUG. The Evangelist now returns to explain why they went, and relate what happened to them while they were crossing the lake: *And it was dark,* he says, *and Jesus was not come to them.* CHRYS. The mention of the time is not accidental, but meant to shew the strength of their love. They did not make excuses, and say, It is evening now, and night is coming on, but in the warmth of their love went into the ship. And now many things alarm them: the time, *And it was now dark;* and the weather, as we read next, *And the sea arose by reason of a great wind that blew;* their distance from land, *So when they had rowed about five and twenty or thirty furlongs.* BEDE. The way of speaking we use, when we are in doubt; about five and twenty, we say, or thirty. CHRYS. And at last He appears quite unexpectedly: *They see Jesus walking upon the sea, drawing nigh.* He reappears after His retirement, teaching them what it is to be forsaken, and stirring them to greater love; His reappearance manifesting His power. They were disturbed, *were afraid,* it is said. Our Lord comforts them: *But He saith unto them, It is I, be not afraid.* BEDE. He does not say, I am Jesus, but only *I am.* He trusts to their easily recognising a voice, which was so familiar to them, or, as is more probable, He shews that He was the same who said to Moses, *I am that I am.* CHRYS. He appeared to them in this way, to shew His power; for He immediately calmed the tempest: *Then they wished to receive Him into the ship; and immediately the ship was at the land, whither they went.* So great was the calm, He did not even enter the ship, in order to work a greater miracle, and to shew his Divinity more clearly[g]. THEOPHYL. Observe the three miracles here; the first, His walking on the sea; the second, His stilling the waves; the third, His putting them immediately on shore, which they were some distance off, when our Lord appeared. CHRYS. Jesus does not shew Himself to the crowd walking on the sea, such a miracle being too much for them to hear. Nor even to the disciples did He shew Himself long, but disappeared immediately. AUG. Mark's[1] account does not contradict this. He says indeed that our Lord told the disciples first to enter the ship, and go before Him over the sea, while He dismissed the crowds, and that when the crowd was

Margin notes: Chrys. Hom. xlii. 1. — Bede in v. cap. — Joan. Chrys. Hom. xliii. 1. — Bede in Matt. c. xiv. — Exod.3, 14. Chrys. Hom. xliii.s.1. — Chrys. Hom. xliii. 1. — [1] Matthew, in Aquinas and Aug. De Con. Ev. l.ii. c. xlvii. Mark 6, 45.

[g] ἤθελον λαβεῖν αὐτὸν in the Greek: our translation, "they willingly received Him."

dismissed, He went up alone into the mountain to pray: while John places His going up alone in the mountain first, and then says, *And when even was now come, His disciples went down unto the sea.* But it is easy to see that John relates that as done *afterwards* by the disciples, which our Lord had ordered *before* His departure to the mountain.

Chrys. Hom. xliii. 1. CHRYS. Or take another explanation. This miracle seems to me to be a different one, from the one given in Matthew: for there they do not receive Him into the ship immediately, whereas here they do[h]: and there the storm lasts for some time, whereas here as soon as He speaks, there is a calm. He often repeats the same miracle in order to impress it on men's minds.

Aug. Tr. xxv. s. 3. et seq. Ps. 7. AUG. There is a mystical meaning in our Lord's feeding the multitude, and ascending the mountain: for thus was it prophesied of Him, *So shall the congregation of the people come about Thee: for their sake therefore lift up Thyself again:* i. e. that the congregation of the people may come about Thee, lift up Thyself again. But why is it fled; for they could not have detained Him against His will? This fleeing has a meaning; viz. that His flight is above our comprehension ; just as, when you do not understand a thing, you say, It escapes me. He fled alone unto the mountain, because He is ascended from above all heavens. But on His ascension aloft a storm came upon the disciples in the ship, i. e. the Church, and it became dark, the light, i. e. Jesus, having gone. As the end of the world draws nigh, error increases, iniquity abounds. Light again is love, ac-
1 John 2, 9. cording to John, *He that hateth his brother is in darkness.* The waves and storms and winds then that agitate the ship, are the clamours of the evil speaking, and love waxing cold. Howbeit the wind, and storm, and waves, and darkness were
Matt. 10, 22. not able to stop, and sink the vessel ; *For he that endureth to the end, the same shall be saved.* As the number five has reference to the Law, the books of Moses being five, the number five and twenty, being made up of five pieces, has the same meaning. And this law was imperfect, before the Gospel came. Now the number of perfection is six, so therefore five is multiplied by six, which makes thirty: i. e.

[h] So in the Catena. But Chrysostom, Why did not they at once receive this? alluding to the disciples seeming to be in doubt longer in St. Matthew whether it was our Lord.

the law is fulfilled by the Gospel.   To those then who fulfil
the law Jesus comes treading on the waves, i. e. trampling
under foot all the swellings of the world, all the loftiness of
men: and yet such tribulations remain, that even they who
believe on Jesus, fear lest they should be lost.   THEOPHYL.
When either men or devils try to terrify us, let us hear
Christ saying, *It is I, be not afraid*, i. e. I am ever near you,
God unchangeable, immoveable; let not any false fears
destroy your faith in Me.   Observe too our Lord did not
come when the danger was beginning, but when it was
ending.   He suffers us to remain in the midst of dangers
and tribulations, that we may be proved thereby, and flee for
succour to Him Who is able to give us deliverance when we
least expect it.   When man's understanding can no longer
help him, then the Divine deliverance comes.   If we are
willing also to receive Christ into the ship, i. e. to live in
our hearts, we shall find ourselves immediately in the place,
where we wish to be, i. e. heaven.   BEDE. This ship, however,
does not carry an idle crew; they are all stout rowers; i. e.
in the Church not the idle and effeminate, but the stre-
nuous and persevering in good works, attain to the harbour
of everlasting salvation.

22. The day following, when the people which stood
on the other side of the sea saw that there was none
other boat there, save that one whereinto his disciples
were entered, and that Jesus went not with his disciples into the boat, but that his disciples were gone
away alone;

23. (Howbeit there came other boats from Tiberias
nigh unto the place where they did eat bread, after
that the Lord had given thanks:)

24. When the people therefore saw that Jesus was
not there, neither his disciples, they also took shipping,
and came to Capernaum, seeking for Jesus.

25. And when they had found him on the other
side of the sea, they said unto him, Rabbi, when
camest thou hither?

26. Jesus answered them and said, Verily, verily, I say unto you, Ye seek me, not because ye saw the miracles, but because ye did eat of the loaves, and were filled.

27. Labour not for the meat which perisheth, but for that meat which endureth unto everlasting life, which the Son of man shall give unto you: for him hath God the Father sealed.

Chrys. Hom. xliii. 2. CHRYS. Our Lord, though He did not actually shew Himself to the multitude walking on the sea, yet gave them the opportunity of inferring what had taken place; *The day following, the people which stood on the other side of the sea saw that there was none other boat there, save that one whereinto His disciples were entered, and that Jesus went not with His disciples into the boat, but that His disciples were gone away alone.* What was this but to suspect that He had walked across the sea, on His going away? For He could not have gone over in a ship, as there was only one there, that in which His disciples had entered; and He had not gone in with them. AUG. Knowledge of the miracle was conveyed to them indirectly. Other ships had come to the place where they had eaten bread; in these they went after Him; *Howbeit there came other boats from Tiberias, nigh unto the place where they did eat bread, after that the Lord had given thanks. When the people therefore saw that Jesus was not there, neither His disciples, they also took shipping, and came to Capernaum, seeking for Jesus.*

Aug. Tr. xxv. 8.

Chrys. Hom. xliii. 1. CHRYS. Yet after so great a miracle, they did not ask Him how He had passed over, or shew any concern about it: as appears from what follows; *And when they had found Him on the other side of the sea, they said unto Him, Rabbi, when camest Thou hither?* Except we say that this *when* meant *how.* And observe their lightness of mind. After saying, *This is that Prophet,* and wishing to take Him by force to make Him king, when they find Him, nothing of the kind is thought of. AUG. So He Who had fled to the mountain, mixes and converses with the multitude. Only just now they would have kept Him, and made Him king.

Aug. Tr. xxv. 8.

But after the sacrament of the miracle, He begins to discourse, and fills their souls with His word, whose bodies He had satisfied with bread. ALCUIN.[1] He who set an example of declining praise, and earthly power, sets teachers also an example of deliverance in preaching. CHRYS. Kindness and lenity are not always expedient. To the indolent or insensible disciple the spur must be applied; and this the Son of God does. For when the multitude comes with soft speeches, *Rabbi, when camest Thou hither?* He shews them that He did not desire the honour that cometh from man, by the severity of His answer, which both exposes the motive on which they acted, and rebukes it. *Jesus answered them and said, Verily, verily, I say unto you, Ye seek Me, not because ye saw the miracles, but because ye did eat of the loaves, and were filled.* AUG. As if He said, Ye seek Me to satisfy the flesh, not the spirit. CHRYS. After the rebuke, however, He proceeds to teach them: *Labour not for the meat which perisheth, but for that meat which endureth unto everlasting life;* meaning, Ye seek for temporal food, whereas I only fed your bodies, that ye might seek the more diligently for that food, which is not temporary, but contains eternal life. ALCUIN. Bodily food only supports the flesh of the outward man, and must be taken not once for all, but daily; whereas spiritual food remaineth for ever, imparting perpetual fulness, and immortality. AUG. Under the figure of food He alludes to Himself. Ye seek Me, He saith, for the sake of something else; seek Me for My own sake. CHRYS. But, inasmuch as some who wish to live in sloth, pervert this precept, *Labour not, &c.* it is well to notice what Paul says, *Let him that stole steal no more, but rather let him labour, working with his hands the thing which is good, that he may have to give to him that needeth.* And he himself too, when he resided with Aquila and Priscilla at Corinth, worked with his hand. By saying, *Labour not for the meat which perisheth,* our Lord does not mean to tell us to be idle; but to work, and give alms. This is that meat which perisheth not; to labour for the meat which perisheth, is to be devoted to the interests of this life. Our Lord saw that the multitude had no thought of believing, and only wished to fill their

Chrys. Hom. xliv. 1.

Aug. Tr. xxv. 10.

Chrys. Hom. xliv. 1.

Aug. Tr. xxv. 10.

Chrys. Hom. xliv. 1.

Ephes. 4, 28.

---

[1] Not found in Alcuin, but in a Gloss.

bellies, without working; and this He justly called the meat

Aug.
Tr. xxv.
10.
c. 4.
which perisheth. AUG. As He told the woman of Samaria
above, *If thou knewest Who it is that saith to thee, Give me
to drink, thou wouldest have asked of Him, and He would
have given thee living water.* So He says here, *Which the
Son of man shall give unto you.* ALCUIN. When, through
the hand of the priest, thou receivest the Body of Christ,
think not of the priest which thou seest, but of the Priest
thou dost not see. The priest is the dispenser of this food,
not the author. The Son of man gives Himself to us, that
we may abide in Him, and He in us. Do not conceive that
Son of man to be the same as other sons of men: He
stands alone in abundance of grace, separate and distinct
from all the rest: for that Son of man is the Son of God, as
it follows, *For Him hath God the Father sealed.* To seal is
to put a mark upon; so the meaning is, Do not despise Me
because I am the Son of man, for I am the Son of man in
such sort, as that the Father hath sealed Me, i. e. given Me
something peculiar, to the end that I should not be confounded with the human race, but that the human race should

Hilar.
viii. de
Trin. c.
44.
be delivered by Me. HILARY. A seal throws out a perfect
impression of the stamp, at the same time that it takes in
that impression. This is not a perfect illustration of the
Divine nativity: for sealing supposes matter, different kinds
of matter, the impression of harder upon softer. Yet He
who was God Only-Begotten, and the Son of man only by
the Sacrament of our salvation, makes use of it to express
the Father's fulness as stamped upon Himself. He wishes to
shew the Jews He has the power of giving the eternal meat,
because He contained in Himself the fulness of God. CHRYS.

Chrys.
Hom.
xliv. 1.
Or sealed, i. e. sent Him for this purpose, viz. to bring us
food; or, sealed, was revealed the Gospel by means of His
witness. ALCUIN. To take the passage mystically: on the
day following, i. e. after the ascension of Christ, the multitude
standing in good works, not lying in worldly pleasures,
expects Jesus to come to them. The one ship is the one
Church: the other ships which come besides, are the con-

Phil. 2,
21.
Aug.
Tr. xxv.
10.
venticles of heretics, who seek their own, not the things of
Jesus Christ. Wherefore He well says, *Ye seek Me, because
ye did eat of the loaves.* AUG. How many there are who

seek Jesus, only to gain some temporary benefit. One man has a matter of business, in which he wants the assistance of the clergy; another is oppressed by a more powerful neighbour, and flies to the Church for refuge: Jesus is scarcely ever sought for Jesus' sake. GREG. In their persons too our Lord condemns all those within the holy Church, who, when brought near to God by sacred Orders, do not seek the recompense of righteousness, but the interests of this present life. To follow our Lord, when filled with bread, is to use Holy Church as a means of livelihood; and to seek our Lord not for the miracle's sake, but for the loaves, is to aspire to a religious office, not with a view to increase of grace, but to add to our worldly means. BEDE. They too seek Jesus, not for Jesus' sake, but for something else, who ask in their prayers not for eternal, but temporal blessings. The mystical meaning is, that the conventicles of heretics are without the company of Christ and His disciples. And other ships coming, is the sudden growth of heresies. By the crowd, which saw that Jesus was not there, or His disciples, are designated those who seeing the errors of heretics, leave them and turn to the true faith.

Greg. xxiii. Moral. (c. xxv.)

28. Then said they unto him, What shall we do, that we might work the works of God?

29. Jesus answered and said unto them, This is the work of God, that ye believe on him whom he hath sent.

30. They said therefore unto him, What sign shewest thou then, that we may see, and believe thee? what dost thou work?

31. Our fathers did eat manna in the desert; as it is written, He gave them bread from heaven to eat.

32. Then said Jesus unto them, Verily, verily, I say unto you, Moses gave you not that bread from heaven; but my Father giveth you the true bread from heaven.

33. For the bread of God is he which cometh down from heaven, and giveth life unto the world.

34. Then said they unto him, Lord, evermore give us this bread.

ALCUIN. They understood that the meat, which remaineth unto eternal life, was the work of God: and therefore they ask Him what to do to work the work of God, i. e. obtain the meat: *Then said they unto Him, What shall we do that we might work the works of God?* BEDE. i. e. By keeping what commandments shall we be able to fulfil the law of God? CHRYS. But they said this, not that they might learn, and do them, but to obtain from Him another exhibition of His bounty. THEOPHYL. Christ, though He saw it would not avail, yet for the good of others afterwards, answered their question; and shewed them, or rather the whole world, what was the work of God: *Jesus answered and said unto them, This is the work of God, that ye believe on Him whom He hath sent.* AUG. He does not say, 'That ye believe Him, but, *that ye believe on Him.* For the devils believed Him, and did not believe on Him; and we believe Paul, but do not believe on Paul. To believe on Him is believing to love, believing to honour Him, believing to go unto Him, and be made members incorporate of His Body. The faith, which God requires of us, is that which worketh by love. Faith indeed is distinguished from works by the Apostle, who says, *That man is justified by faith without the deeds of the law.* But the works indeed which appear good, without faith in Christ, are not really so, not being referred to that end, which makes them good. *For Christ is the end of the law for righteousness to every one that believeth.* And therefore our Lord would not separate faith from works, but said that faith itself was the doing the work of God; He saith not, This is your work, but, *This is the work of God, that ye believe on Him:* in order that he that glorieth might glory in the Lord. AUG. To eat then that meat which endureth unto everlasting life, is to *believe* on Him. Why dost thou make ready thy tooth and thy belly? Only believe, and thou hast eaten already. As He called on them to believe, they still asked for miracles whereby to believe; *They said therefore unto Him, What sign shewest Thou then, that we may see and believe Thee? What dost Thou work?*

Chrys. Hom. xlv. 1.

Aug. Tr. xxv. in Joan.

Rom. 3, 28.

Rom. 10, 4.

Aug. xxv. 12.

CHRYS. Nothing can be more unreasonable than their asking for another miracle, as if none had been given already. And they do not even leave the choice of the miracle to our Lord; but would oblige Him to give them just that sign, which was given to their fathers: *Our fathers did eat manna in the desert.* ALCUIN. And to exalt the miracle of the manna, they quote the Psalm, *As it is written, He gave them bread from heaven to eat.* CHRYS. Whereas many miracles were performed in Egypt, at the Red Sea, and in the desert, they remembered this one the best of any. Such is the force of appetite. They do not mention this miracle as the work either of God, or of Moses, in order to avoid raising Him on the one hand to an equality with God, or lowering Him on the other by a comparison with Moses; but they take a middle ground, only saying, *Our fathers did eat manna in the desert.* AUG. Or thus; Our Lord sets Himself above Moses, who did not dare to say that He gave the meat which perisheth not. The multitude therefore remembering what Moses had done, and wishing for some greater miracle, say, as it were, Thou promisest the meat which perisheth not, and doest not works equal to those Moses did. He gave us not barley loaves, but manna from heaven. CHRYS. Our Lord might have replied, that He had done miracles greater than Moses: but it was not the time for such a declaration. One thing He desired, viz. to bring them to taste the spiritual meat: then *Jesus said unto them, Verily, verily, I say unto you, Moses gave you not that bread from heaven; but My Father giveth you the true bread from heaven.* Did not the manna come from heaven? True, but in what sense did it? The same in which the birds are called, the birds of heaven[k]; and just as it is said in the Psalm, *The Lord thundered out of heaven.* He calls it the true bread, not because the miracle of the manna was false, but because it was the figure, not the reality. He does not say too, Moses gave it you not, but I: but He puts God for Moses, Himself for the manna. AUG. As if He said, That manna was the type of this food, of which I just now spoke; and which all my miracles refer to. You like my miracles, you despise what is signified by them. This bread which God gives, and

Chrys. Hom. xlv. 1.

Chrys. Hom. xlv. 1.

Aug. Tr. xxv. s. 12.

Chrys. Hom. xxv. 1.

Ps. 17.

Aug. Tr. xxv. 31.

[k] Volucres cœli, Vulgate translation of fowls of the air.

Q 2

which this manna represented, is the Lord Jesus Christ, as we read next, *For the bread of God is He which cometh down from heaven, and giveth life unto the world.* BEDE. Not to the physical world, but to men, its inhabitants. THEOPHYL. He calls Himself the true bread, because the only-begotten Son of God, made man, was principally signified by the manna. For manna means literally, what is this? The Israelites were astonished at first on finding it, and asked one another what it was. And the Son of God, made man, is in an especial sense this mysterious manna, which we ask about, saying, What is this? How can the Son of God be the Son of man? How can one person consist of two natures? ALCUIN. Who by the humanity, which was assumed, came down from heaven, and by the divinity, which assumed it, gives life to the world. THEOPHYL. But this bread, being essentially life, (for He is the Son of the living Father,) in quickening all things, does but what is natural to Him to do. For as natural bread supports our weak flesh, so Christ, by the operations of the Spirit, gives life to the soul; and even incorruption to the body, (for at the resurrection the body will be made incorruptible.) Wherefore He says, that He *giveth* Chrys. *life unto the world.* CHRYS. Not only to the Jews, but to Hom. the whole world. The multitude, however, still attached a xlv. 1. low meaning to His words: *Then said they unto Him, Lord, evermore give us this bread.* They say, *Give us this bread,* not, Ask Thy Father to give it us: whereas He had said that Aug. His Father gave this bread. AUG. As the woman of Samaria, Tr. xxv. when our Lord told her, *Whosoever drinketh of this water* 13. *shall never thirst,* thought He meant natural water, and said, *Sir, give me this water,* that she might never be in want of it again: in the same way these say, Give us this bread, which refreshes, supports, and fails not.

35. And Jesus said unto them, I am the bread of life: he that cometh to me shall never hunger; and he that believeth on me shall never thirst.

36. But I said unto you, That ye also have seen me, and believe not.

37. All that the Father giveth me shall come to me; and him that cometh to me I will in no wise cast out.

38. For I came down from heaven, not to do mine own will, but the will of him that sent me.

39. And this is the Father's will which hath sent me, that of all which he hath given me I should lose nothing, but should raise it up again at the last day.

40. And this is the will of him that sent me, that every one which seeth the Son, and believeth on him, may have everlasting life: and I will raise him up at the last day.

CHRYS. Our Lord now proceeds to set forth mysteries; and first speaks of His Divinity: *And Jesus said unto them, I am the bread of life.* He does not say this of His body, for He speaks of that at the end ; *The bread that I will give you is My flesh.* Here He is speaking of His Divinity. The *flesh* is bread, by virtue of the Word; this bread is heavenly bread, on account of the Spirit which dwelleth in it. THEO-PHYL. He does not say, *I am the bread* of nourishment, but *of life,* for, whereas all things brought death, Christ hath quickened us by Himself. But the life here, is not our common life, but that which is not cut short by death : *He that cometh to Me shall never hunger; and He that believeth on Me shall never thirst.* AUG. *He that cometh to Me,* i. e. that believeth on Me, *shall never hunger,* has the same meaning as shall never thirst; both signifying that eternal society, where there is no want. THEO-PHYL. Or, *shall never hunger or thirst,* i. e. shall never be wearied[1] of hearing the word of God, and shall never thirst as to the understanding: as though He had not the water of baptism, and the sanctification of the Spirit. AUG. Ye desire bread from heaven: but, though you have it before you, you eat it not. This is what I told you: *But I said unto you, that ye also have seen Me, and believe not.* ALCUIN. As if He said, I did not say what I did to you about the bread, because I thought you would eat it, but rather to

Chrys. Hom. xlv. 2.

Aug. Tr. xxv. 14.

[1] non famem foret ac- cipiendi sermo- nem.

Aug. Tr. xxv. 14.

conviet you of unbelief. I say, that ye see Me, and believe

Chrys.
Hom.
xliv. 2.
c. 5. not. CHRYS. Or, *I said to you*, refers to the testimony of the Scriptures, of which He said above, *They are they which testify of Me;* and again, *I am come in My Father's name, and ye receive Me not. That ye have seen Me*, is a silent

Aug.
Tr. xxv.
14. allusion to His miracles. AUG. But, because ye have seen Me, and believed not, I have not therefore lost the people of God: *All that the Father giveth Me, shall come unto Me; and him that cometh to Me, I will in no wise cast out.* BEDE. *All*, He saith, absolutely, to show the fulness of the number who should believe. These are they which the Father gives the Son, when, by His secret inspiration, He makes them believe in the Son. ALCUIN. Whomsoever therefore the Father draweth to belief in Me, he, by faith, shall come to Me, that he may be joined to Me. *And those*, who in the steps of faith and good works, *shall come to Me, I will in no wise cast out;* i. e. in the secret habitation of a pure conscience, he shall dwell with Me, and at the last I will receive him to overlasting felicity. AUG. That inner place, whence there is

Aug.
Tr. xxv.
14. no casting out, is a great sanctuary, a secret chamber, where is neither weariness, or the bitterness of evil thoughts, or the

Mat. 25. cross of pain and temptation: of which it is said, *Enter thou*

Chrys.
Hom.
xliv. 2. *into the joy of thy Lord.* CHRYS. The expression, *that the Father giveth Me*, shews that it is no accident whether a man believes or not, and that belief is not the work of human cogitation, but requires a revelation from on high, and a mind devout enough to receive the revelation. Not that they are free from blame, whom the Father does not give, for they are deficient even in that which lies in their own power, the will to believe. This is a virtual rebuke to their unbelief, as it shows that whoever does not believe in Him, transgresses the Father's will. Paul, however, says, that He gives them

1 Cor.
15, 24. up to the Father: *When He shall have given up the kingdom to God, even the Father.* But as the Father, in giving, does not take from Himself, so neither does the Son when He gives up. The Son is said to give up to the Father, because we are brought to the Father by Him. And of the Father at

1 Cor. 1,
9. the same time we read, *By Whom ye were called unto the fellowship of His Son.* Whoever then, our Lord says, cometh to Me, shall be saved, for to save such I took up

flesh: *For I came down from heaven not to do Mine own will, but the will of Him that sent Me.* But what? Hast thou one will, He another? No, certainly. Mark what He says afterwards; *And this is the will of Him that sent Me, that every one which seeth the Son, and believeth on Him, should have everlasting life.* And this is the Son's will too; *For the Son quickeneth whom He will.* He says then, I came to do nothing but what the Father wills, for I have no will distinct from My Father's: all things that the Father hath are Mine. But this not now: He reserves these higher truths for the end of His ministry. AUG. This is the reason why He does not cast out those who come to Him. *For I came down from heaven not to do Mine own will, but the will of Him that sent Me.* The soul departed from God, because it was proud. Pride casts us out, humility restores us. When a physician in the treatment of a disease, cures certain outward symptoms, but not the cause which produces them, his cure is only temporary. So long as the cause remains, the disease may return. That the cause then of all diseases, i. e. pride, might be eradicated, the Son of God humbled Himself. Why art thou proud, O man? The Son of God humbled Himself for thee. It might shame thee, perhaps, to imitate a humble man; but imitate at least a humble God. And this is the proof of His humility: *I came not to do Mine own will, but the will of Him that sent Me.* Pride does its own will; humility the will of God. HILARY. Not that He does what He does not wish. He fulfils obediently His Father's will, wishing also Himself to fulfil that will. AUG. For this very reason therefore, I will not cast out Him that cometh to Me; because I came not to do Mine own will. I came to teach humility, by being humble Myself. He that cometh to Me, is made a member of Me, and necessarily humble, because He will not do His own will, but the will of God; and therefore is not cast out. He was cast out, as proud; he returns to Me humble, he is not sent away, except for pride again; he who keeps his humility, falleth not from the truth. And further, that He does not cast out such, because He came not to do His will, He shews when He says, *And this is the Father's will which hath sent*

Aug.
I c. 5, 21.

Aug.
Tr. xxv.
15.

Hilar.
iii. do
Trin.
c. 9.

Aug.
Tr. xxv
in Joan.
16.

Me, that of all which He hath given Me, I should lose

Mat. 18, 14. *nothing.* Every one of an humble mind is given to Him: *It is not the will of your Father, that one of these little ones should perish.* The swelling ones may perish; of the little ones none

Mat. 18, 3. 5. can; for *except ye be as a little child, ye shall not enter into the kingdom of heaven.* AUG. They therefore who by God's Aug. de Cor. et Gra- tia, c. ix. unerring providence are foreknown, and predestined, called, justified, glorified, even before their new birth, or before they are born at all, are already the sons of God, and cannot possibly perish; these are they who truly come to Christ. By Him there is given also perseverance in good unto the end; which is given only to those who will not perish.

Chrys. Hom. xliv. 3. Those who do not persevere will perish. CHRYS. *I should lose nothing;* He lets them know, he does not desire his own honour, but their salvation. After these declarations, *I will in no wise cast out,* and *I should lose nothing,* He adds, *But should raise it up at the last day.* In the general resurrection the wicked will be cast out, according to Matthew,

Mat. 22, 13. Mat. 10, 28. *Take him, and cast him into outer darkness.* And, *Who is able to cast both soul and body into hell.* He often brings in mention of the resurrection for this purpose: viz. to warn men not to judge of God's providence from present events,

Aug. Tr. xxv. 19. but to carry on their ideas to another world. AUG. See how the twofold resurrection is expressed here. He who cometh to Me, shall forthwith rise again; by becoming humble, and a member of Me. But then He proceeds; *But I will raise him up at the last day.* To explain the words, *All that the Father hath given Me,* and, *I should lose nothing,* He adds; *And this is the will of Him that hath sent Me, that every one which seeth the Son, and believeth on Him, may have everlasting life: and I will raise him up at the last day.*

c. 5, 24. Above He said, *Whoso heareth My word, and believeth on Him that sent Me:* now it is, *Every one which seeth the Son, and believeth on Him.* He does not say, believe on the Father, because it is the same thing to believe on the Father, and on the Son; for *as the Father hath life in Himself, even so hath He given to the Son to have life in Himself;* and again, *That whoso seeth the Son and believeth on Him, should have ever- lasting life;* i. e. by believing, by passing over to life, as at the first resurrection. But this is only the first resurrection, He alludes to the second when He says, *And I will raise him up at the last day.*

41. The Jews then murmured at him, because he said, I am the bread which came down from heaven.

42. And they said, Is not this Jesus, the son of Joseph, whose father and mother we know? how is it then that he saith, I came down from heaven?

43. Jesus therefore answered and said unto them, Murmur not among yourselves.

44. No man can come to me, except the Father which hath sent me draw him: and I will raise him up at the last day.

45. It is written in the prophets, And they shall be all taught of God. Every man therefore that hath heard, and hath learned of the Father, cometh unto me.

46. Not that any man hath seen the Father, save he which is of God, he hath seen the Father.

CHRYS. The Jews, so long as they thought to get food for their carnal eating, had no misgivings; but when this hope was taken away, then, we read, *the Jews murmured at Him because He said, I am the bread which came down from heaven.* This was only a pretence. The real cause of their complaint was that they were disappointed in their expectation of a bodily feast. As yet however they reverenced Him, for His miracle; and only expressed their discontent by murmurs. What these were we read next: *And they said, Is not this Jesus, the Son of Joseph, whose father and mother we know? how is it then that He saith, I came down from heaven?* AUG. But they were far from being fit for that heavenly bread, and did not hunger for it. For they had not that hunger of the inner man. CHRYS. It is evident that they did not yet know of His miraculous birth: for they call Him the Son of Joseph. Nor are they blamed for this. Our Lord does not reply, I am not the Son of Joseph: for the miracle of His birth would have overpowered them.

Chrys. Hom. xlvi. 1.

Aug. Tr. xxvi. 1.

Chrys. Hom. xlvi. 1.

And if the birth according to the flesh were above their belief, how much more that higher and ineffable birth.

Aug.
Tr.xxvi.
AUG. He took man's flesh upon Him, but not after the manner of men; for, His Father being in heaven, He chose a mother upon earth, and was born of her without a father. The answer to the murmurers next follows: *Jesus therefore answered and said unto them, Murmur not among yourselves;* as if to say, I know why ye hunger not after this bread, and so cannot understand it, and do not seek it: *No man can come to Me except the Father who hath sent Me draw him.* This is the doctrine of grace: none cometh, except he be drawn. But whom the Father draws, and whom not, and why He draws one, and not another, presume not to decide, if thou wouldest avoid falling into error. Take the doctrine as it is given thee: and, if thou art not drawn,

Chrys.
Hom.
xlvi. 1.
pray that thou mayest be. CHRYS. But here the Manichees attack us, asserting that nothing is in our own power. Our Lord's words however do not destroy our free agency, but only shew that we need Divine assistance. For He is speaking not of one who comes without the concurrence of his own will, but one who has many hindrances in the way of his coming.

Aug.
Tr.xxvi.
2. et sq.
AUG. Now if we are drawn to Christ without our own will, we believe without our own will; the will is not exercised, but compulsion is applied. But, though a man can enter the Church involuntarily, he cannot believe other than voluntarily; *for with the heart man believeth unto righteousness.* Therefore if he who is drawn, comes without his will, he does not believe; if he does not believe, he does not come. For we do not come to Christ, by running, or walking, but by believing, not by the motion of the body, but the will of the mind. Thou art drawn by thy will. But what

Ps. 36.
is it to be drawn by the will? *Delight thou in the Lord, and He will give thee thy heart's desire.* There is a certain craving of the heart, to which that heavenly bread is pleasant. If the Poet could say, " Trahit sua quemque voluptas," how much more strongly may we speak of a man being drawn to Christ, i. e. being delighted with truth, happiness, justice, eternal life, all which is Christ? Have the bodily senses their pleasures, and has not the soul hers? Give me one who loves, who longs, who burns, who sighs for the source of

his being and his eternal home; and he will know what I
mean. But why did He say, *Except my Father draw him?*
If we are to be drawn, let us be drawn by Him to whom
His love saith, *Draw me, we will run after Thee.* But Cant. 1,
let us see what is meant by it. The Father draws to the ⁴·
Son those who believe on the Son, as thinking that He has
God for His Father. For the Father begat the Son equal to
Himself; and whoso thinks and believes really and seriously
that He on Whom He believes is equal to the Father, him the
Father draws to the Son. Arius believed Him to be a
creature; the Father drew not him. Thomas says, Christ is
only a man. Because he so believes, the Father draws him
not. He drew Peter who said, *Thou art the Christ, the Son* Mat.16.
of the living God; to whom accordingly it was told, *For flesh
and blood hath not revealed it unto thee, but My Father which
is in heaven.* That revelation is the drawing. For if earthly
objects, when put before us, draw us; how much more shall
Christ, when revealed by the Father? For what doth the soul more
long after than truth? But here men hunger, there they will be
filled. Wherefore He adds, *And I will raise him up at the last
day:* as if He said, He shall be filled with that, for which
he now thirsts, at the resurrection of the dead; for I will   .
raise him up. AUG. Or the Father draws to the Son, by the Aug. de
works which He did by Him. CHRYS. Great indeed is the Qu.Nov.
Son's dignity; the Father draws men, and the Son raises them Chrys.
up. This is no division of works, but an equality of power. Hom.
He then shews the way in which the Father draws. *It is
written in the Prophets, And they shall all be taught of
God.* You see the excellence of faith; that it cannot be
learnt from men, or by the teaching of man, but only from
God Himself. The Master sits, dispensing His truth to all,
pouring out His doctrine to all. But if all are to be taught
of God, how is it that some believe not? Because all here
only means the generality, or, all that have the will. AUG. Aug.
Or thus; When a schoolmaster is the only one in a town, we de Præ-
say loosely, This man teaches all here to read; not that all Sancto-
learn of him, but that he teaches all who do learn. And in rum,
the same way we say that God teaches all men to come to Aug.
Christ: not that all do come, but that no one comes in any super
other way. AUG. All the men of that kingdom shall be Tr.xxv.
7.

taught of God; they shall hear nothing from men: for, though in this world what they hear with the outward ear is from men, yet what they understand is given them from within; from within is light and revelation. I force certain sounds into your ears, but unless He is within to reveal their meaning, how, O ye Jews, can ye acknowledge Me, ye whom the Father hath not taught? BEDE. He uses the plural, *In the Prophets*, because all the Prophets being filled with one and the same spirit, their prophecies, though different, all tended to the same end; and with whatever any one of them says, all the rest agree; as with the prophecy of Joel, *All shall be taught of God.* GLOSS. These words are not found in Joel, but something like them; *Be glad then ye children of Sion, and rejoice in the Lord your God, for He hath given you a Teacher.* And more expressly in Isaiah, *And all thy children shall be taught of the Lord.* CHRYS. An important distinction. All men before learnt the things of God through men; now they learn them through the Only Son of God, and the Holy Spirit. AUG. All that are taught of God come to the Son, because they have heard and learnt from the Father of the Son: wherefore He proceeds, *Every man that hath heard, and hath learned of the Father, cometh to Me.* But if every one that hath heard and learnt of the Father cometh, every one that hath not heard of the Father hath not learnt. For beyond the reach of the bodily senses is this school, in which the Father is heard, and men taught to come to the Son. Here we have not to do with the carnal ear, but the ear of the heart; for here is the Son Himself, the Word by which the Father teacheth, and together with Him the Holy Spirit: the operations of the three Persons being inseparable from each other. This is attributed however principally to the Father, because from Him proceeds the Son, and the Holy Spirit. Therefore the grace which the Divine bounty imparts in secret to men's hearts, is rejected by none from hardness of heart: seeing it is given in the first instance, in order to take away hard-heartedness. Why then does He not teach all to come to Christ? Because those whom He teaches, He teaches in mercy; and those whom He teaches not, He teaches not in judgment. But if we say, that those, whom He teaches not, wish to learn, we

Joel 2, 23.

Quia dedit nobis lectorem justitiæ. Vulg.

Isa. 54, 13.

Chrys. Hom. xlvi. 1.

Aug. de Prædest. Sanctorum, c. viii. et seq.

shall be answered, Why then is it said, *Will thou not turn* Ps.84,6. *again, and quicken us?* If God does not make willing minds out of unwilling, why prayeth the Church, according to our Lord's command, for her persecutors? For no one can say, I believed, and therefore He called me: rather the preventing mercy of God called him, that he might believe. AUG. Aug. Behold then how the Father draweth; not by laying a neces-Tr.xxvi. sity on man, but by teaching the truth. To draw, belongeth seq. to God: *Every one that hath heard, and hath learned of the Father, cometh to Me.* What then? Hath Christ taught nothing? Not so. What if men saw not the Father teaching, but saw the Son. So then the Father taught, the Son spoke. As I teach you by My word, so the Father teaches by His Word. But He Himself explains the matter, if we read on: *Not that any man hath seen the Father, save He which is of God, He hath seen the Father;* as if He said, Do not when I tell you, *Every man that hath heard and learnt of the Father,* say to yourselves, We have never seen the Father, and how then can we have learnt from Him? Hear Him then in Me. I know the Father, and am from Him, just as a word is from him who speaks it; i. e. not the mere passing sound, but that which remaineth with the speaker, and draweth the hearer. CHRYS. We are all from God. Chrys. That which belongs peculiarly and principally to the Son, xlvi.s.1. He omits the mention of, as being unsuitable to the weakness of His hearers.

47. Verily, verily, I say unto you, He that believeth on me hath everlasting life.

48. I am that bread of life.

49. Your fathers did eat manna in the wilderness, and are dead.

50. This is the bread which cometh down from heaven, that a man may eat thereof, and not die.

51. I am the living bread which came down from heaven: if any man eat of this bread, he shall live for ever.

AUG. Our Lord wishes to reveal what He is; *Verily, verily,* Aug. Tr.xxvi. s. 10.

I say unto you, He that believeth on Me, hath everlasting life. As if He said; He that believeth on Me hath Me: but what is it to have Me? It is to have eternal life: for the Word which was in the beginning with God is life eternal, and the life was the light of men. Life underwent death,

Chrys. (Nic.) Theoph. that life might kill death. CHRYS. The multitude being urgent for bodily food, and reminding Him of that which was given to their fathers, He tells them that the manna was only a type of that spiritual food which was now to be

Chrys. Hom. xlv. 1. tasted in reality, *I am that bread of life.* CHRYS. He calls Himself the bread of life, because He constitutes one life,

Aug. Tr. xxvi. 11. both present, and to come. AUG. And because they had taunted Him with the manna, He adds, *Your fathers did eat manna in the wilderness, and are dead.* Your fathers they are, for ye are like them; murmuring sons of murmuring fathers. For in nothing did that people offend God more, than by their murmurs against Him. And therefore are they dead, because what they saw they believed, what

Chrys. Hom. xlvi. 2. they did not see they believed not, nor understood. CHRYS. The addition, *In the wilderness,* is not put in without meaning, but to remind them how short a time the manna lasted; only till the entrance into the land of promise. And because the bread which Christ gave seemed inferior to the manna, in that the latter had come down from heaven, while the former was of this world, He adds, *This is the bread which*

Aug. Tr. xxvi. s. 12. *cometh down from heaven.* AUG. This was the bread the manna typified, this was the bread the altar typified. Both the one and the other were sacraments, differing in symbol,

1 Cor. 10. alike in the thing signified. Hear the Apostle, *They did all*

Chrys. Hom. xlvi. 2. *eat the same spiritual meat.* CHRYS. He then gives them a strong reason for believing that they were given for higher privileges than their fathers. Their fathers eat manna and were dead; whereas of this bread He says, that *a man may eat thereof, and not die.* The difference of the two is evident from the difference of their ends. By bread here is meant wholesome doctrine, and faith in Him, or His body: for these

Aug. Tr. xxvi. 11. are the preservatives of the soul. AUG. But are we, who eat the bread that cometh down from heaven, relieved from death? From visible and carnal death, the death of the body, we are not: we shall die, even as they died. But from spiritual death which their fathers suffered, we are delivered. Moses and many acceptable of God, eat the manna, and died not, because they understood that visible food in a spiritual sense, spiritually tasted it, and were spiritually filled with it. And we too at this day receive the visible food; but the Sacrament is one thing, the virtue of the Sacrament another. Many a one receiveth from the Altar, and perisheth in receiving; *eating and drinking his own damnation*, as saith the Apostle. To eat then the heavenly bread spiritually, is to bring to the Altar an innocent mind. Sins, though they be daily, are not deadly. Before you go to the Altar, attend to the prayer you repeat: *Forgive us our debts, as we forgive our debtors.* If thou forgivest, thou art forgiven: approach confidently; it is bread, not poison. None then that eateth of this bread, shall die. But we speak of the virtue of the Sacrament, not the visible Sacrament itself; of the inward, not of the outward eater. ALCUIN. Therefore I say, He that eateth this bread, dieth not: *I am the living bread which came down from heaven.* THEOPHYL. By becoming incarnate, He was not then first man, and afterwards assumed Divinity, as Nestorius fables. AUG. The manna too came down from heaven; but the manna was shadow, this is substance. ALCUIN. But men must be quickened by my life: *If any man eat of this bread, he shall live*, not only now by faith and righteousness, but *for ever*.

1 Cor. 11, 29.

Matt. 6, 12.

Theoph. in v. 33.

Aug. Tr. xxvi. 13.

51. —And the bread that I will give is my flesh, which I will give for the life of the world.

AUG. Our Lord pronounces Himself to be bread, not only in respect of that Divinity, which feeds all things, but also in respect of that human nature, which was assumed by the Word of God: *And the bread*, He says, *that I will give is My flesh, which I will give for the life of the world.* BEDE. This bread our Lord then gave, when He delivered to His disciple the mystery of His Body and Blood, and offered Himself to God the Father on the altar of the cross. *For the life of the world*, i. e. not for the elements, but for mankind, who are called the world. THEOPHYL. *Which I shall give:* this shews His power; for it shews that He was not

Gloss. (Nic.)

crucified as a servant, in subjection to the Father, but of his
own accord; for though He is said to have been given up by
the Father, yet He delivered Himself up also. And observe,
the bread which is taken by us in the mysteries, is not only
the sign of Christ's flesh, but is itself the very flesh of
Christ; for He does not say, *The bread which I will give,* is the
sign of My flesh, but, *is My flesh.* The bread is by a mystical benediction conveyed in unutterable words, and by the
indwelling of the Holy Ghost, transmuted into the flesh of
Christ. But why see we not the flesh? Because, if the flesh
were seen, it would revolt us to such a degree, that we
should be unable to partake of it. And therefore in condescension to our infirmity, the mystical food is given to us
under an appearance suitable to our minds. He gave His
flesh for the life of the world, in that, by dying, He destroyed
death. By the life of the world too, I understand the resurrection; our Lord's death having brought about the resurrection of the whole human race. It may mean too the
sanctified, beatified, spiritual life; for though all have not
attained to this life, yet our Lord gave Himself for the world,
and, as far as lies in Him, the whole world is sanctified.

Aug. Tr.xxvi. 13. AUG. But when does flesh receive the bread which He calls
His flesh? The faithful know and receive the Body of Christ,
if they labour to be the body of Christ. And they become
the body of Christ, if they study to live by the Spirit of
Christ: for that which lives by the Spirit of Christ, is the
body of Christ. This bread the Apostle sets forth, where he
1 Cor. 12, 12. says, *We being many are one body.* O sacrament of mercy,
O sign of unity, O bond of love! Whoso wishes to live,
let him draw nigh, believe, be incorporated, that he may be
quickened.

52. The Jews therefore strove among themselves,
saying, How can this man give us his flesh to eat?

53. Then Jesus said unto them, Verily, verily, I say
unto you, Except ye eat the flesh of the Son of man,
and drink his blood, ye have no life in you.

54. Whoso eateth my flesh, and drinketh my blood,
hath eternal life; and I will raise him up at the last day.

Aug. The Jews not understanding what was the bread of peace, *strove among themselves, saying, How can this man give us His flesh to eat?* Whereas they who eat the bread strive not among themselves, for God makes them to dwell together in unity. Bede. The Jews thought that our Lord would divide His flesh into pieces, and give it them to eat: and so mistaking Him, strove. Chrys. As they thought it impossible that He should do as He said, i. e. give them His flesh to eat, He shews them that it was not only possible, but necessary: *Then said Jesus unto them, Verily, verily, I say unto you, Except ye eat the flesh of the Son of man, and drink His blood, ye have no life in you.* Aug. As if He said, The sense in which that bread is eaten, and the mode of eating it, ye know not; but, *Except ye eat the flesh of the Son of man, and drink His blood, ye have no life in you.* Bede. And that this might not seem addressed to them alone, He declares universally, *Whoso eateth My flesh, and drinketh My blood, hath eternal life.* Aug. And that they might not understand him to speak of this life, and make that an occasion of striving, He adds, *Hath eternal life.* This then he hath not who eateth not that flesh, nor drinketh that blood. The temporal life men may have without Him, the eternal they cannot. This is not true of material food. If we do not take that indeed, we shall not live, neither do we live, if we take it: for either disease, or old age, or some accident kills us after all. Whereas this meat and drink, i. e. the Body and Blood of Christ, is such that he that taketh it not hath not life, and he that taketh it hath life, even life eternal. Theophyl. For it is not the flesh of man simply, but of God: and it makes man divine, by inebriating him, as it were, with divinity. Aug. There are some who promise men deliverance from eternal punishment, if they are washed in Baptism and partake of Christ's Body, whatever lives they live. The Apostle however contradicts them, where he says, *The works of the flesh are manifest, which are these; adultery, fornication, uncleanness, lasciviousness, idolatry, witchcraft, hatred, variance, emulations, wrath, strife, seditions, heresies, envyings, murders, drunkenness, revellings, and such like; of the which I tell you before, as I have also told you in time past, that they which do such things shall not inherit the kingdom of*

Aug. Tr.xxvi. s. 14.

Chrys. Hom. xlvii. 1.

Aug. Tr.xxvi. 15.

Aug. Tr.xxvi. 15.

Theoph. in v. 52.

Aug. de Civ. Dei, lxxi. c. 25.

Gal. 5, 19. et seq.

God. Let us examine what is meant here. He who is in
the unity of His body, (i. e. one of the Christian members,)
the Sacrament of which body the faithful receive when they
communicate at the Altar; he is truly said to eat the body,
and drink the blood of Christ. And heretics and schis-
matics, who are cut off from the unity of the body, may
receive the same Sacrament; but it does not profit them,
nay, rather is hurtful, as tending to make their judgment
heavier, or their forgiveness later. Nor ought they to feel
secure in their abandoned and damnable ways, who, by
the iniquity of their lives, desert righteousness, i. e. Christ;
either by fornication, or other sins of the like kind. Such
are not to be said to eat the body of Christ; forasmuch
as they are not to be counted among the members of Christ.
For, not to mention other things, men cannot be members of
Christ, and at the same time members of an harlot. Aug. By
this meat and drink then, He would have us understand
the society of His body, and His members, which is the
Church, in the predestined, and called, and justified, and
glorified saints and believers. The Sacrament whereof, i. e.
of the unity of the body and blood of Christ, is administered,
in some places daily, in others on such and such days from
the Lord's Table: and from the Lord's Table it is received by
some to their salvation, by others to their condemnation.
But the thing itself of which this is the Sacrament, is for our
salvation to every one who partakes of it, for condemnation
to none. To prevent us supposing that those who, by virtue
of that meat and drink, were promised eternal life, would not
die in the body, He adds, *And I will raise him up at the
last day;* i. e. to that eternal life, a spiritual rest, which the
spirits of the Saints enter into. But neither shall the body
be defrauded of eternal life, but shall be endowed with it at
the resurrection of the dead in the last day.

*Aug.
super
Joan. c.
xxvi.15.*

55. For my flesh is meat indeed, and my blood is
drink indeed.

56. He that eateth my flesh, and drinketh my
blood, dwelleth in me, and I in him.

57. As the living Father hath sent me, and I live

by the Father: so he that eateth me, even he shall live
by me.

58. This is that bread which came down from
heaven: not as your fathers did eat manna, and are
dead: he that eateth of this bread shall live for ever.

59. These things said he in the synagogue, as he
taught in Capernaum.

BEDE. He had said above, *Whoso eateth My flesh and
drinketh My blood, hath eternal life:* and now to shew the
great difference between bodily meat and drink, and the
spiritual mystery of His body and blood, He adds, *For My
flesh is meat indeed, and My blood is drink indeed.* CHRYS. Chrys.
i. e. this is no enigma, or parable, but ye must really eat the Hom. xlvii. 1.
body of Christ; or He means to say that the true meat was
He who saved the soul. AUG. Or thus: Whereas men Aug.
desire meat and drink to satisfy hunger and thirst, this Tr.xxvi. 17.
effect is only really produced by that meat and drink, which
makes the receivers of it immortal and incorruptible; i. e.
the society of Saints, where is peace and unity, full and
perfect. On which account our Lord has chosen for the
types of His body and blood, things which become one out
of many. Bread is a quantity of grains united into one
mass, wine a quantity of grapes squeezed together. Then
He explains what it is to eat His body and drink His blood:
*He that eateth My flesh, and drinketh My blood, dwelleth
in Me, and I in him.* So then to partake of that meat and
that drink, is to dwell in Christ and Christ in thee. He
that dwelleth not in Christ, and in whom Christ dwelleth not,
neither eateth His flesh, nor drinketh His blood: but rather
eateth and drinketh the sacrament of it to his own damnation.
CHRYS. Or, having given a promise of eternal life to those Chrys.
that eat Him, He says this to confirm it: *He that eateth My* Hom. xlvii. 1.
flesh, and drinketh My blood, dwelleth in Me, and I in him.
AUG. As for those, as indeed there are many, who either eat Aug.
that flesh and drink that blood hypocritically, or, who de Verb. Dom.
having eaten, become apostates, do they dwell in Christ, and
Christ in them? Nay, but there is a certain mode of eating
that flesh, and drinking that blood, in the which he that

eateth and drinketh, dwelleth in Christ, and Christ in him.

Aug.   Aug. That is to say, such an one eateth the body and
de Civ.
Dei, l. i. drinketh the blood of Christ not in the sacramental sense,
c. xxv.
Chrys. but in reality. Chrys. And because I live, it is manifest
Hom.   that he will live also: *As the living Father hath sent Me,*
xlvi.
and I live by the Father, even so he that eateth Me, even he
Aug.   *shall live by Me.* As if He said, As the Father liveth,
de Verb.
Dom.   so do I live; adding, lest you should think Him unbegotten,
(Nic.) *By the Father,* meaning that He has His source in the
Father. *He that eateth Me, even he shall live by Me;* the
life here meant is not life simply, but the justified life: for
even unbelievers live, who never eat of that flesh at all. Nor
is it of the general resurrection He speaks, (for all will rise
Aug.   again,) but of the resurrection to glory, and reward. Aug.
Tr.xxvi.
s. 19. He saith not, As I eat the Father, and live by the Father,
so he that eateth Me, even he shall live by Me. For
the Son does not grow better by partaking of the Father,
as we do by partaking of the Son, i. e. of His one body
and blood, which this eating and drinking signifies. So
that His saying, *I live by the Father,* because He is from
Him, must not be understood as detracting from His equality.
Nor do the words, *Even he that eateth Me, the same shall
live by Me,* give us the equality that He has. He does not
equalize, but only mediates between God and man. If,
however, we understand the words, *I live by the Father,* in
c.14,28. the sense of those below, *My Father is greater than I,* then
it is as if He said, That I live by the Father, i. e. refer my
¹ exin- life to Him, as my superior, my¹ humiliation in my incar-
anitio
nation is the cause; but He who lives by Me, lives by Me
by virtue of partaking of My flesh.

Hilar.   HILARY. Of the truth then of the body and blood of Christ,
vii. de
Trin. c. no room for doubting remains: for, by the declaration of our
14.   Lord Himself, and by the teaching of our own faith, the flesh
is really flesh, and the blood really blood. This then is our
principle of life. While we are in the flesh, Christ dwelleth
c.14,19. in us by His flesh. And we shall live by Him, according
as He liveth. If then we live naturally by partaking of Him
according to the flesh, He also liveth naturally by the indwelling of the Father according to the Spirit. His birth
did not give Him an alien or different nature from the

Father. Aug. That we who cannot obtain eternal life of Aug.
ourselves, might live by the eating that bread, He descended _{c. 20.} Tr.xxvi.
from heaven: *This is the bread which cometh down from heaven.*
Hilary. He calls Himself the bread, because He is the origin Hilar.
of His own body. And lest it should be thought that the ^{de Trin.}_{c. 18.}
virtue and nature of the Word had given way to the flesh,
He calls the bread His flesh, that, inasmuch as the bread
came down from heaven, it might be seen that His body was
not of human conception, but a heavenly body. To say that
the bread is His own, is to declare that the Word assumed
His body Himself. Theophyl. For we do not eat God
simply, God being impalpable and incorporeal; nor again,
the flesh of man simply, which would not profit us. But
God having taken flesh into union with Himself, that flesh
is quickening. Not that it has changed its own for the
Divine nature; but, just as heated iron remains iron, with the
action of the heat in it; so our Lord's flesh is quickening, as
being the flesh of the Word of God. Bede. And to shew
the wide interval between the shadow and the light, the
type and the reality, He adds, *Not as your fathers did eat
manna, and are dead: he that eateth of this bread shall live
for ever.* Aug. The death here meant is death eternal. For Aug.
even those who eat Christ are subject to natural death; but _{20.} Tr.xxvi.
they live for ever, because Christ is everlasting life. Chrys. Chrys.
For if it was possible without harvest or fruit of the earth, or ^{Hom.}_{xlvii. 1.}
any such thing, to preserve the lives of the Israelites of old
for forty years, much more will He be able to do this with
that spiritual food, of which the manna is the type. He
knew how precious a thing life was in men's eyes, and
therefore repeats His promise of life often; just as the Old
Testament had done; only that it only offered length of life, Exod.
He life without end. This promise was an abolition of that _{Deut.} 20, 12.
sentence of death, which sin had brought upon us. *These* 22, 7.
things said He in the synagogue, as He taught in Capernaum; ^{1 Kings} 3, 14.
where many displays of His power took place. He taught ^{Ps. 21,} 4; 91,16.
in the synagogue and in the temple, with the view of attract- Prov. 3,
ing the multitude, and as a sign that He was not acting in ^{2.}
opposition to the Father. Bede. Mystically, Capernaum,
which means beautiful town, stands for the world: the
synagogue, for the Jewish people. The meaning is, that our

Lord hath, by the mystery of the incarnation, manifested Himself to the world, and also taught the Jewish people His doctrines.

60. Many therefore of his disciples, when they had heard this, said, This is an hard saying; who can hear it?

61. When Jesus knew in himself that his disciples murmured at it, he said unto them, Doth this offend you?

62. What and if ye shall see the Son of man ascend up where he was before?

63. It is the spirit that quickeneth; the flesh profiteth nothing: the words that I speak unto you, they are spirit, and they are life.

64. But there are some of you that believe not. For Jesus knew from the beginning who they were that believed not, and who should betray him.

65. And he said, Therefore said I unto you, that no man can come unto me, except it were given unto him of my Father.

66. From that time many of his disciples went back, and walked no more with him.

67. Then said Jesus unto the twelve, Will ye also go away?

68. Then Simon Peter answered him, Lord, to whom shall we go? thou hast the words of eternal life.

69. And we believe and are sure that thou art that Christ, the Son of the living God.

70. Jesus answered them, Have not I chosen you twelve, and one of you is a devil?

71. He spake of Judas Iscariot the son of Simon: for he it was that should betray him, being one of the twelve.

AUG. Such is our Lord's discourse. The people did not *Aug.*
perceive that it had a deep meaning, or, that grace went along *Tr.xxvii.* *2.*
with it: but receiving the matter in their own way, and
taking His words in a human sense, understood Him as if
He spoke of cutting of the flesh of the Word into pieces, for
distribution to those who believed on Him: *Many therefore,
not of His enemies, but even of His disciples, when they
heard this, said, This is an hard saying, who can hear it?*
CHRYS. i. e. difficult to receive, too much for their weakness. *Chrys.*
They thought He spoke above Himself, and more loftily than *Hom.* *xlvii. 2.*
He had a right to do; and so said they, *Who can bear it?*
which was answering in fact for themselves, that they could
not. AUG. And if His disciples thought that saying hard, *Aug.*
what would His enemies think? Yet it was necessary to *Tr.xxvii.* *2.*
declare a thing, which would be unintelligible to men. God's
mysteries should draw men's attention, not enmity. THEO-
PHYL. When you hear, however, of His disciples murmuring,
understand not those really such, but rather some who, as
far as their air and behaviour went, seemed to be receiving
instruction from Him. For among His disciples were some
of the people, who were called such, because they stayed
some time with His disciples. AUG. They spoke, however, *Aug.*
so as not to be heard by Him. But He, who knew what was *Tr.xxvii.* *3.*
in them, heard within Himself: *When Jesus knew within Himself that His disciples murmured at it, He said unto them, Doth
this offend you?* ALCUIN. i. e. that I said, you should eat My
flesh, and drink My blood. CHRYS. The revelation however *Chrys.*
of these hidden things was a mark of His Divinity: hence the *Hom.* *xlvii. 2.*
meaning of what follows; *And if ye shall see the Son of man
ascend up where He was before;* supply, What will ye say?
He said the same to Nathanael, *Because I said to thee, I saw
thee under the fig tree, believest thou? Thou shalt see greater
things than these.* He does not add difficulty to difficulty,
but to convince them by the number and greatness of His
doctrines. For if He had merely said that He came down
from heaven, without adding any thing further, he would have
offended His hearers more; but by saying that His flesh is
the life of the world, and that as He was sent by the living
Father, so He liveth by the Father; and at last by adding
that He came down from heaven, He removed all doubt. Nor

does He mean to scandalize His disciples, but rather to remove their scandal. For so long as they thought Him the Son of Joseph, they could not receive His doctrines; but if they once believed that He had come down from heaven, and would ascend thither, they would be much more willing and able to admit them. AUG. Or, these words are an answer to their mistake. They supposed that He was going to distribute His body in bits: whereas He tells them now, that He should ascend to heaven whole and entire: *What and if ye shall see the Son of man ascend up where He was before?* ye will then see that He does not distribute His body in the way ye think. Again; Christ became the Son of man, of the Virgin Mary here upon earth, and took flesh upon Him: He says then, *What and if ye shall see the Son of man ascend up where He was before?* to let us know that Christ, God and man, is one person, not two; and the object of one faith, not a quaternity, but a Trinity. He was the Son of man in heaven, as He was Son of God upon earth; the Son of God upon earth by assumption of the flesh, the Son of man in heaven, by the unity of the person. THEOPHYL. Do not suppose from this that the body of Christ came down from heaven, as the heretics Marcion and Apollinarius say; but only that the Son of God and the Son of man are one and the same. CHRYS. He tries to remove their difficulties in another way, as follows, *It is the spirit that quickeneth, the flesh profiteth nothing:* that is to say, You ought to understand My words in a spiritual sense: he who understands them carnally is profited nothing. To interpret carnally is to take a proposition in its bare literal meaning, and allow no other. But we should not judge of mysteries in this way; but examine them with the inward eye; i. e. understand them spiritually. It was carnal to doubt how our Lord could give His flesh to eat. What then? Is it not real flesh? Yea, verily. In saying then that *the flesh profiteth nothing,* He does not speak of His own flesh, but that of the carnal hearer of His word. AUG. Or thus, *the flesh profiteth nothing.* They had understood by His flesh, as it were, of a carcase, that was to be cut up, and sold in the shambles, not of a body animated by the spirit. Join the spirit to the flesh, and it profiteth

Chrys.
Hom.
xlvii. 3.

Aug.
Tract.
xxvii.
s. 5.

much: for if the flesh profited not, the Word would not have become flesh, and dwelt among us. The Spirit hath done much for our salvation, by means of the flesh. AUG. For the flesh does not cleanse of itself, but by the Word who assumed it: which Word, being the principle of life in all things, having taken up soul and body, cleanseth the souls and bodies of those that believe. *It is the spirit*, then, *that quickeneth: the flesh profiteth nothing;* i. e. the flesh as they understood it. I do not, He seems to say, give My body to be eaten in this sense. He ought not to think of the flesh carnally: *The words that I speak unto you, they are spirit, and they are life.* CHRYS. i. e. are spiritual, have nothing carnal in them, produce no effects of the natural sort; not being under the dominion of that law of necessity, and order of nature established on earth. AUG. If then thou understandest them spiritually, they are life and spirit to thee: if carnally, even then they are life and spirit, but not to thee. Our Lord declares that in eating His body, and drinking His blood, we dwell in Him, and He in us. But what has the power to affect this, except love? *The love of God is shed abroad in our hearts by the Holy Spirit, which is given to us.* CHRYS. Having spoken of His words being taken carnally, He adds, *But there are some of you that believe not.* *Some*, He says, not including His disciples in the number. This insight shews His high nature. AUG. He says not, There are some among you who understand not; but gives the reason why they do not understand. The Prophet said, *Except ye believe, ye shall not understand*.* For how can he who opposes be quickened? An adversary, though he avert not his face, yet closes his mind to the ray of light which should penetrate him. But let men believe, and open their eyes, and they will be enlightened. CHRYS. To let you know that it was before these words, and not after, that the people murmured and were offended, the Evangelist adds, *For Jesus knew from the beginning, who they were that believed not, and who should betray Him.* THEOPHYL. The Evangelist wishes to shew us, that He knew all things before the foundation of the world: which was a proof of His divinity. AUG. And after distinguishing

Chrys. Hom. xlvii. 2.

Aug. Tr.xxxvii.

Rom. 5, 5.

Chrys. Tr.xlvii. 2.

Aug. Tr.xxxvii. s. 7.

Is. 7, 9.

Chrys. Tr.xxxvii. 2.

Aug. Tr.xxxvii. 7.

---

* Be established.   Non permanebitis, Vulg.

those who believed from those who did not believe, our Lord gives the reason of the unbelief of the latter, *And He said, Therefore said I unto you, that no man can come unto Me, except it were given him of My Father.* CHRYS. As if He said, Men's unbelief does not disturb or astonish Me: I know to whom the Father hath given to come to Me. He mentions the Father, to shew first that He had no eye to His own glory; secondly, that God was His Father, and not Joseph. AUG. So then (our) faith is given to us: and no small gift it is. Wherefore rejoice if thou believest; but be not lifted up, for what hast thou which thou didst not receive? And that this grace is given to some, and not to others, no one can doubt, without going against the plainest declarations of Scripture. As for the question, why it is not given to all, this cannot disquiet the believer, who knows that in consequence of the sin of one man, all are justly liable to condemnation; and that no blame could attach to God, even if none were pardoned; it being of His great mercy only that so many are. And why He pardons one rather than another, rests with Him, whose judgments are unsearchable, and His ways past finding out.

And from that time many of the disciples went back, and walked no more with Him. CHRYS. He does not say, withdrew[b], but *went back*, i. e. from being good hearers, from the belief which they once had. AUG. Being cut off from the body, their life was gone. They were no longer in the body; they were created among the unbelieving. There went back not a few, but many after Satan, not after Christ; as the Apostle says of some women, *For some had already turned aside after Satan.* Our Lord says to Peter, *Get thee behind Me.* He does not tell Peter to go after Satan. CHRYS. But it may be asked, what reason was there for speaking words to them which did not edify, but might rather have injured them? It was very useful and necessary; for this reason, they had been just now urgent in petitioning for bodily food, and reminding Him of that which had been given to their fathers. So He reminds them here of spiritual food; to shew that all those miracles were typical. They ought not then to have been offended, but should have

Marginal notes:
Chrys. Hom. xlvi. 2.
Aug. Tr.xxvii. 7.
1 Cor. 4, 7.
Chrys. Hom. xlvii. 3.
Aug. Tr.xxvii. 8.
1 Tim. 5, 15.
Chrys. Hom. xlvi. 2.

[b] οὐκ ἀνεχώρησαν, ἀλλ' ἀπῆλθον εἰς τὰ ὀπίσω.

enquired of Him further. The scandal was owing to their
fatuity, not to the difficulty of the truths declared by our
Lord. Aug. And perhaps this took place for our consola- Aug.
tion; since it sometimes happens that a man says what is Tr.xxvii. g.
true, and what He says is not understood, and they which
hear are offended and go. Then the man is sorry he spoke
what was true; for he says to himself, I ought not to have
spoken it; and yet our Lord was in the same case. He
spoke the truth, and destroyed many. But He is not
disturbed at it, because He knew from the beginning which
would believe. We, if this happens to us, are disturbed.
Let us desire consolation then from our Lord's example; and
withal use caution in our speech. BEDE. Our Lord knew well
the intentions of the other disciples which stayed, as to staying
or going; but yet He put the question to them, in order to
prove their faith, and hold it up to imitation: *Then said
Jesus unto the twelve, Will ye also go away?* CHRYS. This Chrys.
was the right way to retain them. Had He praised them, Hom. xlvii. 3.
they would naturally, as men do, have thought that they
were conferring a favour upon Christ, by not leaving Him:
by shewing, as He did, that He did not need their company,
He made them hold the more closely by Him. He does
not say, however, Go away, as this would have been to cast
them off, but asks whether they wished to go away; thus preventing their staying with Him from any feeling of shame or
necessity: for to stay from necessity would be the same as going
away. Peter, who loved his brethren, replies for the whole
number, *Lord, to whom shall we go?* Aug. As if he said, Thou Aug.
castest us from Thee: give us another to whom we shall go, Tr.xxvii. s. 9.
if we leave Thee. CHRYS. A speech of the greatest love: Chrys.
proving that Christ was more precious to them than father Hom. xlvii. 3.
or mother. And that it might not seem to be said, from
thinking that there was no one whose guidance they could
look to, he adds, *Thou hast the words of eternal life:*
which shewed that he remembered his Master's words,
I will raise Him up, and, *hath eternal life.* The Jews
said, *Is not this the Son of Joseph?* how differently Peter:
*We believe and are sure, that Thou art that Christ, the
Son of the living God.* Aug. For we believed, in order Aug.
to know. Had we wished first to know, and then to Tr.xxvii. s. 9.
believe, we could never have been able to believe. This

we believe, and know, *that Thou art the Christ the Son of God;* i. e. that Thou art eternal life, and that in Thy flesh and blood Thou givest what Thou art Thyself. CHRYS. Peter however having said, *We believe,* our Lord excepts Judas from the number of those who believed: *Jesus answered them, Have not I chosen you twelve, and one of you is a devil?* i. e. Do not suppose that, because you have followed Me, I shall not reprove the wicked among you. It is worth enquiring, why the disciples say nothing here, whereas afterwards they ask in fear, *Lord, is it I?* But Peter had not yet been told, *Get thee behind Me, Satan;* and therefore had as yet no fear of this sort. Our Lord however does not say here, *One of you* shall betray Me, but, *is a devil:* so that they did not know what the speech meant, and thought that it was only a case of wickedness in general, that He was reproving. The Gentiles on the subject of election blame Christ foolishly. His election does not impose any necessity upon the person with respect to the future, but leaves it in the power of His will to be saved or perish. BEDE. Or we must say, that He elected the eleven for one purpose, the twelfth for another: the eleven to fill the place of Apostles, and persevere in it unto the end; the twelfth to the service of betraying Him, which was the means of saving the human race. AUG. He was elected to be an involuntary and unconscious instrument of producing the greatest good. For as the wicked turn the good works of God to an evil use, so reversely God turns the evil works of man to good. What can be worse than what Judas did? Yet our Lord made a good use of his wickedness; allowing Himself to be betrayed, that He might redeem us. In, *Have I not chosen you twelve,* twelve seems to be a sacred number used in the case of those, who were to spread the doctrine of the Trinity through the four quarters of the world. Nor was the virtue of that number impaired, by one perishing; inasmuch as another was substituted in his room. GREG. *One of you is a devil:* the body [b] is here named after its head. CHRYS. Mark the wisdom of Christ: He neither, by exposing him, makes him shameless and contentious; nor again emboldens him, by allowing him to think himself concealed.

Chrys. Hom. xlvii. 3.

Matt. 26, 22. Mat. 16, 23.

Aug. Tr.xxvii. s. 10.

Greg. Moral. l. xiii. c. xxxiv.

Chrys. Hom. xlvii. 4.

---

[b] i. e. the whole body of wicked. Judas, as being one of that body, is named after its head, the devil.

CHAP. VII.

1. After these things Jesus walked in Galilee: for he would not walk in Jewry, because the Jews sought to kill him.

2. Now the Jews' feast of tabernacles was at hand.

3. His brethren therefore said unto him, Depart hence, and go into Judæa, that thy disciples also may see the works that thou doest.

4. For there is no man that doeth any thing in secret, and he himself seeketh to be known openly. If thou do these things, shew thyself to the world.

5. For neither did his brethren believe in him.

6. Then Jesus said unto them, My time is not yet come: but your time is alway ready.

7. The world cannot hate you: but me it hateth, because I testify of it, that the works thereof are evil.

8. Go ye up unto this feast: I go not up yet unto this feast; for my time is not yet fully come.

Aug. As the believer in Christ would have in time to come to hide himself from persecution, that no guilt might attach to such concealment, the Head began with doing Himself, what He sanctioned in the member; *After these things Jesus walked in Galilee: for he would not walk in Jewry, because the Jews sought to kill Him.* Bede. The connexion of this passage admits of much taking place in the interval previously. Judæa and Galilee are divisions of the province of Palestine. Judæa has its name from the tribe of Judah; but it embraces not only the territories of Judah, but of Benjamin, all of which were called Judæa, because Judah

Aug.Tr. xxviii.2.

was the royal tribe. Galilee has its name, from the milky,
i. e. white, colour of its inhabitants; Galilee being Greek for
milk. AUG. It is not meant that our Lord *could* not walk
among the Jews, and escape being killed; for He had this
power, whenever He chose to shew it: but He set the
example of so doing, as an accommodation to our weakness.
He had not lost His power, but He indulged our frailty.
CHRYS. That is to say, He displayed the attribute both of
divinity and humanity. He fled from His persecutors as
man, He remained and appeared amongst them as God;
being really both. THEOPHYL. He withdrew too now to
Galilee, because the hour of His passion was not yet come;
and He thought it useless to stay in the midst of His enemies, when the effect would only have been to irritate them
the more. The time at which this happened is then given;
Now the Jews' feast of tabernacles was at hand. AUG.
What the feast of tabernacles is, we read in the Scriptures.
They used to make tents on the festival, like those in which
they lived during their journey in the desert, after their
departure from Egypt. They celebrated this feast in commemoration of the good things the Lord had done for them;
though they were the very people who were about to slay
the Lord. It is called the day of the feast[*], though it lasted
many days. CHRYS. It appears here, that a considerable
time had passed since the last events. For when our Lord
sat upon the mount, it was near the feast of the Passover,
and now it is the feast of tabernacles: so that in the five
intermediate months the Evangelist has related nothing but
the miracle of the loaves, and the conversation with those
who ate of them. As our Lord was unceasingly working
miracles, and holding disputes with people, the Evangelists
could not relate all; but only aimed at giving those, in which
complaint or opposition had followed on the part of the Jews,
as was the case here. THEOPHYL. His brethren saw that
He was not preparing to go to the feast: *His brethren therefore
said unto him, Depart hence, and go into Judæa.* BEDE.
Meaning to say, Thou doest miracles, and only a few see
them: go to the royal city, where the rulers are, that they
may see Thy miracles, and so Thou obtain praise. And as

Aug.Tr.
xxviii.2.

Chrys.
Hom.
xlviii.1.

Aug.Tr.
xxviii.3.

Chrys.
Hom.
xlviii.1.

---

[*] St. Augustine goes by the Vulgate, dies festus.

our Lord had not brought all His disciples with Him, but left many behind in Judæa, they add, *That Thy disciples also may see the works that Thou doest.* THEOPHYL. i. e. the multitudes that follow Thee. They do not mean the twelve, but the others that had communication with Him. AUG. When you hear of our Lord's brethren, you must understand the kindred of Mary, not her offspring after our Lord's birth. For as the body of our Lord once only lay in the sepulchre, and neither before, nor after that once ; so could not the womb of Mary have possibly conceived any other mortal offspring. Our Lord's works did not escape His disciples, but they escaped His brethren ; hence their suggestion, *That Thy disciples may see the works that Thou doest.* They speak according to the wisdom of the flesh, to the Word that was made flesh, and add, *For there is no man that doeth any thing in secret, and he himself seeketh to be known openly. If Thou do these things, shew Thyself to the world;* as if to say, Thou doest miracles, do them in the eyes of the world, that the world may honour Thee. Their admonitions aim at procuring glory for Him ; and this very thing, viz. aiming at human glory, proved that they did not believe in Him, as we next read, *For neither did His brethren believe on Him.* They were Christ's kindred, but they were on that very account above believing in Him. CHRYS. It is striking to observe the great sincerity of the Evangelists ; that they are not ashamed to mention things which appear to be to our Lord's disadvantage, but take particular care to tell us of them. It is a considerable reflexion on our Lord, that His brethren do not believe on Him. The beginning of their speech has a friendly appearance about it : but there is much bitterness in it, thus charging Him with the motives of fear and vain glory ; *No man,* say they, *doeth any thing in secret :* this was reproaching Him tacitly with fear ; and was an insinuation too that His miracles had not been real and solid ones. In what follows, *And he himself seeketh to be known openly,* they taunt Him with the love of glory. Christ however answers them mildly, teaching us not to take the advice of people ever so inferior to ourselves angrily ; *Then Jesus said unto them, My time is not yet come: but your time is alway ready.* BEDE. This is no contradiction

Aug.Tr. xxviii.3.

Chrys. Hom. xlviii. 1, 2.

Gal. 4, 4. to what the Apostle says, *But when the fulness of time was come, God sent forth His Son.* Our Lord referring here to Aug.Tr. the time not of His nativity, but of His glorification. AUG. xxviii.5. They gave Him advice to pursue glory, and not allow Himself to remain in concealment and obscurity; appealing altogether to worldly and secular motives. But our Lord was laying down another road to that very exaltation, viz. humility: *My time*, He says, i. e. the time of My glory, when I shall come to judge on high, *is not yet come; but your time*, i. e. the glory of the world, *is always ready.* And let us, who are the Lord's body, when insulted by the lovers of this world, say, Your time is ready: ours is not yet come. Our country is a lofty one, the way to it is low. Whoso Chrys. rejecteth the way, why seeketh he the country? CHRYS. Hom. xlviii. 2. Or there seems to be another meaning concealed in the words; perhaps they intended to betray Him to the Jews; and therefore He says, *My time is not yet come*, i. e. the time of My cross and death: *but your time is always ready;* for though you are always with the Jews, they will not kill you, because you are of the same mind with them: *The world cannot hate you; but Me it hateth, because I testify of it, that the works thereof are evil:* as if He said, How can the world hate them who have the same wishes and aims with itself? It hateth Me, because I reprove it. I seek not then glory from men; inasmuch as I hesitate not to reprove them, though I know that I am hated in consequence, and that My life is aimed at. Here we see that the hatred of the Jews was owing to His reproofs, not to His breaking the sabbath. THEOPHYL. Our Lord brings two arguments in answer to their two charges. To the charge of fear He answers, that He reproves the deeds of the world, i. e. of those who love worldly things; which He would not do, if He were under the influence of fear; and He replies to the charge of vain glory, by sending them to the feast, *Go ye up unto this feast.* Had He been possessed at all with the desire for glory, He would have kept them with Him: for Chrys. the vain glorious like to have many followers. CHRYS. This Hom. xlviii.2. is to shew too, that, while He does not wish to humour them, He still allows them to observe the Jewish ordinances. Aug.Tr. xxviii. AUG. Or He seems to say, *Go ye up to this feast,* and seek 5. 8.

for human glory, and enlarge your carnal pleasures, and forget heavenly things.

I go not up unto this feast; CHRYS. i. e. not with you, Chrys. *for My time is not yet full come.* It was at the next passover Hom. xlviii.2. that He was to be crucified. AUG. Or My time, i. e. the Aug. time of My glory, is not yet come. That will be My feast Tract. day; not a day which passeth and is gone, like holidays xxviii. s. here: but one which remaineth for ever. Then will be festivity; joy without end, eternity without stain, sunshine without a cloud.

9. When he had said these words unto them, he abode still in Galilee.

10. But when his brethren were gone up, then went he also up unto the feast, not openly, but as it were in secret.

11. Then the Jews sought him at the feast, and said, Where is he?

12. And there was much murmuring among the people concerning him: for some said, He is a good man: others said, Nay; but he deceiveth the people.

13. Howbeit no man spake openly of him for fear of the Jews.

THEOPHYL. Our Lord at first declares that He will not go up to the feast, (*I go not up with you,*) in order not to expose Himself to the rage of the Jews; and therefore we read, that, *When He had said these words unto them, He abode still in Galilee.* Afterwards, however, He goes up; *But when His brethren were gone up, then went He also up unto the feast.* AUG. He went up, however, not to get temporary glory, but Aug. to teach wholesome doctrine, and remind men of the eternal Tract. xxviii. feast. CHRYS. He goes up, not to suffer, but to teach. And s. He goes up secretly; because, though He could have gone Chrys. openly, and kept the violence and impetuosity of the Jews xlviii. in check, as He had often done before; yet to do this every s. 2. time, would have disclosed His divinity; and he wished to establish the fact of His incarnation, and to teach us the way of life. And He went up privately too, to shew us what

s

we ought to do, who cannot check our persecutors. It is not said, however, in secret, but, *as it were in secret;* to show that it was done as a kind of economy. For had He done all things as God, how should we of this world know what to do, when we fell into danger? ALCUIN. Or, He went up in secret, because He did not seek the favour of men, and took no pleasure in pomp, and being followed about with

non occ. crowds. BEDE. The mystical meaning is, that to all those carnal persons who seek human glory, the Lord remains in Galilee; the meaning of which name is, " passing over;" applying to those his members who pass from vice to virtue, and make progress in the latter. And our Lord Himself delayed to go up, signifying that Christ's members seek not temporal but eternal glory. And He went up secretly,

Ps. 45, 14.
1 Tim. 1, 5.

because all[b] glory is from within: that is, *from a pure heart and good conscience, and faith unfeigned.* AUG. Or the meaning is, that all the ceremonial of the ancient people was

Aug. Tract. xxviii. 9.

the figure of what was to be; such as the feast of tabernacles. Which figure is now unveiled to us. Our Lord went up in secret, to represent the figurative system. He concealed Himself at the feast itself, because the feast itself signified, that the members of Christ were in a strange country. For he dwells in the tents, who regards himself as a stranger in the world. The word scenopegia here means the feast of

Chrys. Hom. xlix. 1.

tabernacles. CHRYS. *Then the Jews sought Him at the feast, and said, Where is He?* out of hatred and enmity; for they would not call Him by His name. There was not much reverence or religion in this observance of the feast, when they wanted to make it an opportunity of seizing

Aug. Tract. xxviii. s. 11.

Christ. AUG. *And there was much murmuring in the people concerning Him.* A murmuring arising from disagreement. *For some said, He is a good man: others said, Nay; but He seduceth the people.* Whoever had any spark of grace, said, *He is a good man;* the rest, *Nay, but He seduceth the people.* That such was said of Him, Who was God, is a consolation to any Christian, of whom the same may be said. If to seduce be to decide, Christ was not a seducer, nor can any Christian be. But if by seducing be meant bringing a person by persuasion out of one way of thinking into another,

[b] The king's daughter is all glorious within.

then we must enquire from what, and to what. If from good to evil, the seducer is an evil man; if from evil to good, a good one. And would that we were all called, and really were, such seducers. CHRYS. The former, I think, was the opinion of the multitude, the one, viz. who pronounced Him a good man; the latter the opinion of the priests and rulers; as is shewn by their saying, *He deceiveth the people*, not, He deceiveth us. AUG. *Howbeit no man spake openly of Him, for fear of the Jews;* none, that is, of those who said, *He is a good man.* They who said, *He deceiveth the people,* proclaimed their opinion openly enough; while the former only dared whisper theirs. CHRYS. Observe, the corruption is in the rulers: the common people are sound in their judgment, but have not liberty of speech, as is generally their case. *(Chrys. Hom. xlix. 1. Aug. Tract. xxviii. 12. Chrys. Hom. xlix. 1.)*

14. Now about the midst of the feast Jesus went up into the temple, and taught.

15. And the Jews marvelled, saying, How knoweth this man letters, having never learned?

16. Jesus answered them, and said, My doctrine is not mine, but his that sent me.

17. If any man will do his will, he shall know of the doctrine, whether it be of God, or whether I speak of myself.

18. He that speaketh of himself seeketh his own glory: but he that seeketh his glory that sent him, the same is true, and no unrighteousness is in him.

CHRYS. Our Lord delays His visit, in order to excite men's attention, and goes up not the first day, but about the middle of the feast: *Now about the midst of the feast Jesus went up into the temple, and taught.* Those who had been searching for Him, when they saw Him thus suddenly appear, would be more attentive to His teaching, both favourers and enemies; the one to admire and profit by it; the other to find an opportunity of laying hands on Him. THEOPHYL. At the commencement of the feast, men would be attending more to the preachings of the festival itself; and afterwards *(Chrys. Hom. xlix. 1. Aug.)*

Aug.
Tract.
xxvii.
s. 60.
would be better disposed to hear Christ. AUG. The feast seems, as far as we can judge, to have lasted several days. And therefore it is said, "about the middle of the feast day^c:" i. e. when as many days of that feast had passed, as were to come. So that His assertion, *I go not up yet to this feast day,* (i. e. to the first or second day, as you would wish me,) was strictly fulfilled. For He went up afterwards, about the

Aug. de
Quæst.
Nov. et
Vet.
Test. 2.
78.
middle of the feast. AUG. In going there too, He went up, not to the feast day, but to the light. They had gone to enjoy the pleasures of the festival, but Christ's feast day was that on which by His Passion He redeemed the world.

Aug.
super
Joan.
Tract.
xxix. 2.
AUG. He who had before concealed Himself, taught and spoke openly, and was not laid hold on. The one was intended for an example to us, the other to testify His power.

Chrys.
Hom.
xlix. 1.
CHRYS. What His teaching is, the Evangelist does not say; but that it was very wonderful is shewn by its effect even upon those who had accused Him of deceiving the people, who turned round and began to admire Him: *And the Jews marvelled, saying, How knoweth this Man letters, having never learned?* See how perverse they are even in their admiration. It is not His doctrine they admire,

Aug.
Tract.
xxix. 2.
but another thing altogether. AUG. All, it would appear, admired, but all were not converted. Whence then the admiration? Many knew where He was born, and how He had been educated; but had never seen Him learning letters. Yet now they heard Him disputing on the law, and bringing forward its testimonies. No one could do this, who had not read the law; no one could read who had not learnt letters;

Chrys.
Hom.
xlix. 1.
and this raised their wonder. CHRYS. Their wonder might have led them to infer, that our Lord became possessed of this learning in some divine way, and not by any human process. But they would not acknowledge this, and contented themselves with wondering. So our Lord repeated it to them: *Jesus answered them and said, My doctrine is not*

Aug.
Tract.
xxix.
s. 3.
Mine, but His that sent Me. AUG. *Mine is not mine,* appears a contradiction; why did He not say, This doctrine is not Mine? Because the doctrine of the Father being the Word of the Father, and Christ Himself being that Word, Christ Himself is the doctrine of the Father. And therefore He

^c Vulgate taken as above literally.

calls the doctrine both His own, and the Father's.   A word
must be a word of some one's.   What is so much Thine as
Thou, and what is so much not Thine as Thou, if what Thou
art, Thou art of another.   His saying then, *My doctrine is
not Mine own*, seems briefly to express the truth, that He is
not from Himself; it refutes the Sabellian heresy, which dares
to assert that the Son is the same as the Father, there being
only two names for one thing.   CHRYS. Or He calls it His ^{Chrys.}
own, inasmuch as He taught it; not His own, inasmuch as ^{Hom.} _{xlix. 2.}
the doctrine was of the Father.   If all things however which
the Father hath are His, the doctrine for this very reason is
His; i. e. because it is the Father's.   Rather that He says,
Is not Mine own, shews very strongly, that His doctrine and
the Father's are one: as if He said, I differ nothing from
Him; but so act, that it may be thought I say and do
nothing else than doth the Father.   AUG. Or thus: In one ^{Aug. de} ^{Trin. i.} _{c. xi.}
sense He calls it His, in another sense not His; according
to the form of the Godhead His, according to the form of
the servant not His.   AUG. Should any one however not ^{Aug.} ^{Tract.} _{xxix.}
understand this, let him hear the advice which immediately
follows from our Lord: *If any man will do His will, he shall* ^{s. 6.}
*know of the doctrine, whether it be of God, or whether I
speak of Myself.*   What meaneth this, *If any man will do
His will?*   To do His will is to believe on Him, as He Him-
self says, *This is the work of God, that ye believe on Him* ^{c. 6, 29.}
whom He hath sent.   And who does not know, that to work
the work of God, is to do His will?   To know is to understand.   Do not then seek to understand in order to believe,
but believe in order to understand, for, *Except ye believe,* ^{Is. 7, 9.}
ye shall not understand.   CHRYS. This is as much as to ^{Vulg.} ^{Chrys.}
say, Put away the anger, envy, and hatred which you have ^{Hom.} _{xlix. 1.}
towards Me, and there will be nothing to prevent your know-
ing, that the words which I speak are from God.   Then He
brings in an irresistible argument taken from human experience: *He that speaketh of himself, seeketh his own
glory:* as if to say, He who aims at establishing some
doctrine of his own, does so for no purpose, but to get glory.
But I seek the glory of Him that sent me, and wish to
teach you for His, i. e. another's, sake: and then it follows,
But he that seeketh His glory that sent Him, the same is

true, and there is no unrighteousness in Him. THEOPHYL.
As if He said, I speak the truth, because.My doctrine containeth the truth : there is no unrighteousness in Me, because

Aug.
Tract.
xxix.
s. 8.

I usurp not another's glory.   AUG. He who seeketh his own
glory is Antichrist.   But our Lord set us an example of
humility, in that being found in fashion as a man, He sought
His Father's glory, not His own.   Thou, when thou doest
good, takest glory to thyself, when thou doest evil, upbraidest

Chrys.
Hom.
xlix 2.

God.   CHRYS. Observe, the reason why He spake so humbly
of Himself, is to let men know, that He does not aim at
glory, or power; and to accommodate Himself to their
weakness, and to teach them moderation, and a humble, as
distinguished from an assuming, way of speaking of themselves.

19. Did not Moses give you the law, and yet none
of you keepeth the law? Why go ye about to kill me?

20. The people answered and said, Thou hast a
devil: who goeth about to kill thee?

21. Jesus answered and said unto them, I have
done one work, and ye all marvel.

22. Moses therefore gave unto you circumcision:
(not because it is of Moses, but of the fathers:) and
ye on the sabbath day circumcise a man.

23. If a man on the sabbath day receive circumcision, that the law of Moses should not be broken;
are ye angry at me, because I have made a man every
whit whole on the sabbath day?

24. Judge not according to the appearance, but
judge righteous judgment.

Chrys.
Hom.
xlix. 2.

CHRYS. The Jews brought two charges against Christ; one,
that He broke the sabbath; the other, that He said God was
His Father, making Himself equal with God.   The latter
He confirmed first by shewing, that He did nothing in
opposition to God, but that both taught the same.   Then
turning to the charge of breaking the sabbath, He says,
Did not Moses give you a law, and none of you keepeth the

law? as much as to say, The law says, Thou shalt not kill,
whereas ye kill. And then, *Why go ye about to kill Me?* As
if to say, If I broke a law to heal a man, it was a transgression, but a beneficial one; whereas ye transgress for an
evil end; so you have no right to judge Me for breaking the
law. He rebukes them then for two things; first, because they
went about to kill Him; secondly, because they were going
about to kill another, when they had not even any right to
judge Him. AUG. Or He means to say, that if they kept
the law, they would see Him pointed to in every part of it,
and would not seek to kill Him, when He came. The
people return an answer quite away from the subject, and
only shewing their angry feelings: *The people answered and
said, Thou hast a devil: who goeth about to kill Thee?* He
who cast out devils, was told that He had a devil. Our
Lord however, in no way disturbed, but retaining all the
serenity of truth, returned not evil for evil, or railing for
railing. BEDE. Wherein He left us an example to take it
patiently, whenever wrong censures are passed upon us,
and not answer them by asserting the truth, though able
to do so, but rather by some wholesome advice to the persons; as doth our Lord: *Jesus answered and said unto
them, I have done one work, and ye all marvel.* AUG. As
if He said, What if ye saw all My works? For all that they
saw going on in the world was of His working, but they saw
not Him Who made all things. But He did one thing, made
a man whole on the sabbath day, and they were in commotion: as if, when any one of them recovered from a
disease on the sabbath, he who made him whole were any
other than He, who had offended them by making one man
whole on the sabbath. CHRYS. *Ye marvel,* i. e. are disturbed, are in commotion. Observe how well He argues with
them from the law. He wishes to prove that this work was
not a violation of the law; and shews accordingly that there
are many things more important than the law for the observance of the sabbath, by the observance of which that law is
not broken but fulfilled. *Moses therefore,* He says, *gave
unto you circumcision, not because it is of Moses, but of the
fathers, and ye on the sabbath day circumcise a man.*
AUG. As if He said, Ye have done well to receive circum-

Marginal notes: Aug. Tr. xxx. 2. — Aug. Tr. xxx. s. 3. — Chrys. Hom. xlix. 3. — Aug. Tr. xxx. s. 4.

cision from Moses, *not because it is of Moses, but of the fathers;* for Abraham first received circumcision from the Lord. *And ye circumcise on the sabbath.* Moses has convicted you: ye received a law to circumcise on the eighth day; and ye received a law to rest on the seventh day. If the eighth day after a child is born happen to be the sabbath, ye circumcise the child; because circumcision appertaineth to, is a kind of sign of, salvation; and men ought not to rest from the work of salvation on the sabbath. ALCUIN. Circumcision was given for three reasons; first, as a sign of Abraham's great faith; secondly, to distinguish the Jews from other nations; thirdly, that the receiving of it on the organ of virility, might admonish us to observe chastity both of body and mind. And circumcision then possessed the same virtue that baptism does now; only that the gate was not yet open. Our Lord concludes: *If a man on the sabbath day receive circumcision, that the law of Moses should not be broken: are ye angry at Me because I have made a man every whit whole on the sabbath day?* CHRYS. Which is as much as to tell them, The breaking of the sabbath in circumcision is a keeping of the law; and in the same way I by healing on the sabbath have kept the law. Ye, who are not the legislators, enforce the law beyond its proper bounds; whereas Moses made the law give way to the observance of a commandment, which did not come from the law, but from the fathers. His saying, *I have made a man every whit whole on the sabbath day,* implies that circumcision was a partial recovering. AUG. Circumcision also was perhaps a type of our Lord Himself. For what is circumcision but a robbing of the flesh, to signify the robbing the heart of its carnal lusts. And therefore it was not without reason that it was applied to that member by which the mortal creature is propagated: *for by one man sin entered into the world.* And therefore every one is born with the foreskin, because every one is born with the fault of his propagation. And God does not change us either from the corruption of our birth, or from that we have contracted ourselves by a bad life, except by Christ: and therefore they circumcised with knives of stone, to prefigure Christ, who is the stone; and on the eighth day, because our Lord's resurrection took place on the day after the seventh day;

Chrys. Hom. xlix. 3.

Aug. Tr. xxx. 5.

Rom. 5, 12.

vite propa-genis

which resurrection circumcises us, i. e. destroys our carnal
appetites. Regard this, saith our Lord, as a type of My
good work in making a man every whit whole on the sabbath
day: for he was healed, that he might be whole in body,
and he believed, that he might be whole in mind. Ye are
forbidden indeed to do servile work on the sabbath; but
is it a servile work to heal on the sabbath? Ye eat and
drink on the sabbath, because it is necessary for your
health: which shews that works of healing are by no means
to be omitted on the sabbath. CHRYS. He does not say, Chrys.
however, I have done a greater work than circumcision; Hom.
but only states the matter of fact, and leaves the judgment xlix. 3.
to them, saying, *Judge not according to the appearance, but
judge righteous judgment:* as if to say, Do not, because
Moses has a greater name with you than I, decide by
degree of personal eminence; but decide by the nature of the
thing itself, for this is to judge righteously. No one however has blamed Moses for making the sabbath give place
to the commandment of circumcision, which was not derived from the law, but from another source. Moses then
commands the law to be broken to give effect to a commandment not of the law: and he is more worthy of credit
than you. AUG. What our Lord here tells us to avoid, in Aug.
judging by the person, is very difficult in this world not to Tr.xxx.
do. His admonition to the Jews is an admonition to us as s. 7.
well; for every sentence which our Lord uttered, was written
for us, and is preserved to us, and is read for our profit.
Our Lord is above; but our Lord, as the truth, is here as
well. The body with which He rose can be only in one
place, but His truth is diffused every where. Who then is
he who judges not by the person? He who loves all alike.
For it is not the paying men different degrees of honour
according to their situation, that will make us chargeable
with accepting persons. There may be a case to decide
between father and son: we should not put the son on an
equality with the father in point of honour; but, in respect
of truth, if he have the better cause, we should give him the
preference; and so give to each their due, that justice do
not destroy desert[d].

---

[d] ut non perdat equitas meritum.

25. Then said some of them of Jerusalem, Is not this he, whom they seek to kill?

26. But, lo, he speaketh boldly, and they say nothing unto him. Do the rulers know indeed that this is the very Christ?

27. Howbeit we know this man whence he is: but when Christ cometh, no man knoweth whence he is.

28. Then cried Jesus in the temple as he taught, saying, Ye both know me, and ye know whence I am: and I am not come of myself, but he that sent me is true, whom ye know not.

29. But I know him: for I am from him, and he hath sent me.

30. Then they sought to take him: but no man laid hands on him, because his hour was not yet come.

Aug. Tr. xxxi. 1. AUG. It was said above that our Lord went up to the feast secretly, not because He feared being taken, (for He had power to prevent it,) but to shew figuratively, that even in the very feast which the Jews celebrated, He was hid, and that it was His mystery. Now however the power appears, which was thought timidity: He spoke publicly at the feast, in so much that the multitude marvelled: *They said some of them at Jerusalem, Is not this He, whom they seek to kill? but, lo, He speaketh boldly, and they say nothing to Him.* They knew the fierceness with which He had been sought for; they marvelled at the power by which he was not taken.

Chrys. Hom. l. 1. CHRYS. The Evangelist adds, *from Jerusalem:* for there had been the greatest display of miracles, and there the people were in the worst state, seeing the strongest proofs of His divinity, and yet willing to give up all to the judgment of their corrupt rulers. Was it not a great miracle, that those who raged for His life, now that they had Him in their grasp, became on a sudden quiet?

Aug. Tr. xxxi. 1. AUG. So, not fully understanding Christ's power, they supposed that it was owing to the knowledge of the rulers that He was spared: *Do the*

Chrys. Hom. l. 1. *rulers know indeed that this is the very Christ?* CHRYS. But they do not follow the opinion of the rulers, but put forth another most perverse and absurd one; *Howbeit we know this Man, whence He is; but when Christ cometh, no man knoweth whence He is.* AUG. This notion did not arise Aug. without foundation. We find indeed that the Scriptures $_{s.\ 2.}^{Tr.xxxi.}$ said of Christ, *He shall be called a Nazarene,* and thus pre- Matt. 2, dicted whence He would come. And the Jews again told $^{23.}$ Herod, when he enquired, that Christ would be born in Bethlehem of Judah, and adduced the testimony of the Prophet. How then did this notion of the Jews arise, that, when Christ came, no one would know whence He was? From this reason, viz. that the Scriptures asserted both. As man, they foretold whence Christ would be; as God, He was hid from the profane, but revealed Himself to the godly. This notion they had taken from Isaiah, *Who shall declare His* Isa. 53. *generation?* Our Lord replies, that they both knew Him, and knew Him not: *Then cried Jesus in the temple as He taught, saying, Ye both know Me, and know whence I am :* that is to say, Ye both know whence I am, and do not know whence I am: ye know whence I am, that I am Jesus of Nazareth, whose parents ye know. The birth from the Virgin was the only part of the matter unknown to them : with this exception, they knew all that pertained to Jesus as man. So He well says, *Ye both know Me, and know whence I am :* i. e. according to the flesh, and the likeness of man. But in respect of His divinity, He says, *I am not come of Myself, but He that sent Me is true.* CHRYS. By which He discloses $_{Hom.}^{Chrys.}$ what was in their minds. I am not, He seems to say, of the l. 1. number of those who have come without reason, but He is true that sent Me ; and if He is true, He hath sent Me in truth ; and therefore He who is sent must needs speak the truth. He then convicts them from their own assertions. For whereas they had said, *When Christ cometh, no man knoweth whence He is,* He shews that Christ did come from one whom they knew not, i. e. the Father. Wherefore He adds, *Whom ye know not.* HILARY. Every man, ever born in Hilar. the flesh, is in a certain sense from God. How then could He $_{ult.\ med.}^{de\ Trin.}$ say that they were ignorant who He was, and whence He was*? Because our Lord is here referring to His own peculiar

---

* Because even considering Him man, He would be born of God in the common sense.

birth from God, which they were ignorant of, because they did not know that He was the Son of God. His very saying then that they did not know whence He was, was telling them whence He was. If they did not know whence He was, He could not be from nothing; for then there would be no *whence* to be ignorant of. He must therefore be from God. And then not knowing *whence* He is, was the reason that they did not know *who* He is. He does not know the Son who does not know His birth from the Father. CHRYS. Or the ignorance, He here speaks of, is the ignorance of a bad life; as Paul saith, *They profess that they know God, but in works they deny Him.* Our Lord's reproof is twofold: He first published what they were speaking secretly, crying out, in order to put them to shame. AUG. Lastly, to shew whence they could get to know Him (who had sent Him), He adds, *I know Him:* so if you would know Him, enquire of Me. *No one knoweth the Father, save the Son, and he to whom the Son will reveal Him. And if I should say, I know Him not, I should be a liar like unto you.* CHRYS. Which is impossible: for He that sent Me is true, and therefore He that is sent must be true likewise. He every where attributes the knowledge of the Father to Himself, as being from the Father: thus here, *But I know Him, for I am from Him.* HILARY. I ask however, does the being from Him express a work of creation, or a birth by generation? If a work of creation, then every thing which is created is from Him. And how then does not all creation know the Father, if the Son knows Him, because He is from Him? But if the knowledge of the Father is peculiar to Him, as being from Him, then the being from Him is peculiar to Him also; i. e. the being the true Son of God by nature. So you have then a peculiar knowledge springing from a peculiar generation. To prevent however any heresy applying the being from Him, to the time of His advent, He adds, *And He hath sent Me:* thus preserving the order of the Gospel sacrament; first announcing Himself born, and then sent. AUG. *I am from Him,* He says, i. e. as the Son from the Father: but that you see Me in the flesh is because *He hath sent Me.* Wherein understand not a difference of nature, but the authority of a father. CHRYS. His saying however, *Whom ye know not,* irritated the Jews, who

Chrys. Hom. l. l.
Tit. 1, 16.

Aug. Tr. xxxi. 4.

c. 8, 55.

Chrys. Hom. l. l.

Hilar. vi. de Trin. ultra med.

Aug. Tr. xxxi. 4.

Chrys. Hom. l. 2.

professed to have knowledge; and *they sought to take Him, but no man laid hands on Him.* Mark the invisible check which is kept upon their fury: though the Evangelist does not mention it, but preserves purposely a humble and human way of speaking, in order to impress us with Christ's humanity; and therefore only adds, *Because His hour was not yet come.* AUG. That is, because He was not so pleased; for our Lord was not born subject to fate. Thou must not believe this even of thyself, much less of Him by Whom thou wert made. And if thine hour is in His will, is not His hour in His own will? His home then here does not mean the time that He was obliged to die, but the time that He deigned to be put to death.

Aug.
Tract.
xxxi.
s. 5.

31. And many of the people believed on him, and said, When Christ cometh, will he do more miracles than these which this man hath done?

32. The Pharisees heard that the people murmured such things concerning him; and the Pharisees and the chief priests sent officers to take him.

33. Then said Jesus unto them, Yet a little while am I with you, and then I go unto him that sent me.

34. Ye shall seek me, and shall not find me : and where I am, thither ye cannot come.

35. Then said the Jews among themselves, Whither will he go, that we shall not find him? will he go unto the dispersed among the Gentiles, and teach the Gentiles?

36. What manner of saying is this that he said, Ye shall seek me, and shall not find me: and where I am, thither ye cannot come?

AUG. *And many of the people believed on Him.* Our Lord brought the poor and humble to be saved. The common people, who soon saw their own infirmities, received His medicine without hesitation. CHRYS. Neither had these

Aug.
Tract.
xxxi. 7.
Chrys.
Hom. l.
2.

however a sound faith; but took up a low way of speaking, after the manner of the multitude: *When Christ cometh, will He do more miracles than this Man hath done?* Their saying, *When Christ cometh,* shews that they were not steady in believing that He was the Christ: or rather, that they did not believe He was the Christ at all; for it is the same as if they said, that Christ, when He came, would be a superior person, and do more miracles. Minds of the grosser sort are influenced not by doctrine, but by miracles. AUG. Or they mean, If there are not to be two Christs, this is He. The rulers however, possessed with madness, not only refused to acknowledge the physician, but even wished to kill Him: *The Pharisees heard that the people murmured such things concerning Him, and the Pharisees and chief priests sent officers to take Him.* CHRYS. He had discoursed often before, but they had never so treated Him. The praises of the multitude however now irritated them; though the transgression of the sabbath still continued to be the reason put forward. Nevertheless, they were afraid of taking this step themselves, and sent officers instead. AUG. Not being able to take Him against His will, they sent men to hear Him teach. Teach what? *Then said Jesus unto them, Yet a little while I am with you.* CHRYS. He speaks with the greatest humility: as if to say, Why do ye make such haste to kill Me? Only wait a little time. AUG. That which ye wish to do now, ye shall do sometime, but not now: because it is not My will. For I wish to fulfil My mission in due course, and so to come to My passion. CHRYS. In this way He astonished the bolder part of the multitude, and made the earnest among them more eager to hear Him; so little time being now left, during which they could have the benefit of His teaching. He does not say, I am here, simply; but, *I am with you:* meaning, Though you persecute Me, I will not cease fulfilling my part towards you, teaching you the way to salvation, and admonishing you. What follows, *And I go unto Him that sent Me,* was enough to excite some fear. THEOPHYL. As if He were going to complain of them to the Father: for if they reviled Him who was sent, no doubt they did an injury to Him that sent. BEDE. *I go to Him that*

Aug. Tract. xxxi. 7.

Aug. Tract. xxxi. s. 8.

Chrys. Hom. l. 2.

Aug. Tract. xxxi. 8.

Chrys. Hom. l. 2.

sent Me: i. e. I return to My Father, at whose command I became incarnate. He is speaking of that departure, from which He has never returned. CHRYS. That they wanted His presence, appears from His saying, *Ye seek Me, and shall not find Me.* But when did the Jews seek Him? Luke relates that the women lamented over Him: and it is probable that many others did the same. And especially, when the city was taken, would they call Christ and His miracles to remembrance, and desire His presence. AUG. Here He foretels His resurrection: for the search for Him was to take place after His resurrection, when men were conscience-stricken. They would not acknowledge Him, when present; afterward they sought Him, when they saw the multitude believing on Him; and many pricked in their hearts said, *What shall we do?* They perceived that Christ's death was owing to their sin, and believed in Christ's pardon to sinners; and so despaired of salvation, until they drank of that blood which they shed. CHRYS. Then lest any should think that His death would take place in the common way, He adds, *And where I am, thither ye cannot come.* If He continued in death, they would be able to go to Him: for we all are going thitherwards. AUG. He does not say, Where I shall be, but *Where I am.* For Christ was always there in that place whither He was about to return: He returned in such a way, as that He did not forsake us. Visibly and according to the flesh, He was upon earth; according to His invisible majesty, He was in heaven and earth. Nor again is it, Ye will not be able, but, Ye are not able to come: for they were not such at the time, as to be able. That this is not meant to drive men to despair, is shewn by His saying the very same thing to His disciples; *Whither I go, ye cannot come;* and by His explanation last of all to Peter, *Whither I go, ye cannot follow Me now, but ye shall follow Me afterwards.* CHRYS. He wants them to think seriously how little time longer He should be with them, and what regret they will feel when He is gone, and they are not able to find Him. *I go unto Him that sent Me;* this shews that no injury was done Him by their plots, and that His passion was voluntary. The words had some effect upon the Jews, who asked each other, where they were to go, which was like

CHRYS. Hom. l. 2.

AUG. Tract. xxxi. 9.

CHRYS. Hom. xlix. 3.

AUG. Tract. xxxi. 9.

CHRYS. Hom. l. 32.

persons desiring to be quit of Him: *Then said the Jews
among themselves, Whither will He go, that we shall not find
Him?　Will He go to the dispersed among the Gentiles, and
teach the Gentiles?*　In the fulness of their self-satisfaction,
they call them Gentiles, as a term of reproach; the Gentiles
being dispersed every where; a reproach which they themselves underwent afterwards.　Of old all the nation was
united together: but now that the Jews were mixed with
the Gentiles in every part of the world, our Lord would not
have said, *Whither I go, ye cannot come,* in the sense of
going to the Gentiles.　Aug. *Whither I go,* i. e. to the
bosom of the Father.　This they did not at all understand:
and yet even their mistake is an unwitting prophecy of our
salvation; i. e. that our Lord would go to the Gentiles, not
in His own person, but by His feet, i. e. His members.　He
sent to us those whom He had made His members, and so
made us His members.　Chrys. They did not mean, that
our Lord was going to the Gentiles for their hurt, but to
teach them.　Their anger had subsided, and they believed
what He had said.　Else they would not have thought of
asking each other, *What manner of saying is this that He
said, Ye shall seek Me, and shall not find Me: and whither
I am, ye cannot come.*

*Aug.
Tract.
xxxi.
10.*

*Chrys.
Hom. l.'
3.*

37. In the last day, that great day of the feast, Jesus
stood and cried, saying, If any man thirst, let him come
unto me, and drink.

38. He that believeth on me, as the Scripture
hath said, out of his belly shall flow rivers of living
water.

39. (But this spake he of the Spirit, which they
that believe on him should receive: for the Holy
Ghost was not yet given; because that Jesus was not
yet glorified.)

*Chrys.
Hom. l.
1.*

Chrys. The feast being over, and the people about to
return home, our Lord gives them provisions for the way: *In
the last day, that great day of the feast, Jesus stood and
cried, saying, If any man thirst, let him come unto Me, and*

drink. AUG. The feast was then going on, which is called Aug. Tract. xxxii. 1. scenopegia, i. e. building of tents. CHRYS. Which lasted seven days. The first and last days were the most important; *In the last day, that great day of the feast,* says the Evangelist. Those between were given chiefly to amusements. He did not then make the offer on the first day, or the second, or the third, lest amidst the excitements that were going on, people should let it slip from their minds, He *cried out,* on account of the great multitude of people present. THEOPHYL. To make Himself audible, inspire confidence in others, and shew an absence of all fear in Himself. CHRYS. Chrys. Hom. li. 1. *If any thirsteth:* as if to say, I use no compulsion or violence: but if any have the desire strong enough, let him come. AUG. Aug. Tract. xxxii. 11. For there is an inner thirst, because there is an inner man: and the inner man of a certainty loves more than the outer. So then if we thirst, let us go not on our feet, but on our affections, not by change of place, but by love. CHRYS. He Chrys. Hom. li. 1. is speaking of spiritual drink, as His next words shew: *He that believeth on Me, as the Scripture hath said, out of his belly shall flow rivers of living water.* But where does the Scripture say this? No where. What then? We should read, *He that believeth in Me, as saith the Scripture,* putting the stop here; and then, *out of his belly shall flow rivers of living water:* the meaning being, that that was a right kind of belief, which was formed on the evidence of Scripture, not of miracles. *Search the Scriptures,* He had said before. JEROME. Or this testimony is taken from the Hierom. in prolog. Gen. Proverbs, where it is said, *Let thy fountains be dispersed abroad, and rivers of waters in the streets.* AUG. The belly Prov. 5, 16. Aug. Tract. xxxii. 4. of the inner man, is the heart's conscience. Let him drink from that water, and his conscience is quickened and purified; he drinks in the whole fountain, nay, becomes the very fountain itself. But what is that fountain, and what is that river, which flows from the belly of the inner man? The love of his neighbour. If any one, who drinks of the water, thinks that it is meant to satisfy himself alone, out of his belly there doth not flow living water. But if he does good to his neighbour, the stream is not dried up, but flows. GREG. When sacred preaching floweth from the soul of the Greg. super Ezech. Hom. x. faithful, rivers of living water, as it were, run down from the

T

bellies of believers. For what are the entrails of the belly but the inner part of the mind; i. e. a right intention, a holy desire, humility towards God, mercy toward man. CHRYS. He says, *rivers*, not river, to shew the copious and overflowing power of grace: and *living water*, i. e. always moving; for when the grace of the Spirit has entered into and settled in the mind, it flows freer than any fountain, and neither fails, nor empties, nor stagnates. The wisdom of Stephen, the tongue of Peter, the strength of Paul, are evidences of this. Nothing hindered them; but, like impetuous torrents, they went on, carrying every thing along with them. AUG. What kind of drink it was, to which our Lord invited them, the Evangelist next explains; *But this He spake of the Spirit, which they that believe on Him should receive.* Whom does the Spirit mean, but the Holy Spirit? For every man has within him his own spirit. ALCUIN. He promised the Holy Spirit to the Apostles before the Ascension; He gave it to them in fiery tongues, after the Ascension. The Evangelist's words, *Which they that believe on Him should receive*, refer to this. AUG. The Spirit of God was, i. e. was with God, before now; but was not yet given to those who believed on Jesus; for our Lord had determined not to give them the Spirit, till He was risen again: *The Holy Ghost was not yet given, because that Jesus was not yet glorified.* CHRYS. The Apostles indeed cast out devils by the Spirit before, but only by the power which they had from Christ. For when He sent them, it is not said, He gave them the Holy Spirit, but, *He gave unto them power.* With respect to the Prophets, however, all agree that the Holy Spirit was given to them: but this grace had been withdrawn from the world. AUG. Yet we read of John the Baptist, *He shall be filled with the Holy Ghost even from his mother's womb.* And Zacharias was filled with the Holy Ghost, and prophesied. Mary was filled with the Holy Ghost, and prophesied of our Lord. And so were Simeon and Anna, that they might acknowledge the greatness of the infant Christ. We are to understand then that the giving of the Holy Spirit was to be certain, after Christ's exaltation, in a way in which it never was before. It was to have a peculiarity at His coming, which it had not before. For we no where read of men under the

Marginal notes:
Chrys. Hom. li. 1.
Aug. Tract. xxxii 5.
Aug. Tract. xxxii.6.
Chrys. Hom. li. 1.
Aug. iv. de Trin. c. xx. Luke 1, 15.

influence of the Holy Spirit, speaking with tongues which they had never known, as then took place, when it was necessary to evidence His coming by sensible miracles. Aug. If the Holy Spirit then is received now, why is there no one who speaks the tongues of all nations? Because now the Church herself speaks the tongues of all nations. Whoso is not in her, neither doth he now receive the Holy Spirit. But if only thou lovest unity, whoever hath any thing in her, hath it for thee. Put away envy, and that which I have is thine. Envy separateth, love unites: have it, and thou hast all things: whereas without it nothing that thou canst have, will profit thee. *The love of God is shed abroad in* Rom. 5, *our hearts by the Holy Spirit which is given to us.* But 9. why did our Lord give the Holy Spirit after His resurrection? That the flame of love might mount upwards to our own resurrection: separating us from the world, and devoting us wholly to God. He who said, *He that believeth in Me, out of his belly shall flow rivers of living water*, hath promised life eternal, free from all fear, and change, and death. Such then being the gifts which He promised to those in whom the Holy Spirit kindled the flame of love, He would not give that Spirit till He was glorified: in order that in His own person He might shew us that life, which we hope to attain to in the resurrection. Aug. If this then is the cause why Aug. the Holy Spirit was not yet given; viz. because Jesus was cont. not yet glorified; doubtless, the glorification of Jesus when l. xxxii. it took place, was the cause immediately of its being given. c. 17. The Cataphryges, however, said that they first received the promised Paraclete, and thus strayed from the Catholic faith. The Manichæans too apply all the promises made respecting the Holy Spirit to Manichæus, as if there were no Holy Spirit given before. Chrys. Or thus; By the glory of Christ, He Chrys. means the cross. For, whereas we were enemies, and gifts Rom. are not made to enemies, but to friends, it was necessary that ii. 2. the victim should be first offered up, and the enmity of the flesh removed; that, being made friends of God, we might be capable of receiving the gift.

40. Many of the people therefore, when they heard this saying, said, Of a truth this is the Prophet.

41. Others said, This is the Christ. But some said, Shall Christ come out of Galilee?

42. Hath not the Scripture said, That Christ cometh of the seed of David, and out of the town of Bethlehem, where David was?

43. So there was a division among the people because of him.

44. And some of them would have taken him; but no man laid hands on him.

45. Then came the officers to the chief priests and Pharisees; and they said unto them, Why have ye not brought him?

46. The officers answered, Never man spake like this man.

47. Then answered them the Pharisees, Are ye also deceived?

48. Have any of the rulers or of the Pharisees believed on him?

49. But this people who knoweth not the law are cursed.

50. Nicodemus saith unto them, (he that came to Jesus by night, being one of them,)

51. Doth our law judge any man, before it hear him, and know what he doeth?

52. They answered and said unto him, Art thou also of Galilee? Search, and look: for out of Galilee ariseth no prophet.

53. And every man went unto his own house.

Aug.
Tract.
xxxiii.1.
Aug. Our Lord having invited those, who believed in Him, to drink of the Holy Spirit, a discussion arose among the multitude: *Many of the people therefore, when they heard this saying, said, Of a truth this is the Prophet.* THEOPHYL. The one, that is, who was expected. *Others*, i. e. the people *said, This is the Christ.* ALCUIN. These had now begun to

[1] Nic.
water
drink in that spiritual thirst[1], and had laid aside the unbe-

licving thirst.　But others still remained dried up in their unbelief: *But some said, Shall Christ come out of Galilee? Hath not the Scripture said, That Christ cometh of the seed of David, and out of the town of Bethlehem, where David was?*　They know what were the predictions of the Prophets respecting Christ, but knew not that they all were fulfilled in Him.　They knew that He had been brought up at Nazareth, but the place of His birth they did not know; and did not believe that it answered to the prophecies.　CHRYS. But be it so, they knew not His birth-place: were they ignorant also of His extraction? that He was of the house and family of David?　Why did they ask, *Hath not the Scripture said, that Christ cometh of the seed of David?* They wished to conceal His extraction, and therefore put forward where He had been educated.　For this reason, they do not go to Christ and ask, How say the Scriptures that Christ must come from Bethlehem, whereas Thou comest from Galilee? purposely and of malice prepense they do not do this.　And because they were thus inattentive, and indifferent about knowing the truth, Christ did not answer them: though He had landed Nathanael, when he said, *Can any good thing come out of Nazareth?* and called Him an Israelite indeed, as being a lover of truth, and well learned in the ancient Scriptures.

So there was a division among the people concerning Him. THEOPHYL. Not among the rulers; for they were resolved one way, viz. not to acknowledge Him as Christ.　The more moderate of them only used malicious words, in order to oppose Christ's path to glory; but the more malignant wished to lay hands on Him: *And some of them would have taken Him.*　CHRYS. The Evangelist says this to shew, that they had no concern for, and no anxiety to learn, the truth.

But no man laid hands on Him.　ALCUIN. That is, because He Who had the power to control their designs, did not permit it.　CHRYS. This were sufficient to have raised some compunction in them; but no, such malignity believes nothing; it looks only to one thing, blood.　AUG. They however who were sent to take Him, returned guiltless of the offence, and full of admiration: *Then came the officers to the chief priests and Pharisees; and they said unto them,*

Chrys. Hom. li. 11.

Chrys. Hom. li. 2.

Chrys. Hom. li. 2.

Aug. Tract. xxxiii. 1.

Why have ye not brought Him? ALCUIN. They who wished to take and stone Him, reprove the officers for not bringing Him. CHRYS. The Pharisees and Scribes profited nothing by seeing the miracles, and reading the Scriptures; but their officers, who had done neither, were captivated with once hearing Him; and they who went to take hold of Him, were themselves taken hold of by the miracle. Nor did they say, We could not because of the multitude: but made themselves proclaimers of Christ's wisdom: *The officers answered, Never man spake like this Man.* AUG. He spoke thus, because He was both God and man. CHRYS. Not only is their wisdom to be admired, for not wanting miracles, but being convinced by His teaching only, (for they do not say, Never man did such miracles as this Man, but, *Never man spake like this Man*,) but also their boldness, in saying this to the Pharisees, who were such enemies of Christ. They had not heard a long discourse, but minds unprepossessed against Him did not require one. AUG. The Pharisees however rejected their testimony: *Then answered them the Pharisees, Are ye also led away?* As if to say, We see that you are charmed by His discourse. ALCUIN. And so they were led away; and laudably too, for they had left the evil of unbelief, and were gone over to the faith. CHRYS. They make use of the most foolish argument against them: *Have any of the rulers or of the Pharisees believed on Him? but this people who knoweth not the law are cursed?* This then was their ground of accusation, that the people believed, but they themselves did not. AUG. They who knew not the law, believed on Him who had given the law, and they who taught the law condemned Him; thus fulfilling our Lord's words, *I am come, that they which see not might see, and that they which see might be made blind.* CHRYS. How then are they cursed, who are convinced by the law? Rather are ye cursed, who have not observed the law. THEOPHYL. The Pharisees answer the officers courteously and gently; because they are afraid of their forthwith separating from them, and joining Christ. CHRYS. As they said that none of the rulers believed on Him, the Evangelist contradicts them: *Nicodemus saith unto them, (he that came to Jesus by night, being one of them.)* AUG. He was not unbelieving, but

Margin notes: Chrys. Hom.lii. 1. — Aug. Tract. xxxiii.1. — Chrys. Hom.lii. 1. — Aug. Tract. xxxiii.1. — Chrys. Hom.lii. 1. — Aug. Tract. xxxiii.1. — c.19,39. — Chrys. Hom.lii. 1. — Chrys. Hom.lii. 1. — Aug. Tract. xxxiii.1.

fearful; and therefore came by night to the light, wishing to be enlightened, but afraid of being known to go. He replies, *Doth our law judge any man before it hear him, and know what he doeth?* He thought that, if they would only hear Him patiently, they would be overcome, as the officers had been. But they preferred obstinately condemning Him, to knowing the truth. Aug. He calls the law of God, *our law;* because it was given to men. Chrys. Nicodemus shews that they knew the law, and did not act according to the law. They, instead of disproving this, take to rude and angry contradiction: *They answered and said unto him, Art thou also of Galilee?* Aug. i. e. led away by a Galilean. Our Lord was called a Galilean, because His parents were of the town of Nazareth; I mean by parents, Mary. Chrys. Then, by way of insult, they direct Him to the Scriptures, as if He were ignorant of them; *Search and look, for out of Galilee ariseth no prophet:* as if to say, Go, learn what the Scriptures say. Alcuin. They knew the place where He had resided, but never thought of enquiring where He was born; and therefore they not only denied that He was the Messiah, but even that He was a prophet. Aug. No prophet indeed ariseth out of Galilee, but the Lord of prophets arose thence.

And every man went unto his own house. Alcuin. Having effected nothing, devoid of faith, and therefore incapable of being benefited, they returned to their home of unbelief and ungodliness.

Chrys. Hom. lii. 1, 2.

Aug. Tract. xxxiii. 2.

Chrys. Hom. lii. 11.

Aug. Tract. xxxiii. 11.

CHAP. VIII.

1. Jesus went unto the mount of Olives.

2. And early in the morning he came again into the temple, and all the people came unto him; and he sat down, and taught them.

3. And the Scribes and Pharisees brought unto him a woman taken in adultery; and when they had set her in the midst,

4. They say unto him, Master, this woman was taken in adultery, in the very act.

5. Now Moses in the law commanded us, that such should be stoned : but what sayest thou?

6. This they said, tempting him, that they might have to accuse him. But Jesus stooped down, and with his finger wrote on the ground, as though he heard them not.

7. So when they continued asking him, he lifted up himself, and said unto them, He that is without sin among you, let him first cast a stone at her.

8. And again He stooped down, and wrote on the ground.

9. And they which heard it, being convicted by their own conscience, went out one by one, beginning at the eldest, even unto the last : and Jesus was left alone, and the woman standing in the midst.

10. When Jesus had lifted up himself, and saw none but the woman, he said unto her, Woman, where are those thine accusers? hath no man condemned thee?

11. She said, No man, Lord. And Jesus said unto her, Neither do I condemn thee: go, and sin no more.

ALCUIN. Our Lord at the time of His passion used to spend the day in Jerusalem, preaching in the temple, and performing miracles, and return in the evening to Bethany, where He lodged with the sisters of Lazarus.   Thus on the last day of the feast, having, according to His wont, preached the whole day in the temple, in the evening He *went to the mount of Olives.*   AUG. And where ought Christ to teach, except on the mount of Olives; on the mount of ointment, on the mount of chrism.   For the name Christ is from chrism, chrism being the Greek word for unction.   He has anointed us, for wrestling with the devil.   ALCUIN. The anointing with oil is a relief to the limbs, when wearied and in pain. The mount of Olives also denotes the height of our Lord's pity, olive in the Greek signifying pity.   The qualities of oil are such as to fit in to this mystical meaning.   For it floats above all other liquids: and the Psalmist says, *Thy mercy is over all Thy works.   And early in the morning, He came again into the temple:* i. e. to denote the giving and unfolding of His mercy, i. e. the now dawning light of the New Testament in the faithful, that is, in His temple.   His returning *early in the morning,* signifies the new rise of grace.   BEDE. And next it is signified, that after He began to dwell by grace in His temple, i. e. in the Church, men from all nations would believe in Him: *And all the people came to Him, and He sat down and taught them.*   ALCUIN. The sitting down, represents the humility of His incarnation. And the people came to Him, when He sat down, i. e. after taking up human nature, and thereby becoming visible, many began to hear and believe on Him, only knowing Him as their friend and neighbour.   But while these kind and simple persons are full of admiration at our Lord's discourse, the Scribes and Pharisees put questions to Him, not for the sake of instruction, but only to entangle the truth in their nets: *And the Scribes and Pharisees brought unto Him a woman taken in adultery; and when they had set her in the midst, they say unto Him, Master, this woman was taken in adultery, in the very act.*   AUG. They had remarked upon Him already, as being over lenient.   Of Him indeed it had been prophesied, *Ride on because of the word of truth, of meekness, and of righteousness.*   So as a teacher He

Aug. Tract. xxxiii. 3.

Ps. 144.

Aug. Tract. xxxiii. s. 4. Ps. 44.

exhibited truth, as a deliverer meekness, as a judge righteousness. When He spoke, His truth was acknowledged; when
against His enemies He used no violence, His meekness was
praised. So they raised the scandal on the score of justice.
For they said among themselves, If He decide to let her go,
He will not do justice; for the law cannot command what is
unjust: *Now Moses in the law commanded us, that such
should be stoned:* but to maintain His meekness, which has
made Him already so acceptable to the people, He must
decide to let her go. Wherefore they demand His opinion:
And what sayest Thou? hoping to find an occasion to accuse
Him, as a transgressor of the law: *And this they said
tempting Him, that they might have to accuse Him.* But
our Lord in His answer both maintained His justice, and
departed not from meekness. *Jesus stooped down, and with
His finger wrote on the ground.* AUG. As if to signify that
such persons were to be written in earth, not in heaven,
where He told His disciples they should rejoice they were
written. Or His bowing His head (to write on the ground),
is an expression of humility; the writing on the ground
signifying that His law was written on the earth which bore
fruit, not on the barren stone, as before. ALCUIN. The
ground denotes the human heart, which yieldeth the fruit
either of good or of bad actions: the finger jointed and
flexible, discretion. He instructs us then, when we see any
faults in our neighbours, not immediately and rashly to condemn them, but after searching our own hearts to begin with,
to examine them attentively with the finger of discretion.
BEDE. His writing with His finger on the ground perhaps
shewed, that it was He who had written the law on stone.

*So when they continued asking Him, He lifted Himself
up.* AUG. He did not say, Stone her not, lest He should
seem to speak contrary to the law. But God forbid that He
should say, Stone her; for He came not to destroy that
which He found, but to seek that which was lost. What
then did He answer? *He that is without sin among you,
let him first cast a stone at her.* This is the voice of justice.
Let the sinner be punished, but not by sinners; the law
carried into effect, but not by transgressors of the law. GREG.
For he who judges not himself first, cannot know how to

Marginal notes:
Aug. de Con. Evang. lib. ii. c. 10.

Aug. Tract. xxxiii. 5.

judge correctly in the case of another. For though He know what the offence is, from being told, yet He cannot judge of another's deserts, who supposing himself innocent, will not apply the rule of justice to himself. AUG. Having with the weapon of justice smitten them, He deigned not even to look on the fallen, but averted His eyes: *And again He stooped down, and wrote on the ground.* ALCUIN. This is like our Lord; while His eyes are fixed, and He seems attending to something else, He gives the bystanders an opportunity of retiring: a tacit admonition to us to consider always both before we condemn a brother for a sin, and after we have punished him, whether we are not guilty ourselves of the same fault, or others as bad. AUG. Thus smitten then with the voice of justice, as with a weapon, they examine themselves, find themselves guilty, and one by one retire: *And they which heard it, went out one by one, beginning at the eldest*[*]. GLOSS. The more guilty of them, perhaps, or those who were more conscious of their faults. AUG. There were left however two, the pitiable[1] and the pitiful, *And Jesus was left alone, and the woman standing in the midst:* the woman, you may suppose, in great alarm, expecting punishment from one in whom no sin could be found. But He who had repelled her adversaries with the word of justice, lifted on her the eyes of mercy, and asked; *When Jesus had lifted Himself up, and saw none but the woman, He said unto her, Woman, where are these thine accusers? hath no man condemned thee? She said, No man, Lord.* We heard above the voice of justice; let us hear now that of mercy: *Jesus said unto her, Neither do I condemn thee;* I, who thou fearedst would condemn thee, because thou foundest no fault in me. What then, Lord? Dost Thou favour sin? No, surely. Listen to what follows, *Go, and sin no more.* So then our Lord condemned sin, but not the sinner. For did He favour sin, He would have said, Go, and live as thou wilt: depend on my deliverance: howsoever great thy sins be, it matters not: I will deliver thee from hell, and its tormentors. But He did not say this. Let those attend, who love the Lord's mercy, and fear His truth. Truly, *Gracious and righteous is the Lord.*

Aug. Tract. xxxiii. b.

Aug. Tract. xxxiii. s. 5.

Aug. Tract. xxxiii. 5, 6. [1] miseria et misericordia.

Ps. 35, 7.

[*] Vulgate omits ὑπὸ τῆς συνειδήσεως ἐλεγχόμενοι ἕως τῶν ἐσχάτων.

12. Then spake Jesus again unto them, saying, I am the light of the world: he that followeth me shall not walk in darkness, but shall have the light of life.

ALCUIN. Having absolved the woman from her sin, lest some should doubt, seeing that He was really man, His power to forgive sins, He deigns to give further disclosure of His divine nature; *Then spake Jesus again unto them, saying, I am the Light of the world.* BEDE. Where it is to be observed, He does not say, *I am* the light of Angels, or of heaven, but *the Light of the world*, i. e. of mankind who live in darkness, as we read, *To give light to them that sit in darkness, and in the shadow of death.* CHRYS. As they had brought Galilee as an objection against Him, and doubted His being one of the Prophets, as if that was all He claimed to be, He wished to shew that He was not one of the Prophets, but the Lord of the whole earth: *Then spake Jesus again unto them, saying, I am the Light of the world:* not of Galilee, or of Palestine, or of Judæa. AUG. The Manichæans suppose the sun of the natural world to be our Lord Christ; but the Catholic Church reprobates such a notion; for our Lord Christ was not made the sun, but the sun was made by Him: inasmuch as *all things were made by Him.* And for our sake did He come to be under the sun, being the light which made the sun: He hid Himself under the cloud of the flesh, not to obscure, but to temper His light. Speaking then through the cloud of the flesh, the Light unfailing, the Light of wisdom says to men, *I am the Light of the world.* THEOPHYL. You may bring these words against Nestorius: for our Lord does not say, In Me is the light of the world, but, *I am the Light of the world:* He who appeared man, was both the Son of God, and the Light of the world; not, as Nestorius fondly holds, the Son of God dwelling in a mere man. AUG. He withdraws you however from the eyes of the flesh, to those of the heart, in that He adds, *He that followeth Me shall not walk in darkness, but shall have the light of life.* He thinks it not enough to say, *shall have light*, but adds, *of life.* These words of our Lord agree with those of the Psalm, *In Thy light shall we see light; for with Thee is the well of life.* For bodily uses, light is one

Luke I, 79.
Chrys. Hom. lii. 2.

Aug. Tract. xxxiv. 2.

c. 1, 3.

Aug. Tract. xxxiv. s. 5.

Ps. 35.

thing, and a well another; and a well ministers to the mouth,
light to the eyes. With God the light and the well are the
same. He who shines upon thee, that thou mayest see Him,
the Same flows unto thee, that thou mayest drink Him. What
He promises is put in the future tense; what we ought to do
in the present. *He that followeth Me,* He says, *shall have;*
i. e. by faith now, in sight hereafter. The visible sun ac-
companieth thee, only if thou goest westward, whither it
goeth also; and even if thou follow it, it will forsake thee, at
its setting. Thy God is every where wholly; He will not
fall from thee, if thou fall not from Him. Darkness is to be
feared, not that of the eyes, but that of the mind; and if of
the eyes, of the inner not the outer eyes; not those by which
white and black, but those by which just and unjust, are
discerned. CHRYS. *Walketh not in darkness,* i. e. spiritually
abideth not in error. Here He tacitly praises Nicodemus
and the officers, and censures those who had plotted against
Him; as being in darkness and error, and unable to come to
the light.

13. The Pharisees therefore said unto him, Thou
bearest record of thyself; thy record is not true.

14. Jesus answered and said unto them, Though
I bear record of myself, yet my record is true: for I
know whence I came, and whither I go; but ye cannot tell whence I come, and whither I go.

15. Ye judge after the flesh; I judge no man.

16. And yet if I judge, my judgment is true: for I
am not alone, but I and the Father that sent me.

17. It is also written in your law, that the testimony
of two men is true.

18. I am one that bear witness of myself, and the
Father that sent me beareth witness of me.

CHRYS. Our Lord having said, *I am the Light of the world;*
and, *he that followeth Me, walketh not in darkness,* the
Jews wish to overthrow what He has said: *The Pharisees
therefore said unto Him, Thou bearest record of Thyself, Thy
record is not true.* ALCUIN. As if our Lord Himself were

the only (one that bore) witness to Himself; whereas the truth was that He had, before His incarnation, sent many witnesses to prophesy of His Sacraments. CHRYS. Our Lord however overthrew their argument: *Jesus answered and said, Though I bear record of Myself, yet My record is true.* This is an accommodation to those who thought Him no more than a mere man. He adds the reason, *For I know whence I come, and whither I go;* i. e. I am God, from God, and the Son of God: though this He does not say expressly, from His habit of mingling lofty and lowly words together. Now God is surely a competent witness to Himself. AUG. The witness of light is true, whether the light shew itself, or other things. The Prophet spake the truth, but whence had he it, but by drawing from the fount of truth? Jesus then is a competent witness to Himself. *For I know whence I come, and whither I go:* this has reference to the Father; for the Son gave glory to the Father who sent Him. How greatly then should man glorify the Creator, who made Him. He did not separate from His Father, however, when He came, or desert us when He returned: unlike that sun which in going to the west, leaves the east. And as that sun throws its light on the faces both of him who sees, and him who sees not; only the one sees with the light, the other sees not: so the Wisdom of God, the Word, is every where present, even to the minds of unbelievers; but they have not the eyes of the understanding, wherewith to see. To distinguish then between believers and enemies among the Jews, as between light and darkness, He adds, *But ye cannot tell whence I come, and whither I go.* These Jews saw the man, and did not believe in the God, and therefore our Lord says, *Ye judge after the flesh,* i. e. in saying, *Thou bearest record of Thyself, Thy record is not true.* THEOPHYL. As if to say: Ye judge untruly, according to the flesh, thinking, because I am in the flesh, that I am flesh only, and not God. AUG. Understanding Me not as God, and seeing Me as man, ye think Me arrogant in bearing witness of Myself. For any man who bears high testimony to himself, is thought proud and arrogant. But men are frail, and may either speak the truth, or lie: the Light cannot lie. CHRYS. As to live according to the flesh is to live

Marginal notes:
Chrys. Hom. liii. 2.
Aug. Tract. xxxv. 6.
s. 5.
Tract. xxxvi.3.
Aug. Tract. xxxvi.3. in Joan.
Chrys. Hom. l. 2.

amiss; so to judge according to the flesh, is to judge un-justly. They might say, however, If we judge wrongly, why dost Thou not convict us, why dost Thou not condemn us? So He adds, *I judge no man.* AUG. Which may be under-stood in two ways; *I judge no man,* i. e. not now: as He says elsewhere, *God sent not His Son into the world to condemn the world, but that the world through Him might be saved:* not that He abandons, but only defers, His justice. Or having said, *Ye judge according to the flesh,* He says immediately, *I judge no man,* to let you know that Christ does not judge according to the flesh, as men judged Him. For that Christ is a judge appears from the next words, *And yet if I judge, My judgment is true.* CHRYS. As if to say: In saying, *I judge no man,* I meant that I did not anticipate judgment. If I judged justly, I should condemn you, but now is not the time for judging. He alludes however to the future judgment, in what follows; *For I am not alone, but I and the Father that sent Me;* which means that He will not condemn them alone, but He and the Father together. This is intended too to quiet suspicion, as men did not think the Son worthy to be believed, unless He had the testimony of the Father also. AUG. But if the Father is with Thee, how did He send Thee? O Lord, Thy mission is Thy incarnation. Christ was here according to the flesh without withdrawing from the Father, because the Father and the Son are every where. Blush, thou Sabellian; our Lord doth not say, I am the Father, and I the self-same person am the Son; but, *I am not alone, because the Father is with Me.* Make a distinction then of persons, and distinction of intelligences: acknowledge that the Father is the Father, the Son the Son: but beware of saying, that the Father is greater, the Son less. Theirs is one substance, one coeternity, perfect equality. Therefore, He says, My judgment is true, because I am the Son of God. But that thou mayest understand how that the Father is with Me, it is not for the Son ever to leave the Father. I have taken up the form of a servant; but I have not lost the form of God. He had spoken of judgment: now He speaks of witness: *It is also written in your law, that the testimony of two men is true.* AUG. Is this made a bad use of by the Manichæans, that our Lord does not say,

Aug. Tract. xxxvi. s. 4.

Chrys. Hom. lii. 2.

Aug. Tract. xxxvi. 7.

in the law of God, but, *in your law?* Who does not recognise here a manner of speaking customary in Scripture ? *In your law,* i. e. the law given to you. The Apostle speaks of *his* Gospel in the same way, though he testifies to having received it not from men, but by the revelation of Jesus Christ. AUG. There is much difficulty, and a great mystery seems to be contained, in God's words, *In the mouth of two or three witnesses, let every word be established.* It is possible that two may speak false. The chaste Susannah was arraigned by two false witnesses: the whole people spake against Christ falsely. How then must we understand the word, *By the mouth of two or three witnesses shall every word be established:* except as an intimation of the mystery of the Trinity, in which is perpetual stability of truth? Receive then our testimony, lest ye feel our judgment. I delay My judgment: I delay not My testimony: *I am one that beareth witnes of Myself, and the Father that sent Me beareth witness of Me.* BEDE. In many places the Father bears witness of the Son; as, *This day have I begotten Thee ;* also, *This is My beloved Son.* CHRYS. *It is written in your law, that the testimony of two men is true.* If this is to be taken literally, in what respect does our Lord differ from men? The rule has been laid down for men, on the ground that one man alone is not to be relied on: but how can this be applicable to God? These words are quoted then with another meaning. When two men bear witness, both to an indifferent matter, their witness is true: this constitutes the testimony of two men. But if one of them bear witness to himself, then they are no longer two witnesses. Thus our Lord means to shew that He is consubstantial with the Father, and does not need another witness, i. e. besides the Father's. *I and the Father that sent Me.* Again, on human principles, when a man bears witness, his honesty is supposed; he is not borne witness to; and a man is admitted as a fair and competent witness in an indifferent matter, but not in one relating to himself, unless he is supported by other testimony. But here it is quite otherwise. Our Lord, though giving testimony in His own case, and though saying that He is borne witness to by another, pronounces Himself worthy of belief; thus shewing His all-sufficiency. He says He

Aug.
Tract.
xxxvi.
10.
Deut.10.

Ps. 2.
Matt. 3,
17.
Chrys.
Hom.
lii. 3.

deserves to be believed.   ALCUIN. Or it is as if He said, If your law admits the testimony of two men who may be deceived, and testify to more than is true ; on what grounds can you reject Mine and My Father's testimony, the highest and most sure of all ?

19. Then said they unto him, Where is thy Father? Jesus answered, Ye neither know me, nor my Father : if ye had known me, ye should have known my Father also.

20. These words spake Jesus in the treasury, as he taught in the temple : and no man laid hands on him ; for his hour was not yet come.

AUG. Those who had heard our Lord say, *Ye judge after the flesh*, shewed that they did so ; for they understood what He said of His Father in a carnal sense: *Then said they unto Him, Where is Thy Father?* meaning, We have heard Thee say, *I am not alone, but I and the Father that sent Me.* We see Thee alone ; prove to us then that Thy Father is with Thee.   THEOPHYL. Some remark that this is said in contumely and contempt ; to insinuate either that He is born of fornication, and knows not who His Father is ; or as a slur on the low situation of His father, i. e. Joseph ; as if to say, Thy father is an obscure, ignoble person ; why dost Thou so often mention him ? So because they asked the question, to tempt Him, not to get at the truth, *Jesus answered, Ye neither know Me, nor My Father.*   AUG. As if He said, *Ye ask where is Thy Father?* As if ye knew Me already, and I were nothing else but what ye see. But ye know Me not, and therefore I tell you nothing of My Father. Ye think Me indeed a mere man, and therefore among men look for My Father. But, forasmuch as I am different altogether, according to My seen and unseen natures, and speak of My Father in the hidden sense according to My hidden nature ; it is plain that ye must first know Me, and then ye will know My Father ; *If ye had known Me, ye would have known My Father also.*   CHRYS. He tells them, it is of no avail for them to say they know the Father,

Aug. Tract. xxxvii. 1.

Aug. Tract. xxxvii. 11.

Chrys. Hom. lii. 3.

Orig.
tom.xix.
1. in
Joan. in
princ.
if they do not know the Son. ORIGEN. *Ye neither know
Me, nor My Father:* this seems inconsistent with what was
said above, *Ye both know Me, and know whence I am.*
But the latter is spoken in reply to some from Jerusalem,
who asked, *Do the rulers know indeed that this is the very
Christ? Ye neither know Me,* is addressed to the Pharisees.
To the former persons from Jerusalem however He said, *He
that sent Me is true, Whom ye know not.* You will ask then,
How is that true, *If ye know Me, ye would know My Father
also?* when they of Jerusalem, to whom He said, *Ye know
Me,* did not know the Father. To this we must reply, that
our Saviour sometimes speaks of Himself as man, and sometimes as God. *Ye both know Me,* He says as man: *ye
neither know Me,* as God. AUG. What does this mean: *If

Aug.
Tract.
xxxvii.
7.
ye knew Me, ye would know My Father also,* but, *I and My
Father are one?* It is a common expression, when you see
one man very like another, If you have seen him, you have
seen the other. You say this, because they are so like. And
thus our Lord says, *If ye had known Me, ye had known My
Father also;* not that the Father is the Son, but that the
Son is like the Father. THEOPHYL. Let the Arian blush: for
if, as he says, the Son be a creature, how does it follow that
he who knows the creature, knows God? For not even by
knowing the substance of Angels, does one know the Divine
Substance? Forasmuch therefore as he who knows the Son,
knows the Father, it is certain that the Son is consubstantial
with the Father. AUG. This word perhaps[c] is used only

Aug.
Tract.
xxxviii.
s. 3.
by way of rebuke, though it seems to express doubt. As
used by men indeed it is the expression of doubt, but He
who knew all things could only mean by that doubt to
rebuke unbelief. Nay, even we sometimes say perhaps,
when they are certain of a thing, e. g. when you are angry
with your slave, and say, Do not you heed me? Consider,
perhaps I am your master. So our Lord's doubt is a reproof
to the unbelievers, when He says, *Ye should have known

Orig.
tom.xix.
1. in
Joan. in
princ.
perhaps My Father also.* ORIGEN. It is proper to observe,
that the followers of other sects think this text proves clearly,
that the God, whom the Jews worshipped, was not the Father
of Christ. For if, say they, our Saviour said this to the

---

[c] forsitan in Vulgate, before *Quæ dr.*

Pharisees, who worshipped God as the Governor of the world, it is evident that the Father of Jesus, whom the Pharisees knew not, was a different person from the Creator. But they do not observe that this is a usual manner of speaking in Scripture. Though a man may know the existence of God, and have learned from the Father that He only must be worshipped, yet if his life is not good, he is said not to have the knowledge of God. Thus the sons of Eli, on account of their wickedness, are said not to have known God. And thus again the Pharisees did not know the Father; because they did not live according to their Creator's command. And there is another thing meant too by knowing God, different from merely believing in Him. It is said, *Be still then, and* Ps. 46, *know that I am God.* And this, it is certain, was written for a people that believed in the Creator. But to know by believing, and believe simply, are different things. To the Pharisees, to whom He says, *Ye neither know Me, nor My Father,* He could with right have said, Ye do not even believe in My Father; for he who denies the Son, has not the Father, either by faith or knowledge. But Scripture gives us another sense of knowing a thing, viz. being joined to that thing. Adam knew his wife, when he was joined to her. And if he who is joined to a woman knows that woman, he who is joined to the Lord is one spirit, and knows the Lord. And in this sense the Pharisees neither knew the Father, nor the Son. But may not a man know God, and yet not know the Father? Yes; these are two different conceptions. And therefore among an infinite number of prayers offered up in the Law, we do not find any one addressed to God the Father. They only pray to Him as God and Lord; in order not to anticipate the grace shed by Jesus over the whole world, calling all men to the Sonship, according to the Psalm, *I will declare Thy name unto my brethren.*

These words spake Jesus in the treasury, as He taught in the temple. ALCUIN. Treasury (Gazophylacium): Gaza is the Persian for wealth: phylattein is to keep. It was a place in the temple, where the money was kept. CHRYS. He spake in the temple magisterially, and now He was speaking to those who railed at and accused Him, for making Himself

Aug.
Tract.
xxxvii.
8. equal to the Father. AUG. Great however is His confidence and fearlessness: it not being possible that He should undergo any suffering, but that which He voluntarily undertook. Wherefore it follows, *And no man laid hands on Him, for His hour was not yet come.* Some, when they hear this, think Christ to have been under the control of fate. But if fate comes from the verb fari, to speak, as some derive it, how can the Word of God be under the control of fate? Where are the fates? In the heavens, you say, in the courses and revolutions of the stars. How then can fate have power over Him, by Whom the heavens and stars were made; when even thy will, if thou exert it aright, transcends the stars? Dost thou think that because the flesh of Christ was placed beneath the heavens, that therefore His power was subjected to the heavens? *His hour* then *had not yet come;* i. e. the hour, not on which he should be obliged to die, but on Orig.
tom.xix.
in Joan. which He should deign to be put to death. ORIGEN. Whenever it is added, Jesus spoke these words in such a place, you will, if you attend, discover a meaning in the addition. γαζοφυλακίῳ The treasury was a place for keeping the money, which was given for the honour of God, and the support of the poor. The coins are the divine words, stamped with the likeness of the great King. In this sense then let every one contribute to the edification of the Church, carrying into that spiritual treasury all that he can collect, to the honour of God, and the common good. But while all were thus contributing to the treasury of the temple, it was especially the office of Jews to contribute his gifts, which were the words of eternal life. While Jesus therefore was speaking in the treasury, no one laid hands on Him; His discourse being stronger than those who wished to take Him; for there is no weakness in that which the Word of God utters. BEDE. Or thus; Christ speaks in the treasury; i. e. He had spoken in parables to the Jews; but now that He unfolded heavenly things to His disciples, His treasury began to be opened, which was the meaning of the treasury being joined to the temple; all that the Law and the Prophets had foretold in figure, appertained to our Lord.

21. Then said Jesus again unto them, I go my way,

and ye shall seek me, and shall die in your sins: whither I go, ye cannot come.

22. Then said the Jews, Will he kill himself? because he saith, Whither I go, ye cannot come.

23. And he said unto them, Ye are from beneath; I am from above: ye are of this world, I am not of this world.

24. I said therefore unto you, that ye shall die in your sins: for if ye believe not that I am he, ye shall die in your sins.

AUG. In accordance with what was just, He said that *no man laid hands on Him, because His hour was not yet come;* He now speaks to the Jews of His passion, as a free, and not a compulsory sacrifice on His part: *Then said Jesus again unto them, I go My way.* Death to our Lord was a return to the place whence He had come. BEDE. The connexion of these words is such, that they might have been spoken at one place and one time, or at another place and another time: as either nothing at all, or some things, or many may have intervened. ORIGEN. But some one will object: If this was spoken to men who persisted in unbelief, how is it He says, *Ye shall seek Me?* For to seek Jesus is to seek truth and wisdom. You will answer that it was said of His persecutors, that they sought to take Him. There are different ways of seeking Jesus. All do not seek Him for their health and profit: and only they who seek Him aright, find peace. And they are said to seek Him aright, who seek the Word which was in the beginning with God, in order that He may lead them to the Father. AUG. *Ye shall seek Me,* then, He says, not from compassionate regret, but from hatred: for after He had departed from the eyes of men, He was sought for both by those who hated, and those who loved Him: the one wanting to persecute, the other to have His presence. And that ye may not think that ye shall seek Me in a good sense, I tell you, *Ye shall die in your sin.* This is to seek Christ amiss, to die in one's sin: this is to hate Him, from Whom alone cometh salvation. He pronounces sentence on them prophetically, that they shall die in their

[margin notes:] Aug. Tract. xxxviii. 2.

Orig. tom. xix. in Joan. s. 3.

Aug. Tract. xxxviii. 2.

ἁμαρτίᾳ plural in our Transl.

sins. BEDE. Note: *sin* is in the singular number, *your* in the plural; to express one and the same wickedness in all.

Orig. tom.xix. in Joan. s. 3.   ORIGEN. But I ask, as it is said below that many believed on Him, whether He speaks to all present, when He says, *Ye shall die in your sins?* No: He speaks to those only, whom He knew would not believe, and would therefore die in their sins, not being able to follow Him. *Whither I go,* He says, *ye cannot come;* i. e. there where truth and wisdom are, for with them Jesus dwells. They cannot, He says, because they will not: for had they wished, He could not reasonably have said, *Ye shall die in your sin.*

Aug. Tract. xxviii. s. 2.   AUG. This He tells His disciples in another place; without saying to them, however, *Ye shall die in your sin,* He only says, *Whither I go, ye cannot follow Me now;* not preventing, but only delaying their coming.

Orig. tom.xix. 3.   ORIGEN. The Word, while still present, yet threatens to depart. So long as we preserve the seeds of truth implanted in our minds, the Word of God does not depart from us. But if we fall into wickedness, then He says to us, *I go away;* and when we seek Him, we shall not find Him, but shall die in our sin, die caught in our sin. But we should not pass over without notice the expression itself: *Ye shall die in your sins.* If *ye shall die* be understood in the ordinary sense, it is manifest that sinners die in their sins, the righteous in their righteousness. But if we understand it of death in the sense of sin; then the meaning is, that not their bodies, but their souls were sick unto death. The Physician seeing them thus grievously sick, says, *Ye shall die in your sins.* And this is evidently the meaning of the words, *Whither I go ye cannot come.* For when a man dies in his sin, he cannot go where Jesus goes: no dead man

Ps. 113.   can follow Jesus: *The dead praise not Thee, O Lord.*

Aug. Tract. xxviii.   AUG. They take these words, as they generally do, in a carnal sense, and ask, *Will He kill Himself, because He saith, Whither I go, ye cannot come?* A foolish question. For why? Could they not go where He went, if He killed Himself? Were they never to die themselves? *Whither I go,* then, He says; meaning not His departure at death, but where He went after death. THEOPHYL. He shews here that He will rise again

Orig. tom.xix. in Joan. s. 4.   in glory, and sit at the right hand of God. ORIGEN. May they not however have a higher meaning in saying this?

For they had opportunities of knowing many things from their apocryphal books or from tradition. As then there was a prophetical tradition, that Christ was to be born at Bethlehem, so there may have been a tradition also respecting His death, viz. that He would depart from this life in the way which He declares, *No man taketh it from Me, but I lay it down* c.10,18. *of Myself.* So then the question, *Will He kill Himself,* is not to be taken in its obvious sense, but as referring to some Jewish tradition about Christ. For His saying, *I go My way,* shews that He had power over His own death, and departure from the body; so that these were voluntary on His part. But I think that they bring forward this tradition which had come down to them, on the death of Christ, contemptuously, and not with any view to give Him glory. *Will He kill Himself?* say they: whereas, they ought to have used a loftier way of speaking, and have said, Will His soul wait His pleasure, to depart from His body? Our Lord answers, *Ye are from beneath,* i. e. ye love earth; your hearts are not raised upwards. He speaks to them as earthly men, for their thoughts were earthly. CHRYS. As if to say, No wonder Chrys. that ye think as ye do, seeing ye are carnal, and understand Hom. nothing spiritually. *I am from above.* AUG. From whom Aug. above? From the Father Himself, Who is above all. *Ye are* Tract. *of this world, I am not of this world.* How could He be of 4. the world, by Whom the world was made? BEDE. And Who was before the world, whereas they were of the world, having been created after the world had begun to exist. CHRYS. Or He says, *I am not of this world,* with reference Chrys. to worldly and vain thoughts. THEOPHYL. I affect nothing Hom. worldly, nothing earthly: I could never come to such mad-liii. 1. ness as to kill Myself. Apollinarius, however, falsely infers . from these words, that our Lord's body was not of this world, but came down from heaven. Did the Apostles then, to whom our Lord says below, *Ye are not of this world,* derive c.15,19. all of them their bodies from heaven? In saying then, *I am not of this world,* He must be understood to mean, I am not of the number of you, who mind earthly things. ORIGEN. Orig. *Beneath,* and, *of this world,* are different things. *Beneath,* tom.xix. in Joan. refers to a particular place; this material world embraces s. 5.

different tracts[d], which all are beneath, as compared with things immaterial and invisible, but, as compared with one another, some beneath, some above. Where the treasure of each is, there is his heart also. If a man then lay up treasure upon earth, he is beneath: if any man lay up treasure in heaven, he is above; yea, ascends above all hearers, attains to a most blissful end. And again, the love of this world makes a man of this world: whereas he who loveth not the world, neither the things that are in the world, is not of the world. Yet is there beyond this world of sense, another world, in which are things invisible, the beauty of which shall the pure in heart behold, yea, the First-born of every creature may be called the world, insomuch as He is absolute wisdom, and in wisdom all things were made. In Him therefore was the whole world, differing from the material world, in so far as the [1] scheme divested of the matter, differs from the subject matter itself. The soul of Christ then says, *I am not of this world;* i. e. because it has not its conversation in this world.

[1] ratio

Aug. Our Lord expresses His meaning in the words, *Ye are of this world,* i. e. ye are sinners. All of us are born in sin; all have added by our actions to the sin in which we were born. The misery of the Jews then was, not that they had sin, but that they would die in their sin: *I said therefore unto you, that ye shall die in your sin.* Amongst the multitude, however, who heard our Lord, there were some who were about to believe; whereas this most severe sentence had gone forth against all: *Ye shall die in your sin;* to the destruction of all hope even in those who should hereafter believe. So His next words recall the latter to hope: *For if ye believe not that I am He, ye shall die in your sin:* therefore if ye believe that I am He, ye shall not die in your sin.

Aug.
Tract.
xxxviii.
6.

CHRYS. For if He came in order to take away sin, and a man cannot put that off, except by washing, and cannot be baptized except he believe; it follows, that he who believes not must pass out of this life, with the old man, i. e. sin, within him: not only because he believes not, but because he departs hence, with his former sins upon him.

Chrys.
Hom.
liii. 1.

AUG. His saying, *If ye believe not that I am,* without adding any thing,

Aug.
Tract.
xxxviii.
8.

[d] e. g. earth beneath, sky above.

proves a great deal. For thus it was that God spoke to
Moses, *I am that I am.* But how do I understand, *I am* Exod. 3.
that I am, and, *If ye believe not that I am?* In this
way. All excellence, of whatever kind, if it be mutable,
cannot be said really to be, for there is no real *to be*, where there
is a *not to be.* Analyze the idea of mutability, and you will find,
was, and *will be;* contemplate God, and you will find, *is,*
without possibility of a past. In order to be, thou must leave
him behind thee. So then, *If ye believe not that I am,* means
in fact, If ye believe not that I am God; this being the condition, on which we shall not die in our sins. God be
thanked that He says, *If ye believe not,* not, If ye understand not; for who could understand this? ORIGEN. It is Orig.
manifest, that he, who dies in his sins, though he say that he tom.xix.
in Joan.
believes in Christ, does not really believe. For he who
believes in His justice does not do injustice; he who believes
in His wisdom, does not act or speak foolishly; in like
manner with respect to the other attributes of Christ, you
will find that he who does not believe in Christ, dies in his
sins: inasmuch as he comes to be the very contrary of what
is seen in Christ.

25. Then said they unto him, Who art thou? And
Jesus saith unto them, Even the same that I said
unto you from the beginning.

26. I have many things to say and to judge of you:
but he that sent me is true; and I speak to the world
those things which I have heard of him.

27. They understood not that he spake to them of
the Father.

AUG. Our Lord having said, *If ye believe not that I am,* Aug.
ye shall die in your sins; they enquire of Him, as if wishing to Tract.
xxxviii.
know in whom they are to believe, that they might not die s. 11.
in their sin: *Then said they unto Him, Who art Thou?* For
when Thou saidst, *If ye believe not that I am,* Thou didst
not add, who Thou art. But our Lord knew that these were
some who would believe, and therefore after being asked,
Who art Thou? that such might know what they should
believe Him to be, *Jesus saith unto them, The beginning,*

who also speak to you; not as if to say, *I am the beginning,* but, Believe Me to be the beginning; as is evident from the Greek, where beginning is feminine. Believe Me then to be the beginning, but ye die in your sins: for the beginning cannot be changed; it remains fixed in itself, and is the source of change to all things. But it is absurd to call the Son the beginning, and not the Father also. And yet there are not two beginnings, even as these are not two Gods. The Holy Spirit is the Spirit of the Father and the Son; not being either the Father, or the Son. Yet Father, Son, and Holy Spirit are one God, one Light, one beginning. He adds, *Who also speak to you,* i. e. Who humbled Myself for your sakes, and condescended to those words. Therefore believe Me to be the beginning; because that ye may believe this, not only am I the beginning, but I also speak with you, that ye may believe that I am. For if the Beginning had remained with the Father in its original nature, and not taken upon it the form of a servant, how could men have believed in it? Would their weakly minds have taken in the spiritual Word, without the medium of sensible sound? BEDE. In some copies we find, *Who also speak to you;* but it is more consistent to read *for* (quia), not, *who* (qui): in which case the meaning is: Believe Me to be the beginning, for for your sakes have I condescended to these words. CHRYS. See here the madness of the Jews; asking after so long time, and after all His miracles and teaching, *Who art Thou?* What is Christ's answer? From the beginning I speak with you; as if to say, Ye do not deserve to hear any thing from Me, much less this thing, Who I am. For ye speak always, to tempt Me. But I could, if I would, confound and punish you: *I have many things to say, and to judge of you.* AUG. Above He said, *I judge no man;* but, *I judge not,* is one thing, *I have to judge,* another. *I judge not,* He says, with reference to the present time. But the other, *I have many things to say, and to judge of you,* refers to a future judgment. And I shall be true in My judgment, because I am truth, the Son of the true One. *He that sent Me is true.* My Father is true, not by partaking of, but begetting truth. Shall we say that truth is greater than one who is true? If we say this, we shall

Marginal notes:

Tract. xxxix. 1, 2.

Tract. xx.xviii. 11.'

Chrys. Hom. liii. 1.

Aug. Tract. xxxix.

begin to call the Son greater than the Father. CHRYS. He says this, that they may not think that He allows them to talk against Him with impunity, from inability to punish them; or that He is not alive to their contemptuous designs. THEOPHYL. Or having said, *I have many things to say, and to judge of you,* thus reserving His judgment for a future time, He adds, But He that sent Me is true: as if to say, Though ye are unbelievers, My Father is true, Who hath appointed a day of retribution for you. CHRYS. Or thus: As My Father hath sent Me not to judge the world, but to save the world, and My Father is true, I accordingly judge no man now; but speak thus for your salvation, not your condemnation: *And I speak to the world those things that I have heard of Him.* ALCUIN. And to hear from the Father is the same as to be from the Father; He has the hearing from the same sense that He has the being. AUG. The coequal Son gives glory to the Father: as if to say, I give glory to Him whose Son I am: how proudly thou detractest from Him, whose servant Thou art. ALCUIN. They did not understand however what He meant by saying, *He is true that sent Me: they understand not that He spake to them of the Father.* For they had not the eyes of their mind yet opened, to understand the equality of the Father with the Son.

28. Then said Jesus unto them, When ye have lifted up the Son of man, then shall ye know that I am he, and that I do nothing of myself; but as my Father hath taught me, I speak these things.

29. And he that sent me is with me: the Father hath not left me alone; for I do always those things that please him.

30. As he spake these words, many believed on him.

AUG. When our Lord said, He is true that sent Me, the Jews did not understand that He spake to them of the Father. But He saw some there, who, He knew, would believe on Him after His passion. *Then said Jesus unto them, When ye have lifted up the Son of man, then ye shall*

Chrys. Hom. liii. 1.

Chrys. Hom. liii. 1.

Aug. Tract. xxxix. s. 6.

Aug. Tract. xl. 2.

Exod.
3, 14. *know that I am.* Recollect the words, *I am that I am,* and
ye will know why I say, *I am.* I pass over your knowledge,
in order that I may fulfil My passion. In your appointed
time ye will know who I am; when ye have lifted up the
Son of man. He means the lifting up of the cross; for He
was lifted up on the cross, when He hung thereon. This
was to be accomplished by the hands of those who should
afterwards believe, whom He is now speaking to; with what
intent, but that no one, however great his wickedness and
consciousness of guilt might despair, seeing even the mur-
Chrys.
Hom.
liii. 1, 2. derers of our Lord forgiven. Chrys. Or the connection is
this: When His miracles and teaching had failed to convert
men, He spoke of the cross; *When ye have lifted up the
Son of man, then ye shall know that I am He:* as if to say,
Ye think that ye have killed Me; but I say that ye shall
then, by the evidence of miracles, of My resurrection, and
your captivity, know most especially, that I am Christ the
Son of God, and that I do not act in opposition to God;
But that as My Father hath taught Me, I speak these things.
Here He shews the likeness of His substance to the Father's;
and that He says nothing beyond the Paternal intelligence.
If I were contrary to God, I should not have moved His
Aug.
Tr. xl.
s. 3. et
seq. anger so much against those who did not hear Me. Aug.
Or thus: Having said, *Then shall ye know that I am,* and in
this, *I am,* implied the whole Trinity: lest the Sabellian error
should creep in, He immediately adds, *And I do nothing
of Myself;* as if to say, I am not of Myself; the Son is God
from the Father. Let not what follows, *as the Father hath
taught Me, I speak these things,* suggest a carnal thought to
any of you. Do not place as it were two men before your
eyes, a Father speaking to his son, as you do when you
speak to your sons. For what words could be spoken to the
only Word? If the Father speaks in your hearts without
sound, how does He speak to the Son? The Father speaks
to the Son incorporeally, because He begat the Son incorporeally: nor did He teach Him, as having begotten Him
untaught; rather the teaching Him, was the begetting Him
knowing. For if the nature of truth be simple, to be, in the
Son, is the same as to know. As then the Father gave the
Son existence by begetting, so He gave Him knowledge also.

CHRYS. He gives now a humbler turn to the discourse: *And* Chrys. Hom. liii. 2. *He that sent Me.* That this might not be thought however to imply inferiority, He says, *Is with Me.* The former is His dispensation, the latter His divinity. AUG. And though Aug. both are together, yet one is sent, the other sends. For the Tr xl. 6. mission is the incarnation; and the incarnation is of the Son only, not of the Father. He says then, *He that sent Me,* meaning, By whose Fatherly authority I am made incarnate. The Father however, though He sent the Son, did not withdraw from Him, as He proceeds to say: *The Father hath not left Me alone.* For it could not be that where He sent the Son, there the Father was not; He who says, *I fill* Jer. 33. *heaven and earth.* And He adds the reason why He did not leave Him: *For I do always those things that please Him;* always, i. e. not from any particular beginning, but without beginning and without end. For the generation from the Father hath no beginning in time. CHRYS. Or, He Chrys. means it as an answer to those who were constantly saying that Hom. liii. 2. He was not from God, and that because He did not keep the sabbath; *I do always,* He says, *do those things that please Him;* shewing that the breaking the sabbath even was pleasing to Him. He takes care in every way to shew that He does nothing contrary to the Father. And as this was speaking more after a human fashion, the Evangelist adds, *As He spake these words, many believed on Him;* as if to say, Do not be disturbed at hearing so humble a speech from Christ; for those who had heard the greatest doctrines from Him, and were not persuaded, were persuaded by these words of humility. These then believed on Him, yet not as they ought; but only out of joy, and approbation of His humble way of speaking. And this the Evangelist shews in his subsequent narration, which relates their unjust proceedings towards Him.

31. Then said Jesus to those Jews which believed on him, If ye continue in my word, then are ye my disciples indeed;

32. And ye shall know the truth, and the truth shall make you free.

33. They answered him, We be Abraham's seed, and were never in bondage to any man: how sayest thou, Ye shall be made free?

34. Jesus answered them, Verily, verily, I say unto you, Whosoever committeth sin is the servant of sin.

35. And the servant abideth not in the house for ever: but the Son abideth ever.

36. If the Son therefore shall make you free, ye shall be free indeed.

Aug.
(Chrys.
Nic.)
Hom.
liv. 1.
CHRYS. Our Lord wished to try the faith of those who believed, that it might not be only a superficial belief: *Then said Jesus to those Jews which believed on Him, If ye continue in My word, then are ye My disciples indeed.* His saying, *if ye continue,* made it manifest what was in their hearts. He knew that some believed, and would not continue. And He makes them a magnificent promise, viz. that they shall become His disciples indeed; which words are a tacit rebuke to some who had believed and afterwards withdrawn.

Aug.
de Verb.
Dom.
s. xlvii.
AUG. We have all one Master, and are fellow disciples under Him. Nor because we speak with authority, are we therefore masters; but He is the Master of all, Who dwells in the hearts of all. It is a small thing for the disciple to come to Him in the first instance: he must continue in Him: if we continue not in Him, we shall fail. A little sentence this, but a great work; *if ye continue.* For what is it to continue in God's word, but to yield to no temptations? Without labour, the reward would be gratis; if with, then a great reward indeed.

Aug.
Tr.xli.1.
xl. 9.
And ye shall know the truth. AUG. As if to say: Whereas ye have now belief, by continuing, ye shall have sight. For it was not their knowledge which made them believe, but rather their belief which gave them knowledge. Faith is to believe that which you see not: truth to see that which you believe? By continuing then to believe a thing, you come at last to see the thing; i. e. to the contemplation of the very truth as it is; not conveyed in words, but revealed by light. The truth is unchangeable; it is the bread of the soul, refreshing others, without diminution to itself; changing

him who eats into itself, itself not changed. This truth is the Word of God, which put on flesh for our sakes, and lay hid; not meaning to bury itself, but only to defer its manifestation, till its suffering in the body, for the ransoming of the body of sin, had taken place. CHRYS. Or, *ye shall know the truth*, i. e. Me: for I am the truth. The Jewish was a typical dispensation; the reality ye can only know from Me. AUG. Some one might say perhaps, And what does it profit me to know the truth? So our Lord adds, *And the truth shall free you;* as if to say, If the truth doth not delight you, liberty will. To be freed is to be made free, as to be healed is to be made whole. This is plainer in the Greek; in the Latin we use the word free chiefly in the sense of escape of danger, relief from care, and the like. THEOPHYL. As He said to the unbelievers alone, *Ye shall die in your sin*, so now to them who continue in the faith He proclaims absolution. AUG. From what shall the truth free us, but from death, corruption, mutability, itself being immortal, uncorrupt, immutable? Absolute immutability is in itself eternity. CHRYS. Men who really believed could have borne to be rebuked. But these men began immediately to shew anger. Indeed if they had been disturbed at His former saying, they had much more reason to be so now. For they might argue; If He says we shall know the truth, He must mean that we do not know it now: so then the law is a lie, our knowledge a delusion. But their thoughts took no such direction: their grief is wholly worldly; they know of no other servitude, but that of this world: *They answered Him, We be Abraham's seed, and were never in bondage to any man. How sayest Thou then, we shall be made free?* As if to say, They of Abraham's stock are free, and ought not to be called slaves: we have never been in bondage to any one. AUG. Or it was not those who believed, but the unbelieving multitude that made this answer. But how could they say with truth, taking only secular bondage into account, that *we have never been in bondage to any man?* Was not Joseph sold? were not the holy prophets carried into captivity? Ungrateful people! Why does God remind you so continually of His having taken you out of the house of bondage if you never were in bondage? Why do you who are now

Chrys.
Hom.
liv. 1.

Aug.
de Verb.
Dom.
Serm.
xlviii.

Aug.
iv. de
Trin. c.
18.

Chrys.
Hom.
liv. 1.

Aug.
Tr. xli. 2.

talking, pay tribute to the Romans, if you never were in
bondage? CHRYS. Christ then, who speaks for their good,
not to gratify their vainglory, explains His meaning to have
been that they were the servants not of men, but of sin, the
hardest kind of servitude, from which God only can rescue:
Jesus answered them, Verily, verily, I say unto you, Who-
soever committeth sin is the servant of sin. AUG. This
asseveration is important: it is, if one may say so, His
oath. *Amen* means true, but is not translated. Neither the
Greek nor the Latin Translator have dared to translate it.
It is a Hebrew word; and men have abstained from trans-
lating it, in order to throw a reverential veil over so
mysterious a word: not that they wished to lock it up, but
only to prevent it from becoming despised by being exposed.
How important the word is, you may see from its being
repeated. *Verily I say unto you,* says Verity itself; which
could not be, even though it said not verily. Our Lord however has recourse to this mode of enforcing His words, in
order to rouse men from their state of sleep and indifference.
Whosoever, He saith, *committeth sin,* whether Jew or Greek,
rich or poor, king or beggar, *is the servant of sin.* GREG.
Because whoever yields to wrong desires, puts his hitherto
free soul under the yoke of the evil one, and takes him for
his master. But we oppose this master, when we struggle
against the wickedness which has laid hold upon us, when
we strongly resist habit, when we pierce sin with repentance,
and wash away the spots of filth with tears. GREG. And
the more freely men follow their perverse desires, the more
closely are they in bondage to them. AUG. O miserable
bondage! The slave of a human master when wearied with
the hardness of his tasks, sometimes takes refuge in flight.
But whither does the slave of sin flee? He takes it along
with him, wherever he goes; for his sin is within him. The
pleasure passes away, but the sin does not pass away: its
delight goes, its sting remains behind. He alone can free
from sin, who came without sin, and was made a sacrifice
for sin. And thus it follows: *The servant abideth not in the*
house for ever. The Church is the house: the servant is the
sinner; and many sinners enter into the Church. So He
does not say, *The servant* is, not in the house; but, *The*

Chrys.
Hom.
liv.1.

Aug.
Tr. xli.
3.

Greg.
iv. Mor.
c. 42. in
Nov.
Ex. 21.

Greg.
xxv.
Moral.
c. 20.
not in
Nov.
Ex. 14.

servant abideth not in the house for ever. If a time then is
to come, when there shall be no servant in the house; who
will there be there? Who will boast that he is pure from sin?
Christ's are fearful words. But He adds, *The Son abideth
for ever.* So then Christ will live alone in His house. Or
does not the word Son, imply both the body and the head?
Christ purposely alarms us first, and then gives us hope.
He alarms us, that we may not love sin; He gives us hope,
that we may not despair of the absolution of our sin. Our
hope then is this, that we shall be freed by Him who is
free. He hath paid the price for us, not in money, but in
His own blood: *If the Son therefore shall make you free,
ye shall be free indeed.* AUG. Not from the barbarians, but Aug.
from the devil; not from the captivity of the body, but from de Verb.
the wickedness of the soul. AUG. The first stage of freedom Ser.
is, the abstaining from sin. But that is only incipient, it is xlvii.
not perfect freedom: for the flesh still lusteth against the super
spirit, so that ye do not do the things that ye would. Full Joan.
and perfect freedom will only be, when the contest is over, 10. et
and the last enemy, death, is destroyed. CHRYS. Or thus: Chrys.
Having said that *whosoever committeth sin, is the servant* Hom.
of sin, He anticipates the answer that their sacrifices saved
them, by saying, *The servant abideth not in the house for
ever, but the Son abideth ever.* The house, He says, meaning the Father's house on high; in which, to draw a comparison from the world, He Himself had all the power, just
as a man has all the power in his own house. *Abideth not,*
means, has not the power of giving; which the Son, who is
the master of the house, has. The priests of the old law had
not the power of remitting sins by the sacraments of the law;
for all were sinners. Even the priests, who, as the Apostle
says, were obliged to offer up sacrifices for themselves. But
the Son has this power; and therefore our Lord concludes:
If the Son shall make you free, ye shall be free indeed;
implying that that earthly freedom, of which men boasted so
much, was not true freedom. AUG. Do not then abuse your Aug.
freedom, for the purpose of sinning freely; but use it in order Tr. xli.
not to sin at all. Your will will be free, if it be merciful: 8.
you will be free, if you become the servant of righteousness.

x

37. I know that ye are Abraham's seed; but ye seek to kill me, because my word hath no place in you.

38. I speak that which I have seen with my Father: and ye do that which ye have seen with your father.

39. They answered and said unto him, Abraham is our father. Jesus saith unto them, If ye were Abraham's children, ye would do the works of Abraham.

40. But now ye seek to kill me, a man that hath told you the truth, which I have heard of God: this did not Abraham.

41. Ye do the deeds of your father.

Aug. Tr. xlii. 1. AUG. The Jews had asserted they were free, because they were Abraham's seed. Our Lord replies, *I know that ye are Abraham's seed;* as if to say, I know that ye are the sons of Abraham, but according to the flesh, not spiritually and by faith. So He adds, *But ye seek to kill Me.* CHRYS. Chrys. Hom. liv. 2. He says this, that they might not attempt to answer, that they had no sin. He reminds them of a present sin; a sin which they had been meditating for some time past, and which was actually at this moment in their thoughts: putting out of the question their general course of life. He thus removes them by degrees out of their relationship to Abraham, teaching them not to pride themselves so much upon it: for that, as bondage and freedom were the consequences of works, so was relationship. And that they might not say, We do so justly, He adds the reason why they did so; *Because* Aug. Tr. xlii. 1. *My word hath no place in you.* AUG. That is, hath not place in your heart[1], because your heart does not take it in. The word of God to the believing, is like the hook to the fish; it takes when it is taken: and that not to the injury of those who are caught by it. They are caught for their Chrys. Hom. liv. 2. salvation, not for their destruction. CHRYS. He does not say, Ye do not take in My word, but *My word has not room in you;* shewing the depth of His doctrines. But they might say; What if thou speakest of thyself? So He adds, *I speak that which I have seen of My Father;* for I

[1] capit Vulg. for χωρεῖ ἐν. Aug. goes off upon the Latin word.

have not only the Father's substance, but His truth. AUG. Aug.
Our Lord by His Father wishes us to understand God: as Tr. xlii.
if to say, I have seen the truth, I speak the truth, because I 11.
am the truth. If our Lord then speaks the truth which He
saw with the Father, it is Himself that He saw, Himself
that He speaks; He being Himself the truth of the
Father. ORIGEN. This is proof that our Saviour was Orig.
witness to what was done with the Father: whereas men, to tom. xx.
whom the revelation is made, were not witnesses. THE- in Joan.
OPHYL. But when you hear, *I speak that which I have seen*, s. 7.
do not think it means bodily vision, but innate knowledge,
sure, and approved. For as the eyes when they see an object,
see it wholly and correctly; so I speak with certainty what I
know from My Father.

And ye do that which ye have seen with your father. Orig.
ORIGEN. As yet He has not named their father; He men- tom. xx.
tioned Abraham indeed a little above, but now He is going 13.
to mention another father, viz. the devil: whose sons they
were, in so far as they were wicked, not as being men. Our
Lord is reproaching them for their evil deeds. CHRYS.
Another reading has, *And¹ do ye do that which ye have seen* ¹ καιεῖτε,
with your father; as if to say, As I both in word and deed *ye do,*
declare unto you the Father, so do ye by your works shew *or do.*
forth Abraham. ORIGEN. Also another reading has; *And* Orig.
do ye do what ye have heard from the Father. All that was tom. xx.
written in the Law and the Prophets they had heard from 7.
the Father. He who takes this reading, may use it to prove
against them who hold otherwise, that the God who gave the
Law and the Prophets, was none other than Christ's Father.
ᵈAnd we use it too as an answer to those who maintain two
original natures in men, and explain the words, *My word* c. s.
hath no place in you, to mean that these were by nature
incapable of receiving the word. How could those be of an
incapable nature, who had *heard from the Father*ᵉ? And
how again could they be of a blessed nature, who sought to
kill our Saviour, and would not receive His words. *They
answered and said unto Him, Abraham is our father.* This
answer of the Jews is a great falling off from our Lord's

ᵈ This is the meaning of the original;   ᵉ The reading in Origen for, *have
it is slightly altered in the Catena.   seen with your father.*

meaning. He had referred to God, but they take Father in
the sense of the father of their nature, Abraham. AUG. As if
to say, What art thou going to say against Abraham? They
seem to be inviting Him to say something in disparagement
of Abraham; and so to give them an opportunity of executing
their purpose. ORIGEN. Our Saviour denies that Abraham
is their father: *Jesus saith unto them, If ye were Abraham's
children, ye would do the works of Abraham.* AUG. And
yet He says above, *I know that ye are Abraham's seed.*
So He does not deny their origin, but condemns their deeds.
Their flesh was from him; their life was not. ORIGEN. Or
we may explain the difficulty thus. Above it is in the Greek,
I know that ye are Abraham's seed. So let us examine
whether there is not a difference between a bodily seed and a
child. It is evident that a seed contains in itself all the
proportions of him whose seed it is, as yet however dormant,
and waiting to be developed; when the seed first has changed
and moulded the material it meets with in the woman, derived nourishment from thence and gone through a process
in the womb, it becomes a child, the likeness of its begetter.
So then a child is formed from the seed: but the seed is not
necessarily a child. Now with reference to those who are
from their works judged to be the seed of Abraham, may we
not conceive that they are so from certain seminal proportions implanted in their souls? All men are not the seed of
Abraham, for all have not these proportions implanted in
their souls. But he who is the seed of Abraham, has yet
to become his child by likeness. And it is possible for him
by negligence and indolence even to cease to be the seed.
But those to whom these words were addressed, were not yet
cut off from hope: and therefore Jesus acknowledged that
they were as yet the seed of Abraham, and had still the
power of becoming children of Abraham. So He says, *If ye
are the children of Abraham, do the works of Abraham.* If
as the seed of Abraham, they had attained to their proper
sign and growth, they would have taken in our Lord's words.
But not having grown to be children, they cared not; but
wish to kill the Word, and as it were break it in pieces, since
it was too great for them to take in. If any of you then be
the seed of Abraham, and as yet do not take in the word of

Margin notes:
Aug. Tr. xlii. s. 3.
Orig. tom. xx. 9.
Aug. Tr. xlii. 4.
Orig. tom. xx. 2. et sq.

God, let him not seek to kill the word; but rather change himself into being a son of Abraham, and then he will be able to take in the Son of God. Some select one of the works of Abraham, viz. that in Genesis, *And Abraham be-* Gen. 15, *lieved God, and it was counted to him for righteousness.* 6. But even granting to them that faith is a work, if this were so, why was it not, *Do the work of Abraham:* using the singular number, instead of the plural? The expression as it stands is, I think, equivalent to saying, Do all the works of Abraham : i. e. in the spiritual sense, interpreting Abraham's history allegorically. For it is not incumbent on one, who would be a son of Abraham, to marry his maidservants, or after his wife's death, to marry another in his old age.

But now ye seek to kill Me, a man that hath told you the truth. CHRYS. This truth, that is, that He was equal to Chrys. the Father: for it was this that moved the Jews to kill Him. Hom. liv. 2. To shew, however, that this doctrine is not opposed to the Father, He adds, *Which I have heard from God.* ALCUIN. Because He Himself, Who is the truth, was begotten of God the Father, to hear, being in fact the same with to be from the Father. ORIGEN. *To kill Me,* He says, *a man.* I say Orig. nothing now of the Son of God, nothing of the Word, because tom. xx. the Word cannot die; I speak only of that which ye see. It 11. is in your power to kill that which you see, and offend Him Whom ye see not.

This did not Abraham. ALCUIN. As if to say, By this you prove that you are not the sons of Abraham; that you do works contrary to those of Abraham. ORIGEN. It might Orig. seem to some, that it were superfluous to say that Abraham tom. xx. did not this; for it were impossible that it should be; Christ 12. was not born at that time. But we may remind them, that in Abraham's time there was a man born who spoke the truth, which he heard from God, and that this man's life was not sought for by Abraham. Know too that the Saints were never without the spiritual advent of Christ. I understand then from this passage, that every one who, after regeneration, and other divine graces bestowed upon him, commits sin, does by this return to evil incur the guilt of crucifying the Son of God, which Abraham did not do.

Ye do the works of your father. AUG. He does not say Aug. Tr. xlii. 6.

Chrys.
Hom.
liv. 2.
as yet who is their father.   CHRYS. Our Lord says this with
a view to put down their vain boasting of their descent; and
persuade them to rest their hopes of salvation no longer on
the natural relationship, but on the adoption.   For this it
was which prevented them from coming to Christ; viz. their
thinking that their relationship to Abraham was sufficient for
their salvation.

41. Then said they to him, We be not born of fornication; we have one Father, even God.

42. Jesus said unto them, If God were your Father,
ye would love me: for I proceeded forth and came from
God; neither came I of myself, but he sent me.

43. Why do ye not understand my speech? even
because ye cannot hear my word.

Aug.
Tr. xlii.
7.
AUG. The Jews had begun to understand that our Lord
was not speaking of sonship according to the flesh, but of
manner of life.   Scripture often speaks of spiritual fornication, with many gods, and of the soul being prostituted,
as it were, by paying worship to false gods.   This explains
what follows: *Then said they to Him, We be not born of
fornication; we have one Father, even God.*   THEOPHYL.
As if their motive against Him was a desire to avenge God's

Orig.
tom. xx.
14.
honour.   ORIGEN. Or their sonship to Abraham having been
disproved, they reply by bitterly insinuating, that our Saviour
was the offspring of adultery.   But perhaps the tone of the
answer is disputatious, more than any thing else.   For
whereas they have said shortly before, *We have Abraham
for our father*, and had been told in reply, *If ye are
Abraham's children, do the works of Abraham;* they declare
in return that they have a greater Father than Abraham, i. e.
God; and that they were not derived from fornication.   For

qui nihil
facit ex
se
the devil, who has no power of creating any thing from himself, begets not from a spouse, but a harlot, i. e. matter, those
who give themselves up to carnal things, that is, cleave to

Chrys.
Hom.
liv. 3.
matter.   CHRYS. But what say ye?   Have ye God for your
Father, and do ye blame Christ for speaking thus?   Yet
true it was, that many of them were born of fornication, for

people then used to form unlawful connexions. But this is not the thing our Lord has in view. He is bent on proving that they are not from God. *Jesus said unto them, If God were your Father, ye would love Me: for I proceeded forth and came from God.* HILARY. It was not that the Son of God condemned the assumption of so religious a name; that is, condemned them for professing to be the sons of God, and calling God their Father; but that He blamed the rash presumption of the Jews in claiming God for their Father, when they did not love the Son. *For I proceeded forth, and came from God.* To *proceed forth*, is not the same with to *come*. When our Lord says that those who called God their Father, ought to love Him, because He *came forth* from God, He means that His being born of God was the reason why He should be loved: the proceeding forth, having reference to His incorporeal birth. Their claim to be the sons of God, was to be made good by their loving Christ, Who was begotten from God. For a true worshipper of God the Father must love the Son, as being from God[t]. And he only can love the Father, who believes that the Son is from Him. AUG. This then is the eternal procession, the proceeding forth of the Word from God: from Him It proceeded as the Word of the Father, and came to us: *The Word was made flesh.* His advent is His humanity: His staying, His divinity. Ye call God your Father; acknowledge Me at least to be a brother. HILARY. In what follows, He teaches that His origin is not in Himself; *Neither came I of Myself, but He sent Me.* ORIGEN. This was said, I think, in allusion to some who came without being sent by the Father, of whom it is said in Jeremiah, *I have not sent these prophets, yet they ran.* Some, however, use this passage[1] to prove the existence of two natures[g]. To these we may reply, Paul hated Jesus when he persecuted the Church of God, at the time, viz. that our Lord said, *Why persecutest thou Me?* Now if it is true, as is here said, *If God were your Father, ye would love Me;* the converse is true, If ye do not love Me, God is not your Father. And Paul for some time did

Marginal references: Hilar. vi. de Trin. c. 30. Aug. Tr. xlii. 8. c. 1, 14. Hilar. lib. v. ibid. Orig. tom. xx. 15. Jer. 23, 21. [1] i. e. if God were your Father, &c. Acts 9, 4.

---

[t] The Son *is from God* not by reason of His advent, but His nativity.

[g] Alluding to the belief that some men were of a good nature, being the creation of God, others evil, being made by the devil.

not love Jesus. There was a time when God was not Paul's father. Paul therefore was not by nature the son of God, but afterwards was made so. And when does God become any one's Father, except when he keeps His commandments?

Chrys. Hom. liv. 3.

CHRYS. And because they were ever enquiring, *What is this which He saith, Whither I go ye cannot come?* He adds here, *Why do ye not understand My speech? even because ye cannot hear My word.*

Aug. Tr. xlii. 9.

AUG. And they could not hear, because they would not believe, and amend their lives.

Orig. tom. xx. 18. (Nic.)

ORIGEN. First then, that virtue must be sought after, which hears the divine word; that by degrees we may be strong enough to embrace the whole teaching of Jesus. For so long as a man has not had his hearing restored by the Word,

Mark 7, 34.

which says to the deaf ear, *Be opened:* so long he cannot hear.

44. Ye are of your father the devil, and the lusts of your father ye will do. He was a murderer from the beginning, and abode not in the truth, because there is no truth in him. When he speaketh a lie, he speaketh of his own: for he is a liar, and the father of it.

45. And because I tell you the truth, ye believe me not.

46. Which of you convinceth me of sin? And if I say the truth, why do ye not believe me?

47. He that is of God heareth God's words: ye therefore hear them not, because ye are not of God.

Chrys. Hom. liv. 3.

CHRYS. Our Lord, having already cut off the Jews from relationship to Abraham, overthrows now this far greater claim, to call God their Father, *Ye are of your father the*

Aug. Tr. xlii. 10.

devil. AUG. Here we must guard against the heresy of the Manichæans, who hold a certain original nature of evil, and a nation of darkness with princes at their head, whence the devil derives his existence. And thence they say our flesh is produced; and in this way interpret our Lord's speech,

Ye are of your father the devil: viz. to mean that they were by nature evil, drawing their origin from the opposite seed of darkness. ORIGEN. And this seems to be the same mistake, as if one said, that an eye which saw right was different in kind from an eye which saw wrong. For just as in these there is no difference of kind, only one of them for some reason sees wrong; so, in the other case, whether a man receives a doctrine, or whether he does not, he is of the same nature. AUG. The Jews then were children of the devil by imitation, not by birth: *And the lusts of your father ye will do,* our Lord says. Ye are his children then, because ye have such lusts, not because ye are born of him: for *ye seek to kill Me, a man that hath told you the truth:* and he envied man, and killed him: *he was a murderer from the beginning;* i. e. of the first man on whom a murder could be committed: man could not be slain, before man was created. The devil did not go, girt with a sword, against man: he sowed an evil word, and slew him. Do not suppose therefore that you are not guilty of murder, when you suggest evil thoughts to your brother. The very reason why ye rage against the flesh, is that ye cannot assault the soul. ORIGEN. Consider too; it was not one man only that he killed, but the whole human race, inasmuch as in Adam all die; so that he is truly called a murderer from the beginning. CHRYS. He does not say, his works, but *his lusts ye will do,* meaning that both the devil and the Jews were bent on murder, to satisfy their envy. *And stood not in the truth.* He shews whence sprang their continual objection to Him, that He was not from God. AUG. But it will be objected perhaps, that if from the beginning of his existence, the devil stood not in the truth, he was never in a state of blessedness with the holy angels, refusing, as he did, to be subject to his Creator, and therefore false and deceitful; unwilling at the cost of pious subjection to hold that which by nature he was; and attempting in his pride and loftiness to simulate that which he was not. This opinion is not the same with that of the Manichæans, that the devil has his own peculiar nature, derived as it were from the opposite principle of evil. This foolish sect does not see that our Lord says not, Was alien from the truth, but

Orig. tom. xx.

Aug. Tr. xlii. 11.

Orig. tom. xx. 21.

Chrys. Hom. liv. 3.

Aug. xi. de Civ. Dei, c. 13.

Stood not in the truth, meaning, fell from the truth. And thus they interpret John, *The devil sinneth from the beginning,* not seeing that if sin is natural, it is no sin. But what do the testimonies of the prophets reply? Isaiah, setting forth the devil under the figure of the prince of Babylon, says, *How art thou fallen from heaven, O Lucifer, son of the morning!* Ezekiel says, *Thou hast been in Eden, the garden of God.* Which passages, as they cannot be interpreted in any other way, shew that we must take the word, *He stood not in the truth,* to mean, that he was in truth, but did not remain in it; and the other, that the devil sinneth from the beginning, to mean, that he was a sinner not from the beginning of his creation, but from the beginning of sin. For sin began in him, and he was the beginning of sin.

ORIGEN. There is only one way of standing in the truth; many and various of not standing in it. Some try to stand in the truth, but their feet tremble and shake so, they cannot. Others are not come to that pass, but are in danger of it, as we read in the Psalms, *My feet were almost gone:* others fall from it. *Because the truth is not in him,* is the reason why the devil did not stand in the truth. He imagined vain things, and deceived himself; wherein He was so far worse than others, in that, while others are deceived by him, he was the author of his own deception. But farther; does *the truth is not in him,* mean that he holds no true doctrine, and that every thing he thinks is false; or that he is not a member of Christ, who says, *I am the truth?* Now it is impossible that any rational being should think falsely on every subject and never be even ever so slightly right in opinion. The devil therefore may hold a true doctrine, by the mere law of his rational nature: and therefore his nature is not contrary to truth, i. e. does not consist of simple error and ignorance; otherwise he could never have known the truth.

AUG. Or when our Lord says, *The truth is not in him,* He intends it as an index: as if we had asked Him, how it appeared that the devil stood not in the truth; and He said, *Because the truth is not in him.* For it would be in him, if he stood in it.

When he speaketh a lie, he speaketh of his own: for he is a liar, and the father of it. AUG. Some have thought from

1 John 3, 8.

Ezek. 28, 13.

Orig. tom. xx. 22.

Ps. 72.

c. 14, 6.

Aug. xi. de Civ. Dei, c. xiv.

Aug. Tr. xlii. s. 12, 13.

these words that the devil had a father, and asked who was the father of the devil. This is the error of the Manichæans. But our Lord calls the devil the father of a lie for this reason: Every one who lies is not the father of his own lie; for you may tell a lie, which you have received from another; in which case you have lied, but are not the father of the lie. But the lie wherewith, as with a serpent's bite, the devil slew man, had no source but himself: and therefore he is the father of a lie, as God is the Father of the truth. THEOPHYL. For he accused God to man, saying to Eve, But of envy He hath forbidden you the tree: and to God he accused man, as in Job, *Doth Job serve God for nought?* ORIGEN. Note however; this word, liar, is applied to man, as well as to the devil, who begat a lie, as we read in the Psalm, *All men are liars.* If a man is not a liar, he is not an ordinary man, but one of those, to whom it is said, *I have said, Ye are Gods.* When a man speaketh a lie, he speaketh of his own; but the Holy Spirit speaketh the word of truth and wisdom; as he said below, *He shall receive of Mine, and shall shew it unto you.* AUG. Or thus: The devil is not a singular, but a common name. In whomsoever the works of the devil are found, he is to be called the devil. It is the name of a work, not of a nature. Here then our Lord means by the father of the Jews, Cain; whom they wished to imitate, by killing the Saviour: for he it was who set the first example of murdering a brother. That he spoke a lie of his own, means that no one sins but by his own will. And inasmuch as Cain imitated the devil, and followed his works, the devil is said to be his father. ALCUIN. Our Lord being the truth, and the Son of the true God, spoke the truth; but the Jews, being the sons of the devil, were averse to the truth; and this is why our Lord says, *Because I tell you the truth, ye believe not.* ORIGEN. But how is this said to the Jews who believed on Him? Consider: a man may believe in one sense, not believe in another; e. g. that our Lord was crucified by Pontius Pilate, but not that He was born of the Virgin Mary. In this same way, those whom He is speaking to, believed in Him as a worker of miracles, which they saw Him to be; but did not believe in His doctrines, which were too deep for them. CHRYS. Ye wish to kill Me then, be-

Marginal references:
Job I, 9.
Orig. tom. xx. 23.
Ps. 111.
Ps. 81.
c. 16, 15.
Aug. de Quæst. Nov. et Vet. Test. 2, 90.
Orig. tom. xx. 24.
Chrys. Hom. liv. s. 3.

cause ye are enemies of the truth, not that ye have any fault to find in Me: for, *which of you convinceth Me of sin?* THEOPHYL. As if to say: If ye are the sons of God, ye ought to hold sinners in hatred. If ye hate Me, when ye cannot convince Me of sin, it is evident that ye hate Me because of the truth: i. e. because I said I was the Son of God. ORIGEN. A bold speech this; which none could have had the confidence to utter, but he Who did no sin; even our Lord.

Orig. tom. xx. in Joan. s. 25.

GREG. Observe here the condescension of God. He who by virtue of His Divinity could justify sinners, deigns to shew from reason, that He is not a sinner. It follows: *He that is of God heareth God's words; ye therefore hear them not, because ye are not of God.* AUG. Apply this not to their nature, but to their faults. They both are from God, and are not from God at the same time; their nature is from God, their fault is not from God. This was spoken too to those, who were not only faulty, by reason of sin, in the way in which all are: but who it was foreknown would never possess such faith as would free them from the bonds of sin.

Greg. Hom. xviii. in Evang.

Aug. Tr. xlii. 16.

GREG. Let him then, who would understand God's words, ask himself whether he hears them with the ears of his heart. For there are some who do not deign to hear God's commands even with their bodily ears; and there are others who do this, but do not embrace them with their heart's desire; and there are others again who receive God's words readily, yea and are touched, even to tears: but who afterwards go back to their sins again; and therefore cannot be said to hear the word of God, because they neglect to practise it.

Greg. ut sup.

48. Then answered the Jews, and said unto him, Say we not well that thou art a Samaritan, and hast a devil?

49. Jesus answered, I have not a devil; but I honour my Father, and ye do dishonour me.

50. And I seek not mine own glory; there is one that seeketh and judgeth.

51. Verily, verily, I say unto you, If a man keep my saying, he shall never see death.

CHRYS. Whenever our Lord said any thing of lofty mean- Chrys. Hom.lv. 1.
ing, the Jews in their insensibility set it down madness:
*Then answered the Jews and said unto Him, Say we not
well that Thou art a Samaritan, and hast a devil?* ORIGEN. Orig. tom. xx. 28.
But how, we may ask, when the Samaritans denied a future
life, and the immortality of the soul, could they dare to call
our Saviour, Who had preached so much on the resurrection
and the judgment, a Samaritan? Perhaps they only mean
a general rebuke to Him for teaching, what they did not approve of. ALCUIN. The Samaritans were hated by the Jews;
they lived in the land that formerly belonged to the ten
tribes, who had been carried away. ORIGEN. It is not un- Orig. tom. xx. 28.
likely too, some may have thought that He held the Samaritan opinion of there being no future state really, and only
put forth the doctrine of a resurrection and eternal life, in
order gain to the favour of the Jews. They said that He had
a devil, because His discourses were above human capacity,
those, viz. in which He asserted that God was His Father,
and that He had come down from heaven, and others of a
like kind: or perhaps from a suspicion, which many had,
that He cast out devils by Beelzebub, the prince of the devils.
THEOPHYL. Or they called Him a Samaritan, because He
transgressed the Hebrew ordinances, as that of the sabbath:
the Samaritans not being correct observers of the law. And
they suspected Him of having a devil, because He could
disclose what was in their thoughts. When it was that
they called Him a Samaritan, the Evangelist no where says:
a proof that the Evangelists left out many things. GREG. Greg. Hom. xviii. in Evang.
See; when God suffers a wrong, He does not reply reproach-
fully: *Jesus answered, I have not a devil.* An intimation this
to us, that when reproached by our neighbours falsely, we
should not retort upon them by bringing forward their evil
deeds, however true such charges might be; lest the vehicle
of a just rebuke turn into a weapon of rage. CHRYS. Chrys. Hom.lv. 1.
And observe, when He had to teach them, and pull down
their pride, He used roughness; but now that He has to
suffer rebuke, He treats them with the utmost mildness: a
lesson to us to be severe in what concerns God, but careless
of ourselves. AUG. And to imitate His patience first, if Aug. Tr. xliv. 1. 2.
we would attain to His power. But though being reviled,

He reviled not again, it was incumbent on Him to deny the charge. Two charges had been made against Him: *Thou art a Samaritan, and hast a devil.* In reply He does not say, *I am not a Samaritan:* for Samaritan means keeper; and He knew He was a keeper: He could not redeem us, without at the same time preserving us. Lastly, He is the Samaritan, who went up to the wounded, and had compassion on him. ORIGEN. Our Lord, even more than Paul, wished to become all things to all men, that He might gain some: and therefore He did not deny being a Samaritan. *I have not a devil,* is what Jesus alone can say; as He alone can say, *The prince of this world cometh, and hath nothing in Me.* None of us are quite free from having a devil. For even lesser faults come from him. AUG. Then after being so reviled, all that He says to vindicate His glory, is, *But I honour My Father:* as if to say, That you may not think Me arrogant, I tell you, I have One, Whom I honour. THEOPHYL. He honoured the Father, by revenging Him, and not suffering murderers or liars to call themselves the true sons of God. ORIGEN. Christ alone honoured the Father perfectly. No one, who honours any thing which is not honoured by God, honours God. GREG. As all who have zeal toward God are liable to meet with dishonour from wicked men, our Lord has Himself set us an example of patience under this trial; *And ye do dishonour Me.* AUG. As if to say, I do my duty: ye do not do yours. ORIGEN. And this was not addressed to them only, but to all who by unrighteous deeds inflict injury upon Christ, who is righteousness; or by scoffing at wisdom wrong Him who is wisdom: and the like. GREG. How we are to take injuries, He shews us by His own example, when He adds, *I seek not Mine own glory, there is one that seeketh and judgeth.* CHRYS. As if to say, I have told you this[h] on account of the honour which I have for My Father; and for this ye dishonour Me. But I concern not myself for your reviling: ye are accountable to Him, for whose sake I undergo it. ORIGEN. God seeks Christ's glory, in every one of those who receive Him: which glory He finds in those who cultivate the seeds of virtue implanted in them. And those in whom He finds

Marginal notes:
Orig. tom. xx. s. 28.
s. 29.
c. 14, 30.
Aug. Tr. xliii. 3.
Orig. tom. xx. 29.
Greg. Hom. xliii. 3.
Aug. Tr. xliii. 3.
Orig. tom. xx. 29.
ut sup.
Chrys. Hom. lv. 1.
Orig. tom. xx. s. 30.

[h] i. e. that they had no right to call God their Father.

not His Son's glory, He punishes: *There is one that seeketh and judgeth.* AUG. Meaning of course the Father. But how is it then that He says in another place, *The Father judgeth no man, but hath committed all judgment unto the Son.* Judgment is sometimes put for condemnation, whereas here it only stands for trial: as if to say, There is one, even My Father, who distinguishes My glory from yours; ye glory after this world, I not after this world. The Father distinguishes the glory of the Son, from that of all men: for that He has been made man, does not bring us to a comparison with Him. We men have sin: He was without sin, even when He was in the form of a servant; for, as the Word which was in the beginning, who can speak worthily of Him? ORIGEN. Or thus; If that is true which our Saviour says below, *All men are thine*, it is manifest that the judgment itself of the Son, is the Father's. GREG. As the perversity of the wicked increases, preaching so far from giving way, ought even to become more active. Thus our Lord, after He had been accused of having a devil, imparts the treasures of preaching in a still larger degree: *Verily, verily, I say unto you, If a man keep My saying, he shall never see death.* AUG. *See* is put for experience. But since, about to die Himself, He spoke with those about to die, what means this, *If a man keep My saying, he shall never see death?* What, but that He saw another death from which He came to free us, death eternal, the death of the damned, which is shared with the devil and his angels! That is the true death: the other is a passage only. ORIGEN. We must understand Him, as it were, to say, If a man keep My light, he shall not see darkness for ever; *for ever* being taken as common to both clauses, as if the sentence were, *If a man keep My saying for ever, He shall not see death for ever:* meaning that a man does not see death, so long as he keeps Christ's word. But when a man, by becoming sluggish in the observance of His words, and negligent in the keeping of his own heart, ceases to keep them, he then sees death; he brings it upon himself. Thus taught then by our Saviour, to the prophet who asks, *What man is he that liveth, and shall not see death?* we are able to answer, He who keepeth Christ's word. CHRYS. He says, *keep*, i. e. not by faith, but

[margin notes:]
Aug. Tr. xliii. 4.
c. 5, 22.

Orig. tom. xx. 31.
(Nic.)
c. 17, 10.
Greg. Hom. xviii. in Evang.

Aug. Tr. xliii. 10, 11.

Orig. tom. xx. s. 31.

Ps. 88.
Chrys. Hom. lv. 1.

by purity of life. And at the same time too He means it as a tacit intimation that they can do nothing to Him. For if whoever keepeth His word, shall never die, much less is it possible that He Himself should die.

52. Then said the Jews unto him, Now we know that thou hast a devil. Abraham is dead, and the prophets; and thou sayest, If a man keep my saying, he shall never taste of death.

53. 'Art thou greater than our father Abraham, which is dead? and the prophets are dead; whom makest thou thyself?

54. Jesus answered, If I honour myself, my honour is nothing; it is my Father that honoureth me; of whom ye say, that he is your God:

55. Yet ye have not known him; but I know him: and if I should say, I know him not, I shall be a liar like unto you: but I know him, and keep his saying.

56. Your father Abraham rejoiced to see my day: and he saw it, and was glad.

at sup. GREG. As it is necessary that the good should grow better by contumely, so are the reprobate made worse by kindness. On hearing our Lord's words, the Jews again blaspheme: *Then said the Jews unto Him, Now we know Thou hast a* Orig. *devil.* ORIGEN. Those who believe the Holy Scriptures, tom. xx. 32, 33. understand that what men do contrary to right reason, is not done without the operation of devils. Thus the Jews thought that Jesus had spoken by the influence of the devil, when He said, *If a man keep My saying, he shall never see death.* And this idea they laboured under, because they did not know the power of God. For here He was speaking of that death ἐχθροὶ τῷ λόγῳ of enmity to reason, by which sinners perish: whereas they understand Him of that death which is common to all; and therefore blame Him for so speaking, when it was certain that Abraham and the Prophets were dead: *Abraham is dead, and the Prophets; and Thou sayest, If a man keep My saying, he shall never taste of death. Shall never taste of death*, they say, instead of, *shall not see death*; though between tasting and seeing death there is a difference. Like careless hearers, they mistake what our Lord said. For as our Lord, in that He is the true bread, is good to taste; in that He is wisdom, is beautiful to behold; in like manner His adversary death is both to be tasted and seen. When then a man stands by Christ's help in the spiritual place ἐν τῷ Ἰησοῦ. pointed out to him, he shall not taste of death if he preserves μένω that state: according to Matthew, *There be those standing* μέντοι τινες HERE, *which shall not taste of death*. But when a man hears Mat. 16, Christ's words and keeps them, he shall not see death. 28.

CHRYS. Again, they have recourse to the vainglorious Chrys. argument of their descent: *Art Thou greater than our* Hom. iv. 1. *father Abraham, which is dead?* They might have said, Art Thou greater than God, whose words they are dead who heard? But they do not say this, because they thought Him inferior even to Abraham. ORIGEN. For they do not see Orig. that not Abraham only, but every one born of woman, is less tom. xx. 33. than He who was born of a Virgin. Now were the Jews right in saying that Abraham was dead? for he heard the word of Christ, and kept it, as did also the Prophets, who, they say, were dead. For they kept the word of the Son of God, when the word of the Lord came to Hosea, Isaiah, or Jeremiah; if any one else kept the word, surely those Prophets did. They utter a lie then when they say, *We know that Thou hast a devil;* and when they say, *Abraham is dead, and the Prophets*. GREG. For being given over to ut sup. eternal death, which death they saw not, and thinking only, as they did, of the death of the body, their minds were darkened, even while the Truth Himself was speaking. They add: Whom makest Thou Thyself? THEOPHYL. As if to say, Thou a person of no account, a carpenter's son of Galilee, to take glory to Thyself! BEDE. *Whom makest Thou Thyself?* i. e. Of what merit, of what dignity wouldest Thou be accounted? Nevertheless, Abraham only died in the body; his soul lived. And the death of the soul which is to live for ever, is greater than the death of the body that must die some time. ORIGEN. This was the speech of persons spiritually Orig. blind. For Jesus did not make Himself what He was, but tom. xx. received it from the Father: *Jesus answered and said, If I* 33.

Y

Chrys.
Hom.
liv. 1, 2.
c. 5.

honour Myself, My honour is nothing. CHRYS. This is to answer their suspicions; as above, *If I bear witness of Myself, My witness is not true.* BEDE. He shews in these words that the glory of this present life is nothing. AUG.

Aug.
Tr. xliii.
14.

This is to answer those who said, *Whom makest Thou Thyself?* He refers His glory to the Father, from Whom He is: *It is My Father that honoureth Me.* The Arians take occasion from those words to calumniate our faith, and say, Lo, the Father is greater, for He glorifieth the Son. Heretics, have ye not read that the Son also glorifieth the Father? ALCUIN. The Father glorified the Son, at His baptism, on the mount, at the time of His passion, when a voice came to Him, in the midst of the crowd, when He raised Him up again after His passion, and placed Him at the right

Chrys.
Hom.
lv. 2.

hand of His Majesty. CHRYS. He adds, *Of whom ye say that He is your God;* meaning to tell them that they were not only ignorant of the Father, but even of God. THEOPHYL. For had they known the Father really, they would have reverenced the Son. But they even despise God, who in the Law forbad murder, by their clamours against Christ. Wherefore He says, *Ye have not known Him.* ALCUIN. As if to say, Ye call Him your God, after a carnal manner, serving Him for temporal rewards. Ye have not known Him, as He should be known; ye are not able to serve Him

Aug.
Tr. xliii.
15.

spiritually. AUG. Some heretics say that the God proclaimed in the Old Testament is not the Father of Christ, but a kind of prince of bad angels. These He contradicts when He calls Him His Father, whom the Jews called their God, and knew not. For had they known Him, they would have received His Son. Of Himself however He adds, *But I know Him.* And here too, to men judging after the flesh, He might appear arrogant. But let not arrogance be so guarded against, as that truth be deserted. Therefore our Lord says, *And if I should say I know Him not, I*

Chrys.
Hom.
lv. 2.

should be a liar like unto you. CHRYS. As if to say, As ye, saying that ye know Him, lie; so were I a liar, did I say I knew Him not. It follows, however, (which is the greatest proof of all that He was sent from God,) *But I know Him.* THEOPHYL. Having that knowledge by nature; for as I am, so is the Father also; I know Myself, and therefore I know

Him. And He gives the proof that He knows Him: *And I keep His saying,* i. e. His commandments. Some understand, *I keep His saying,* to mean, I keep the nature of His substance unchanged; for the substance of the Father and the Son is the same, as their nature is the same; and therefore I know the Father. *And* here has the force of *because: I know Him* because *I keep His saying.* AUG. He spoke the saying of the Father too, as being the Son; and He was Himself that Word of the Father, which He spoke to men. CHRYS. In answer then to their question, *Art Thou greater than our father Abraham,* He shews them that He is greater than Abraham; *Your father Abraham rejoiced to see My day: he saw it, and was glad;* he must have rejoiced, because My day would benefit him, which is to acknowledge Me greater than himself. THEOPHYL. As if to say, He regarded My day, as a day to be desired, and full of joy; not as if I was an unimportant or common person. AUG. He did not fear, but *rejoiced to see:* he rejoiced in hope, believing, and so by faith *saw.* It admits of doubt whether He is speaking here of the temporal day of the Lord, that, viz. of His coming in the flesh, or of that day which knows neither rising or setting. I doubt not however that our father Abraham knew the whole: as he says to his servant whom he sent, *Put thy hand under my thigh, and swear to me by the God of heaven.* What did that oath signify, but that the God of heaven was to come in the flesh, out of the stock of Abraham. GREG. Abraham saw the day of the Lord even then, when he entertained the three Angels, a figure of the Trinity. CHRYS. They are aliens from Abraham if they grieve over what he rejoiced in. By this day perhaps He means the day of the cross, which Abraham prefigured by the offering up of Isaac and the ram: intimating hereby that He did not come to His passion unwillingly. AUG. If they rejoiced to whom the Word appeared in the flesh, what was his joy, who beheld in spiritual vision the light ineffable, the abiding Word, the bright illumination of pious souls, the indefectible wisdom, still abiding with God the Father, and sometime to come in the flesh, but not to leave the Father's bosom,

Marginal notes: Aug. Tr. xliii. 15. — Chrys. Hom. lv. 2. — Aug. Tr. xliii. 16. — Gen. 24, 2. — Greg. Hom. xv. in Evang. — Chrys. Hom. liv. 2. — Aug. Tr. xliii. 16.

57. Then said the Jews unto him, Thou art not yet fifty years old, and hast thou seen Abraham?

58. Jesus said unto them, Verily, verily, I say unto you, Before Abraham was, I am.

59. Then took they up stones to cast at him: but Jesus hid himself, and went out of the temple, going through the midst of them, and so passed by.

Greg. Hom. xviii. in Evang. GREG. The carnal minds of the Jews are intent on the flesh only; they think only of His age in the flesh: *Then said the Jews unto Him, Thou art not fifty years old, and hast Thou seen Abraham?* that is to say, Many ages have passed since Abraham died; and how then could he see thy day? For they took His words in a carnal sense. THEOPHYL. Christ was then thirty-three years old. Why then do they not say, Thou art not yet forty years old, instead of *fifty?* A needless question this: they simply spoke as chance led them at the time. Some however say that they mentioned the fiftieth year on account of its sacred character, as being the year of jubilee, in which they redeemed their captives, and gave up the possessions they had bought.

ut sup. GREG. Our Saviour mildly draws them away from their carnal view, to the contemplation of His Divinity; *Jesus said unto them, Verily, verily, I say unto you, Before Abraham was, I am.* *Before* is a particle of past time, *am*, of present. Divinity has no past or future, but always the present; and therefore He does not say, Before Abraham was, I was: but,

Exod.3, 14. *Before Abraham was, I am:* as it is in Exodus, *I am that I am.* *Before* and *after* might be said of Abraham with reference to different periods of his life; *to be*, in the present, is said of the truth only.

Aug. Tr. xliii. 18. AUG. Abraham being a creature, He did not say *before Abraham* was, but, *before Abraham was made.* Nor does He say, I am made; because that, *in the beginning* WAS *the*

ut sup. *Word.* GREG. Their unbelieving minds, however, were unable to support these indications of eternity; and not understanding Him, sought to destroy Him: *Then they took up*

Aug. Tr. xliii. 18. *stones to cast at Him.* AUG. Such hardness of heart, whither was it to run, but to its truest likeness, even the

stones? But now that He had done all that He could do
as a teacher, and they in return wished to stone Him, since
they could not bear correction, He leaves them: *Jesus hid
Himself, and went out of the temple.* He did not hide
Himself in a corner of the temple, as if He was afraid, or
take refuge in a house, or run behind a wall, or a pillar; but
by His heavenly power, making Himself invisible to His
enemies, went through the midst of them: *Jesus hid Himself, and went out of the temple.* GREG. Who, had He
chosen to exert the power of His Divinity, could, without
a word, by His mere nod, have seized them, with the very
stones in their hands, and delivered them to immediate
death. But He who came to suffer, was slow to execute
judgment. AUG. For His part was more to exhibit patience Aug.
than exercise power. ALCUIN. He fled, because His hour Tr.xliii.
was not yet come; and because He had not chosen this 18.
kind of death. AUG. So then, as a man, He flies from the Aug.
stones; but woe to them, from whose stony hearts God flies. Tr.xliii.
BEDE. Mystically, a man throws a stone at Jesus, as often as 18.
he harbours an evil thought; and if he follows it up, so far
as lies in him, he kills Jesus. GREG. What does our Lord ut sup.
mean by hiding Himself, but that the truth is hidden to
them, who despise His words. The truth flies the company
of an unhumbled soul. His example shews us, that we should
in all humility rather retreat from the wrath of the proud,
when it rises, than resist it, even though we might be able.

CHAP. IX.

1. And as Jesus passed by, he saw a man which was blind from his birth.

2. And his disciples asked him, saying, Master, who did sin, this man, or his parents, that he was born blind?

3. Jesus answered, Neither hath this man sinned, nor his parents: but that the works of God should be made manifest in him.

4. I must work the works of him that sent me, while it is day: the night cometh, when no man can work.

5. As long as I am in the world, I am the light of the world.

6. When he had thus spoken, he spat on the ground, and made clay of the spittle, and he anointed the eyes of the blind man with the clay,

7. And said unto him, Go, wash in the pool of Siloam, (which is by interpretation, Sent.) He went his way therefore, and washed, and came seeing.

Chrys.
Hom.
lvi. 1. CHRYS. The Jews having rejected Christ's words, because of their depth, He went out of the temple, and healed the blind man; that His absence might appease their fury, and the miracle soften their hard hearts, and convince their unbelief. *And as Jesus passed by, He saw a man which was blind from his birth.* It is to be remarked here that, on going out of the temple, He betook Himself intently to this manifestation of His power. He first saw the blind man, not the blind man Him: and so intently did He fix His eye upon him, that His disciples were struck, and asked, *Rabbi,*

who did sin, this man or his parents, that he was born blind? BEDE. Mystically, our Lord, after being banished from the minds of the Jews, passed over to the Gentiles. The passage or journey here is His descent from heaven to earth, where He saw the blind man, i. e. looked with compassion on the human race. AUG. For the blind man here is the human race. Blindness came upon the first man by reason of sin: and from him we all derive it: i. e. man is blind from his birth. AUG. *Rabbi* is Master. They call Him Master, because they wished to learn: they put their question to our Lord, as to a Master. THEOPHYL. This question does not seem a proper one. For the Apostles had not been taught the fond notion of the Gentiles, that the soul has sinned in a previous state of existence. It is difficult to account for their putting it. CHRYS. They were led to ask this question, by our Lord having said above, on healing the man sick of the palsy, *Lo, thou art made whole; sin no more.* Thinking from this that the man had been struck with the palsy for his sins, they ask our Lord of the blind man here, whether he *did sin, or his parents;* neither of which could have been the reason of his blindness; the former, because he had been blind from his birth; the latter, because the son does not suffer for the father.

Jesus answered, Neither hath this man sinned, nor his parents. AUG. Was he then born without original sin, or had he never added to it by actual sin? Both this man and his parents had sinned, but that sin was not the reason why he was born blind. Our Lord gives the reason; viz. *That the works of God should be made manifest in him.* CHRYS. He is not to be understood as meaning that others had become blind, in consequence of their parents' sins: for one man cannot be punished for the sin of another. But had the man therefore suffered unjustly? Rather I should say that that blindness was a benefit to him: for by it he was brought to see with the inward eye. At any rate He who brought him into being out of nothing, had the power to make him in the event no loser by it. Some too say, that the *that* here, is expressive not of the cause, but of the event, as in the passage in Romans, *The law entered that sin might abound;* the effect in this case being, that our Lord by

[margin notes: non occ. / Aug. Tr. xliv. 1, 2. / Aug. Tr. xliv. 1, 2. / Chrys. Hom. liv. 1. c. 5. / Aug. Hom. xliv. 3. / Chrys. Hom. lvi. 1, 2. / Rom. 5, 20.]

opening the closed eye, and healing other natural infirmities,

Greg. in Praef. Moral. c. 5.

demonstrated His own power. GREG. One stroke falls on the sinner, for punishment only, not conversion; another for correction; another not for correction of past sins, but prevention of future; another neither for correcting past, nor preventing future sins, but by the unexpected deliverance following the blow, to excite more ardent love of the Saviour's goodness.

Chrys. Hom. liv. 2.

CHRYS. *That the glory of God should be made manifest,* He saith of Himself, not of the Father; the Father's glory was manifest already. *I must work the works of Him that sent Me:* i. e. I must manifest Myself, and shew that I do the same that My Father doeth. BEDE. For when the Son declared that He worked the works of the Father, He proved that His and His Father's works were the same: which are, to heal the sick, to strengthen the weak, and enlighten man.

Aug. Tr. xliv. 4.

AUG. By His saying, *Who sent Me,* He gives all the glory to Him from Whom He is. The Father hath a Son Who is from Him, but hath none from whom He Himself is.

Chrys. Hom. lvi. 2.

CHRYS. *While it is day,* He adds; i. e. while men have the opportunity of believing in Me; while this life lasts; *The night cometh, when none can work.*

Mat. 22, 13.

Night here means that spoken of in Matthew, *Cast him into outer darkness.* Then will there be night, wherein none can work, but only receive for that which he has worked. While thou livest, do that which thou wilt do: for beyond it is neither faith, nor labour, nor repentance.

Aug. Tr. xliv. 5.

AUG. But if we work now, now is the day time, now is Christ present; as He says, *As long as I am in the world, I am the light of the world.* This then is the day. The natural day is completed by the circuit of the sun, and contains only a few hours: the day of Christ's presence will last to the end of the world:

Mat. 28, 20.

for He Himself has said, *Lo, I am with you alway, even unto the end of the world.*

Chrys. Hom. lvi. 2.

CHRYS. He then confirms His words by deeds: *When He had thus spoken, He spat on the ground, and made clay of the spittle, and anointed the eyes of the blind man with the clay.* He who had brought greater substances into being out of nothing, could much more have given sight without the use of any material: but He wished to shew that He was the Creator, Who in the beginning used clay for the formation of man.

Hom. lvii. 1.

He makes the clay with spittle, and

not with water, to make it evident that it was not the pool of
Siloam, whither He was about to send him, but the virtue
proceeding from His mouth, which restored the man's
sight.   And then, that the cure might not seem to be the
effect of the clay, He ordered the man to wash: *And He
said unto him, Go, wash in the pool of Siloam.*   The
Evangelist gives the meaning of Siloam, *which is by interpretation, Sent,* to intimate that it was Christ's power that
cured him even there.   As the Apostle says of the rock in
the wilderness, that *that Rock was Christ,* so Siloam had a 1 Cor.
spiritual character: the sudden rise of its water being a 10, 14.
silent figure of Christ's unexpected manifestation in the flesh.
But why did He not tell him to wash immediately, instead
of sending him to Siloam?   That the obstinacy of the Jews
might be overcome, when they saw him going there with the
clay on his eyes.   Besides which, it proved that He was
not averse to the Law, and the Old Testament.   And there
was no fear of the glory of the case being given to Siloam:
as many had washed their eyes there, and received no such
benefit.   And to shew the faith of the blind man, who
made no opposition, never argued with himself, that it was
the quality of clay rather to darken, than give light, that He
had often washed in Siloam, and had never been benefited;
that if our Lord had the power, He might have cured him by
His word; but simply obeyed: *he went his way therefore,
and washed, and came seeing.*   Thus our Lord manifested Hom.
His glory: and no small glory it was, to be proved the Creator lvi. 2.
of the world, as He was proved to be by this miracle.   For
on the principle that the greater contains the less, this act of
creation included in it every other.   Man is the most honourable of all creatures; the eye the most honourable member of
man, directing the movements, and giving him sight.   The eye
is to the body, what the sun is to the universe; and therefore
it is placed aloft, as it were, upon a royal eminence.   THE-
OPHYL. Some think that the clay was not laid upon the eyes,
but made into eyes.   AUG. Our Lord spat upon the ground, Aug.
and made clay of the spittle, because He was the Word made Tr. xlv.
flesh.   The man did not see immediately as he was anointed; 2.
i. e. was, as it were, only made a catechumen.   But he was

sent to the pool which is called Siloam, i. e. he was baptized in Christ; and then he was enlightened. The Evangelist then explains to us the name of this pool: *which is by interpretation, Sent:* for, if He had not been sent, none of us

Greg.
viii.
Moral.
c. xxx.
(49.)

would have been delivered from our sins. GREG. Or thus: By His spittle understand the savour of inward contemplation. It runs down from the head into the mouth, and gives us the taste of revelation from the Divine splendour even in this life. The mixture of His spittle with clay is the mixture of supernatural grace, even the contemplation of Himself with our carnal knowledge, to the soul's enlightenment, and restoration of the human understanding from its original blindness.

8. The neighbours therefore, and they which before had seen him that he was blind, said, Is not this he that sat and begged?

9. Some said, This is he: others said, He is like him: but he said, I am he.

10. Therefore said they unto him, How were thine eyes opened?

11. He answered and said, A man that is called Jesus made clay, and anointed mine eyes, and said unto me, Go to the pool of Siloam, and wash: and I went and washed, and I received sight.

12. Then said they unto him, Where is he? He said, I know not.

13. They brought to the Pharisees him that aforetime was blind.

14. And it was the sabbath day when Jesus made the clay, and opened his eyes.

15. Then again the Pharisees also asked him how he had received his sight. He said unto them, He put clay upon mine eyes, and I washed, and do see.

16. Therefore said some of the Pharisees, This man is not of God, because he keepeth not the sabbath

lay. Others said, How can a man that is a sinner
do such miracles? And there was a division among
them.

17. They say unto the blind man again, What
sayest thou of him, that he hath opened thine eyes?
He said, He is a prophet.

CHRYS. The suddenness of the miracle made men incredulous: *The neighbours therefore, and they which had seen
him that he was blind, said, Is not this he that sat and
begged?* Wonderful clemency and condescension of God!
Even the beggars He heals with so great considerateness:
thus stopping the mouths of the Jews; in that He made not
the great, illustrious, and noble, but the poorest and meanest,
the objects of His providence. Indeed He had come for
the salvation of all. *Some said, This is he.* The blind man
having been clearly recognised in the course of his long walk
to the pool; the more so, as people's attention was drawn by
the strangeness of the event; men could no longer say,
This is not he; *Others said, Nay, but he is like him.* AUG.
His eyes being opened had altered his look. *But he said,
I am he.* He spoke gratefully; a denial would have convicted
him of ingratitude. CHRYS. He was not ashamed of his
former blindness, nor afraid of the fury of the people, nor
verse to shew himself, and proclaim his Benefactor. *Therefore
said they unto him, How were thine eyes opened?* How they
were, neither he nor any one knew: he only knew the fact; he
could not explain it. *He answered and said, A man that is
called Jesus made clay, and anointed mine eyes.* Mark his
exactness. He does not say how the clay was made; for he
could not see that our Lord spat on the ground; he does not say
that he does not know; but that He anointed him he could feel.
And said unto me, Go to the pool of Siloam, and wash. This
too he could declare from his own hearing; for he had heard
our Lord converse with His disciples, and so knew His
voice. Lastly, he shews how strictly he had obeyed our
Lord. He adds, *And I went, and washed, and received
sight.* AUG. Lo, he is become a proclaimer of grace, an
evangelist, and testifies to the Jews. That blind man testi-

Margin notes: Chrys. Hom. lvii. s. 1. Aug. Tr. xliv. 8. Chrys. Hom. lvii. s. 2. Aug. Tr. xliv. s. 8.

fied, and the ungodly were vexed at the heart, because they had not in their heart what appeared upon his countenance.

Chrys.
Hom.
lvii. 2.

Then said they unto him, Where is He? CHRYS. This they said, because they were meditating His death, having already begun to conspire against Him. Christ did not appear in company with those whom He cured; having no desire for glory, or display. He always withdrew, after healing any one; in order that no suspicion might attach to the miracle. His withdrawal proved the absence of all connexion between Him and the healed; and therefore that the latter did not publish a false cure out of favour to Him. *He said, I know*

Aug.
Tr. xliv.
8.

not. AUG. Here he is like one anointed, but unable yet to see: he preaches, and knows not what he preaches. BEDE. Thus he represents the state of the catechumen, who believes in Jesus, but does not, strictly speaking, know Him, not being yet washed. It fell to the Pharisees to confirm or deny the

Chrys.
Hom.
lvii. 2.

miracle. CHRYS. The Jews, whom they asked, *Where is He?* were desirous of finding Him, in order to bring Him to the Pharisees; but, as they could not find Him, they bring the blind man. *They brought to the Pharisees him that aforetime was blind;* i. e. that they might examine him still more closely. The Evangelist adds, *And it was the sabbath day, when Jesus made the clay, and opened his eyes;* in order to expose their real design, which was to accuse Him of a departure from the law, and thus detract from the miracle: as appears from what follows, *Then again the Pharisees also asked him how he had received his sight.* But mark the firmness of the blind man. To tell the truth to the multitude before, from whom he was in no danger, was not so great a matter; but it is remarkable, now that the danger is so much greater, to find him disavowing nothing, and not contradicting any thing that he said before: *He said unto them, He put clay upon mine eyes, and I washed, and do see.* He is more brief this time, as his interrogators were already informed of the matter: not mentioning the name of Jesus, nor His saying, *Go, and wash;* but simply, *He put clay upon mine eyes, and I washed, and do see;* the very contrary answer to what they wanted. They wanted a disavowal, and they receive a confirmation of the story.

Aug.
Tr. xliv.
9.

Therefore said some of the Pharisees. AUG. Some, no

all: for some were already anointed. But they, who neither saw, nor were anointed, said, *This man is not of God, because he keepeth not the sabbath day.* Rather He kept it, in that He was without sin; for to observe the sabbath spiritually, is to have no sin. And this God admonishes us of, when He enjoins the sabbath, saying, *In it thou shalt do no ser-* **Exod.20,** *vile work.* What servile work is, our Lord tells us above, **10.** *Whosoever committeth sin, is the servant of sin.* They **c. 8, 34.** observed the sabbath carnally, transgressed it spiritually. CHRYS. Passing over the miracle in silence, they give all **Chrys.** the prominence they can to the supposed transgression; **Hom.** **lvii. 2.** not charging Him with healing on the sabbath, but with not keeping the sabbath. *Others said, How can a man that is a sinner do such miracles?* They were impressed by His miracles, but only in a weak and unsettled way. For whereas such might have shewn them, that the sabbath was not broken; they had not yet any idea that He was God, and therefore did not know that it was the Lord of the sabbath who had worked the miracle. Nor did any of them dare to say openly what his sentiments were, but spoke ambiguously; one, because he thought the fact itself improbable; another, from his love of station. It follows, *And there was a division among them.* That is, the people were divided first, and then the rulers. AUG. It was Christ, who divided the day into light **Aug.** and darkness. CHRYS. Those who said, Can a man that is **Hom.** **xliv.4,5.** a sinner do such miracles? wishing to stop the others' mouths, **Chrys.** make the object of our Lord's goodness again come forward; **Hom.** **lviii. 1.** but without appearing to take part with Him themselves: *They say unto the blind man again, What sayest thou of Him, that He hath opened thine eyes?* THEOPHYL. See with what good intent they put the question. They do not say, What sayest thou of Him that keepeth not the sabbath, but mention the miracle, *that He hath opened thine eyes;* meaning, it would seem, to draw out the healed man himself; He hath benefited them, they seem to say, and thou oughtest to preach Him. AUG. Or they sought how they could throw reproach **Aug.** upon the man, and cast him out of their synagogue. He **Tr. xliv.** declares however openly what he thinks: *He said, He is a* **9.** *Prophet.* Not being anointed yet in heart, he could not confess the Son of God; nevertheless, he is not wrong in what he

Luke 4, 24. says: for our Lord Himself says of Himself, *A prophet is not without honour, save in his own country.*

18. But the Jews did not believe concerning him, that he had been blind, and received his sight, until they called the parents of him that had received his sight.

19. And they asked them, saying, Is this your son, who ye say was born blind? how then doth he now see?

20. His parents answered them and said, We know that this is our son, and that he was born blind:

21. But by what means he now seeth, we know not; or who hath opened his eyes, we know not: he is of age; ask him: he shall speak for himself.

22. These words spake his parents, because they feared the Jews: for the Jews had agreed already, that if any man did confess that he was Christ, he should be put out of the synagogue.

23. Therefore said his parents, He is of age; ask him.

Chrys. Hom. lviii. 1. CHRYS. The Pharisees being unable, by intimidation, to deter the blind man from publicly proclaiming his Benefactor, try to nullify the miracle through the parents: *But the Jews did not believe concerning him, that he had been blind, and received his sight, until they had called the parents of him that had received his sight.* Aug. Tr. xliv. s. 10. AUG. i. e. had been blind, and now saw. Chrys. Hom. lviii. 3. CHRYS. But it is the nature of truth, to be strengthened by the very snares that are laid against it. A lie is its own antagonist, and by its attempts to injure the truth, sets it off to greater advantage: as is the case now. For the argument which might otherwise have been urged, that the neighbours knew nothing for certain, but spoke from a mere resemblance, is cut off by introduction of the parents, who could of course testify to their own son. Having brought these before the assembly, they interrogate them with great sharpness, saying, *Is this your son,* (they

say not, who was born blind, but) *who ye say was born blind?*
Say. Why what father is there, that would say such things of
a son, if they were not true? Why not say at once, Whom ye
made blind? They try two ways of making them deny the
miracle: by saying, *Who ye say was born blind,* and by
adding, *How then doth he now see?* THEOPHYL. Either, say
they, it is not true that he now sees, or it is untrue that he
was blind before: but it is evident that he now sees; therefore
it is not true that he was born blind. CHRYS. Three things Chrys.
then being asked,—if he were their son, if he had been blind, Hom.
lviii. 2.
and how he saw,—they acknowledge two of them: *His*
parents answered them and said, We know that this is our
son, and that he was born blind. But the third they refuse
to speak to: *But by what means he now seeth, we know not.*
The enquiry in this way ends in confirming the truth of the
miracle, by making it rest upon the incontrovertible evidence
of the confession of the healed person himself; *He is of*
age, they say, *ask him; he can speak for himself.* AUG. As Aug.
if to say, We might justly be compelled to speak for an infant, Tr. xliv.
10.
that could not speak for itself: but he, though blind from
his birth, has been always able to speak. CHRYS. What Chrys.
Hom.
sort of gratitude is this in the parents; concealing what they lvii. 2.
knew, from fear of the Jews? as we are next told; *These*
words spake his parents, because they feared the Jews. And
then the Evangelist mentions again what the intentions and
dispositions of the Jews were: *For the Jews had agreed*
already, that if any man did confess that He was Christ, he
should be put out of the synagogue. AUG. It was no disad- Aug.
Tr. xliv.
vantage to be put out of the synagogue: whom they cast out, 10.
Christ took in.

Therefore said his parents, He is of age, ask him. ALCUIN.
The Evangelist shews that it was not from ignorance, but
fear, that they gave this answer. THEOPHYL. For they were
fainthearted; not like their son, that intrepid witness
to the truth, the eyes of whose understanding had been
enlightened by God.

24. Then again called they the man that was blind,
and said unto him, Give God the praise: we know that
this man is a sinner.

25. He answered and said, Whether he be a sinner or no, I know not: one thing I know, that, whereas I was blind, now I see.

26. Then said they to him again, What did he to thee? how opened he thine eyes?

27. He answered them, I have told you already, and ye did not hear: wherefore would ye hear it again? will ye also be his disciples?

28. Then they reviled him, and said, Thou art his disciple; but we are Moses' disciples.

29. We know that God spake unto Moses: as for this fellow, we know not from whence he is.

30. The man answered and said unto them, Why herein is a marvellous thing, that ye know not from whence he is, and yet he hath opened mine eyes.

31. Now we know that God heareth not sinners: but if any man be a worshipper of God, and doeth his will, him he heareth.

32. Since the world began was it not heard that any man opened the eyes of one that was born blind.

33. If this man were not of God, he could do nothing.

34. They answered and said unto him, Thou wast altogether born in sins, and dost thou teach us? And they cast him out.

CHRYS. The parents having referred the Pharisees to the healed man himself, they summon him a second time: *Then again called they the man that was blind.* They do not openly say now, Deny that Christ has healed thee, but conceal their object under the pretence of religion: *Give God the praise,* i. e. confess that this man has had nothing to do with the work. AUG. Deny that thou hast received the benefit. This is not to give God the glory, but rather to blaspheme Him. ALCUIN. They wished him to give glory to God, by calling Christ a sinner, as they did: *We know that this man is a sinner.* CHRYS. Why then did ye not

[margin: Chrys. Hom. lviii. 2.]
[margin: Aug. Tr. xliv. s. 11.]
[margin: Chrys. Hom. lviii. 2.]

convict Him, when He said above, *Which of you convinceth* c. 8, 46.
Me of sin? ALCUIN. The man, that he might neither expose
himself to calumny, nor at the same time conceal the truth,
answers not that he knew Him to be righteous, but, *Whether
He be a sinner or no, I know not.* CHRYS. But how comes Chrys.
this, *whether He be a sinner, I know not,* from one who had Hom. lviii. 2.
said, *He is a Prophet?* Did the blind fear? far from it: he
only thought that our Lord's defence lay in the witness of
the fact, more than in another's pleading. And he gives
weight to his reply by the mention of the benefit he had
received: *One thing I know, that, whereas I was blind, now
I see:* as if to say, I say nothing as to whether He is a sinner; but only repeat what I know for certain. So being
unable to overturn the fact itself of the miracle, they fall
back upon former arguments, and enquire the manner of the
cure: just as dogs in hunting pursue wherever the scent
takes them: *Then said they to him again, What did He do to
thee? How opened He thine eyes?* i. e. was it by any charm?
For they do not say, How didst thou see? but, *How opened
He thine eyes?* to give the man an opportunity of detracting
from the operation. So long now as the matter wanted ex-
amining, the blind man answers gently and quietly; but, the
victory being gained, he grows bolder: *He answered them,
I have told you already, and ye did not hear: wherefore
would ye hear it again?* i. e. Ye do not attend to what is
said, and therefore I will no longer answer you vain questions, put for the sake of cavil, not to gain knowledge: *Will ye
also be His disciples?* AUG. *Will ye also?* i. e. I am already, Aug.
do ye wish to be? I see now, but do not envy. He says Tr. xliv. s. 11.
this in indignation at the obstinacy of the Jews; not tole- video,
rating blindness, now that he is no longer blind himself. non inviden.
CHRYS. As then truth is strength, so falsehood is weakness: Chrys.
truth elevates and ennobles whomever it takes up, however Hom. lviii. 2.
mean before: falsehood brings even the strong to weakness
and contempt.

Then they reviled him, and said, Thou art His disciple. Aug.
AUG. A malediction only in the intention of the speakers, Tr. xliv. 12.
not in the words themselves. May such a malediction be ἐλοιδ·
upon us, and upon our children! It follows: *But we are* ησαν, male-
Moses' disciples. We know that God spake unto Moses. But dixe- runt, Vulg

Z

ye should have known, that our Lord was prophesied of

by Moses, after hearing what He said, *Had ye believed Moses,
ye would have believed Me, for he wrote of Me.* Do ye
follow then a servant, and turn your back on the Lord?
Even so, for it follows: *As for this fellow, we know not*

whence He is. CHRYS. Ye think sight less evidence than
hearing; for what ye say, ye know, is what ye have heard
from your fathers. But is not He more worthy of belief, who
has certified that He comes from God, by miracles which ye
have not heard only, but seen? So argues the blind man:
*The man answered and said, Why herein is a marvellous
thing, that ye know not whence He is, and yet He hath
opened mine eyes.* He brings in the miracle every where,
as evidence which they could not invalidate: and, inasmuch
as they had said that a man that was a sinner could not do
such miracles, he turns their own words against them; *Now
we know that God heareth not sinners;* as if to say, I quite

agree with you in this opinion. AUG. As yet however He
speaks as one but just anointed[1], for God hears sinners too.

Else in vain would the publican cry, *God be merciful to me
a sinner.* By that confession he obtained[2] justification, as

the blind man had his sight. THEOPHYL. Or, that God

heareth not sinners, means, that God does not enable sinners
to work miracles. When sinners however implore pardon
for their offences, they are translated from the rank of sinners

to that of penitents. CHRYS. Observe then, when he said
above, *Whether He be a sinner, I know not,* it was not that
he spoke in doubt; for here he not only acquits him of all
sin, but holds him up as one well pleasing to God: *But if
any man be a worshipper of God, and doeth His will, him
He heareth.* It is not enough to know God, we must do
His will. Then he extols His deed: *Since the world
began, was it not heard that any man opened the eyes of
one that was born blind:* as if to say, If ye confess that God
heareth not sinners; and this Man has worked a miracle,
such an one, as no other man has; it is manifest that the
virtue whereby He has wrought it, is more than human: *If*

this Man were not of God, He could do nothing. AUG.
Freely, stedfastly, truly. For how could what our Lord
did, be done by any other than God, or by disciples even

except when their Lord dwelt in them? CHRYS. So then Chrys. Hom. viii. 3. because speaking the truth he was in nothing confounded, when they should most have admired, they condemned him: *Thou wast altogether born in sins, and dost thou teach us?* AUG. What meaneth *altogether?* That he was quite blind. Aug. Tr. xliv. 14. Yet He who opened his eyes, also saves him altogether. CHRYS. Or, *altogether*, that is to say, from thy birth thou art Chrys. Hom. viii. 3. in sins. They reproach his blindness, and pronounce his sins to be the cause of it; most unreasonably. So long as they expected him to deny the miracle, they were willing to believe him, but now *they cast him out.* AUG. It was they Aug. Tr. xliv. 14. themselves who had made him teacher; themselves, who had asked him so many questions; and now they ungratefully cast him out for teaching. BEDE. It is commonly the way with great persons to disdain learning any thing from their inferiors.

35. Jesus heard that they had cast him out; and when he had found him, he said unto him, Dost thou believe on the Son of God?

36. He answered and said, Who is he, Lord, that I might believe on him?

37. And Jesus said unto him, Thou hast both seen him, and it is he that talketh with thee.

38. And he said, Lord, I believe. And he worshipped him.

39. And Jesus said, For judgment I am come into this world, that they which see not might see; and that they which see might be made blind.

40. And some of the Pharisees which were with him heard these words, and said unto him, Are we blind also?

41. Jesus said unto them, If ye were blind, ye should have no sin: but now ye say, We see: therefore your sin remaineth.

CHRYS. Those who suffer for the truth's sake, and con- Chrys. Hom. lix. 1. fession of Christ, come to greatest honour; as we see in the instance of the blind man. For the Jews cast him out of the temple, and the Lord of the temple found him; and received him as the judge doth the wrestler after his labours, and crowned him: *Jesus heard that they had cast him out; and when He had found him, He saith unto him, Dost thou believe on the Son of God?* The Evangelist makes it plain that Jesus came in order to say this to him. He asks him, however, not in ignorance, but wishing to reveal Himself to him, and to shew that He appreciated his faith; as if He said, The people have cast reproaches on Me, but I care not for them; one thing only I care for, that thou mayest believe. Better is he that doeth the will of God, than ten thousand of the wicked. HILARY. If any mere confession whatsoever of Christ were the perfection of faith, it would have been said, *Dost thou believe in Christ?* But inasmuch as all heretics would have had this name in their mouths, confessing Christ, and yet denying the Son, that which is true of Christ alone, is required of our faith, viz. that we should believe in the Son of God. But what availeth it to believe on the Son of God as being a creature, when we are required to have faith in Christ, not as a creature of God, but as the Son of God. CHRYS. But the blind man did not yet know Christ, for before he went to Christ he was blind, and after his cure, he was taken hold of by the Jews: *He answered and said, Who is He, Lord, that I might believe on Him?* The speech this of a longing and enquiring mind. He knows not who He is for whom he had contended so much; a proof to thee of his love of truth. The Lord however says not to him, I am He who healed thee; but uses a middle way of speaking, *Thou hast both seen Him.* THEOPHYL. This He says to remind him of his cure, which had given him the power to see. And observe, He that speaks is born of Mary, and the Son is the Son of God, not two different Persons, according to the error of Nestorius: *And it is He that talketh with thee.* AUG. First, He washes the face of his heart. Then, his heart's face being washed, and his conscience cleansed, he acknowledges Him as not only the Son of man, which he believed before, but as the Son of God, Who had taken flesh upon Him: *And he said, Lord, I believe.* I believe, is a small thing. Wouldest thou see what he believes of Him?

Hilar.
vi. de
Trin.
circa
fin.

Chrys.'
Hom.
lix. 1.

Aug.
Tr. xliv.
15.

And falling down, he worshipped Him. BEDE. An example ^{Vulgate} to us, not to pray to God with uplifted neck, but prostrate upon earth, suppliantly to implore His mercy. CHRYS. He ^{Chrys.} adds the deed to the word, as a clear acknowledgment of ^{Hom.} ^{lix. 1.} His divine power. The Lord replies in a way to confirm His faith, and at the same time stirs up the minds of His followers: *And Jesus said, For judgment have I come into this world.* AUG. The day then was divided between light and ^{Aug.} darkness. So it is rightly added, *that they which see not,* ^{Tr.xliv.} ^{16, 17.} *may see;* for He relieved men from darkness. But what is that which follows: *And that they which see might be made blind.* Hear what comes next. Some of the Pharisees were moved by these words: *And some of the Pharisees which were with Him heard these words, and said unto Him, Are we blind also?* What had moved them were the words, *And that they which see might be made blind.* It follows; *Jesus saith unto them, If ye were blind, ye should have no sin;* i. e. If ye called yourselves blind, and ran to the physician. *But now ye say, We see; therefore your sin remaineth:* for in that saying, *We see,* ye seek not a physician, ye shall remain in your blindness. This then which He has just before said, *I came, that they that see not might see;* i. e. they who confess they cannot see, and seek a physician, in order that they may see: and that they which see not may be made blind; i. e. they which think they can see, and seek not a physician, may remain in their blindness. This act of division He calls judgment, saying, *For judgment have I come into this world:* not that judgment by which He will judge quick and dead at the end of the world. CHRYS. Or, ^{Chrys.} *for judgment,* He saith; i. e. for greater punishment, shewing ^{Hom.} ^{lix. 1.} that they who condemned Him, were the very ones who were condemned. Respecting what He says, *that they which see not might see, and that they which see might be made blind;* it is the same which St. Paul says, *The Gentiles which* ^{Rom. 9,} *followed not after righteousness, have attained to righteous-* ^{30. 31.} *ness, even the righteousness which is of faith. But Israel, which followed after the law of righteousness, hath not attained to the law of righteousness.* THEOPHYL. As if to say, Lo, he that saw not from his birth, now sees both in body and soul; whereas they who seem to see, have had their

Chrys.
Hom.
lix. 1.

understanding darkened. CHRYS. For there is a twofold vision, and a twofold blindness; viz. that of sense, and that of the understanding. But they were intent only on sensible things, and were ashamed only of sensible blindness: wherefore He shews them that it would be better for them to be blind, than seeing so: *If ye were blind, ye should have no sin;* your punishment would be easier; *But now ye say, We see.* THEOPHYL. Overlooking the miracle wrought on the blind man, ye deserve no pardon; since even visible miracles make no impression on you. CHRYS. What then they thought

Chrys.
Hom.
lix. 1, 2.

their great praise, He shews would turn to their punishment; and at the same time consoles him who had been afflicted with bodily blindness from his birth. For it is not without reason that the Evangelist says, *And some of the Pharisees which were with him, heard these words;* but that he may remind us that those were the very persons who had first withstood Christ, and then wished to stone Him. For there were some who only followed in appearance, and were easily changed to the contrary side. THEOPHYL. Or, if ye were blind, i. e. ignorant of the Scriptures, your offence would be by no means so heavy a one, as erring out of ignorance: but now, seeing ye call yourselves wise and understanding in the law, your own selves condemn you.

CHAP. X.

1. Verily, verily, I say unto you, He that entereth not by the door into the sheepfold, but climbeth up some other way, the same is a thief and a robber.

2. But he that entereth in by the door is the shepherd of the sheep.

3. To him the porter openeth; and the sheep hear his voice: and he calleth his own sheep by name, and leadeth them out.

4. And when he putteth forth his own sheep, he goeth before them, and the sheep follow him: for they know his voice.

5. And a stranger will they not follow, but will flee from him : for they know not the voice of strangers.

CHRYS. Our Lord having reproached the Jews with blindness, they might have said, We are not blind, but we avoid Thee as a deceiver. Our Lord therefore gives the marks which distinguish a robber and deceiver from a true shepherd. First come those of the deceiver and robber: *Verily, verily, I say unto you, He that entereth not by the door into the sheepfold, but climbeth up some other way, the same is a thief and a robber.* There is an allusion here to Antichrist, and to certain false Christs who had been, and were to be. The Scriptures He calls *the door.* They admit us to the knowledge of God, they protect the sheep, they shut out the wolves, they bar the entrance to heretics. He that useth not the Scriptures, but climbeth up some other way, i. e. some self-chosen [1], some unlawful way, is a thief. Climbeth up, He says, not, enters, as if it were a thief getting over a wall, and running all risks. *Some other way,* may refer too

Chrys.
Hom.
lix. 2.

[1] ἕτεραι
ἑαυτῷ

to the commandments and traditions of men which the
Scribes taught, to the neglect of the Law. When our Lord
further on calls Himself the Door, we need not be surprised.
According to the office which He bears, He is in one
place the Shepherd, in another the Sheep. In that He introduces us to the Father, He is the Door; in that He takes
care of us, He is the Shepherd. AUG. Or thus: Many go
under the name of good men according to the standard of
the world, and observe in some sort the commandments of
the Law, who yet are not Christians. And these generally
boast of themselves, as the Pharisees did; *Are we blind
also?* But inasmuch as all that they do they do foolishly,
without knowing to what end it tends, our Lord saith of
them, *Verily, verily, I say unto you, He that entereth not
by the door into the sheepfold, but climbeth up some other
way, the same is a thief and a robber*. Let the Pagans then,
the Jews, the Heretics, say, " We lead a good life;" if they
enter not by the door, what availeth it? A good life only
profiteth, as leading to life eternal. Indeed those cannot be
said to lead a good life, who are either blindly ignorant of,
or wilfully despise, the end of good living. No one can hope
for eternal life, who knows not Christ, who is the life, and
by that door enters into the fold. Whoso wisheth to enter
into the sheepfold, let him enter by the door; let him preach
Christ; let him seek Christ's glory, not his own. Christ is a
lowly door, and he who enters by this door must be lowly,
if he would enter with his head whole. He that doth not
humble, but exalt himself, who wishes to climb up over the
wall, is exalted that he may fall. Such men generally try to
persuade others that they may live well, and not be Christians. Thus they climb up by some other way, that they
may rob and kill. They are thieves, because they call that
their own, which is not; robbers, because that which they
have stolen, they kill. CHRYS. You have seen His description of a robber, now see that of the Shepherd: *But he that
entereth in by the door is the shepherd of the sheep*. AUG.
He enters by the door, who enters by Christ, who imitates
the suffering of Christ, who is acquainted with the humility
of Christ, so as to feel and know, that if God became man
for us, man should not think himself God, but man. He

Aug.
Tr. xiv.
2. et sq.

Chrys.
Hom.
lix. 2.

Aug.
deVerb.
Dom.
Serm.
xlix.

who being man wishes to appear God, does not imitate Him,
who being God, became man. Thou art bid to think less of
thyself than thou art, but to know what thou art.

To Him the porter openeth. CHRYS. The porter perhaps
is Moses; for to him the oracles of God were committed.
THEOPHYL. Or, the Holy Spirit is the porter, by whom the
Scriptures are unlocked, and reveal the truth to us. AUG.
Or, the porter is our Lord Himself; for there is much less
difference between a door and a porter, than between a door
and a shepherd. And He has called Himself both the door
and the shepherd. Why then not the door and the porter?
He opens Himself, i. e. reveals[1] Himself. If thou seek[1]
another person for porter, take the Holy Spirit, of whom our
Lord below saith, *He will guide you into all truth.* The
door is Christ, the Truth; who openeth the door, but He
that *will guide you into all Truth?* Whomsoever thou
understand here, beware that thou esteem not the porter
greater than the door; for in our houses the porter ranks
above the door, not the door above the porter. CHRYS. As
they had called Him a deceiver, and appealed to their own
unbelief as the proof of it; (*Which of the rulers believeth
on Him?*) He shews here that it was because they refused to
hear Him, that they were put out of His flock. *The sheep
hear His voice.* The Shepherd enters by the lawful door;
and they who follow Him are His sheep; they who do not,
voluntarily put themselves out of His flock.

And He calleth His own sheep by name. AUG. He knew
the names of the predestinated; as He saith to His disciples,
Rejoice that your names are written in heaven.

And leadeth them out. CHRYS. He led out the sheep,
when He sent them not out of the reach of, but into the
midst of, the wolves. There seems to be a secret allusion to
the blind man. He called him out of the midst of the Jews;
and he heard His voice. AUG. And who is He who leads
them out, but the Same who loosens the chain of their sins,
that they may follow Him with free unfettered step? GLOSS.
*And when He putteth forth His own sheep, He goeth before
them,* He leadeth them out from the darkness of ignorance
into light, while He goeth before in the pillar of cloud, and
fire. CHRYS. Shepherds always go behind their sheep; but

Margin notes:
Chrys. Hom. xlix. 2.
Aug. Tr. xlvi. 2.
[1] expo- nit.
c.16,13.
Chrys. Hom. lix. 2.
c. 7, 48.
Aug. Tr. xlv. 12.
Luke 19, 14.
Chrys. Hom. lix. 2.
Aug. Tr. xlv. 14.
Chrys. Hom. lix. 2.

He, on the contrary, goes before, to shew that He would lead

Aug.
Tr. xlv.
c. 14.
Rom. 6,
9.
Infra
17, 24.
all to the truth. AUG. And who is this that goeth before the sheep, but He who *being raised from the dead, dieth no more;* and who said, *Father, I will also that they, whom Thou hast given Me, be with Me where I am?*

And the sheep follow Him, for they know His voice. And a stranger will they not follow, but will flee from him; for they know not the voice of strangers.

Chrys.
Hom.
xlix. 3.
CHRYS. The strangers are Theudas, and Judas, and the false apostles who came after Christ. That He might not appear one of this number, He gives many marks of difference between Him and them. First, Christ brought men to Him by teaching them out of the Scriptures; they drew men from the Scriptures. Secondly, the obedience of the sheep; for men believed on Him, not only during His life, but after death: their followers ceased, as soon as they were gone. THEOPHYL. He alludes to Antichrist, who shall deceive for a time, but lose all his followers when he dies. AUG.

Aug.
Tr. xlv.
10. et
seq.
But here is a difficulty. Sometimes they who are not sheep hear Christ's voice; for Judas heard, who was a wolf. And sometimes the sheep hear Him not; for they who crucified Christ heard not; yet some of them were His sheep. You will say, While they did not hear, they were not sheep; the voice, when they heard it, changed them from wolves to sheep. Still I am disturbed by the Lord's rebuke to the

Ezek. 34,
4.
shepherds in Ezekiel, *Neither have ye brought again that which strayed.* He calls it a stray sheep, but yet a sheep all the while; though, if it strayed, it could not have heard the voice of the Shepherd, but the voice of a stranger. What

2 Tim.
2, 19.
I say then is this; *The Lord knoweth them that are His.* He knoweth the foreknown, he knoweth the predestinated. They are the sheep: for a time they know not themselves, but the Shepherd knows them; for many sheep are without the fold, many wolves within. He speaks then of the predestinated. And now the difficulty is solved. The sheep do hear the Shepherd's voice, and they only. When

Mat. 10,
32.
is that? It is when that voice saith, *He that endureth to the end shall be saved.* This speech His own hear, the alien hear not.

6. This parable spake Jesus unto them: but they understood not what things they were which he spake unto them.

AUG. Our Lord feedeth by plain words, exerciseth by *ut sup.* obscure. For when two persons, one godly, the other ungodly, hear the words of the Gospel, and they happen to be such that neither can understand them; one says, What He saith is true and good, but we do not understand it: the other says, It is not worth attending to. The former, in faith, knocks, yea, and, if he continue to knock, it shall be opened unto him. The latter shall hear the words in Isaiah, *If ye will not believe, surely ye shall not be established*[1]. Isa.7,9.
[1] non intelligetis

7. Then said Jesus unto them again, Verily, verily, Aug. I say unto you, I am the door of the sheep. non permanebi-

8. All that ever came before me are thieves and tis Vulg. robbers: but the sheep did not hear them.

9. I am the door: by me if any man enter in, he shall be saved, and shall go in and out, and find pasture.

10. The thief cometh not, but for to steal, and to kill, and to destroy: I am come that they might have life, and that they might have it more abundantly.

CHRYS. Our Lord, to waken the attention of the Jews, Chrys. unfolds the meaning of what He has said; *Then said Jesus* Hom. lix. 3. *unto them again, Verily, verily, I say unto you, I am the door of the sheep.* AUG. Lo, the very door which He had Aug. shut up, He openeth; He is the Door: let us enter, and let Tr. xlv. us enter with joy. 8.

All that ever came before Me are thieves and robbers. CHRYS. He saith not this of the Prophets, as the heretics Chrys. think, but of Theudas, and Judas, and other agitators. So Hom. lix. 3. he adds in praise of the sheep, *The sheep heard them not;* but he no where praises those who disobeyed the prophets, but condemns them severely. AUG. Understand, All that Aug. ever came at variance with Me. The Prophets were not at Tr. xlv. variance[2] with Him. They came with Him, who came with [2] præter. 8.

the Word of God, who spake the truth. He, the Word, the
Truth, sent heralds before Him, but the hearts of those whom
He sent were His own. They came with Him, inasmuch
as He is always, though He assumed the flesh in time: *In
the beginning was the Word.* His humble advent in the
flesh was preceded by just men, who believed on Him as
about to come, as we believe on Him come. The times are
different, the faith is the same. Our faith knitteth together
both those who believed that He was about to come, and
those who believe that He has come. All that ever came at
variance with Him were thieves and robbers; i. e. they
came to steal and to kill; *but the sheep did not hear them.*
They had not Christ's voice; but were wanderers, dreamers,
deceivers. Why He is the Door, He next explains, *I am
the Door; by Me if any man enter in he shall be saved.*
ALCUIN. As if to say, The sheep hear not them, but Me
they hear; for I am the Door, and whoever entereth by
Me not falsely but in sincerity, shall by perseverance be
saved. THEOPHYL. The door admits the sheep into the
pasture; *And shall go in and out, and find pasture.* What
is this pasture, but the happiness to come, the rest to
which our Lord brings us? AUG. What is this, *shall go in
and out?* To enter into the Church by Christ the Door, is
a very good thing, but to go out of the Church is not. Going
in must refer to inward cogitation; going out to outward
action; as in the Psalm, *Man goeth forth to his work.*
THEOPHYL. Or, to *go in* is to watch over the inner man; to
go out, to mortify the outward man, i. e. our members which
are upon the earth. He that doth this shall find pasture in
the life to come. CHRYS. Or, He refers to the Apostles who
went in and out boldly; for they became the masters of the
world, none could turn them out of their kingdom, and they
found pasture. AUG. But He Himself explains it more satisfac-
torily to me in what follows: *The thief cometh not, but for to
steal, and for to kill: I am come that they might have life, and
that they might have it more abundantly.* By going in they
have life; i. e. by faith, which worketh by love; by which
faith they go into the fold. *The just liveth[1] by faith.* And
by going out they will *have it more abundantly:* i. e. when
true believers die, they have life more abundantly, even a

Aug.
Tr. xlv.
c. 15.

Ps. 103,
24.

Colos. 3.

Chrys.
Hom.
lix. 3.

A g.
Tr. xlv.
15.

[1] vivit
Vulg.

Heb. 10,
38.

life which never ends. Though in this fold there is not wanting pasture, then they will find pasture, such as will satisfy them. *To-day shalt thou be with Me in paradise.* Luke23, GREG. *Shall go in,* i. e. to faith: *shall go out,* i. e. to sight: Greg. *and find pasture,* i. e. in eternal fulness. ALCUIN. *The thief* super cometh not but for to steal, and to kill.* As if He said, And well Hom. may the sheep not hear the voice of the thief; for he cometh xiii. not but for to steal: he usurpeth another's office, forming his followers not on Christ's precepts, but on his own. And therefore it follows, *and to kill,* i. e. by drawing them from the faith; *and to destroy,* i. e. by their eternal damnation. CHRYS. *The thief cometh not but for to steal, and to kill,* Chrys. *and to destroy;* this was literally fulfilled in the case of those lix. 1. movers of sedition³, whose followers were nearly all destroyed; deprived by the thief even of this present life. But came, He saith, for the salvation of the sheep; *That they might have life, and that they might have it more abundantly,* in the kingdom of heaven. This is the third mark of difference between Himself, and the false prophets. THEOPHYL. Mystically, the thief is the devil, steals by wicked thoughts, kills by the assent of the mind to them, and destroys by acts.

11. I am the good shepherd: the good shepherd giveth his life for the sheep.

12. But he that is an hireling, and not the shepherd, whose own the sheep are not, seeth the wolf coming, and leaveth the sheep, and fleeth : and the wolf catcheth them, and scattereth the sheep.

13. The hireling fleeth, because he is an hireling, and careth not for the sheep.

AUG. Our Lord has acquainted us with two things which Aug. were obscure before; first, that He is the Door; and now Tr. xlvi. again, that He is the Shepherd: *I am the good Shepherd.* Above He said that the shepherd entered by the door. If c. xlvii. He is the Door, how doth He enter by Himself? Just as He knows the Father by Himself, and we by Him; so He enters into the fold by Himself, and we by Him. We enter

---

ª Theudas, Judas, mentioned above.

by the door, because we preach Christ; Christ preaches Himself. A light shews both other things, and itself too.

Tr. xliv. 5. There is but one Shepherd. For though the rulers of the Church, those who are her sons, and not hirelings, are shep- Tr. xlvii. 3. herds, they are all members of that one Shepherd. His office of Shepherd He hath permitted His members to bear. Peter is a shepherd, and all the other Apostles: all good Bishops are shepherds. But none of us calleth himself the door. He could not have added *good*, if there were not bad shepherds as well. They are thieves and robbers; or at forma bonitatis. Greg. Hom. xiv. in Evang. least mercenaries. Greg. And He adds what that goodness is, for our imitation: *The good Shepherd giveth His life for the sheep.* He did what He bade, He set the example of what He commanded: He laid down His life for the sheep, that He might convert His body and blood in our Sacrament, and feed with His flesh the sheep He had redeemed. A path is shewn us wherein to walk, despising death; a stamp is applied to us, and we must submit to the impression. Our first duty is to spend our outward possessions upon the sheep; our last, if it be necessary, is to sacrifice our life for the same sheep. Whoso doth not give his substance to the Aug. Tr. xlvii. sheep, how can he lay down his life for them? Aug. Christ was not the only one who did this. And yet if they who did it are members of Him, one and the same Christ did it always. He was able to do it without them; they were not Aug. de Verb. Dom. Serm. l. without Him. Aug. All these however were good shepherds, not because they shed their blood, but because they did it for the sheep. For they shed it not in pride, but in love. Should any among the heretics suffer trouble in consequence of their errors and iniquities, they forthwith boast of their martyrdom; that they may be the better able to steal under so fair a cloak: for they are in reality wolves. But not all who give their bodies to be burned, are to be thought to shed their blood for the sheep; rather against the sheep; for the 1 Cor. 13, 3. Apostle saith, *Though I give my body to be burned, and have not charity, it profiteth me nothing.* And how hath he even convictus the smallest charity, who does not love connexion with Christians? to command which, our Lord did not mention Chrys. Hom. lx. 5. many shepherds, but one, *I am the good Shepherd.* Chrys. Our Lord shews here that He did not undergo His passion

unwillingly; but for the salvation of the world.   He then
gives the difference between the shepherd and the hireling :
*But he that is an hireling, and not the shepherd, whose own
the sheep are not, seeth the wolf coming, and leaveth the
sheep, and fleeth.*   GREG. Some there are who love earthly ^Greg.
possessions more than the sheep, and do not deserve the ^Hom. in
name of a shepherd.   He who feeds the Lord's flock for the ^xiv.
sake of temporal hire, and not for love, is an hireling, not
a shepherd.   An hireling is he who holds the place of
shepherd, but seeketh not the gain of souls, who panteth
after the good things of earth, and rejoices in the pride of
station.   AUG. He seeketh therefore in the Church, not God, ^Aug.
but something else.   If he sought God he would be chaste; ^de Verb.
for the soul hath but one lawful husband, God.   Whoever ^Serm.
seeketh from God any thing beside God, seeketh unchastely. ^xlix.
GREG. But whether a man be a shepherd or an hireling, ^Greg.
cannot be told for certain, except in a time of trial.   In ^Hom. in
tranquil times, the hireling generally stands watch like the ^xiv.
shepherd.   But when the wolf comes, then every one shews
with what spirit he stood watch over the flock.   AUG. The ^Aug.
wolf is the devil, and they that follow him; according to ^de Verb.
Matthew, *Which come to you in sheeps' clothing, but inwardly* ^Serm.
they are ravening wolves.   AUG. Lo, the wolf hath seized ^Matt. 7,
a sheep by the throat, the devil hath enticed a man into ^15.
adultery.   The sinner must be excommunicated.   But if he ^Tr. xlvi.
is excommunicated, he will be an enemy, he will plot, ^8.
he will do as much harm as he can.   Wherefore thou
art silent, thou dost not censure, thou hast seen the wolf
coming, and fled.   Thy body has stood, thy mind has fled.
For as joy is relaxation, sorrow contraction, desire a reaching forward of the mind; so fear is the flight of the mind.
GREG. The wolf too cometh upon the sheep, whenever any ^Greg.
spoiler and unjust person oppresses the humble believers. ^Hom. in
And he who seems to be shepherd, but leaves the sheep and ^xiv.
flees, is he who dares not to resist his violence, from fear of
danger to himself.   He flees not by changing place, but
by withholding consolation from his flock.   The hireling
is inflamed with no zeal against this injustice.   He only
looks to outward comforts, and overlooks the internal suffering of his flock.   *The hireling fleeth, because he is an*

hireling, and careth not for the sheep. The only reason that the hireling fleeth, is *because he is an hireling;* as if to say, He cannot stand at the approach of danger, who doth not love the sheep that he is set over, but seeketh earthly gain. Such an one dares not face danger, for fear he should lose what he so much loves. AUG. But if the Apostles were shepherds, not hirelings, why did they flee in persecution? And why did our Lord say, *When they persecute you in this city, flee ye into another?* Let us knock, then will come one, who will explain. AUG. A servant of Christ, and minister of His Word and Sacraments, may flee from city to city, when he is specially aimed at by the persecutors, apart from his brethren; so that his flight does not leave the Church destitute. But when all, i. e. Bishops, Clerics, and Laics, are in danger in common, let not those who need assistance be deserted by those who should give it. Let all flee together if they can, to some place of security; but, if any are obliged to stay, let them not be forsaken by those who are bound to minister to their spiritual wants. Then, under pressing persecution, may Christ's ministers flee from the place where they are, when none of Christ's people remain to be ministered to, or when that ministry may be fulfilled by others who have not the same cause for flight. But when the people stay, and the ministers flee, and the ministry ceases, what is this but a damnable flight of hirelings, who care not for the sheep? AUG. On the good side are the door, the porter, the shepherd, and the sheep; on the bad, the thieves, the robbers, the hirelings, the wolf. AUG. We must love the shepherd, beware of the wolf, tolerate the hireling. For the hireling is useful so long as he sees not the wolf, the thief, and the robber. When he sees them, he flees. AUG. Indeed he would not be an hireling, did he not receive wages from the hirer. Sons wait patiently for the eternal inheritance of their father; the hireling looks eagerly for the temporal wages from his hirer; and yet the tongues of both speak abroad the glory of Christ. The hireling hurteth, in that he doeth wrong, not in that he speaketh right: the grape bunch hangeth amid thorns; pluck the grape, avoid the thorn. Many that seek temporal advantages in the Church, preach Christ, and through them Christ's voice is heard; and the

Aug.
Tr. xlvi.
7.
Mat. 10,
23.

Aug. ad
Honor.
Ep.
clxxx.

Aug.
Tr. xlvi.
1.
Aug. de
Verb.
Dom.
s. xlix.
Aug.
Tr. xlvi.
5.

c. 6.

sheep follow not the hireling, but the voice of the Shepherd heard through the hireling.

14. I am the good shepherd, and know my sheep, and am known of mine.

15. As the Father knoweth me, even so know I the Father: and I lay down my life for the sheep.

16. And other sheep I have, which are not of this fold: them also I must bring, and they shall hear my voice; and there shall be one fold, and one shepherd.

17. Therefore doth my Father love me, because I lay down my life, that I might take it again.

18. No man taketh it from me, but I lay it down of myself. I have power to lay it down, and I have power to take it again. This commandment have I received of my Father.

19. There was a division therefore again among the Jews for these sayings.

20. And many of them said, He hath a devil, and is mad; why hear ye him?

21. Others said, These are not the words of him that hath a devil. Can a devil open the eyes of the blind?

CHRYS. Two evil persons have been mentioned, one that Chrys. kills, and robs the sheep, another that doth not hinder: the Hom. ix. 1. one standing for those movers of seditions; the other for the rulers of the Jews, who did not take care of the sheep committed to them. Christ distinguishes Himself from both; from the one who came to do hurt by saying, *I am come that they might have life;* from those who overlook the rapine of the wolves, by saying that He giveth His life for the sheep. Wherefore He saith again, as He said before, *I am the good Shepherd.* And as He had said above that the sheep heard the voice of the Shepherd and followed Him, that no one might have occasion to ask, What sayest Thou then of those

that believe not? He adds, *And I know My sheep, and am*
Rom.
11, 12. *known of Mine.* As Paul too saith, *God hath not cast away*
Greg. *His people, whom He foreknew.* GREG. As if He said, I
Hom. in
Evang. love My sheep, and they love and follow Me. For he who
xiv. loves not the truth, is as yet very far from knowing it. THEO-
PHYL. Hence the difference of the hireling and the Shepherd.
The hireling does not know his sheep, because he sees them
so little. The Shepherd knows His sheep, because He is so at-
Chrys. tractive to them. CHRYS. Then that thou mayest not attribute to
Hom.
lx. 1. the Shepherd and the sheep the same measure of knowledge, He
adds, *As the Father knoweth Me, even so know I the Father:*
i. e. I know Him as certainly as He knoweth Me. This then
Luke 10,
23. is a case of like knowledge, the other is not; as He saith, *No*
Greg. *man knoweth who the Son is, but the Father.* GREG. *And I*
Hom. in
Evang. *lay down My life for My sheep.* As if to say, This is why
xiv. I know My Father, and am known by the Father, because I
lay down My life for My sheep; i. e. by My love for My
Chrys. sheep, I shew how much I love My Father. CHRYS. He
Hom.
lx. 1. gives it too as a proof of His authority. In the same way
the Apostle maintains his own commission in opposition to
the false Apostles, by enumerating his dangers and sufferings. THEOPHYL. For the deceivers did not expose their
lives for the sheep, but, like hirelings, deserted their followers.
infr. 18,
8. Our Lord, on the other hand, protected His disciples: *Let*
Greg. *these go their way.* GREG. But as He came to redeem not
Hom.
xiv. only the Jews, but the Gentiles, He adds, *And other sheep*
Aug. *I have, which are not of this fold.* AUG. The sheep hitherto
de Verb.
Dom. spoken of are those of the stock of Israel according to the
s. 1. flesh. But there were others of the stock of Israel, according to faith, Gentiles, who were as yet out of the fold; predestinated, but not yet gathered together. *They are not of*
this fold, because they are not of the race of Israel, but they
Chrys. will be of this fold: *Them also I must bring.* CHRYS. What
Hom.
lx. 2. wonder that these should hear My voice, and follow Me,
when others are waiting to do the same. Both these flocks
are dispersed, and without shepherds; for it follows, *And they*
shall hear My voice. And then He foretells their future
Greg. union: *And there shall be one fold and one Shepherd.* GREG.
Hom.
Evang. Of two flocks He maketh one fold, uniting the Jews and
xiv. Gentiles in His faith. THEOPHYL. For there is one sign of

baptism for all, and one Shepherd, even the Word of God.
Let the Manichean mark; there is but one fold and one
Shepherd set forth both in the Old and New Testaments.
AUG. What does He mean then when He says, *I am not
sent but unto the lost sheep of the house of Israel?* Only,
that whereas He manifested Himself personally to the Jews,
He did not go Himself to the Gentiles, but sent others.
CHRYS. The word *must* here (*I must bring*) does not signify
necessity, but only that the thing would take place. *Therefore doth My Father love Me, because I lay down My life,
that I might take it again.* They had called Him an alien
from His Father. AUG. i. e. Because I die, to rise again.
There is great force in, *I lay down.* Let not the Jews, He
says, boast; rage they may; but if I should not choose to lay
down My life, what will they do by raging? THEOPHYL. The
Father does not bestow His love on the Son as a reward for
the death He suffered in our behalf; but He loves Him, as
beholding in the Begotten His own essence, whence proceeded such love for mankind. CHRYS. Or He says, in condescension to our weakness, Though there were nothing
else which made Me love you, this would, that ye are so
loved by My Father, that, by dying for you, I shall win His
love. Not that He was not loved by the Father before, or
that we are the cause of such love. For the same purpose
He shews that He does not come to His Passion unwillingly:
No man taketh it from Me, but I lay it down of Myself.
AUG. Wherein He shewed that His natural death was not
the consequence of sin in Him, but of His own simple will,
which was the why, the when, and the how: *I have power to
lay it down.* CHRYS. As they had often plotted to kill Him,
He tells them their efforts will be useless, unless He is willing.
I have such power over My own life, that no one can take
it from Me, against My will. This is not true of men. We
have not the power of laying down our own lives, except we put
ourselves to death. Our Lord alone has this power. And this
being true, it is true also that He can take it again when He
pleases: *And I have power to take it again:* which words declare beyond a doubt a resurrection. That they might not
think His death a sign that God had forsaken Him, He adds,
This commandment have I received from My Father; i. e. to

lay down My life, and take it again. By which we must not understand that He first waited to hear this commandment, and
had to learn His work; He only shews that that work which
He voluntarily undertook, was not against the Father's will.
THEOPHYL. He only means His perfect agreement with His
Father. ALCUIN. For the Word doth not receive a command
by word, but containeth in Himself all the Father's commandments. When the Son is said to receive what He possesseth
of Himself, His power is not lessened, but only His generation declared. The Father gave the Son every thing in
begetting Him. He begat Him perfect. THEOPHYL. After
declaring Himself the Master of His own life and death
which was a lofty assumption, He makes a more humble confession; thus wonderfully uniting both characters; shewing
that He was neither inferior to or a slave of the Father on
the one hand, nor an antagonist on the other; but of the same

Aug. power and will. AUG. How doth our Lord lay down His
Tr. xlvii. own life? Christ is the Word, and man, i. e. in soul and
body. Doth the Word lay down His life, and take it again
or doth the human soul, or doth the flesh? If it was the
¹ ψυχὴ, Word of God that laid down His soul¹ and took it again, that
life. soul was at one time separated from the Word. But, though
death separated the soul and body, death could not separate
the Word and the soul. It is still more absurd to say that
the soul laid down itself; if it could not be separated from
the Word, how could it be from itself? The flesh therefore
layeth down its life and taketh it again, not by its own power
but by the power of the Word which dwelleth in it. This
refutes the Apollinarians, who say that Christ had not a
human, rational soul. ALCUIN. But the light shined in darkness, and the darkness comprehended it not. There was a
division among the Jews for these sayings. And many of
Chrys. them said, He hath a devil, and is mad. CHRYS. Because
Hom. He spoke as one greater than man, they said He had a devil
lx. 3. But that He had not a devil, others proved from His works
Others said, These are not the words of Him that hath a
devil. Can a devil open the eyes of the blind? As if to say
Not even the words themselves are those of one that had
a devil; but if the words do not convince you, be persuaded
by the works. Our Lord having already given proof why

He was by His works, was silent. They were unworthy of an answer. Indeed, as they disagreed amongst themselves, an answer was unnecessary. Their opposition only brought out, for our imitation, our Lord's gentleness, and long suffering. ALCUIN. We have heard of the patience of God, and of salvation preached amid revilings. They obstinately preferred tempting Him to obeying Him.

22. And it was at Jerusalem the feast of the dedication, and it was winter.

23. And Jesus walked in the temple in Solomon's porch.

24. Then came the Jews round about him, and said unto him, How long dost thou make us to doubt? If thou be the Christ, tell us plainly,

25. Jesus answered them, I told you, and ye believed not: the works that I do in my Father's name, they bear witness of me.

26. But ye believe not, because ye are not of my sheep, as I said unto you.

27. My sheep hear my voice, and I know them, and they follow me.

28. And I give unto them eternal life; and they shall never perish, neither shall any man pluck them out of my hand.

29. My Father, which gave them me, is greater than all; and no man is able to pluck them out of my Father's hand.

30. I and my Father are one.

AUG. *And it was at Jerusalem the feast of the dedication.* Encænia is the feast of the dedication of the temple; from the Greek word καινὸν, signifying new. The dedication of any thing new was called encænia. CHRYS. It was the feast of the dedication of the temple, after the return from the Babylonish captivity. ALCUIN. Or, it was in memory of the dedication under Judas Maccabeus. The first dedi-

Aug. Tract. xlviii. 2.

Chrys. Hom. lxi. 1.

cation was that of Solomon in the autumn; the second that
of Zorobabel, and the priest Jesus in the spring. This was
in winter time. BEDE. Judas Maccabeus instituted an an-
nual commemoration of this dedication. THEOPHYL. The
Evangelist mentions the time of winter, to shew that it was
near His passion. He suffered in the following spring; for
which reason He took up His abode at Jerusalem. GREG. Or
because the season of cold was in keeping with the cold
malicious hearts of the Jews. CHRYS. Christ was present
with much zeal at this feast, and thenceforth stayed ¹in
Judæa; His passion being now at hand. *And Jesus walked
in the temple in Solomon's porch.* ALCUIN. It is called
Solomon's porch, because Solomon went to pray there. The
porches of a temple are usually named after the temple. If
the Son of God walked in a temple where the flesh of brute
animals was offered up, how much more will He delight to
visit our house of prayer, in which His own flesh and blood
are consecrated? THEOPHYL. Be thou also careful, in the
winter time, i. e. while yet in this stormy wicked world, to
celebrate the dedication of thy spiritual temple, by ever
renewing thyself, ever rising upward in heart. Then will
Jesus be present with thee in Solomon's porch, and give
thee safety under His covering. But in another life no man
will be able to dedicate Himself. AUG. The Jews cold in
love, burning in their malevolence, approached Him not to
honour, but persecute. *Then came the Jews round about
Him, and said unto Him, How long dost Thou make us to
doubt? If Thou be the Christ, tell us plainly.* They did not
want to know the truth, but only to find ground of accusation.
CHRYS. Being able to find no fault with His works, they
tried to catch Him in His words. And mark their perversity.
When He instructs by His discourse, they say, *What sign
shewest Thou?* When He demonstrates by His works, they
say, *If Thou be the Christ, tell us plainly.* Either way
they are determined to oppose Him. There is great malice
in that speech, *Tell us plainly.* He had spoken plainly¹,
when up at the feasts, and had hid nothing. They preface
however with flattery: *How long dost Thou make us² to doubt?*
as if they were anxious to know the truth, but really only
meaning to provoke Him to say something that they might

Greg.
i. Mor.
c. 11.

Chrys.
Hom.
lxi. 1.
¹ συνεχῶς
ἰσχυ-
ρίαζεν

τῇ σκέπῃ
αὐτοῦ

Aug.
Tract.
xlviii. 3.

Chrys.
Hom.
lxi.

¹ παῤῥη-
σία
openly
before
a'l
²V. tollis
αἴρεις

lay hold of. ALCUIN. They accuse Him of keeping their minds in suspense and uncertainty, who had come to save their souls[a]. AUG. They wanted our Lord to say, *I am the* Aug. *Christ.* Perhaps, as they had human notions of the Messiah, Tract. xlviii. having failed to discern His divinity in the Prophets, they wanted Christ to confess Himself the Messiah, of the seed of David; that they might accuse Him of aspiring to the regal power. ALCUIN. And thus they intended to give Him into the hands of the Proconsul for punishment, as an usurper against the emperor. Our Lord so managed His reply as to stop the mouths of His calumniators, open those of the believers; and to those who enquired of Him as a man, reveal the mysteries of His divinity: *Jesus answered them, I told you, and ye believed not: the works that I do in My Father's name, they bear witness of Me.* CHRYS. Chrys. He reproves their malice, for pretending that a single word Hom. lxi. 2. would convince them, whom so many words had not. If you do not believe My works, He says, how will you believe My words? And He adds why they do not believe: *But ye believe not, because ye are not of My sheep.* AUG. He saw Aug. that they were persons predestinated to eternal death, and Tract. xlviii. c. not those for whom He had bought eternal life, at the price 4. of His blood. The sheep believe, and follow the Shepherd. THEOPHYL. After He had said, *Ye are not of My sheep,* He exhorts them to become such: *My sheep hear My voice.* ALCUIN. i. e. Obey My precepts from the heart. *And I know them, and they follow Me,* here by walking in gentleness and innocence, hereafter by entering the joys of eternal life; *And I give unto them eternal life.* AUG. This is the *pasture* Aug. of which He spoke before: *And shall find pasture.* Eternal Tract. xlviii. 5, life is called a goodly pasture: the grass thereof withereth 6. not, all is spread with verdure. But these cavillers thought only of this present life. *And they shall not perish eternally;* ὁ μὴ as if to say, Ye shall perish eternally, *because ye are not of* ἀπόλ- λυνται *My sheep.* THEOPHYL. But how then did Judas perish? εἰς τὸν Because he did not continue to the end. Christ speaks of αἰῶνα them who persevere. If any sheep is separated from the flock, and wanders from the Shepherd, it incurs danger im-

---

[a] Alc. literally, Christ did not come to make them doubt, but to give them life: they made themselves to doubt, tempting Christ, not believing in Him.

Aug.
Tract.
xlviii. 6.
2 Tim.
2, 19.

mediately. AUG. And He adds why they do not perish: *Neither shall any man pluck them out of My hand.* Of those sheep of which it is said, *The Lord knoweth them that are His,* the wolf robbeth none, the thief taketh none, the robber killeth none. Christ is confident of their safety; and He knows what He gave up for them.

Hilar.
de Trin.
vii.c.22.

HILARY. This is the speech of conscious power. Yet to shew, that though of the Divine nature He hath His nativity from God, He adds, *My Father which gave Me them is greater than all.* He does not conceal His birth from the Father, but proclaims it. For that which He received from the Father, He received in that He was born from Him. He received it in the birth itself, not after it; though He was

Aug.
Tract.
xlviii.

born when He received it. AUG. The Son, born from everlasting of the Father, God from God, has not equality with the Father by growth, but by birth. This is that greater than all which the Father gave Him [b]; viz. to be His Word, to be His Only-Begotten Son, to be the brightness of His light. Wherefore no man taketh His sheep out of His hand, any more than from His Father's hand: *And no man is able to pluck them out of My Father's hand.* If by hand we understand power, the power of the Father and the Son is one, even as Their divinity is one. If we understand the Son, the Son is the hand of the Father, not in a bodily sense, as if God the Father had limbs, but as being He by Whom all things were made. Men often call other men hands, when they make use of them for any purpose. And sometimes a man's work is itself called his hand, because made by his hand; as when a man is said to know his own hand, when he recognises his own handwriting. In this place, however, *hand* signifies power. If we take it for Son, we shall be in danger of imagining that if the Father has a hand, and that

Hilar.
vii. de
Trin.
c. 22.

hand is His Son, the Son must have a Son too. HILARY. The hand of the Son is spoken of as the hand of the Father, to let thee see, by a bodily representation, that both have the same nature, that the nature and virtue of the Father is in

Chrys.
Hom.
lxi.

the Son also. CHRYS. Then that thou mayest not suppose that the Father's power protects the sheep, while He is Himself too weak to do so, He adds, *I and My Father are*

[b] Pater meus quod dedit mihi majus omnibus est. V.

one. AUG. Mark both those words, *one* and *are,* and thou Aug. Tract. xxxvi. non occ. wilt be delivered from Scylla and Charybdis. In that He says, *one* the Arian, in *we are* the Sabellian, is answered. There are both Father and Son. And if *one,* then there is no difference of persons between them. AUG. *We* are *one.* Aug. vii. de Trin. What He is, that am I, in respect of essence, not of relation. HILARY. The heretics, since they cannot gainsay these c. 2. Hilar. viii. de Trin. c. 5. words, endeavour by an impious lie to explain them away. They maintain that this unity is unanimity only; a unity of will, not of nature; i. e. that the two are one, not in that they *are* the same, but in that they will the same. But they are one, not by any economy merely, but by the nativity of the Son's nature, since there is no falling off of the Father's divinity in begetting Him. They are one whilst the sheep that are not plucked out of the Son's hand, are not plucked out of the Father's hand: whilst in Him working, the Father worketh; whilst He is in the Father, and the Father in Him. This unity, not creation but nativity, not will but power, not unanimity but nature accomplisheth. But we deny not therefore the unanimity of the Father and Son; for the heretics, because we refuse to admit concord in the place of unity, accuse us of making a disagreement between the Father and Son. We deny not unanimity, but we place it on the ground of unity. The Father and Son are one in respect of nature, honour, and virtue: and the same nature cannot will different things.

31. Then the Jews took up stones again to stone him.

32. Jesus answered them, Many good works have I shewed you from my Father; for which of those works do ye stone me?

33. The Jews answered him, saying, For a good work we stone thee not; but for blasphemy; and because that thou, being a man, makest thyself God.

34. Jesus answered them, Is it not written in your law, I said, Ye are gods?

35. If he called them gods, unto whom the word of God came, and the scripture cannot be broken;

36. Say ye of him, whom the Father hath sanctified, and sent into the world, Thou blasphemest; because I said, I am the Son of God?

37. If I do not the works of my Father, believe me not.

38. But if I do, though ye believe not me, believe the works: that ye may know, and believe, that the Father is in me, and I in him.

Aug. Tract. xlviii. 8. AUG. At this speech, *I and My Father are one*, the Jews could not restrain their rage, but ran to take up stones, after their hardhearted way: *Then the Jews took up stones again* Hilar. vii. de Trin. c. 23. *to stone Him.* HILARY. The heretics now, as unbelieving and rebellious against our Lord in heaven, shew their impious hatred by the stones, i. e. the words they cast at Him; as if they would drag Him down again from His throne to the cross. THEOPHYL. Our Lord remonstrates with them; *Many good works have I shewed you from My Father*, shewing that they had no just reason for their anger. ALCUIN. Healing of the sick, teaching, miracles. He shewed them of the Father, because He sought His Father's glory in all of them. *For which of these works do ye stone Me?* They confess, though reluctantly, the benefit they have received from Him, but charge Him at the same time with blasphemy, for asserting His equality with the Father; *For a good work we stone Thee not, but for blasphemy; and because that Thou, being a man, makest Thyself God.* Aug. Tract. xlviii. 8. AUG. This is their answer to the speech, *I and My Father are one.* Lo, the Jews understood what the Arians understand not. For they are angry for this very reason, that they could not conceive but that by saying, *I and My Father are one*, He meant the equality of the Father and the Son. Hilar. vii. de Trin. c. 23. HILARY. The Jew saith, *Thou being a man*, the Arian, Thou being a creature: but both say, *Thou makest Thyself God.* The Arian supposes a God of a new and different substance, a God of another kind, or not a God at all. He saith, Thou art not Son by birth, Thou art not God of truth; Thou Chrys. Hom. lxi. 2. art a superior creature. CHRYS. Our Lord did not correct the Jews, as if they misunderstood His speech, but confirmed and defended it, in the very sense in which they had taken it. *Jesus answered them, Is it not written in your law,* Aug. i. e. the Law given to you, *I have said, Ye are Gods?* God saith this by the Prophet in the Psalm. Our Lord calls all those Scriptures the Law generally, though elsewhere He spiritually distinguishes the Law from the Prophets. *On these two commandments hang all the Law and the Prophets.* In another place He makes a threefold division of the Scriptures; *All things must be fulfilled which were written in the Law of Moses, and in the Prophets, and in the Psalms concerning Me.* Now He calls the Psalms the Law, and thus argues from them; *If he called them gods unto whom the word of God came, and the scripture cannot be broken, say ye of Him whom the Father hath sanctified, and sent into the world, Thou blasphemest, because I said, I am the Son of God?* HILARY. Before proving that He and His Father are one, He answers the absurd and foolish charge brought against Him, that He being man made Himself God. When the Law applied this title to holy men, and the indelible word of God sanctioned this use of the incommunicable name, it could not be a crime in Him, even though He were man, to make Himself God. The Law called those who were mere men, gods; and if any man could bear the name religiously, and without arrogance, surely that man could, who was sanctified by the Father, in a sense in which none else is sanctified to the Sonship; as the blessed Paul saith, *Declared[1] to be the Son of God with power, according to the Spirit of holiness.* For all this reply refers to Himself as man; the Son of God being also the Son of man. AUG. Or *sanctified,* i. e. in begetting, gave Him holiness, begat Him holy. If men to whom the word of God came were called gods, much more the Word of God Himself is God. If men by partaking of the word of God were made gods, much more is the Word of which they partake, God. THEOPHYL. Or, *sanctified,* i.e. set apart to be sacrificed for the world: a proof that He was God in a higher sense than the rest. To save the world is a divine work, not that of a man made divine by grace. CHRYS. Or, we must consider this a speech of humility,

Aug. Tract. xlviii. Ps.82,6.

Matt. 22, 40.

Luke 24, 44.

Hilar. vii. do Trin. c. 24.

[1] predestinatus v.

Rom. 1, 4.

Aug. Tract. xlviii.

Chrys. Hom. lxi.

made to conciliate men. After it he leads them to higher things; *If I do not the works of My Father, believe Me not;* which is as much as to say, that He is not inferior to the Father. As they could not see His substance, He directs them to His works, as being like and equal to the Father's. For the equality of their works, proved the equality of their power. HILARY. What place hath adoption, or the mere conception of a name then, that we should not believe Him to be the Son of God by nature, when He tells us to believe Him to be the Son of God, because the Father's nature shewed itself in Him by His works? A creature is not equal and like to God: no other nature has power comparable to the divine. He declares that He is carrying on not His own work, but the Father's, lest in the greatness of the works, the nativity of His nature be forgotten. And as under the sacrament[1] of the assumption of a human body in the womb of Mary, the Son of God was not discerned, this must be gathered from His work; *But if I do, though ye believe not Me, believe the works.* Why doth the sacrament of a human birth hinder the understanding of the divine, when the divine birth accomplishes all its work by aid of the human? Then He tells them what they should gather from His works; *That ye may know and believe, that the Father is in Me, and I in Him.* The same declaration again, *I am the Son of God: I and the Father are one.* AUG. The Son doth not say, *The Father is in Me, and I in Him,* in the sense in which men who think and act aright may say the like; meaning that they partake of God's grace, and are enlightened by His Spirit. The Only-begotten Son of God is in the Father, and the Father in Him, as an equal in an equal.

Margin notes:
Hilar. vii. de Trin. 26.

[1] sacramenta corporis

Aug. Tract. xlviii. 10.

39. Therefore they sought again to take him: but he escaped out of their hand,

40. And went away again beyond Jordan into the place where John at first baptized; and there he abode.

41. And many resorted unto him, and said, John

did no miracle : but all things that John spake of this man were true.

42. And many believed on him there.

BEDE. The Jews still persist in their madness ; *Therefore they sought again to take Him.* AUG. To lay hold of Him, not by faith and the understanding, but with bloodthirsty violence. Do thou so lay hold of Him, that thou mayest have sure hold ; they would fain have laid hold on Him, but they could not : for it follows, *But He escaped out of their hand.* They did lay hold of Him with the hand of faith. It was no great matter for the Word to rescue His flesh from the hands of flesh. CHRYS. Christ, after discoursing on some high truth, commonly retires immediately, to give time to the fury of people to abate, during His absence. Thus He did now : *He went away again beyond Jordan, into the place where John at first baptized.* He went there that He might recall to people's minds, what had gone on there ; John's preaching and testimony to Himself. BEDE. He was followed there by many : *And many resorted unto Him, and said, John did no miracle.* AUG. Did not cast out devils, did not give sight to the blind, did not raise the dead. CHRYS. Mark their reasoning, *John did no miracle,* but this Man did ; wherefore He is the superior. But lest the absence of miracles should lessen the weight of John's testimony, they add, *But all things that John spake of this Man were true.* Though he did no miracle, yet every thing he said of Christ was true, whence they conclude, if John was to be believed, much more this Man, who has the evidence of miracles. Thus it follows, *And many believed on Him.* AUG. These laid hold of Him while abiding, not, like the Jews, when departing. Let us approach by the candle to the day. John is the candle, and gave testimony to the day. THEOPHYL. We may observe that our Lord often brings out the people into solitary places, thus ridding them of the society of the unbelieving, for their furtherance in the faith : just as He led the people into the wilderness, when He gave them the old Law. Mystically, Christ departs from Jerusalem, i. e. from the Jewish people ;

(margin notes:) Aug. Tract. xlviii. 11. Chrys. Hom. lxi. 3. non occ. Aug. Tract. xlviii. c. 12. Chrys. Hom. lxi. 3. Aug. Tract. xlviii. c. 12.

and goes to a place where are springs of water, i. e. to
the Gentile Church, that hath the waters of baptism.   And
many resort unto Him, passing over the Jordan, i. e. through
baptism.